VOICES FROM THE
WATERLOO

VOICES FROM THE PAST
WATERLOO 1815

John Grehan
with additional research by Sara Mitchell

FRONTLINE BOOKS

WATERLOO 1815

This edition published in 2015 and reprinted in this format in 2022
by Frontline Books,
an imprint of Pen & Sword Books Ltd,
47 Church Street, Barnsley, S. Yorkshire, S70 2AS

ISBN: 9-781-39909-207-4

CIP data records for this title are available from the British Library

Printed and bound by CPI Group (UK) Ltd, Croydon, CR0 4YY [TBC]
Typeset in 10.5/12.5 Palatino

For more information on our books, please email: info@frontline-books.com, write to us at the above address, or visit:
www.frontline-books.com

Contents

WATERLOO CAMPAIGN
1815.

English Miles

0 1 2 3 4 5   10

Introduction

'The past is a foreign country'

The Battle of Waterloo has been the subject of thousands of books, pamphlets, magazines and journals. Indeed, 18 June 1815, is the single most documented and discussed day in history – and therein lies the problem. Which amongst this vast assortment are those that can be relied upon to present us with the unbiased truth. It might be assumed that history is a succession of acknowledged facts and that it is the function of the historian merely to gather those facts together and present them to his or her readers in a comprehensible form. This is on the presumption that most contemporary commentators record the event that they are witnessing with a reasonable degree of accuracy and honesty, otherwise historians would have no basis at all to work from. Of course, this is sometimes far from being the case.

Firstly, any conclusions drawn from contemporary comments would have to be tempered by known or assumed prejudice or predisposition. How and to what degree such influences affect the individual can, at best, only be estimated. Added to this is the fact that, as we all know from experience, not everyone witnessing an event will agree in detail on what they have seen. Also, when the mists of time mingle with the fog of war our ability to discern the reliability or otherwise of those witnesses is considerably obscured.

These problems were recognised by Napoleon who knew only too well that his actions would be the subject of much historical examination:

> Historical fact, which is so often invoked, to which everyone so readily appeals, is so often a mere word: it cannot be ascertained when events actually occur in the heat of contrary passions; and, if later on, there is a consensus, this is only because there is no-one left to contradict.
>
> In all such things there are two very distinct essential elements – material fact and moral intent. Material facts, one should think, ought to be incontrovertible; and yet, go and see if any two accounts agree.

There are facts that remain in eternal litigation. As for moral intent, how is one to find his way, supposing that the narrators are in good faith? And what if they are prompted by bad faith, self-interest and bias? Suppose I have given an order: who can read the bottom of my thoughts, my true intention? And yet everyone will take hold of that order, measure it by his own yardstick, make it bend to conform to his plans, his individual way of thinking ... And everybody will be so confident of his own version! The lesser mortals will hear it from privileged mouths, and they will be so confident in turn. Then the flood of memoirs, diaries, anecdotes, drawing-room reminiscences; and yet, my friend, that is history.

In spite of his cynical view of history, or perhaps because of it, Napoleon wrote his own history in the form of his memoirs. Not so Wellington, who steadfastly refused to put pen to paper. His take on history, though, was not dissimilar to that of his great rival. In far fewer words than Napoleon, Wellington famously declared that,

The history of a battle is not unlike the history of a ball. Some individuals may recollect all the little events of which the great result is the battle won or lost, but no individual can recollect the order in which, or the exact moment at which, they occurred, which makes all the difference as to their value or importance.

Wellington's solution to this was, therefore, that only the official accounts of a battle or campaign should be considered:

The duty of the Historian of a battle ... is to prefer that which has been officially recorded and published by public responsible authorities; next to attend to that which proceeds from Official Authority ... and to pay least attention to the statements of Private Individuals.

In terms of the Battle of Waterloo, in 1817 Wellington said the following to the British Ambassador to the Netherlands:

The truth regarding the battle of Waterloo is this: there exists in England an insatiable curiosity upon every subject which has occasioned a mania for travelling and writing. The battle of Waterloo having been fought within reach, every creature who could afford it, travelled to the field; and almost every one who came could write, wrote an account. It is inconceivable the number of lies that were published and circulated in this manner by English travellers; and other nations, seeing how successfully this could be done, thought it as well to adopt the same means of circulating their own stories. This has been done with such industry, that it is now quite certain that I was not present and did not command in the battle of Quatre Bras, and it is very doubtful whether I was present in the battle of Waterloo. It is not easy to dispose of the British army as it is of an individual: but although it is admitted they were present, the brave Belgians, or the brave Prussians, won the battle; neither in histories, pamphlets, plays, nor pictures, are the British troops ever noticed. But I must say that our travellers began this warfare of lying; and we must make up our minds to the consequences.

Wellington was equally contemptuous of the efforts of historians to refight the Battle of Waterloo in print and the Duke, who was twice Commander-in-Chief of the Army let alone twice being Prime Minister, held such an unassailable position in the years after the battle, no-one dare question his opinion. The result was that the official, or Wellingtonian version of the battle, was the only one that could hope to be published. The most egregious example of this is the most highly regarded of all the histories produced during the Duke's lifetime, William Siborne's *History of the Waterloo Campaign*. This was first published in June 1844, and remained for a very long time the most accurate and detailed history of the campaign. It sold in large numbers and more than 150 years later it is still in print.

The story behind Siborne's book began in 1829 when he was commissioned by the then Commander-in-Chief of the British Army, General Rowland Hill, to create a vast scale model of the Battle of Waterloo which would form the centre-piece of the new United Services Museum in London. Siborne populated his diorama with an astonishing 80,000 model figures representing the British, French and Prussian armies at a ratio of one model to two actual soldiers. Siborne chose to portray one moment in time and he decided upon what was defined as the 'Crisis of the Battle' at around 19.00 hours, as the Imperial Guard reached the crest of the Mont St Jean.

In order to establish exactly where every regiment was positioned at that particular moment in time, Siborne received permission to write to every surviving officer to solicit information. He had been advised to simply use Wellington's official despatch as his guide, but Siborne felt he needed more detailed information. Yet he did not see that there would be any conflict with Wellington's despatch. No-one could contemplate that Wellington, widely regarded as the greatest living Briton, had been economical with the truth. The Duke's integrity was considered beyond question. If Wellington said that was what happened on 18 June 1815, then that was what happened.

The response to Siborne's request for information produced a wonderful collection of first-hand accounts. However, this did not impress Wellington. His stated reason was that if Siborne 'went to one gentleman and said, 'What did you do?' [he would reply] 'I did so and so.' To another, 'What did you do? [and he would also reply] 'I did such and such a thing.' One did it at ten and another at twelve, and they have mixed up the whole. The fact is, a battle is like a ball; they keep footing it all the day through.' Wellington believed that Siborne should have chosen the start of the battle for his model as the exact position of all the troops was beyond doubt at that stage.

Wellington's wish for the start of the battle to be portrayed in Siborne's model may not have been driven by the desire for historical accuracy, however. In his official despatch from Waterloo the day after the battle, he paid little regard to the efforts of the Prussians. Though Napoleon had to employ increasing numbers of men to hold back the Prussians from mid-afternoon onwards, in his despatch Wellington only mentions them 'about seven in the evening'.

Siborne, though, was gradually reaching a somewhat different conclusion. He had sent out his circular asking the officers where their units had been at about 19.00 hours, what enemy formations were to their front and what the crops had been like in their vicinity. He also enquired if the officers had any further comments they would like to make regarding the part played by their regiments. He appended a plan of the battlefield and asked the officers if they could mark the positions of their own and the enemy's units on it. He advised them that they should not worry about making mistakes after such a long period of time had elapsed as 'by fairly weighting and comparing the data thus afforded me, I shall be enabled to deduce a most faithful and authentic record of the Battle'.

In total Siborne received around 700 replies and gradually he assembled the most comprehensive collection of eye-witness accounts of the battle. He also made contact with the Prussian Minister of War and was given much useful information but received a mute response from the French.

As the replies came in, Siborne would amend the position of the relevant regiments on a map. If the information in one letter contradicted that of another, Siborne went to considerable lengths to resolve the discrepancy. Finally, after some three years, he was ready to finalize the positioning of his figures on the model. Unfortunately what the model showed was that the Prussians, far from being scarcely involved in the action at the time of the 'Crisis', were in fact on the battlefield in large numbers. By 19.00 hours, 49,886 Prussians with 123 guns were in action.

This contradicted Wellington's despatch. The silent figures on the model landscape loudly challenged the great man's veracity. 'The result did indeed surprise me,' wrote Siborne, 'so greatly at variance was this historical evidence with the general notions which had previously prevailed on the subject'.

Unfortunately for Siborne there had been a change of government since he had been commissioned to start the model and the new administration refused funding. Having started, Siborne was determined to finish the project, using his own money.

In October 1838 the 'Model of the Battle of Waterloo' went on display at the Egyptian Hall, Piccadilly. The model proved to be an immediate success, with around 100,000 people paying 1 shilling each to view it. One person who was conspicuous by his absence was the Duke of Wellington.

Despite the model's popularity Siborne received little money from the man who put it on display and Siborne, who had spent thousands of pounds on the model, faced the sad prospect of having to sell the model to recoup his losses. Severely short of funds, Siborne even volunteered to change the model in any way that a purchaser might require. He was prepared to sacrifice all the years of painstaking effort to ensure the model's accuracy rather than face a debtor's court.

He even wrote to the Army and the Government for help in preserving the model but he knew that one major obstacle stood in his way – the Duke of Wellington.

Siborne was well aware of Wellington's disapproval of the moment in time that he had chosen to represent, and he knew that he had contradicted Wellington's despatch so, with his creditors closing in, he felt that he had no choice but to re-arrange the figures on the model to fit Wellington's version of events in the hope that he would therefore receive some official backing. The only way he could do that was by moving the Prussians further from the action to indicate that they arrived on the battlefield far later than had been established by Siborne. But, limited by the scope of the model, this would have actually meant completely removing the equivalent of 40,000 Prussians from the model. No-one in the Establishment, however, was interested.

Siborne, having accumulated so many first-hand accounts, knew that he was in a unique position to write the first truly comprehensive history of the Waterloo campaign. Having had his fingers burnt with his model, however, Siborne had no intention of stoking the fire of controversy further with his book. It would follow the Wellingtonian version of events. He squared this circle by stating in his *History* that 'the evidence I had collected ... was of too vague a nature, as regards *time* and *situation* [Siborne's italics] to enable me either to corroborate or to rectify the details with which I had been furnished by the Prussian authorities'. He concluded that 'according to the *original* [Siborne's italics once again] arrangement of the figures upon the model, the Prussian troops distributed along that intervening space, immediately in front of Lobau's corps, were represented in too forward a position'.

Siborne then went even further in his bid to placate Wellington by writing:

> It was only subsequently, when collecting that further information which has enabled me in this present work to describe with such minuteness of detail those brilliant dispositions of the Duke of Wellington, by which he not only defeated the French imperial guard upon his position, but secured the victory.

All this, however, did him no good. He had earlier cast aspersions on Wellington's honour and he would never be forgiven. The Duke wrote:

> It is curious that the Historian of the Battle of Waterloo, Captain Siborne, having discovered that in his capacity of artist he had failed in producing an accurate, and even intelligible, representation of the Battle of Waterloo, on his beautiful and accurate model of the ground, by having listened to every hero of his own tale ... the consequences of which have been to render ridiculous and useless that beautiful work ... should in his History of this great military event, have fallen into the same error, so far at least to have listened to every individual who chose to tell his own tale, to insert into his work as facts ... while he lays aside and unnoticed the authentic [sic] reports by the General Commanding-in-Chief.

Siborne's embarrassment served as a dire warning to any others that sought to challenge Wellington's version of events. The result was exactly as Napoleon predicted – the consensus history.

We must, in fairness to Wellington, point out that there was another reason, one not normally associated with Wellington, why he was loth to be drawn into a detailed analysis of the battle – that of not wishing to taint the reputation of any individual officers or individual regiments. This was revealed in a report from Ernst von Vinche, who commanded the 5th Hanoverian Brigade. At one point in the battle, the square formed by the Hildesheim and Peine battalions suddenly retired down the road towards Brussels. Vinche had not ordered the battalions to move and he demanded to know what was happening. It transpired that Major Count von Westphalan, whose command of English was limited, had received an order he did not understand. He was under the impression that he was to take his battalions and 'assemble the numerous fugitives who were streaming to the rear'.

When Vinche asked for an inquiry into the incident he was told by Sir E. Barnes, the Adjutant-General, that 'it was the irrevocable intention of the Duke of Wellington that all these kinds of events were to be consigned to oblivion'.

In the heat of battle mistakes are made and people do not always behave as well as might be expected. Wellington understood this and he had no desire to cause anyone any embarrassment. It was far better, in Wellington's opinion, not to look too deeply into such things. His official despatch lavishes praise; it does not ascribe blame. And that, the Duke believed, was where matters should rest. As John Gurwood, the man who edited Wellington's collected despatches, observed, when the Duke was pressed about certain incidents during the battle, he would reply, 'Oh! I know nothing of the services of particular regiments: there was glory enough for us all.'

This was understood by many in the military, including Lieutenant Colonel Henry Murray of the 18th Hussars, who warned Siborne that, 'too critical an inquiry as of who has the greatest claim to praise engenders a jealously which never should exist between companions in arms'.

*

An historian's interpretation of past events is coloured by the times in which he or she lives. As the historian and author Peter Hofschröer discovered during research for his ground-breaking books on the Waterloo campaign, 'it was fascinating to observe how the way in which it [the Battle of Waterloo] has been treated has varied according to fashion and the contemporary political circumstances'.

In the nineteenth century Britain was experiencing its greatest era. In the wealthiest and most powerful nation on the planet there was an air of positivity throughout the country, especially amongst the educated classes. The histories of that period sought only to glorify the deeds of its statesmen and its armed forces. In the words of the diligent Francophile historian Andrew W. Fields the British were guilty of 'insufferable self-congratulation and arrogance in our wallowing in the warm and prolonged afterglow of victory'. In such an environment authors did not question the established versions of events, for such publications would find few readers.

The modern era could not be more different. Now, we actively seek the alternative view. Indeed, merely repeating the standard version of past events would attract little attention. Everyone is looking for a different perspective, even something controversial, to challenge the accepted, or consensus, view of events. In order to be able to achieve this, the historian must be able to call on previously undisclosed information or draw fresh conclusions from the existing evidence. In both instances the historian will select the material which best supports his or her new theory. As Peter Hofschröer concedes, 'every historian has an axe to grind'. This can lead, perhaps will always lead, to a distortion of the facts.

We are left, therefore, to wonder which histories can be depended upon to deliver the truth, which brings us to the present volume. It is a compilation of documents, from the simplest personal diary to the considered orders of the great commanders. It is history without the complications or the bias of the historian.

The collection is random and eclectic, and draws no particular conclusions, but all the documents were written either during the course of that tumultuous spring and summer of 1815 or subsequently by those individuals that, in one capacity or another, were involved. As David Howarth portrayed so brilliantly in his *A Near Run Thing*, 'critical analysis is the essence of military history, and it has an intellectual interest of its own. But it is not the essence of a battle; it does not describe a human experience.'

The purpose of this book is to describe that human experience. But is aim is not just to tell the story of the Hundred Days campaign through the words of those who were there at the time, for this is no new technique, but more to re-kindle the atmosphere of those exciting, if terrifying weeks using the voice of the people – voices that are heard through a selection of varied means including letters, official documents, parliamentary debates and newspaper reports.

As L.P. Hartley famously wrote, 'The past is a different country, they do things differently there', and as it is only possible to truly appreciate a different country by visiting it, likewise with the past. For all the brilliant interpretations and insightful analyses of historians, we can only really understand the past if we let the people that inhabit it speak for themselves. This is what we have done.

Yet, even though we have stood aside and allowed the participants to command the field, a note of caution needs to be sounded. One of the officers that replied to William Siborne's request for information on the 'Crisis' of the battle bluntly declared that,

> it is fully within my memory that the fog and smoke lay so heavily upon the ground that we could only ascertain the approach of the enemy by the noise and clashing of arms which the French usually make in their advance to attack, and it has often occurred to me from the above circumstances, that the accuracy and particulars with which the crisis has so frequently and so minutely discussed, must have had a good deal of fancy in the narrative.

Another of Siborne's correspondents wrote that, 'if ever truth lies at the bottom of a well, she does so immediately after a great battle, and it takes an amazingly long time before she can be lugged out'.

Wellington himself conceded that, in regard to his despatches, he 'never told a falsehood in them, but I never told the whole truth, nor anything like it. Either one or the other would have been contradicted by 5,000 officers in my army in their letters to their mothers, wives, brothers or sisters and cousins, all of whom imagined they as well understood what they saw as did.' Well, there have been far more than 5,000 letters, articles and books written on the Battle of Waterloo and yet there remain aspects of the battle that are still in dispute and are contested as fiercely now as the Mont St Jean was 200 years ago.

*

Readers will see that in the remote country of the past some words were spelt differently than today. We see that after the battle the various parties engaged in 'negociations', and instead of show we have 'shew'. We find not only unusual spellings, but also new words being coined. So, for example, we have 'massy' columns in one letter to the *Caledonian Mercury*, describing the main French attack, and a visitor to Waterloo shortly after the battle used an entirely inexplicable word, 'notious' in a letter published in the *Chester Chronicle*, as well as an account from July 1815 naming the famous farm on the right of the Anglo-Netherlands' line 'Haugemont'. One visitor to Waterloo after the battle described the battlefield as varied by 'inequalities and indulations' meaning, of course undulations. Favour and favor, honour and honor were interchangeable; capital letters for common and proper nouns were used indiscriminately by some authors even in the same document. If we are to let the people of the past speak for themselves, then we must allow them to do so in their own vernacular, so such spellings, and the often anachronistic grammar, have been left unaltered.

SKETCH of the BATTLE

of

WATERLOO,

fought on the 18th June 1815, between the Allied
Army under the Command of His Grace the Duke
of WELLINGTON and that of the French led by
NAPOLEON BUONAPARTE.

TABLE OF REFERENCE.

A. British Troops in Position.
B. The Infantry which formed Squares & were repeatedly
  charged by the Enemys Cavalry.
C. The French Cuirassiers before & after their charge.
D. The Wood which the Enemy so obstinately endeavoured to
  obtain but without success.
E. The French Columns of Infantry of the Guard formed
  for the attack.
F. High Hill on which there is a Telegraph, from which
  Buonaparte directed the movements of his Troops.
G. Road by which the Prussians advanced in the evening
  of the 18th.
H. Road by which the Enemy retreated.

Royal Engineer Department.

SCALE OF MILES

WATERLOO

Forest of Sougne

1

Boney Returns

On 11 April 1814, the Emperor Napoleon issued the following Act of Abdication from the Palace of Fontainebleau:

> The Allied Powers having declared that Emperor Napoleon was the sole obstacle to the restoration of peace in Europe, Emperor Napoleon, faithful to his oath, declares that he renounces, for himself and his heirs, the thrones of France and Italy, and that there is no personal sacrifice, even that of his life, which he is not ready to do in the interests of France.[1]

Following his abdication, Napoleon was exiled to the tiny Mediterranean island of Elba. That, it seemed, was the end of the 'scourge' of Europe. The world turned its back on Napoleon Bonaparte.

The nations of Europe, after more than twenty years of almost continuous warfare, sought to find a means of ensuring peace. The representatives of the great powers and the smaller nations met at Vienna in September 1814, to re-draw the map of Europe. Britain was represented by Viscount Castlereagh, Secretary of State for Foreign Affairs, who was in turn replaced by the Duke of Wellington on 3 February 1815. Despite the months of talks, agreement on the future shape of Europe was not achieved and it seemed that much negotiation still remained. That was until 7 March, as Field Marshal the Duke of Wellington wrote to Viscount Castlereagh, from Vienna, on 12 March, 1815:

> I received here on the 7th inst. a dispatch from Lord Burghersh, of the 1st, giving an account that Buonaparte had quitted the island of Elba, with all his civil and military officers, and about 1200 troupes, on the 26th Feb. I immediately communicated this account to the Emperors of Austria and Russia, and to the King of Prussia, and to the ministers of the different Powers; and I found among all one prevailing

sentiment, of a determination to unite their efforts to support the system established by the peace of Paris.

As it was uncertain to what quarter Buonaparte had gone, whether he would not return to Elba, or would even land on any part of the continent, it was agreed that it was best to postpone the adoption of any measure till his farther progress should be ascertained; and we have since received accounts from Genoa, stating that he had landed in France, near Cannes, on the 1st March; had attempted to get possession of Antibes, and had been repulsed, and that he was on his march towards Grasse. No accounts had been received at Paris as late as the middle of the day of the 5th of his having quitted Elba, nor any accounts from any quarter of his farther progress. In the meantime the Sovereigns, and all persons assembled here, are impressed with the importance of the crisis which this circumstance occasions in the affairs of the world.

All are desirous of bringing to an early conclusion the business of the Congress, in order that the whole and undivided attention and exertion of all may be directed against the common enemy; and I don't entertain the smallest doubt that, even if Buonaparte should be able to form a party for himself in France, capable of making head against the legitimate government of that country, such a force will be assembled by the Powers of Europe, directed by such a spirit in their councils, as must get the better of him.

The Emperors of Austria and Russia and the King of Prussia have dispatched letters to the King of France, to place at His Majesty's disposal all their respective forces; and Austrian and Prussian officers are dispatched with the letters, with powers to order the movement of the troops of their respective countries placed on the French frontiers, at the suggestion of the King of France. The Plenipotentiaries of the eight Powers who signed the Treaty of Paris assembled this evening, and have resolved to publish a declaration, in which they will, in the name of their Sovereigns, declare their firm resolution to maintain the peace and all its articles with all their force, if necessary … Upon the whole, I assure your Lordship that I am perfectly satisfied with the spirit which prevails here upon this occasion; and I don't entertain the smallest doubt that, if unfortunately it should be possible for Buonaparte to hold at all against the King of France, he must fall under the cordially united efforts of the Sovereigns of Europe.[2]

Napoleon had been kept informed of the lack of unanimity in Vienna and the dissatisfaction that had grown in France under the restored monarchy of Louis XVIII and he believed that not only would he be welcomed back by the people of France, but that he would also be able to exploit the discord between the nations at the Congress of Vienna.

In France, with the country no longer on a war footing, large numbers of Napoleon's former soldiers were out of work. The army had been reduced from 500,000 to just 200,000, with the ranks of the unemployed being swollen by the return of 400,000 prisoners of war. One of them had declared that, in losing Napoleon, 'French military men had lost everything'.[3]

Napoleon left Elba, as Wellington noted, on three Elban ships along with 1,100 loyal soldiers, forty horses and two cannon. It was, as has been remarked, probably the smallest invasion force that ever set out to conquer a nation of fifty million people.[4]

Colonel Marie Antoine de Reiset was an officer in Louis XVIII's bodyguard and was present at the Tuileries Palace when, on 4 March 1815, the king received the news of Napoleon's landing at Golfe-Juan. De Reiset noted the following in his journal:

> An astounding piece of news arrived yesterday. We learnt, by telegraph, that Bonaparte had landed at Cannes, near Fréjus.
>
> Monsieur de Vitrolles [one of the King's secretaries] had come back to his office at about one o'clock, after the Sunday court, when Monsieur Chappe brought him, for handing to His Majesty, a sealed dispatch which had just been transmitted by means of the apparatus he had invented. The Director of Telegraphs seemed extremely agitated. He is a large and corpulent man and had run so fast that he was all out of breath and unable to speak. When he was eventually in a state to articulate a few words, he merely begged Monsieur de Vitrolles personally to take the message, as the news was important. The King, who is very unwell, is at present suffering from an attack of gout which principally affects his hands, so much that he had great difficulty in opening the envelope. Having read its contents he remained silent, then spent several moments with his head in his hands, deep in thought.
>
> 'Do you know what this telegraph contains?' he at length asked Monsieur de Vitrolles, who was waiting for orders.
>
> 'No, Sir, I do not.'
>
> 'Well I will tell you. It is revolution once more. Bonaparte has landed on the coast of Provence. Have this letter taken instantly to the Minister of War, so that he can come and speak to me at once and decide what steps are to be taken.'[5]

3

The Minister of War was Jean-de-Dieu Soult, the Duke of Dalmatia, formally one of Napoleon's most able generals who had accepted a position under the restored monarchy. The step that Soult decided to take was to warn the National Guard and its commanders that, should Napoleon seize power again, it would inevitably lead to war, with all its inherent evils. His 'Order of the Day' to the 'National Guards of France' was dated Tuesday, 7 March 1815:

A telegraphic dispatch and a courier have announced to the King that Buonaparte has quitted the Island of Elba, and disembarked at Cannes, in the department of the Var, with a thousand men and four pieces of cannon; and that he was marching in the direction of Gap, across the mountains, the only road which the weakness of his detachment allowed him to take. An advanced body which presented itself at the gates of Antibes has been disarmed and arrested by the Governor. The same dispatches announce that the Governors and Commanders of military divisions have marched to meet him with the troops and the National Guards, Monsieur is gone towards Lyons with Marshal Gouvion St. Cyr, and several general officers.

A proclamation of the King convokes the two Chambers. An ordinance of the King prescribes the urgent measures requisite for the suppression of this attempt. The National Guards of the kingdom are called upon to give their assistance to the execution of these measures. In consequence of which, the Prefects, the Sub-Prefects, and the Mayors, officially, or on the demand of the competent authority, will require, and the inspectors and commanders of the National Guards will execute all those measures, whose object is to second the acts of the troops and of the gendarmerie, to maintain the public tranquillity, to protect persons and property, to restrain and repress the factious and the treasonable. For this purpose, the inspectors and commanders, under the authority of magistrates, will complete and perfect, as well as circumstances permit, the organization of the national guards which exist, and will organize provisionally those whose lists and skeletons are ready.

At the same time that the King convokes the Chambers, he calls to the defence of the country and of the throne, the army whose glory is without stain, and the national guards, who are no other than the nation itself armed to defend its institutions. It is, then, the interest of the nation itself which the national guards must have before their eyes.

Whether the measures adopted at the Congress of Vienna to settle the peace of Europe, by removing still further the only man interested

4

in troubling it, have thrown this man upon a desperate enterprize; whether criminal intelligence has flattered him with the support of some traitors, his very partizans know him, and will serve him less from affection than in hate, in defiance of the established Government, or from personal motives of ambition or avarice.

Free from such passions, strangers to such calculations, the national guards will see with other eyes the re-appearance of that man, who, himself destroying his own institutions, and under the pretence of a regular government, exercising the most arbitrary and despotic power, has sacrificed the population, the riches, the industry, the commerce of France to the desire of extending his rule beyond all limits, and of destroying all the dynasties of Europe to establish his own family. That man who, to say all in one word, gave to the world a new and terrible example of the abuse of power and fortune, when ambition is without bounds, passions without check, and talents without virtues. He re-appears at a time when France is just recovering its breath under a moderate government: when violent parties, checked by the charter, are reduced to vain murmurs, and are without power to disturb the public peace: when the nation is about to receive from the King and the Chambers the completion of its institutions: when capital so long shut up is applied to agriculture, to industry, to foreign commerce, with a development which awaits only the proclamation of the basis adopted by the Congress for the balance and peace of Europe. He returns; and conscription, continental blockade, indefinite war, arbitrary power, public discredit, re-appear in his train, preceded by civil war and revenge. Does he hope that France is willing to reassume his yoke, to be again the slave of his passions, to combat again for 15 years, and to give its blood and treasures to glut the ambition or the hatred of a single man?[6]

It was all very well for Soult to issue such orders from Paris, but just how the French troops would react when they came face to face with Napoleon remained to be seen. That question was answered on the same day that Soult issued his Order of the Day:

Three leagues from Gorp the Emperor found a battalion of the fifth regiment, a company of sappers, &c. in all, seven or eight hundred men, stationed to oppose him. He accordingly sent [Captain] Raoul to parley with the men, but they would not hear him. Napoleon then alighting from his horse, marched straight for the detachment, followed by his guard, with arms turned downwards:— 'What, my friends,' said he 'do you not know me? I am your Emperor; if there be a soldier among you, who is willing to kill his General, his Emperor, he may do it: here I am,' placing his hand upon his breast. 'Long live the Emperor!' was the answer, in an unanimous shout.[7]

These are the words of Colonel Charles Angélique François Huchet comte de La Bédoyère, who commanded the 7th Regiment. He had managed to hide his regiment's Imperial eagle and *tricolore* and now, with these emblems at its head, the 7th Regiment marched to join the Emperor's tiny band.

Worried that the French National Guard appeared unable to stop Napoleon, the dignitaries in Vienna put aside their differences and agreed to combine forces to resist Bonaparte should he succeed in re-establishing himself at the head of the French nation. Rough plans were quickly made by the various representatives at Vienna. This was explained by Wellington to Castlereagh on 12 March:

I have but little to add to my dispatch regarding Buonaparte's invasion of France. The intention is, as soon as it shall be ascertained that he can make head against the King, to assemble three large corps: one in Italy, solely Austrian, which will consist of 150,000 men; one on the Upper Rhine, Austrian, Bavarian, troops of Baden and Wurtemberg, which will eventually consist of 200,000 men, but will at first consist of only the troops of Bavaria, Baden, and Wurtemberg; the third on the Lower Rhine, consisting of the Prussian corps of Kleist, the Austrian garrison of Mayence, and other troops on the Moselle, to be joined to the British and Hanoverians in Flanders. Of this corps they wish me to take the command. The Russian army, 200,000 men, is to be formed in reserve at Wurtzburg, &c. &c.; the remainder of the Prussian army in reserve on the Lower Rhine. The Emperor of Russia seems reconciled to the notion of the old system, of managing the great concern in a council, consisting of himself, the King of Prussia, and Schwarzenberg. He expressed a wish that I should be with him, but not a very strong one; and, as I should have neither character nor occupation in such a situation, I should prefer to carry a musket.

The Emperor [of Austria] intimated to me this day that, in case the movement of his troops became necessary, he could do nothing without the assistance of money from England. I told him I should write to your Lordship upon the subject by this courier; and that, in my opinion, the first measure to be adopted was one something of the nature of the treaty of Chaumont, in which he agreed; and afterwards to think of subsidy, if England could grant such a thing. It is my opinion that Buonaparte has acted upon false or no information, and that the King will destroy him without difficulty, and in a short time. If he does not, the affair will be a serious one, and a great and immediate effort must be made, which will doubtless be successful.

All the measures above stated to be in contemplation tend to this effort; and it will remain for the British government to determine how far they will act themselves, and how far second the effort of the Continent. I now recommend to you to put all your force in the Netherlands at the disposition of the King of France. I will go and join it if you like it, or do any thing else that government choose. I think we shall have settled our concerns here, and signed the treaty … by the end of the month. We shall have finished every thing that is important much sooner, so that I shall be ready whenever you please to call for me.[8]

The Treaty of Chaumont which Wellington refers to was a document offered to Napoleon in early March 1814 which had been put together by the allied nations of the Sixth Coalition. In this treaty, the Coalition partners offered reasonable terms to Napoleon if he agreed on a ceasefire. If he did not, then the allies vouched that they would not stop fighting Napoleon until he was defeated. Napoleon rejected the treaty.

At this stage, however, just what would happen in France was not known, as Wellington wrote to Lord Burghersh, a former aide-de-camp of his, and the then Minister to Tuscany, on 13 March 1815:

Many thanks for your letters, which I have received to the 6th inclusive. Bony's conduct is very extraordinary, and is, in my opinion, certainly an effet d'illusion. But, if not fit for Bedlam, as I believe, ought to be hanged. We ought to have known of his intention before he put it in execution, and then we might have hoped to have had some of our 6 sail of the line, with their &c. &c., now in the Mediterranean, off the island by the 26th. Here we are all zeal, and, I think, anxious to take the field. I moderate these sentiments as much as possible, and get them on paper; and in the mean time am working at a great exertion, in case things should become serious in France. But I think the King will settle the business himself.[9]

The news of Napoleon's escape from Elba was, of course, reported in the British and French press. This was the story carried in *Le Moniteur* on 8 March:

We have hitherto delayed giving accounts of Buonaparte's landing on the coast of Provence, because the telegraphic dispatches which first made it known still communicated no details.

Buonaparte left Porto Ferrajo on the 26th of February, at nine o'clock in the evening, in extremely calm weather, which lasted until the 1st of March. He embarked in a brig, and was followed by four other vessels, such as pinks and feluccas, having on board from 1,000 to 1,100 men at most, of whom a few were French, and the rest Poles, Corsicans, Neapolitans, and natives of Elba.

The vessels anchored in the road of the Gulph of Juan, near Cannes, on the 1st of March, and the troops landed. Fifty men advanced the same day to Cannes, where they urged the Mayor to proceed to the Gulph of Juan, to receive the orders of the person whom they called the Commander in Chief: but the Mayor returned an absolute refusal. He immediately received order to prepare 3,000 rations the same evening.

The same day fifteen men belonging to the expedition made their appearance before Antibes, soliciting permission to enter as deserters from the Isle of Elba. General Baron Corsin, the Commandant, an officer of distinction, and covered with honourable wounds, received them by causing them to be disarmed. Shortly after, an officer came to summon the place in the name of Buonaparte; he was arrested and imprisoned. In time, a third emissary presented himself before the Commandant, to claim the fifteen men detained, and to invite him in the name of General Drouot, to repair with the Civil Authorities to the Gulph of Juan; the only answer the emissary had, was his arrest. Next day, the men who had disembarked, began their march for Grasse; avoiding, however, the direct road through that town, and taking the road to Digne, where it is said they bivouacked on the 4th.

On the 2d, General Morangier, who commands in the department of the Var, assembled at Frejus the garrison of Draguignan and the National Guards of the adjacent communes. All the roads affording to the persons disembarked any communication with the sea, or any possibility of returning, are well guarded, and entirely intercepted.

A dispatch from Marshal the Prince of Essling announces that he has sent, in the direction of Aix, a corps under the orders of General Miollis, to intercept the route which the expedition had taken.

General Marchand has assembled at Grenoble an imposing force, with which he may act according to circumstances.

The first accounts of these events reached Paris on the 5th, and Monsieur set off the following night for Lyons, where he must have arrived yesterday evening.

The Paris-based *Le Moniteur*, which was, in effect, an organ of the French government, continued its report on the following day:

The weather being extremely cloudy and tempestuous the whole of yesterday morning, totally interrupted the telegraphic communications, and permitted the arrival only of the ordinary correspondence from the South.

A letter from Digne of the 4th, to Marshal Moncey, says, that Buonaparte had arrived with his small band at Bareine, four leagues from Digne, and imposed a requisition upon that town of 3000 rations.

A letter from the Maritime Prefect of Toulon, dated the 5th, adds the following details to those which are already known:-

'The detachment which occupied Cannes consisted of 80 men, including three officers and a drummer, there then arrived a General named Cambrone, who was constantly at the head of the detachment posted at St. Pierre, the French gate; two officers demanded passports for Marseilles and Toulon, which were positively refused; and Lieutenant General Abbé was immediately informed of this fact, that he might be on his guard against the emissaries which Buonaparte might wish to send to the said two towns. General Cambrone arrested the Prince of Monaco, who happened to be at Cannes, and who was proceeding to his principality. He conducted him to an inn, where he placed him under a corporal's guard; and then proceeded to make requisitions of provisions, ordering the fronts of the houses to be illuminated. The whole town was in motion, all the streets crowded; some questions put by the General and his officers as to the dispositions of the inhabitants in regard to Buonaparte, were only replied to by gloomy silence.

'At half an hour past midnight, Buonaparte arrived, preceding his troop by some paces. He fixed his bivouac close to the town.

'At one o'clock he caused the Prince of Monaco to be brought to him, and asked where he was going, and whether he would follow him. Every one could easily perceive, by the Prince's gestures, that he begged to be excused, and permitted to continue his journey, which was immediately granted.

'At three o'clock Buonaparte set off on horseback; his troop followed him, with drums beating and music at their head, preceded by four field pieces and a superb carriage. On arriving within a league of Grasse, he sent a General to sound the dispositions of the inhabitants: he found there great agitation, but in no respect favourable to his views; on approaching he was convinced of this, and did not deem it prudent to enter. He then took the road to St. Vallier, leaving his 4 field pieces, and his carriage, at the gate of Grasse. It is presumed that his plan is to advance towards Grenoble, by way of Castellane, Digne, Sesteron, and Gap, spreading every where reports calculated to encourage his band. But it was already observed, that his soldiers were selling their cartouch boxes, and that arms and cockades were found abandoned in the bivouac, and on the roads, which shews that desertions had taken place. Four men were arrested, drunk, in a village: ten others have entered Grasse, and remained there. It is not known that a single individual has taken part with Buonaparte, or made the least demonstration in his favour.

'This event has had only a happy effect on all minds at Toulon. All the inhabitants and all the military have at once declared their attachment and fidelity to the Government. Order and tranquillity reigned in the city, the most perfect discipline and the best spirit among the troops.'

Letters from Grenoble, dated the morning of the 5th, announce that the moment the news of the landing was spread in the town, a great number of the inhabitants proceeded to the Staff of the National Guard to enrol themselves for active service; the white cockade was spontaneously resumed, and cries of *Vive le Roi* were heard on all sides. The troops composing the garrison participated in these feelings; they shewed themselves animated with the best spirit, full of ardour, fidelity, and absolute confidence in their chiefs, who second with zeal the wise measures taken by General Marchand. The most perfect union reigns between the troops and the national guard, between the heads of the military and civil departments.

'All the official and private accounts from Marseilles agree in giving the following details:-

'On the first news of the landing of Buonaparte, an unanimous feeling was displayed by all classes of the inhabitants of that large city. Almost at the same moment, and as in the first days of the restoration, the white flag was waved from all the windews. The whole population spread through the streets, with cries of *Vive le Roi! Vive la Famille Royale!* The National Guard ran to arms, and demanded instantly to march against the men disembarked. The most perfect concord, in every measure, reigns between the civil and military authorities, and the faithful Marseillese.'[10]

Le Moniteur sought to present a far more positive view of what was happening in the south of France than was really the case. The statesmen at the Congress were either better informed or more suspicious of the sentiments of the people in France and they were taking no chances, as revealed in this letter from Wellington to Castlereagh:

10

We have received here the accounts of the state of affairs in France, and of Buonaparte's progress as known at Paris on the night of the 11th, and of the intentions of the King and of the government; and I am happy to inform your Lordship that what has occurred in that country has augmented the eagerness of the different Powers to put forth the general strength for the common protection ...

I am not certain that I am correct in the estimate I have formed of the extent of the disposable allied force in the Low Countries; but I believe I have rather underrated it. I have this moment returned from a conference of the Ministers of the four allied courts; at which it has been determined to renew the treaty of Chaumont between the four courts, and to invite the accession of the King of France, the Sovereign of the Low Countries, the King of Sardinia, the King of Bavaria, and the Kings of Spain, Portugal, Hanover, Wurtemberg, and Denmark ... I stated that, supposing Great Britain should have it in her power to give any subsidy, it was very obvious that she could not give more than had been stipulated by the treaty of Chaumont; but that it was equally so, that other Powers, particularly Bavaria and Hesse, would require some assistance of this description; and that this must fall upon those Powers with whose armies the contingents of those smaller Powers should be employed. I likewise stated that, seeing that Great Britain engaged to employ 150,000 men for the common cause, and that it was probable she could likewise afford further assistance in subsidy, I hoped all the Powers would attend to the Low Countries, by which our interests were more particularly united with those of the continent, although I believed that all ought to feel the same interest in their preservation from the hands of the enemy; and that I trusted they would take care to support properly the efforts which should be made in that quarter by the Sovereign of the Netherlands and the Prince Regent.

In this sentiment they all cordially agreed; and I then consented that the sums to be paid by Great Britain for any deficiency of the numbers stipulated to be employed by her should be paid to the smaller Powers, under the selection of Great Britain, whose troops should be employed in the common cause, in proportion to their numbers. The treaty then will contain an article by which the Prince Regent will engage to take into consideration the desire of the three Powers to be assisted by subsidies, and nothing more.

It is very desirable that government should without loss of time send their orders regarding treaties and subsidies; but I must state it as my decided opinion that none of the Powers can act at all unless they receive assistance of this description at least to the amount stipulated by the treaty of Chaumont.[11]

It was on 13 March that the representatives at Vienna issued the famous statement which made Napoleon an international outlaw:

> Napoleon Bonaparte, by again appearing in France with projects of confusion and disorder, has deprived himself of the protection of the law, and in consequence has placed himself without the pale of civil and social relations; and, as an enemy and disturber of the tranquillity of the world, has rendered himself liable to public vengeance.[12]

With the major Powers agreeing to each put at least 150,000 troops into the field, and Britain accepting that she would provide subsidies if she was unable to find that number of troops, the main concern of the Allies was with the newly created Kingdom of the United Netherlands. This nation had been put together at the Congress of Vienna, made up of the former Dutch Republic and Belgium and Luxemburg. At its head was the Dutch *Stadtholder*, who became the king. Its joint capitals were Amsterdam and Brussels.

Not only did this new country border France, its component parts had previously been under Napoleonic rule and a very large proportion of its solders had fought in Napoleon's armies. Consequently, the Congress members decided to send the finest allied general to take charge of the situation in the Netherlands, the Duke of Wellington. On 18 March, Wellington wrote to Castlereagh:

> You will see in both the protocols of the military conferences, the desire expressed by the Allied Powers that I should proceed to the Netherlands to take the command of the troops in that country, and particularly in the last that I should lose no time.
>
> As this desire is so strongly expressed, and as the principal business here is nearly settled, and, at all events, will fall into the hands of the Earl of Clancarty, who is in every way qualified in so superior a degree to bring it to the conclusion wished by His Majesty's government, and as I think it probable that the wishes of His Majesty's government would coincide with those expressed by the Allied Powers in the military conferences, I propose to quit Vienna and to proceed to Bruxelles immediately that I shall have concluded the treaty for renewing that of Chaumont, which I hope will be in the course of to-morrow. I shall of course wait at Bruxelles till I shall receive your Lordship's orders.[13]

As Napoleon progressed further inland, his support grew. At Grenoble, the garrison surrendered to Napoleon's no longer inconsiderable army, and from there he wrote a proclamation which, within days, was being reproduced across France:

Soldiers! In my exile I heard your voice ... Put up your *tricolore* cockade! You wore it in our great battles ... Come and place yourselves under the flags of your leader ... Victory will advance at the charge; the Eagle, with the national colours, will fly from steeple to steeple all the way to the towers of Notre-Dame ... In your old age, surrounded and esteemed by your fellow citizens, they will listen to you and you will say with pride: 'And I too, I was part of that grand army which twice entered the walls of Vienna, of Rome, of Berlin, of Madrid, of Moscow, which delivered Paris from the stain of treason and the presence of the enemy imprinted there.'[14]

Events were moving with astonishing speed, and *The Times* presented a comprehensive summary to its readers under the title of *Narrative of Events from the Landing of Buonaparte to the Departure of His Most Christian Majesty Louis XVIII*:

A catastrophe equally disastrous and unexpected has struck Europe with the greatest astonishment. A King, who was surrounded by the confidence and the love of his people, has been compelled to abandon his capital, and soon after his states, which had been invaded by that man whose name recalls only calamities and crimes: and France has in less than three weeks been re-plunged, from the state of profound peace and progressive prosperity to which she had been restored, into that abyss of evils which was believed to have been ever closed. It is important to make known by what progression of irresistible causes treason has under such circumstances been enabled to enchain the public force, and the national will.

On the 5th of March the King received information by a telegraphic dispatch of the landing of Buonaparte on the French territory, at the head of eleven hundred men. This enterprise was to be considered in two different views. It was either the result of a plot, supported by extensive communications, or the act of a madman whose ambition and violence of character prevented him from longer supporting a retirement which could afford to him only the agitations of remorse. In this double supposition, it was necessary to adopt every measure suggested by prudence, and which the most imminent peril would have dictated. No precaution was neglected. Orders were issued with the greatest dispatch for the assembling of troops at Lyons. Satisfactory accounts were received from the Commandant of

Grenoble, and the conduct of the garrison of Antibes caused it to be conjectured that Buonaparte had been deceived in his hopes of being joined by the King's troops. If, however, he had formed any communications, they might be expected to favour his first progress; but it was hoped that a corps which had been stationed at Lyons would, at all events, stop him. Monsieur departed on the 6th to take the command of that corps, and was followed the next day by the Duke of Orleans.

All the Marshals and Generals employed in the Department received orders to proceed to their respective commands, and immediately departed.

Marshal Ney, who commanded at Besancon, and who might effectually have seconded the operations of Monsieur, took leave of the King; and on kissing the hand of his Majesty, said, with a tone of affection and an energy which seemed to proceed from the frankness of a soldier, that '*if he should subdue the enemy of the King and of France, he would bring him prisoner in an iron cage*'. The event soon shewed by what base dissimulation he had been inspired. Thus was disclosed the project of a traitor, which every soldier in Europe will learn with horror.

Monsieur was received with enthusiasm at Lyons. All was prepared for the most vigorous resistance, but unfortunately no ammunition was to be procured.

It was soon made known that the garrison of Grenoble had opened the gates of the town to the enemy, and that a regiment which had departed from Chambery, under the orders of M. de la Bedoyere, had joined the rebels; only a small number of troops has as yet arrived at Lyons; but Monsieur, who had been eagerly joined by Marshal Macdonald, did not hesitate in determining to maintain himself behind the works, which had been hastily constructed. However, on the approach of the first dragoons, which preceded Buonaparte, a general disaffection appeared among the troops of Monsieur. All the remonstrances of the Duke of Tarentum were vain; and then, as afterwards, the forces collected to resist the torrent, only served to increase it, and to add to its violence.

It was learned on the 10th, by a telegraphic dispatch, and consequently without any details, that Buonaparte had entered Lyons that day. The return of the Duke of Orleans, who arrived at Paris on the 14th, and that of Monsieur, were quickly followed by accounts which carried to the highest pitch the alarm which so rapid a continuation of disasters could not fail to create.

Meanwhile opinion, agitated by alarm and distrust, sought to discover otherwise than in the fatal ascendancy of a detested man the cause of his deplorable success. No one would believe that the mere seduction of his presence could produce such an effect on the troops. The Marshal Duke of Dalmatia, Minister of War, had been the last to support in France, by force of arms, the already lost cause of Napoleon. Some pretended to infer from this former mark of attachment, a proof of treason. The public voice was raised against the Marshal, and he himself came and delivered into the hands of the King his resignation and his sword.[15]

The French people and soldiers had made their feelings known and Napoleon had been cheered at every town on his march to Paris. The enthusiasm of the troops certainly appears to have been quite genuine, if the scene described by Captain Lonwy of the *9ème Régiment d'Infanterie Légère* is typical:

We were at the place where brave Colonel D'Eslon resides. Without knowing why, he formed us up and conducted us to beneath his windows.

Imagine seeing 80 officers in two ranks, asking one another what was going on? What was there? In the end we were filled with worry when we saw Colonel D'Eslon appear, holding in his hands, what? You would not guess what in a hundred years ... Our eagle under which we had marched so many times to victory and which the brave colonel had hidden inside the mattress of his bed when *that rotten race of Bourbons* (an expression of the Prince of the Moskva) ascended the throne and exchanged our cherished colours with those that reminded us of slavery.

At the sight of the cherished standard cries of '*Vive l'Empereur!*' could be heard; soldiers and officers, all overwhelmed, wanted not only to see, but to embrace and touch it; this incident made every eye flow with tears of emotion, and all, in a spontaneous motion; we have promised to die beneath our eagle for the country and Napoleon.[16]

The French capital was buzzing with excitement on the morning of 20 March, as demonstrated by an account written by one Captain Routier:

At dawn some of us were already assembled in the square at the end of the Paris road. There we were told the King had abandoned the capital and that he'd passed through Saint-Denis during the night, fleeing from Napoleon's impeding arrival and making for Belgium. We all clustered together, consulted together. Finally our long pent up feelings exploded, a shout of *Vive l'Empereur!* burst from all throats. The white cockade is ripped off and trampled underfoot. Lieutenant-General Maison [military governor of Paris], whose present at this scene, jumps on his horse and flees.[17]

Finally, on the evening of that day, the 20th, Napoleon entered the French capital in triumph. The approach to the Tuileries,

> was filled with such a solid mass of generals, officers, guardsmen and a large quantity of distinguished persons, however, that the carriage could not proceed to the stairs of the main entrance. Seeing that he could advance no further, the Emperor descended in the midst of the immense crowd, which quickly engulfed him.[18]

The 'madman' who had recklessly attempted to conquer France with just 1,000 men was back in power. It had taken him less than a month. His progress from forgotten man to national hero was exemplified in a broadsheet that was hawked around the streets of Paris:

> The Tiger has broken out of his den
> The Ogre has been three days at sea
> The Wretch has landed at Fréjus
> The Buzzard has reached Antibes
> The Invader has arrived at Grenoble
> The General has entered Paris
> Napoleon slept at Fontainebleau last night
> The Emperor will proceed to the Tuileries today.[19]

The news of Napoleon's welcome in Paris hit the headlines in the country most likely to be immediately affected by Napoleon's return, Belgium. These reports are from a Brussels newspaper and repeated in *The Times*:

> We received yesterday the news of Napoleon's entrance into Paris. It would be difficult to describe the effect which this event has produced. We had flattered ourselves that the King, who since his return has consecrated every moment to the happiness of France, and who had done everything to alleviate the fate of the soldiers prisoners of war, would have been able to collect round his standard a number of faithful Frenchmen considerable enough to combat with advantage

the small corps of Napoleon; but it seems that the defection has been complete. There remains, then, no way except that of arms. The immense preparations which the powers make to support their declaration leaves no doubt as to the issue of this new war.

As if by magic, all is changed here within a few weeks. The silence of the Cabinet is succeeded by the din of arms. Very large bodies of troops continually march through Vienna.[20]

Europe then was set on war. The only question still to be resolved was whether or not Napoleon would take the offensive or wait to be attacked by the combined armies of the Allies. This was the subject that occupied the mind of the Duke of Wellington who had arrived in Brussels to take command of the Anglo-Netherlands forces that were gathering in the south of Belgium.

2

Peace and War

Wellington arrived in Brussels on the evening of 4 April 1815. The only military force there was assembled from the body of the army which had taken part in Sir Thomas Graham's unsuccessful attempt to seize Bergen-op-Zoom the previous year. This force, composed mainly of British and King's German Legion regiments, had been broken up following Napoleon's abdication, but the nucleus remained in the United Netherlands to ensure the peaceful transition of that country from the rule of Napoleon to that of the House of Orange.

To this was added a number of troops from the new Netherlands Army which consisted of an approximately equal number of veterans who had, until his fall from power in 1814, served under Napoleon, and of raw recruits. The British contingent amounted to six regiments of cavalry, twenty-five battalions of infantry and supporting artillery, numbering, in all around 14,000 men. As Wellington was to explain to his Government, this force was wholly inadequate for the task ahead. He wrote to the Secretary of State for War and the Colonies, the Earl of Bathurst, on 6 April:

> I arrived here the night before last, and received from the Prince of Orange your Lordship's letters; and a dispatch from H.R.H. the Commander in Chief, containing His Majesty's Commission of Commander of the Forces on the Continent of Europe, and His Royal Highness' instructions for my guidance. Although I have not yet formally taken upon myself the command, I have inquired into the state of the forces here, upon which subject I will address your Lordship hereafter; and now enclose the copy of a letter which I have thought it proper to address to Gen. Ziethen , who commands on the Rhine and Meuse.
>
> Your Lordship will see by my letter to Gen. Ziethen in what state we stand as to numbers. I am sorry to say that I have a very bad account of the troops; and he appears unwilling to allow them to be

mixed with ours, which, although they are not our best, would afford a chance of making something of them. Although I have given a favorable opinion of ours to Gen. Ziethen, I cannot help thinking, from all accounts, that they are not what they ought to be to enable us to maintain our military character in Europe. It appears to me that you have not taken in England a clear view of your situation, that you do not think war certain, and that in your message to Parliament, by which measure your troops of the line in Ireland or elsewhere might become disposable; and how we are to make out 150,000 men, or even the 60,000 of the defensive part of the treaty of Chaumont, appears not to have been considered.

If you could let me have 40,000 good British infantry, besides those you insist upon having in garrisons, the proportion settled by treaty that you are to furnish of cavalry, that is to say, the eighth of 150,000 men, including in both the old German Legion, and 150 pieces of British field artillery fully horsed, I should be satisfied, and take my chance for the rest, and engage that we would play our part in the game. But, as it is, we are in a bad way.

I beg that your Lordship will take this proposition into consideration. I beg you also to send here the Waggon train, and all the spring waggons for the carriage of sick and wounded; and that you will ask Lord Mulgrave to send here, in addition to the ordnance above mentioned fully horsed, 200 musket ball cartridge carts at present, and as many more hereafter; and an intrenching tool cart for each battalion of infantry, and 200 more for the corps of Engineers, and the whole corps of Sappers and Miners. It would be also desirable that we should have the whole Staff corps. I request your Lordship likewise to mention to Lord Mulgrave that it is desirable that measures should be taken to horse the 40 pontoons already here, and that 40 more should be sent out immediately, fully horsed. Without these equipments, military operations are out of the question.[1]

Having set out his requirements, Wellington began to organise all around him with his usual energy, and despite the size of the army under his control, and regardless of what he had just told Bathurst, the Duke began to consider attacking Paris before Napoleon had fully re-established himself. He explained his plans on 10 April to the Earl of Clancarty, who was both a Dutch and an Irish peer, who had taken over from Wellington at the Congress of Vienna.

I went to Ghent on the day before yesterday to pay my respects to the King of France, and I returned yesterday, having acquired there some information with which it is desirable that the ministers of the Allied Powers should be made acquainted.

It appears certain, from all accounts, that the great majority of the population in France are decidedly adverse to Buonaparte, and that many General and other officers, the whole of the National Guard, and even some of the regiments of the line, have remained faithful to the King. The National Guards and population of all the fortified towns on this frontier are in favor of His Majesty, and hopes are entertained of being able to get possession of some towns, of which Dunkirk is particularly mentioned as one.

35,000 men are stated to be in arms in the West, under the directions of the Duc de Bourbon; and the Duc d'Angoulême is in the South, at or near Nismes, where he is making some progress in organising a large force. The Duchesse d'Angoulême has certainly been obliged to quit Bordeaux. It would appear that, notwithstanding what is stated in the Paris newspapers regarding the defeat of the force under the Due d'Angoulême, it still gives some uneasiness to Buonaparte's government; as a person employed by me, who left Paris on Wednesday last, the 5th, states that all the troops of the line in and about Paris broke up on the preceding day, and marched on the road towards Fontainebleau.

I enclose the report made by this person; and I likewise enclose a memoir given to me by the Duc de Feltre, regarding the state and distribution of the French forces. In my opinion, this memoir gives an erroneous idea of their strength. I am certain the regiments of infantry have more than 1000 men each. Those which I saw last autumn at Paris, before they were completed to the peace establishment, had more than that number; I should say 1200 men on an average; and I should imagine they cannot now have fewer than 2000 each regiment. I believe the account of the cavalry, artillery, &c., to be correct.

With this information before them, the ministers of the Allied Powers, and the august Sovereigns, will see how important it is that no time should be lost in commencing our offensive operations. This point is so clear, that it would be a useless waste of your time and mine to discuss it; but there is a period approaching, before which it is desirable that our forces should enter France, and that France should see what she has to expect from the government of the usurper.

He has called together for the 15th May, what he denominates 'An 'l' Assemblée du Champ de Mai,' and it must be expected that his means and resources will be thereby considerably augmented, particularly in men; which augmentation, owing to the general detestation of his government, the resistance to it in some parts of the country, and the necessity under which he labors to employ his troops to overcome that resistance, he cannot obtain in any other manner.

It remains then to be seen with what force the Allies can commence their offensive operations on the 1st May.

The British, Hanoverian, and Dutch Corps will at that period consist of about 60,000 men, of which about 9000 will be cavalry; and not reckoning the contingents of Saxony, Brunswick, Oldenburg, Nassau, and the Hanse towns, eventually destined to join this army. Towards the latter end of April, the Prussian army between the Rhine and the Meuse will consist of 63,000 men, as appears by a letter from the Earl Cathcart of the 1st inst.; and there will be on the Upper Rhine an Austro-Bavarian corps, according to the same authority, at the same period of time, consisting of about 146,000 men; so that at the end of April the Allies could enter France with 270,000 men.

As well as I can recollect, the Russian troops will then begin to arrive on the Mayn; and it appears by Lord Cathcart's report that, by the middle of May, the Prussian army will be augmented to 156,000; and the contingents above referred to, probably to the amount of 30,000 men, and other reinforcements from England, &c., probably to the amount of 10,000 more, will have arrived in this country.

It remains then to be considered whether it will not be expedient to commence our operations on the 1st May, considering the relative force of the two contending parties at that period, rather than wait till the middle of May, and thus give to Buonaparte the advantages which he will certainly derive from the 'Assemble du Champ de Mai.'[2]

The assembly of the Champ de Mai that Wellington referred to was a form of national gathering in which Napoleon was formally adopted by the people and where he re-distributed the Eagles to each regiment of the Army and the National Guard. This latter act signified the dissolution of the Bourbon forces and the re-establishment of the Napoleonic army.[3]

Napoleon once famously said that 'it is with baubles that men are led' and the whole event was conducted with the usual Napoleonic pageantry and drama, the Emperor himself sitting on his throne dressed in Imperial robes:

Soldiers of the National Guard of the Empire! Soldiers of the land and sea forces! To your hands I confide the Imperial Eagle with the National Colours. Swear to defend it with the sacrifice of your blood, against the enemies of France, and of this throne. Swear that it shall always be your rallying signal.

Predictably, the soldiers responded with 'We swear it.' Napoleon then went to another gilded throne on the Champs de Mars, a large public green space in Paris, to actually hand over the Eagles:

> Soldiers of the National Guard of Paris! Soldiers of the Imperial Guard! I confide to you the National Eagles, and the National Colours. You swear to perish, if necessary, in defending them against the enemies of the country and the throne.

Once again the troops shouted out their allegiance. Drums then rolled to quieten the excited soldiers. Napoleon then continued:

> You swear never to acknowledge any other rallying sign. You soldiers of the National Guard of Paris swear never to suffer foreigners again to pollute by their presence the capital of this great nation![4]

After more vocal demonstrations of their support for Napoleon, the solders marched past their Emperor. Despite this display of martial might, Napoleon claimed that he wanted the position of a constitutional monarch, declaring that, 'I am growing old. The repose of a constitutional king may suit me. It will more surely suit my son.' In declaring that he was no longer interested in wars and conquests, he said, 'Can one be as fat as I am and have ambition?'[5] He wrote to Viscount Castlereagh, the British Foreign Secretary, stating that he had,

> No other wish, than ... the blessings of a happy tranquillity. It is to the duration of peace that the Emperor looks forward for the accomplishment of his noblest intentions. With a disposition to respect the rights of other nations, his Majesty has the pleasing hope, that those of the French nation will remain inviolate.[6]

Napoleon, though, would not be allowed his happy tranquillity and he knew only too well that if he wanted peace he had to plan for war. Wellington was making his own plans, especially as he had been told that he was to be given supreme command of all the Allied armies in Belgium.

The decision to increase the number of troops for the coming conflict was debated in Parliament and, perhaps surprisingly, it met with a degree of opposition. Samuel Whitbread was against a 'fresh crusade for the purpose of determining who should fill the throne of France'. Sir Francis Burdett argued that if Napoleon was 'the French people's choice', Britain had no right to interfere and that an invasion of France was 'an unjustifiable and ruinous enterprise'. Castlereagh put the Government's case for intervention:

> It might be thought that an armed peace would be preferable to a state of war, but the danger ought fairly to be looked at: and, knowing that good faith was opposite to the system of the [Napoleonic] party to be treated with, knowing that the rule of his conduct was self-interest, regardless of every other consideration, whatever decision they came to, must rest on the principle of power, and not on that of reliance on the man.

Britain was justified, Whitbread declared, 'in holding Buonaparté out as an object of terror, and in endeavouring, by all legitimate means, to destroy and extinguish his power'.[7]

When all was said and done, when the House divided, 273 were in favour of deposing Napoleon and seventy-two against.

To help the Duke in extinguishing Napoleon's power, as many troops as could be spared were despatched to Belgium from the UK, including the Household Cavalry and a large number of other cavalry and infantry regiments including the 23rd Regiment of Foot, otherwise known as the Royal Welch Fusiliers. Amongst their number was Drummer Richard Bentinck, speaking in the third person to an interviewer:

> They landed at Ostend, the first Regiment at the rendezvous. After one day's delay they proceeded by canal to the ancient city of Bruges, remained there for about a week and then, making room for troops that by this time were rapidly coming up, they pushed on to Ghent. They were then overtaken by the 51st Regiment, whom they then kept company with for a fortnight, before marching rapidly on up the country. They found the inhabitants were kindly disposed and were well treated by them.[8]

Captain Cavalié Mercer's troop of the Royal Horse Artillery was one the units which were ordered to join Wellington's force:

> On the 8th of April, the post brought our order to march forthwith to Harwich, there to embark for Ostend – an order received with unfeigned joy by officers and men, all eager to plunge into danger and bloodshed, all hoping to obtain glory and distinction.
>
> On the morning of the 9th, the troop paraded at half-past seven o'clock with as much regularity and as quietly as if only going to a

field-day; not a man either absent or intoxicated, and every part of the guns and appointments in the most perfect order. At eight, the hour named in orders, we marched off the parade.[9]

Captain Digby of the 7th Foot was an aide-de-camp to General Hill who was to take command of the Anglo-Dutch II Corps. He noted the following on his arrival at Ostend on 31 March:

We arrived here this evening at 5 o'clock ... The whole town was in confusion from the number of English troops lately disembarked, all of whom, true to their English nature, were wandering about with their hands in their pockets, and their eyes and mouths wide open, staring at the wonderful sight of a few dozen heavy stupid Flemmings.[10]

Despite the transporting of such troops, Wellington was far from impressed – as he made clear in a letter to Lieutenant General Charles Stewart on 8 May:

I have got an infamous army, very weak and ill equipped, and a very inexperienced Staff. In my opinion they are doing nothing in England. They have not raised a man; they have not called out the militia either in England or Ireland; are unable to send me anything; and they have not sent a message to Parliament about the money. The war spirit is therefore evaporating as I am informed.[11]

Happy or not with the force at his disposal, Wellington had already begun to consider how his troops would be organised. This was relayed to key individuals, including the Earl of Clancarty:

H.R.H. the Prince Regent having appointed Field Marshal the Duke of Wellington to be Commander of His Majesty's forces on the continent of Europe, all reports are in future to be made to his Grace ... It being desirable to amalgamate the two armies, Anglo-Hanoverian, and that of the Netherlands, in order that the troops which are to act together may be accustomed to each other, and that the whole consolidated force may with facility move in one uniform manner, having one great object in view:

The infantry and artillery, therefore, of the allied armies, will for the present be divided into two great corps; the first of which will be under the orders of H.R.H. the Prince of Orange, and the second under the command of Lieut. Gen. Lord Hill.

The 1st corps will be composed of the troops Anglo-Hanoverian, as follows, viz.: The 1st and 3d divisions of infantry, with the artillery attached to them, and the following troops of the Netherlands, viz., the 2d and 3d divisions of the army of the Netherlands, with a battery of foot artillery, and a battery of horse artillery, and the division of cavalry of the Netherlands. The 2d corps will be composed of the troops Anglo-Hanoverian, as follows, viz.: The 2d and 4th divisions of infantry, with the artillery attached to them, and the 2d brigade of cavalry of the King's German Legion, and the troops of the Netherlands as follows, viz., the Indian brigade and the 1st division, with a battery of foot artillery, and a battery of horse artillery. H.R.H. Prince Frederick of Orange will command the troops attached to H.R.H. the Prince of Orange, and His Royal Highness will have the goodness to make arrangements for attaching to the 2d corps such Staff officers as may be necessary.

Notwithstanding this amalgamation, everything which regards the discipline of the officers and soldiers of each nation, the provisioning, the clothing, the equipping, the means of transport, &c. &c., will be under the direction of the officers, civil and military, of each nation. The General commanding each *corps d'armée* will give orders for all other matters.[12]

As soon as he had notified the respective commanders of the nature of his reorganisation, Wellington set out his plans for the invasion of France, with his intention of pre-empting any moves made by Napoleon, spelling out these in a memorandum, once again to the Earl of Clancarty:

The object of the operations … to be undertaken by the corps of the Allies, which will probably be assembled in Flanders and on the Rhine in the end of the month of April, is, that by their rapidity they might be beforehand with the plans and measures of Buonaparte. His power now rests upon no foundation but the army; and if we can introduce into the country such a force as is capable either to defeat the army in the field, or to keep it in check, so that the various parties interested in the defeat of Buonaparte's views may have the power of acting, our object will be accomplished. The Allies have no views of conquest; there is no territory which requires in particular to be covered by the course of their operations; their object is to defeat the army, and to destroy the power of one individual; and the only military points to be considered are:

1st; To throw into France, at the earliest possible period, the largest body of men that can be assembled:

2dly; To perform this operation in such a manner that it can be supported by the forces of the Allies, which are known to be following immediately:

3dly; That the troops which shall enter France shall be secure of a retreat upon the supporting armies, in case of misfortune. The troops to be employed in this operation should be the allied British, Hanoverian, and Dutch troops, under the command of the Duke of Wellington; the Prussian troops, as reinforced, under the command of Comte Gneisenau; the allied Austrian, Bavarian, Wurtemberg, and Baden troops, to be assembled on the Upper Rhine, under Prince Schwarzenberg. The two former should enter France between the Sambre and the Meuse; the Duke of Wellington endeavoring to get possession of Maubeuge, or, at all events, of Avesnes; and Gen. Gneisenau directing his march upon Rocroy and Chimay. Luxembourg; and, while his left should observe the French fortresses of Longwy, Thionville, and Metz, he should possess himself of the forts of Sedan, Stenay, and Dun, and cross the Meuse. The first object would then be accomplished, and we should have in France a larger body of troops than it is probable the enemy can assemble.

It is expected that the British and Dutch army would be followed in the course of a fortnight by about 40,000 men, and the Prussian army in the same period by 90,000 men; and that the allied Austrian and Bavarian army would be followed by a Russian army of 180,000. Supposing, then, that the enemy should have the facility of attacking the line of communication of the English, Hanoverian, and Dutch army, by Maubeuge, and that of the allied Austrian army from their fortresses on the Upper Moselle and Upper Meuse, they could not prevent the junction of those troops. It must, besides, be observed, that the enemy could not venture to leave their fortresses entirely without garrisons of troops of the line, on account of the disgust which the usurpation of Buonaparte has occasioned universally; and the operations upon our communications will therefore necessarily be carried on by a diminished body of troops.

However inconvenient, then, they may be to those troops which will have advanced, they can neither prevent the junction of the armies which will be following the first that will enter France, nor can they prevent the retreat of these upon those which are moving to their support. According to this scheme, then, we should have in the centre of France a body of above 200,000 men, to be followed up by nearly 300,000 more, and their operations would be directed upon Paris, between the Meuse and the Oise.[13]

From the above it would seem Wellington still believed that, despite the remarkable nature of his return to power, Napoleon did not command the support of the French people. That view was about to change, as he told the Earl of Clancary the following day:

> I now enclose the plan according to which I conceived it possible to carry on our operations against the enemy with the force which the Allies would have at their disposal for that purpose in the latter end of April and beginning of May. Since I wrote to your Lordship, however, some important events have occurred to increase it at an early period. You will see, by the enclosed papers, that ... Buonaparte, besides having called for the soldiers recently discharged, amounting, as I understand, to about 127,000, of which 100,000 may be deemed immediately disposable, has organised 200 battalions of grenadiers of the National Guards. I imagine that the latter will not be a very formidable force; but still numbers were too nearly equal.[14]

It was far from being all work and no play though for Wellington and the British soldiers stationed in Brussels. Cricket matches became a frequent distraction for the troops, prompted by the Duke of Richmond, who commanded a reserve force at Brussels and was a keen cricketer and the man who formed the MCC. There were also parades and reviews as well as regular horse races, but with a large part of London Society having followed its aristocratic officers to Brussels the Belgian city was alive in the evenings with great social events, as Captain Digby Mackworth wrote on 27 May:

> Lord Wellington gave a grand ball yesterday at which all the principal people in Brussels were present, a most magnificent supper was prepared and the gardens so well illuminated as almost to resemble day. The Duke himself danced and always with the same person, a Lady Caroline Webster to whom he paid so much attention that scandal who is supreme Goddess here, began to whisper all sorts of stories.[15]

Wellington's behaviour was the subject of much interest and intrigue amongst the social elite, as Lady Caroline Capel wrote:

> Balls are going on here as if we had had none for a year. Nothing ever was so fine or so magnificent as the review of English cavalry 3 days ago ... The Duke of Wellington has not improved the morality of our

society, as he has given several things & makes a point of asking all of the ladies of loose character. Everyone was surprised at seeing Lady John Campbell at his house and one of his staff told me it had been represented to him her not being received for that her Character was more than suspicious. 'Is it, by God,' said he, 'then I will go and ask her myself.' Upon which he immediately took his hat and went out for the purpose.[16]

There was a popular 'dark walk' close to the Parc de Bruxelles, the latter being a city park in the centre of the city:

There his Grace of Wellington is sometimes to be seen with a fair lady under his arm. He generally dresses in plain clothes, to the astonishment of all the foreign officers. He is said to be as successful in the fields of Idalia as in those of Bellona, and the ladies whom he honours with his attentions suffer not a little in their reputation.[17]

Clearly concerned less with Brussels gossip than with how many troops Napoleon was raising, Wellington sought to bring every soldier he could into the field to crush the Emperor before the French forces became too formidable. He knew, however, that despite his rapidly growing strength Napoleon did not have the resources to fight on more than one front and so Wellington urged the Portuguese Prince Regent to open up a second front in the south. The following was sent to H.R.H. the Prince Regent of Portugal from Brussels on 16 April:

Your Royal Highness will have learned that I signed, on the 25th March last, with the Plenipotentiaries of Austria, Russia, and Prussia, as the Plenipotentiary of His Majesty, a treaty of alliance and co-operation, applicable to the circumstances of the moment in Europe, occasioned by the return of Buonaparte to France, and of the usurpation of the supreme power in that country. All the Powers of Europe are invited to accede to that treaty; and I imagine that the Plenipotentiaries of your Royal Highness consider themselves authorised to accede to it on the part of your Royal Highness. The object of the treaty is to put in operation against Buonaparte the largest force which the contracting or acceding parties can bring into the field; and that upon which I wish to trouble your Royal Highness is the seat to be chosen for the operations of your Royal Highness' troops.

The natural seat for their operations would be the frontiers of Spain; but I am very apprehensive that the financial resources of His

Catholic Majesty are not of a nature, nor in a situation, to enable him to equip and maintain an army to co-operate actively with that of your Royal Highness; and yet, without that co-operation, and the assistance which your Royal Highness would expect to derive from the country, it does not appear that your Royal Highness' army could carry on their operations with their accustomed credit in that quarter. Under these circumstances, it has appeared to me that it would be expedient, and I have recommended to your Royal Highness' ministers at Vienna, and have requested His Majesty's ministers to recommend to the Regency at Lisbon, that your Royal Highness' troops should be employed with the allied army assembling in Flanders, and destined to act, under my command, against the common enemy.

I need not point out to your Royal Highness' penetration the advantages to your Royal Highness' reputation of appearing in the field in this part of Europe; but as your troops cannot serve actively in the natural seat for their operations, and they will serve here with their old companions and under their old commanders, it appears to me that this measure is to be recommended, if only as one of military expediency. I trust, then, that your Royal Highness will approve of my having recommended it to your ministers and to the Regency.[18]

Until he was in a position to mount an offensive into France, and with the likelihood that Napoleon would seize the initiative and take the offensive before the Allied armies were fully deployed, Wellington had to look to the defence of Belgium. This was explained to H.R.H. the Prince of Orange, on 17 April:

As I passed Ghent yesterday, I went to look at the works which had been executed by your Royal Highness' orders at the Tournay gate, which are nearly completed, and perfectly answer the purpose for which they were intended. In order, however, to complete the scheme at Ghent, it would be necessary to strengthen the Bruges gate, and to repair the works of the citadel; and I should then consider Ghent quite secure from any attack likely to be made upon it, under existing circumstances.

Adverting to the King's objections to occupy any of these works, and feeling that I cannot occupy them with the troops under my command with justice to the King's Allies, who have really but a secondary interest to that of His Majesty in their occupation, I have not thought it proper to give the engineer any directions regarding the continuance of the works at Ghent; and I beg your Royal Highness to make me acquainted with His Majesty's wishes upon that point, and that you will also take His Majesty's pleasure respecting the mode of defending the works already executed at Ghent.

His Majesty should, in my opinion, consider that he has but a small and very young army to oppose to possibly a numerous and well disciplined one; and that he has a large extent of country to cover but lately brought under His Majesty's government, whose inhabitants are supposed to be very well disposed towards it. I know of no mode so well calculated for the defence of such a country by such an army, as works well chosen.

In the supposition that the Allies will enter France, including those more immediately allied to His Majesty, and his own army under your Royal Highness, it must be expected that the enemy will keep his fortresses on the frontier well garrisoned. If these garrisons should collect to the amount only of 15,000 men, after the Allies shall have passed them, and should make an irruption into His Majesty's dominions (an event by no means improbable), will His Majesty, under existing circumstances, have in his power the means of stopping them at least short of Bruxelles? In my opinion, certainly not, unless he should occupy Ghent, Tournay, Ath, and Mons. There is no danger of any of these points being seriously attacked; and they will be so strong that, unless seriously attacked, they cannot be carried; and there is no chance that such an enemy as I have supposed may make an irruption into the country, will venture to pass them.

This is my decided opinion regarding these posts, and it rests with His Majesty to occupy them or not, as he may think proper. As far as the King's Allies will be concerned, I shall take measures to render it a matter of total indifference to their particular interests, whether the enemy does or does not occupy Bruxelles as soon as we shall have advanced.[19]

One of Wellington's principal concerns was with the lack of artillery available to him, especially being aware that Napoleon, an ex-artilleryman, always sought to employ more guns than his opponents, as indeed would be the case at Waterloo. He wrote on this subject to the Earl of Bathurst, Secretary of State for War and the Colonies, on 21 April:

I have received a letter from Lord Mulgrave of the 15th, from which I see that, after doing all he can for us, we shall have only 84 pieces of artillery equipped, instead of 150, for which I asked. We have now only 72, including German artillery, 30 pieces, leaving 42 as the number which the British artillery can supply!

Then for the musket ball cartridge carts, intrenching tools, carts for the engineers, pontoons, and the heavy artillery to move with the army, I must call upon the Commissariat for horses. We shall easily purchase the number of horses required at the rate of 25 guineas each, which money for the exchange will cost the country about 30 guineas; but I had already stopped the purchase because we had no drivers to take care of them. I conclude that, in consequence of the reduction, they can no more furnish drivers than they can horses; and, that being the case, I beg leave to point out to your Lordship that, as the drivers of the country cannot be depended upon, and as at all events I have not time to form them, I have no other means of providing for this absolutely necessary service, than to take soldiers from the British infantry to perform it, and that very badly. If you will look at our returns, you will see how little able we are to afford a soldier to take care of each pair of horse we require.

Our demand for horses for the whole equipments demanded was above 6000, of which above 4000 deficient. As the equipment is reduced to the amount of half the field artillery, which would have required about 1200 horses to draw them, we shall have about 2800 horses to purchase, for which we shall want 1400 soldiers to take care of them, or about four regiments of infantry of their present strength. I hope that government will be able to adopt some measures to relieve us from this demand. The only thing I can suggest is, to send us dismounted dragoons to perform this service. In the last war I used the Portuguese dismounted dragoons to perform the service of the artillery, and I now recommend that some dismounted dragoons may be sent, with a proportion of officers and non-commissioned officers, to take charge of them.

I assure your Lordship that the demand which I have made of field artillery is excessively small. The Prussian corps on the Meuse of 40,000 men has with it 200 pieces of cannon; and you will see by reference to Prince Hardenberg's return of the Prussian army that they take into the field nearly 80 batteries, manned by 10,000 artillery. Their batteries are of 8 guns each, so that they will have about 600 pieces. They don't take this number for show or amusement; and, although it is impossible to grant my demand, I hope it will be admitted to be small.[20]

Wellington continued to press his Government with demands for more of everything, and to urge his allies to greater efforts, particularly as evidence was mounting that Napoleon was gathering his forces on France's border with Belgium. The following is a secret memorandum that he sent on 1 May to the Prince of Orange, and to his senior commanders, the Earl of Uxbridge, who commanded the cavalry and who was nominally Wellington's second-in-command, and to Lieutenant General Roland Hill, who commanded II Corps and was described by Wellington as his 'right hand':

1st; Having received reports that the Imperial guard had moved from Paris upon Beauvais, and a report having been for some days prevalent in the country that Buonaparte was about to visit the northern frontier, I deem it expedient to concentrate the cantonments of the troops, with a view to their early junction in case this country should be attacked, for which concentration the Quarter Master General now sends orders.

2d; In this case, the enemy's line of attack will be either between the Lys and the Scheldt, or between the Sambre and the Scheldt, or by both lines.

3d; In the first case, I should wish the troops of the 4th division to take up the bridge on the Scheldt, near Avelghem, and with the regiment of cavalry at Courtrai, to fall back upon Audenarde, which post they are to occupy, and to inundate the country in the neighbourhood.

4th; The garrison of Ghent are to inundate the country in the neighbourhood likewise, and that point is to be held at all events.

5th; The cavalry in observation between Menin and Fumes are to fall back upon Ostend, those between Menin and Tournay upon Tournay, and thence to join their regiments.

6th; The 1st, 2d, and 3d divisions of infantry are to be collected at the head quarters of the whole to be in readiness to march at a moment's notice.

7th; The troops of the Netherlands to be collected at Soignies and Nivelles.

8th; In case the attack should be made between the Sambre and the Scheldt, I propose to collect the British and Hanoverians at and in the neighbourhood of Enghien, and the army of the Low Countries at and in the neighbourhood of Soignies and Braine le Comte.

9th; In this case, the 2d and 3d divisions will collect at their respective head quarters, and gradually fall back towards Enghien with the cavalry of Col. Arentschildt's and the Hanoverian brigade.

10th; The garrisons of Mons and Tournay will stand fast; but that of Ath will be withdrawn, with the 2d division, if the works should not have been sufficiently advanced to render the place tenable against a coup de main.

11th; Gen. Sir W. Ponsonby's, Sir J. Vandeleur's, and Sir H.Vivian's brigades of cavalry will march upon Hal.

12th; The troops of the Low Countries will collect upon Soignies and Braine le Comte.

13th; The troops of the 4th division and the 2d hussars, after taking up the bridge at Avelghem, will fall back upon Audenarde, and there wait for further orders.

14th; In case of the attack being directed by both lines supposed, the troops of the 4th division and 2d hussars, and the garrison of Ghent, will act as directed in Nos. 3 and 4 of this memorandum; and the 2d and 3d divisions, and the cavalry, and the troops of the Low Countries, as directed in Nos. 8, 9, 10, 11, and 12.[21]

Wellington also wrote to Lieutenant General Sir William Stewart on 8 May, revealing both his hopes and his fears:

I have received your letters of the 28th April, for which I am very much obliged to you; and I have perused with the greatest attention the memorandum which you enclosed. I saw Clarke [the Duc de Feltre, the French Minister of War under Louis] yesterday, and he told me that a person of the War Office, upon whom he could depend, had informed him that on the 30th April the enemy's regular army amounted to 130,000 men; and the Guard to 25,000; the gendarmerie and national guards raised, and expected to be raised, would make it 280,000. This was the utmost expected.

Beurnonville, who ought to know, told me this day that we ought to reckon that the enemy had an effective force of 200,000 men. He says the King had 155,000 when he quitted Paris, and that he had granted above 100,000 *congés*, which had been called in; but that not above half could be reckoned upon as likely to join. I understand, likewise, that there were above 100,000 deserters wandering about France.

In reference to these different statements, I beg you to observe that Clarke speaks from positive information; Beurnonville from conjecture. According to Clarke's account, the army gained in strength only 3000 men in the last 15 days; but then it must be observed, that the Guard have gained about 19,000, being the difference between 6000, which they were, and 25,000, which they are now.

In respect to periods of commencing operations, you will have seen that I had adopted the opinion that it was necessary to wait for more troops, as far back as the 13th April. After, however, that we shall have waited a sufficient time to collect a force, and to satisfy military men that their force is what it ought to be to enable them to accomplish the object in view, the period of attack becomes a political question, upon which there can be no difference of opinion. Every day's experience convinces me that we ought not to lose a moment which could be spared.

I say nothing about our defensive operations, because I am inclined to believe that Blücher [*Generalfeldmarschall* Gebhard Leberecht von Blücher, Commander of the Prussian Army in the West] and I are so well united, and so strong, that the enemy cannot do us much mischief. I am at the advanced post of the whole; the greatest part of the enemy's force is in my front; and, if I am satisfied, others need be under no apprehension. In regard to offensive operations, my opinion is, that, however strong we shall be in reference to the enemy, we should not extend ourselves farther than is absolutely necessary in order to facilitate the subsistence of the troops. I don't approve of an extension from the Channel to the Alps; and I am convinced that it will be found not only fatal, but that the troops at such a distance on the left of our line will be entirely out of the line of the operations.

We are now, or shall be shortly, placed on the French frontier in the form of an echelon, of which the right, placed here, is the most advanced of the echelon, and the left, upon the Upper Rhine, is the most retired.

Paris is our object, and the greatest force and greatest military difficulties are opposed to the movements of the right, which is the most advanced part of our general line. Indeed, such force and difficulties are opposed to us in this part, that I should think that Blucher and I cannot move till the movements of others of the allied corps shall have relieved us from part of the enemy's force opposed to us. Then, it must be observed that we cannot be relieved by movements through Luxembourg.

In my opinion, then, the movement of the Allies should begin with the left, which should cross the Rhine between Basle and Strasbourg. The centre collected upon the Sarre should cross the Meuse on the day the left should be expected to be at Langres. If these movements should not relieve the right, they should be continued; that is to say, the left should continue its movement on both banks of the Marne, while the centre should cross the Aisne; and the distance between the two bodies, and between each and Paris, should be shortened daily.

But this last hypothesis is not probable: the enemy would certainly move from this front upon the earliest alarm of the movements on the Upper Rhine; and the moment he did move, or that the operation should be practicable, Blücher's corps and mine should move forward, and the former make the siege of Givet, the latter of Maubeuge; and the former likewise to aid the movement of the centre across the Meuse.

If the enemy should fall upon the centre, it should either retire upon Luxembourg or fight, according to the relative strength; and in either case Blücher should act upon the enemy's communication upon the Aisne.

But the most probable result of these first movements would be the concentration of the enemy's forces upon the Aisne; and accordingly we hear of the fortifications of Soissons and Laon, of an entrenched camp at Beauvais, etc. etc. We must, in this case, after the first operation, throw our whole left across the Marne, and strengthen it if necessary from the centre, and let it march upon Paris, between the Seine and the Marne, while the right and the centre should either attack the enemy's position upon the Aisne, or endeavor to turn its left; or the whole should cooperate in one general attack upon the enemy's position.

I come now to consider the strength required for these operations. The greatest strength the enemy is supposed to have is 200,000 effective men, besides national guards for his garrisons. Of this number it can hardly be believed that he can bring 150,000 to bear upon any one point.

Upon this statement let our proceedings be founded. Let us have 150,000 men upon the left, and 150,000 men upon the right; and all the rest, whatever they may be, in the centre; or after a sufficient centre is formed, let the remainder be in reserve for the right, left, or centre, as may be most convenient for their march and subsistence, and I will engage for the result, as they may be thrown where we please. Let us begin when we shall have 450,000 men. Before the Austrians upon the left shall be at Langres, the Russians will have passed the Rhine, and the whole Prussian army will be in line.

These are my general ideas ... Mind, when I think of the siege of Givet and Maubeuge, I don't mean by the whole of the two armies of the right, but to be carried on by detachments from them. The centre should seize Sedan, which is not strong or garrisoned, and observe Longwy, Thionville, and Metz. The left will have to observe Huningue and the fortresses in Alsace.

In regard to the force in Piedmont, I confess that I wish that the whole Austrian army in Italy was actively employed against Murat, with the exception of the garrisons. Murat must be destroyed early, or he will hang heavily upon us. If any force should be employed from

Piedmont, its operations should be separate from those of the great confederacy. They cannot be connected without disconnecting those of what I have hitherto considered the left from the remainder of our great line, however they may be calculated to aid that left, particularly by being directed upon Chambery, or by keeping that post in check. Their basis is, however, different, and cannot easily be made otherwise.

These opinions are for yourself; God knows whether they can be acted upon, or whether the Allies will allow their forces to be divided as I suppose; and particularly whether the Prussians will act in two corps, one under Blucher here, and another from Luxembourg with the centre; or whether the other Allies will like to commence till the whole Russian army is *en mesure*. But I am convinced that what I have proposed is so clearly the plan of operations, that I don't doubt it will be adopted, with but little variation.[22]

Wellington refers here to Joachim Murat, Napoleon's brother-in-law, who was the King of Naples. Napoleon knew that he could count on Murat's support and before the Emperor had left Elba he had warned Murat to prepare for war, but not to take any action until Napoleon instructed him. The small and unreliable Neapolitan Army had little fighting value, but it could well play an important role in the coming conflict. Italy was in Austria's sphere of influence and if Murat took to the field the Austrians would have no choice but to despatch an army to deal with the Neapolitans. Though Murat was certain to eventually be overwhelmed, he would be able to tie down the Austrians during the initial, and most important, stages of the coming war

Murat, always headstrong and unpredictable, did not follow Napoleon's instructions. As soon as he heard that the Emperor had landed in France he declared war on the Allied Powers. As soon as his army was ready for operations he sent a detachment of some 10,000 to 12,000 men to take Rome whilst he personally led his main force of around 30,000 men up the Adriatic coast.

Taking the Austrians by surprise, Murat advanced northwards, and seized Bologna before uniting his whole force on an assault upon the powerful fortress-city of Mantua. Napoleon needed Murat to stay in the field as long as he was able in order to keep as many Austrian troops occupied as possible. Throwing his army against the strongest fortification in northern Italy was exactly the opposite of what Napoleon wanted.

Predictably, Murat failed to take Mantua and he had to fall back. On 2 May he met the Austrians at Bianchi. In a two-day battle the

Neapolitans were defeated, losing approximately 4,000 men. Murat's army broke up in disarray, with thousands of his soldiers deserting. Napoleon was furious at Murat's stupidity and he refused to meet him or give him a command in the French Army. Napoleon had lost his only ally. He stood alone against the combined might of Europe.[23]

The following note was sent on 16 May to Lieutenant Colonel Sir Henry Harding who had served with Wellington in the Peninsular War and who was given command of a brigade for the coming campaign:

> I enclose a memorandum which I have drawn from intelligence I have recently received, from which the Marshal will see the strength and disposition of the French army; and that with the 1st, 2d, 3d, and 6th corps, and the Guard, and the 3d division of cavalry of reserve, we have a good lot of them in our front. I should think not less than 110,000 men.
>
> I heard yesterday that Vandamme's corps had moved to its left, and had brought its right upon Givet. There are a great number of troops about Maubeuge, Avesnes, &c.
>
> I heard also that measures had been taken to move the Guard from Paris to Maubeuge in forty-eight hours; and that an aide de camp of the Emperor was there on the 12th. It is reported, also, that Soult has accepted the office of Major General, which is important, as it will induce many officers to serve Buonaparte; and I believe it to be true, as I see that Mortier is employed.[24]

Wellington was surprisingly accurate with his assessment of the strength of Napoleon's *l'armée du Nord*. Altogether, this amounted to 83,753 infantry, 20,959 cavalry and 11,412 artillery, engineers, and wagon-train personnel. Wellington mentions Marshal Mortier, duc de Trévise, who was given command of the newly-raised Young Guard.[25]

Wellington may well have been well informed, but there was very little information being leaked to the newspapers, as the *Haarlem Courant*, of 20 May would seem to show:

> The main body of the French force that was about Valenciennes has marched, according to a telegraphic dispatch, in three columns of 10,000 men each, towards the Maese, taking the direction of Givet. This movement, the object of which it is hard to conceive, has been executed with remarkable precipitation. The Prussian army on the Meuse has again been reinforced by a great many troops, particularly cavalry. Charleroi and the Sambre are covered with a powerful force. The English and Hanoverians continue to concentrate their army on

the frontiers. The French have broken down all the bridges on the whole line from Donay to Gravelines.

Wellington was anxious that with Belgium having until the previous year been under French control, there would be very many French sympathizers across the country who would try to pass on intelligence concerning the nature and disposition of the Anglo-Dutch forces to Napoleon. With all the appearances being that Napoleon was preparing to take the offensive into Belgium, Wellington issued strict instructions concerning border security. Under the heading 'The Adjutant-General to Major-General Dörnberg and Officers commanding at Ypres, Tournay, and Nieuport', these were dated 20th May, 1815:

> I am commanded by the Duke of Wellington to desire that you will take the most effectual means in your power to prevent all communications between this country and France on the line of the frontier, excepting under the following regulations: viz., That no person shall be permitted to pass from this country into France without a passport signed by the Field Marshal, or by Monsieur de Nagell, or Baron Capellan. Should any persons attempt to pass from France into this country, you will be pleased to cause them to be arrested and conveyed under escort to Brussels to be delivered over to the Mayor. You will, at the same time, have the goodness to report to me, for the information of the Commander of the Forces, the names and qualities of the persons arrested under this order.[26]

Tension was quickly mounting, as the following commentary which was printed in *The Times* of 12 June 1815 indicates:

> Every day may be expected to bring news of the actual commencement of hostilities. BUONAPARTE having at length put into action the machinery of the rebel government, has formally announced that he will soon put himself at the head of the army ... The report which was prevalent on Saturday, of an attempt to assassinate BUONAPARTE by a sort of infernal machine, turns out to be a very accident which befell a Saxon chemist, who accidentally exploded some fulminating powder near the Chamber of Representatives.

Wellington, however, presented a calm facade, as the Reverend Spencer Madan, tutor to the children of the Lennox family (the Duke and Duchess of Richmond), disclosed in a letter dated just one day after the above featured edition of *The Times*:

38

Though I have some pretty good reasons for supposing that hostilities will soon commence, yet no one would suppose it, judging by the Duke of Wellington. He appears to be thinking of anything else in the world, gives a ball every week, attends every party, partakes of every amusement that offers. [Yesterday] he took Lady Jane Lennox [daughter of the Duke and Duchess of Richmond] to Enghein for the cricket match, and brought her back at night, apparently having gone for no other object but to amuse her. At the time Bonaparte was said to be at Maubeuge, thirty or forty miles off.[27]

The Duke, of course, was fully aware that Napoleon might attack at any moment. That moment came just four weeks later and despite all the plans and preparations, he would be taken by surprise.

As late as 13 June, just two days before Napoleon launched his offensive, Wellington wrote to General Thomas Graham (later Lord Lynedoch):

There is nothing new here. We have reports of Bonaparte's joining the army and attacking us; but I have accounts from Paris of the 10th, on which day he was still there; and I judge from his speech to the Legislature that his departure was not likely to be immediate. I think we are now too strong for him here.[28]

The next few days would put Wellington's confidence to the test.

3

Advance to Contact

Wellington and Blücher were convinced that Napoleon was not going to wait for France to be invaded. They believed that the Emperor would try to seize the initiative, something that Wellington in particular wished to prevent, by attacking first. Just how close Wellington was to opening hostilities can be seen from a letter sent by the British Prime Minister, Lord Liverpool, to George Canning, who had been Foreign Secretary but who was at the time Ambassador to Portugal, on 13 June:

> We may now be in daily expectation of hearing that the Allied armies have entered France. The operations will probably begin on the upper Rhine, as the most distant point from Paris; but we know that the Duke of Wellington and Blücher are ready to move; and fortunately there subsists between them the most perfect union and cordiality.[1]

Napoleon, though, was already on the move, as documents named later as 'French Movements and previous Arrangements to the Battles of the 15th, 16th, 17th, and I8th of June', which were subsequently found in Napoleon's portfolio, reveal:

> June 11.—Monsieur Count Lavellette,—As I said in my speech this day, that I should depart this night, I wish you would look to it, that no post-horses be taken from the road by which I travel: that particular attention be paid to the persons to whom horses are given on the neighbouring roads, and that no courier, or *estaffette*, be sent off.
>
> Other letters, written this day, request Marshal Massena to take the command of the third and fourth divisions, and say, 'let Ney come if he wishes to be present at the first battle: he must be at Avesnes by the 13th, where my head quarters will be.'

Acquaint Marshal Sucht, that hostilities will commence on the 16th, and on that day to make himself master of Montmeillan.

I may be without anxiety about the city of Paris ...

June 11.—To the Minister of Marine.—I suppose that you have broken off all communication by sea, and that no person or packet boat dare to pass any more, under any pretence.

June 12.—Set off from Paris and slept at Laon.

June 13.—Slept at Avesnes ...

June 14th.—Slept at Beaumont. I shall advance to Charleroi, where the Prussian army is, which will occasion a battle, or the retreat of the enemy. The army is fine, and the weather pretty fair; the country perfectly well disposed. I shall write this evening, if the communications are to be made on the 16th, meantime we must prepare ...

To the Minister at War. — I hope to pass the Sambre to-morrow, the 16th. If the Prussians do not evacuate, we shall have a battle.[2]

Napoleon writes here about Marshal Ney, whose relationship with the Emperor had been ambivalent for some time. It had been Ney that had demanded Napoleon's abdication the previous year, informing Napoleon that the army would no longer fight. 'The army will obey me,' declared Ney. 'The army will not march.' Napoleon saw Ney's actions as nothing but betrayal and, since his return from exile, Napoleon had not involved Ney in any of his planning nor had he included his name in any of the despatches he had issued since the start of operations.

As it transpired Ney would soon join Napoleon and be given a position of considerable importance. It is also interesting to observe how accurate Napoleon was with regard to his prediction of a battle with the Prussians on the 16th.

The following 'Orders of March for *l'armée du Nord*' were issued from Beaumont, 'By Order of the Emperor, Marshal of the Empire and Major-General, Duke of Dalmatia', on 14 June 1815:

To-morrow, the 15th, at 2.30 a.m. General Vandamme's Light Cavalry Division will advance along the Charleroi road. Patrols will be sent out in every direction to reconnoitre the country, and to capture the enemy's advanced posts; each patrol will consist of not less than fifty men. Before marching off General Vandamme will make sure that the cavalry are provided with small-arms ammunition ...

At the same time Lieut.-General Pajol will parade the 1st Cavalry Corps, and will follow the advance of General Demon's Division; the latter is placed under General Pajol's orders. The divisions of the 1st

Cavalry Corps will furnish no detachments, the 3rd Division will furnish such as are necessary. General Demon's Horse Battery will follow, marching immediately behind the leading battalion of the III Infantry Corps, and consequently will come under General Vandamme's orders …

The Emperor will accompany the Advanced Guard on the Charleroi road. The Lieut.-Generals will take care to keep His Majesty informed of their various movements, and to transmit all information which they happen to collect.

They are warned that His Majesty intends to have passed the Sambre before noon, and to cross the whole army over to the left bank of that river.

The bridging train will be divided into two sections, the first section being subdivided into three parts, each consisting of 5 pontoons and 5 Advanced Guard boats, so as to throw 3 bridges over the Sambre. There will be a company of pontoon personnel accompanying each of these subdivisions. The first section will follow in rear of the Engineer Park, and after the III Corps. The second section will remain with the Artillery Reserve Park, in the baggage column, it will have with it the fourth company of the bridging train [personnel].

The Emperor's baggage, and that of the Headquarter Staff, will be collected and marched off at 10 a.m.; as soon as they have defiled, the Director-General of Transport will put in motion that of the Imperial Guard, followed in succession by that of the III and VI Corps; at the same time he will send orders to the baggage columns of the Cavalry Reserve to proceed in the direction already taken by the Cavalry.

The ambulances of the army will follow the Headquarters, and will march ahead of the baggage; but, in no case, will the baggage, or the Artillery Reserve Park, or the second section of the bridging train equipment, approach within 3 leagues of the army, without express orders from the Major-General, and they will only cross the Sambre when specially ordered to do so.

The Director-General of Transport will subdivide the baggage into divisions, each to be placed under an officer, so that anything required by Headquarters, or for the use of officers, can be detached.

The Commissariat-General will have collected in this column all the administrative baggage and transport vehicles, and their precise places in the column will be assigned.

Carriages which are delayed will go to the left, and will only be able to leave their allotted place under orders from the Director-General of Transport.

The Emperor commands that all transport vehicles found in Infantry, Cavalry, or Artillery columns are to be burned, as well as the vehicles in the baggage column which leave their allotted place and thus change the order of march, unless they have previously obtained special permission to do so from the Director-General of Transport.

For this purpose a detachment of 50 Military Police will be placed under the orders of the Director-General of Transport; and the latter officer is held personally responsible, as well as the officers of the Military Police and also the Military Police themselves, for the due execution of these arrangements on which the success of the campaign may depend.[3]

Here we have Napoleon's orders for the movement of his army from their concentration points in France up to and over the border into Belgium. His instructions call for *l'armée du Nord* to be across the Sambre and into Belgium before midday. It is notable that bridging equipment was provided in case the bridges over the river had been destroyed. Speed was essential if Napoleon was to take the allies by surprise which is why any unauthorised vehicles trying to join the marching columns would be burnt.

It is also of note that Soult, the Duke of Dalmatia, had accepted the position of Major-General under Napoleon. In other words, he had become the chief-of-staff and the man who would put into effect the orders of the Emperor.

Napoleon knew the power of words and that his men were inspired by visions of victory and *la gloire*. He also knew that his words as well as his deeds would be recorded for posterity. His address to his troops was therefore couched in phrases certain to rouse the men to great efforts whilst also justifying his decision to attack the allied nations. It was issued to his men on 14 June:

Behold the anniversary of Marengo and Friedland which has twice decided the destinies of Europe. It was then, as at Austerlitz, as at Wagram, that we were too generous to an enemy at our feet. We gave our easy faith to the protestations and oaths of those princes to whom we left their thrones. These same princes, having leagued amongst themselves, are now in arms against the independence of France. Let us march to give them the meeting, both they and we are still the same.

Soldiers, at Jena, against these same Prussians, we were one against three; and at Montmirail, one against six.

As many of you as have been prisoners amongst the English, relate to your comrades what you suffered in their prisons and hulks.

43

The Saxons, Belgians, and Hanoverians, and soldiers of the Confederation of the Rhine, lament that unhappy force which compels them to obey those princes who are the enemies of justice and liberty. They know the insatiable cupidity of this coalition. They know that these princes have already devoured twelve millions of Poles, twelve millions of Italians, a million of Saxons, and six millions of Belgians, and thus all the German states of the second order are their next destined prey.

Madmen! a moment of prosperity has blinded them. The oppression and humiliation of the French people are beyond their power; if they enter France, they will find in it only their grave.

Soldiers, we have marches to make, battles to give, and dangers to incur; but with constancy, discipline, and a resolution to conquer, the victory will be ours; and the glory and liberty of France will be reconquered.

For all Frenchman who have a heart, the moment is come to conquer or to die.[4]

As planned, *l'armée du Nord* began its move across the Sambre early on the morning of the 15th. Despite the care which Marshal Soult had taken with his orders of march, things did not go entirely according to plan.

Firstly, the horse of the officer carrying Soult's instructions to General Vandamme fell and broke its leg. This meant III Corps did not move off on time and in fact did not move until VI Corps, which had set off as arranged, bumped into Vandamme's men.

The delay that this caused led to Pajol's and Demon's (usually given as Domon) cavalry arriving at the River Sambre at Charleroi unsupported. There General von Ziethen's Prussian I Corps had barricaded the bridge and resisted tenaciously. The comte de la Bédoyère, who had become one of Napoleon's aides, wrote:

A corps of infantry, under General Ziethen, attempted to dispute the passage of the Sambre, but the fourth corps of chasseurs, supported by the ninth, broke it, sword in hand, and took three hundred prisoners. The sappers and miners of the guard, sent after the enemy, to repair the bridges, did not allow the latter time to destroy them, following as sharp shooters, and penetrating into the great square. The dauntless General Pajole soon arrived with his cavalry, and Charleroy was taken, when the inhabitants, rejoiced on once more seeing the French, saluted them with continued shouts of 'Long live the Emperor! France for ever!'[5]

II Corps, meanwhile, forced the river at Marchiennes, 'overthrowing every thing before it,' continued de la Bédoyère:

> The Prussians, however, rallied, and attempted to oppose some resistance; but General Reille broke them with his light cavalry, took two hundred prisoners, and killed or dispersed the rest. Beaten in every direction, they retired to the heights of Fleurus ... Napoleon reconnoitred the ground at a glance, and the French rushed on the Prussians at full gallop, when three squares of infantry, supported by several squadrons and artillery, sustained the shock with intrepidity.
>
> Wearied at such resistance, the Emperor ordered General Letort to charge with the dragoons of the guard, at the same moment Excelmans fell upon the left flank of the enemy; while the twentieth dragoons, commanded by Brigueville, rushed on the Prussians on one side, Letort attacking them on the other They were then broken and annihilated; the French, however, paid dearly for that victory, Letort being killed. That affair, though of little importance in its results, as it only cost the enemy five pieces of artillery, and three thousand men, killed and prisoners, produced the happiest effects on the French army.[6]

The crossing of the Sambre was achieved just after midday. Ziethen withdrew, pursued by Grouchy's Cavalry Corps. Finally the Prussians made a stand at Gilly. This news was relayed to Napoleon who was still at Charleroi, to which place Grouchy went to ask for infantry support. At the same time Ney rode up to Charleroi. Napoleon now had with him the two men to whom he would entrust his army:

> Bonjour Ney [said the Emperor]. I want you to take command of I and II Corps. I will give you besides, the light cavalry of my Guard, but do not make use of it. Tomorrow you will be joined by Kellermann's cuirassiers. Now go and drive away all the enemy along the Brussels road and take up a position at Quatre Bras and await further orders.[7]

Napoleon had decided to divide his army, with Ney pushing up the road to Brussels with I and II Corps, whilst he went with the rest of his force directly towards the Prussians. His aim was to hold back Wellington whilst he dealt with the Prussians.

As early as 09.00 hours Wellington received the first intimation that Napoleon had invaded. He took no action at that time. It was only at 15.00 hours, when a messenger from General Ziethen rode to General von Müffling, the Prussian liaison officer at Wellington's headquarters in Brussels, with more concrete information, that the Duke responded.

Wellington did not think that it was the main French army that was engaged with Ziethen and he continued to believe that Napoleon would try to cut his communications with the coast. Nevertheless, he accepted that the campaign had begun and, as he told Müffling, 'the departure of the troops is certain, and only the place of rendezvous remains uncertain, I will order all to be in readiness'.[8]

Wellington, therefore, through his Deputy Quartermaster-General, Sir William Howe De Lancey, issued the first of his orders to Uxbridge, Hill and the Prince of Orange, timed at 17.00 hours on 15 June 1815:

1. Gen. Dornberg's brigade and the Cumberland hussars to march this night upon Vilvorde.
2. Lord Uxbridge to collect his cavalry this night upon Ninhove, leaving the 2d hussars looking out between the Scheldt and the Lys.
3. The 1st division to remain as they are at Enghien, and all in readiness to march at a moment's notice.
4. The 2d division to collect this night at Ath and adjacents, and to be in readiness to march at a moment's notice.
5. The 3d division at Braine le Comte, the same.
6. The 4th division to be collected at Grammont, with the exception of the troops beyond the Scheldt, which are to be brought to Audenarde.
7. The 5th and 6th divisions in readiness at a moment's notice.
8. The brigade at Ghent to march to Bruxelles in the evening.
9. The Duke of Brunswick to collect to-night on the high road from Bruxelles to Vilvorde, the Nassau troops on the Louvain road, and both ready to march in the morning.
10. The Prince of Orange, who is now at Alava's, to be directed to collect at Nivelles the 2d and 3d divisions of the army of the Low Countries; and in case that point should have been attacked this day, to move the 3d division and 1st division upon Nivelles as soon as collected. This movement not to take place until it is quite certain that the enemy's attack is upon the Prussian right or our left.
11. Lord Hill to be directed to order Prince Frederick of Orange to occupy Audenarde with 500 men, and to collect the 1st division of the army of the Low Countries and the Indian brigade at Sotteghem, so as to be ready to march in the morning at daylight.
12. The reserve artillery, &c. to be in readiness to move at daylight.[9]

Nothing in these orders gave an indication of urgency and everything remained relatively calm in Brussels during the day. To the south-east, however, the French attack was developing, with Napoleon concentrating the right wing of his army against the Prussians at Gilly.

At 18.00 hours the French attack was delivered against Major-General von Pirch's II Corps and Major-General von Steinmetz's I Brigade of I Corps. Such was the strength of the French forces opposing the Prussians, it certainly appeared that it was not simply a diversion. It was important that the Anglo-Netherlands army moved up to support Blücher otherwise the allies would be defeated in detail, which was exactly what Napoleon hoped for. Further messages were consequently sent to Brussels to urge Wellington to commit his troops to supporting his allies.

Ahead of the left wing of *l'armée du Nord*, Lefebvre-Desnoëttes's Guard cavalry had been sent along the road towards Brussels with orders to occupy and hold the vital crossroads of Quatre Bras. He reached there around 18.30 hours, and reported back to Ney. His communication, written at Frasnes at 21.00 hours on 15 June 1815, was addressed 'To the Marshal, Prince of the Moskowa, Commanding the Left Wing of *l'armée du Nord'*. 'My Lord,' he began,

> When we reached Frasnes, in accordance with your orders, we found it occupied by a regiment of Nassau Infantry (some 1,500 men), and 8 guns. As they observed that we were manoeuvring to turn them, they retired from the village where we had practically enveloped them with our squadrons. General Colbert [with the Lancers of the Guard] reached within musket shot of Quatre Bras on the high road, but as the ground was difficult and the enemy fell back for support to the Bossu Wood, keeping up a vigorous fire from their 8 guns, it was impossible for us to carry it.
>
> The troops which were found at Frasnes had not advanced this morning and were not engaged at Gosselines. They are under the orders of Lord Wellington and appear to be retiring towards Nivelles. They set light to a beacon at Quatre Bras, and fired their guns a great deal. None of the troops who fought this morning at Gosselies have passed this way, they marched towards Fleurus.
>
> The peasants can give no information about a large assembly of troops in this neighbourhood, only that there is a Park of Artillery at Tubize, composed of 100 ammunition wagons and 12 guns; they say that the Belgian Army is in the neighbourhood of Mons, and that the headquarters of the Prince of Orange is at Braine-le-Comte. We took about 15 prisoners, and we have had 10 men killed and wounded.
>
> Tomorrow at daybreak, if it is possible, I shall send a reconnoitring party to Quatre Bras so as to occupy that place, for I think that the Nassau troops have left it.

47

A battalion of Infantry has just arrived [from Bachelu's Division], and I have placed it in front of the village. My Artillery not having joined me, I have sent orders for it to bivouac with Bachelu's Division, it will rejoin me tomorrow morning.

I have not written to the Emperor, as I have nothing more important to report to him than what I am telling your Excellency.

The Nassau troops who were holding Quatre Bras were commanded by Prince Bernhard of Saxe Weimar, who was in charge of General de Perponcher's 2nd Brigade. Prince Bernhard wrote the following letter from his bivouac near Waterloo three days later:

Dear Father, Thank God, I am still alive and have escaped unhurt from two bloody battles. The first was on the 16th of June, the second was yesterday, I beg when you read this, to take Ferrari's map in your hand. For four weeks I was in cantonments in Genappe, with the regiment of Orange Nassau, of which I am Colonel. On the 15th I was appointed Brigadier of the second brigade, of the division Perponcher; my predecessor had had the misfortune to break his leg. Besides my two battalions of Orange Nassau, I now had under my command three battalions of the Duchy of Nassau; – when my brigade was 4000 strong: – to-day I have not 1200 left! –.

On the 15th, the French fell upon the Prussian army, and pressed it very much. My brigade continued on the left wing of the Dutch army, the head-quarters of which were at Braine-le-Comte – my division lay in Nivelles. A battalion of Nassau were at Frasnes, and also a battery of Dutch horse-artillery. When the Prussians retreated towards Fleurus, the post at Frasnes was attacked and driven back.

The infantry threw itself into a wood on the right, and the artillery retired fighting to Quatre Bras. At this important post, I had drawn my brigade together, and cannonaded the Enemy, whom I succeeded in keeping off. I maintained this post through the whole night.[10]

The French had failed to take control of Quatre Bras, with fatal consequences for the success of the entire campaign. As can be seen from Prince Bernhard's letter, Lefebvre-Desnoëttes was mistaken in believing that the Nassau troops had withdrawn during the night and they were still in control of the crossroads on the morning of the 16th.

That Prince Bernhard's troops were at Quatre Bras to stop the French gaining control of those vital crossroads was due to the foresight of the Quartermaster-General and Chief of Staff of the Netherlands army, Jean-Victor de Constant-Rebècque:

Towards midday I received a communication from General Behr [at Mons] that the Prussians had been attacked that morning in front of Thuin and that the Prussian detachment which was occupying Binche had retreated to Gosselies. The enemy had not shown themselves at Binche. I immediately forwarded this information to the Prince [of Orange] at Bruxelles; at the same time I sent an order to General de Perponcher to assemble his 1st Brigade on the high road near Nivelles on the side of Quatre Bras, and his 2nd Brigade at Quatre Bras itself. I then sent orders to Generals Chassé [3rd Netherlands Division] and Collaert [Netherlands Cavalry Division] to assemble their divisions, the first at Fayt the second behind la Haine.[11]

That night a ball was being held by the Duchess of Richmond in a coach house in Brussels. The duchess's husband, Charles Lennox, the Duke of Richmond, commanded a reserve force stationed in Brussels, and all but three of Wellington's senior officers made a point in attending the ball despite the fact that the enemy were known to have crossed the border just a few miles to the south. Wellington himself was determined to maintain an appearance of calm and normality and he also went to the ball.

Müffling likewise, was going to this glamorous social event. As he was getting ready to go he received a note from Wellington, which read:

I have a report from General Dörnberg [in command of the 3rd Cavalry Brigade] at Mons that Napoleon has moved on Charleroi with all his force, and that he, General Dörnberg, has nothing in his front. I have therefore sent orders for the concentration of my people on Nivelles and Quatre Bras.[12]

Magdalene De Lancey, the wife of Wellington's Assistant Quartermaster-General, Sir William Howe De Lancey, left a 'narrative' of that day in Brussels as she watched her husband write those fateful orders:

On Thursday the 15th of June ... He was to dine at the Spanish Ambassador's; it was the first time he had left me to spend an evening away since our marriage [on 4 April] ... A short time after a message came from the Duke of Wellington to Sir William. He returned from the dinner and told me that news had been received of the near approach of the French, and that a battle was to be expected immediately, and that he had all the orders and arrangements to write as the army was to leave Bruxelles at daybreak.

I entreated to remain in the room with him, promising not to speak. He wrote for several hours without any interruption but the entrance and departure of various messengers who were to take the orders.[13]

Sir William's 'Additional Instructions', were issued at 22.00 hours. These stated that:

The troops in Bruxelles (5th and 6th divisions, Duke of Brunswick's and Nassau troops) to march when assembled from Bruxelles by the road of Namur to the point where the road to Nivelles separates; to be followed by Gen. Dornberg's brigade and the Cumberland hussars.

The 3d division to move from Braine le Comte upon Nivelles.

The 1st division from Enghien upon Braine le Comte.

The 2d and 4th divisions upon Enghien from Ath and Grammont; also from Audenarde, and to continue their movement upon Enghien.

The cavalry upon Enghien from Ninhove.[14]

So off went the Duke and his officers to the ball. It has become probably the most famous ball in history, and was widely reported in the British press, such as this account in the *Chester Courant* on Tuesday, 8 August 1815:

It is reported that many of the English officers were at a ball given by the Duchess of Richmond, at Brussels, during the battle of the 16th. At three o'clock in the morning they hastened to the field of battle, without having time to change their ball dresses, in which many were killed.

When a reporter described the event for the *Bury and Norwich Post* on Wednesday, 13 September 1815, it bore the headline 'The Richmond Ball':

Bonaparte, it is said, had made a complete arrangement, previous to the battle of Waterloo, to entrap the British Staff by finesse. He had engaged the Ladies of Brussels to apply to the Duchess of Richmond to give a ball; her grace consented. On the evening of the day of the fete, he posted 600 men dressed in blue frocks, with arms underneath them, in an appropriate situation, where they remained unobserved.

The dancing commenced, and the hour rapidly approached when the signal was to be given; and Bonaparte meant to enter at the head of the force already named. Providentially one of the Ladies became violently enamoured with the personal attractions of her partner, so much so that she could not resist the impulse to disclose to him the situation of himself and his gallant brethren. She took him aside, and communicated to him the plan. The Commander in Chief was directly apprised of his situation, and as promptly took the necessary steps to seize the enemy in ambuscade. The counterplot succeeded. – The credibility of this story may be suspected.

This was not the last time that 'The Richmond Ball' featured in the pages of the *Bury and Norwich Post*, as this report from the edition of Wednesday, 3 January 1816, testifies:

At the ball at Brussels, it is stated in a German paper, the Duke of Brunswick was the first person whose ear instinctively caught the sound of the French cannon. He went up to the Duke of Wellington, who was dancing, and told him his apprehensions. The Duke said it was no such thing, that Buonaparte could not be come, and that it was the Prussians saluting the King on his arrival.

The Duke of Brunswick was not satisfied, but went and sat down somewhat melancholy at a window, when presently another roar came, deep and hollow, over his ear. He started up, and begged of Lord Wellington, for God's sake, to let him go. He went, and fell in the same cause in which his father fell 23 years before. The D. of Wellington danced on.

Wellington, though, did not stay long at the ball. His final moments there were watched by Captain George Bowles:

At the Duchess of Richmond's ball at Brussels the Prince of Orange, who commanded the 1st Division of the army, came back suddenly, just as the Duke of Wellington had taken his place at the supper table, and whispered some minutes to his grace, who only said he had no fresh orders to give, and recommended the Prince to go back to his quarters and go to bed.

The Duke of Wellington remained nearly twenty minutes after this, and then said to the Duke of Richmond, 'I think it is time for me to go to bed likewise,' and then, whilst wishing him goodnight, whispered to ask him if he had a good map in his house. The Duke of Richmond said he had, and took him into his dressing-room, which opened into the supper-room. The Duke of Wellington shut the door and said, 'Napoleon has humbugged me, by God, he has gained twenty-four hours' march on me.' The Duke of Richmond said, 'What do you intend doing?'

The Duke of Wellington replied, 'I have ordered my army to concentrate at Quatre Bras; but we shall not stop him there, and if so I must fight him here' (at the same time passing his thumb-nail over the position of Waterloo). He then said adieu and left the house by another way out … He [the Duke of Richmond] marked the Duke of Wellington's thumb-nail with his pencil on the map, and we often looked at it together some months afterwards.[15]

There was nothing further Wellington could do until morning when the enemy was certain to be engaged, as he later told the Earl of Bathurst in his official despatch, dated the day after the Battle of Waterloo:

Buonaparte, having collected the 1st, 2nd, 3rd, 4th, and 6th corps of the French army, and the Imperial Guards, and nearly all the cavalry, on the Sambre, and between that river and the Meuse, between the 10th and 14th of the month, advanced on the 15th and attacked the Prussian posts at Thuin and Lobbes, on the Sambre, at day-light in the morning.

I did not hear of these events till in the evening of the 15th; and I immediately ordered the troops to prepare to march, and afterwards to march to their left, as soon as I had intelligence from other quarters to prove that the enemy's movement upon Charleroi was the real attack.

The enemy drove the Prussian posts from the Sambre on that day; and General Ziethen, who commanded the corps which had been at Charleroi, retired upon Fleurus; and Marshal Prince Blücher concentrated the Prussian army upon Sombref, holding the villages in front of his position of St. Amand and Ligny.

The enemy continued his march along the road from Charleroi towards Bruxelles; and, on the same evening, the 15th, attacked a brigade of the army of the Netherlands, under the Prince de Weimar, posted at Frasnes, and forced it back to the farm house, on the same road, called Les Quatre Bras.[16]

Many of the officers were still dining in Brussels when they received their orders to prepare their regiments for imminent departure. Amongst these was Sir James Kempt who commanded the 8th British Brigade in Lieutenant General Picton's 5th Division. That evening he was dining with Harry Ross-Lewin, who wrote:

Coffee and a young aide-de-camp from the Duke of Wellington came together. This officer was the bearer of a note from the Duke, and while Sir James was reading it, said: 'Old Blücher has been hard at it; a Prussian officer has just come to the Beau [Wellington's nickname], all covered with sweat and dirt, and says they have had much fighting'. Our host then rose, and, addressing the regimental officers at the table, said: 'Gentlemen, you will proceed without delay to your respective regiments, and let them get under arms immediately.'[17]

The scene in Brussels that evening was a mixture of excitement and anxiety. The following description was provided by an un-named witness, who was only referred to as 'a near observer':

On the evening of Thursday the 15th of June, a Courier arrived at Brussels, from Marshal Blucher to announce, that hostilities had commenced. The Duke of Wellington was sitting after dinner, with a party of officers, over the desert and wine, when he received the dispatches, containing this unexpected news. Marshal Blucher had been attacked that day, by the French; but he seemed to consider it as a mere affair of outposts, which was not likely to proceed much further at present, though it might probably prove the prelude to a more important engagement.

It was the opinion of most military men in Brussels, that the enemy intended by this feint, to induce the allies to concentrate their chief military force in that quarter, in order that he might more successfully make a serious attack upon some other point, and that it was against Brussels and the English army, that the blow would be aimed. The troops were ordered to hold themselves in readiness, to march at a moment's notice; but no immediate movement was expected, and for some hours all was quiet.

It was past midnight, and profound repose seemed to reign over Brussels, when suddenly the drums beat to arms, and the trumpet's loud call was heard from every part of the city. It is impossible to describe the effect of these sounds, heard in the silence of the night. We were not long left in doubt of the truth. A second courier had arrived from Blucher, the attack had become serious; the enemy were in considerable force; they had taken Charleroi, and had gained some advantage over the Prussians, and our troops were ordered to march immediately to support them; instantly every place resounded with the sound of martial preparations. There was not a house in which military were not quartered, and consequently, the whole town was one universal scene of bustle: the soldiers were seen assembling from all parts in the Place Royale, with their knap sacks upon their backs; some taking leave of their wives and children; others sitting down unconcernedly upon the sharp pavement, waiting for their comrades; others sleeping upon packs of straw, surrounded by all the din of war, draught horses, and baggage waggons, artillery, and commissariat trains – carts clattering, hammers knocking, chargers neighing, bugles sounding, drums beating, and colours flying.

A most laughable contrast to this martial scene was presented by a long procession of carts, coming quietly in, as usual, from the country to market, filled with old Flemish women, who looked irresistibly comic, seated among their piles of cabbages, baskets of green peas, early potatoes, totally ignorant of what might be the meaning of all these warlike preparations, and moving merrily along, one after another, through the Place Royale, amidst the crowds of soldiers, and the confusion of baggage waggons, gazing at the scene before them, with many a look of gaping wonder.

Yet there was order amidst all this apparent confusion. Regiment after regiment formed with the utmost regularity, and marched out of Brussels. About four o'clock in the morning, the 42nd and 92nd Highland regiments marched through the Place Royale, and the Plaza. One could not but admire their fine appearance; their firm, collected, steady, military demeanour, as they went rejoicing to battle, with their bagpipes playing before them, and the partial gleams of the rising sun shining upon their glittering arms ...

Thousands were parting with their nearest and dearest to them, and to every British heart; it was a moment of the deepest interest. Our countrymen were marching out to battle – they might return victorious – and we proudly indulged the hope of their triumph; but they were going to meet an Enemy formidable by their numbers, their discipline, and under the command of a leader, whose military talents had made him the terror, and the Tyrant of Europe, whose remorseless crimes and unbounded ambition had so long been its scourge. Not only was the safety of our brave army at stake, but the glory which Britain had so dearly purchased and so nobly won. – Her prosperity – her greatness – her name among other nations – the security and the fate of Europe, depended upon the issue of that eventful contest, which was now on the eve of being decided.

Our troops, however, cheered in the confidence and recollection they were fighting under the command of a General, who had already beaten a victorious army from the shores of the Tagus, over the Mountains of the Pyrenees; who had carried conquest and dismay into the heart of France, and whose brightest victories had ever been graced with humanity. What could not British soldiers do under such a general? What could not such a general do with such soldiers?[18]

In her narrative, Magdalene De Lancey also wrote of the military preparations that were taking place in Brussels at this moment:

> The *reveille* was sounded all night, and the troops actively prepared for their march. I stood with my husband at a window of the house, which overlooked a gate of the city, and saw the whole army go out. Regiment after regiment passed through and melted away in the mist of the morning. At length my husband was summoned.[19]

De Lancey was mortally wounded at the Battle of Waterloo. He died with his young bride by his side a week after the battle.

Serving in the 95th Rifles, Edward Costello was amongst the soldiers who marched to war that fateful day in June 1815:

> All things arranged, we passed the gates of Brussels, and descended the wood of Soignies, that leads to the little village of Waterloo. It was the 16th – a beautiful summer morning – the sun slowly rising above the horizon and peeping through the trees, while our men were as merry as crickets, laughing and joking with each other, and at times pondered in their minds what all this fuss, as they called it, could be about for even the old soldiers could not believe the enemy were so near.[20]

As for the French, Napoleon was satisfied with the opening moves of the campaign, as he himself subsequently wrote:

> All the Emperor's manoeuvres had succeeded to his wishes; he had thenceforth in his power to attack the armies of the enemy in detail. To avoid this misfortune, the greatest that could befall them, the only means they had left was to abandon the ground, and assemble at Brussels or beyond that city.[21]

This, however, was the exact opposite course of action to that which both Wellington and Blücher had chosen. Events would soon show who was right.

4

Quatre Bras

An officer of the 8th Brigade wrote the following from the camp at Clichy near Paris, which became the main British encampment during the occupation of the French capital at the end of the campaign:

> All the sharers of my tent having gone to Paris, and my servant having manufactured a window-shutter into a table, and a pack-saddle into a seat, I will no longer delay answering your two affectionate letters, and endeavour to comply with your demand of an account of the battle such as it offered to my own eyes.

The following officer was a member of the Brigade of Guards and, like most of the Anglo-Netherlands army, he was marching throughout the morning of 16 June towards Quatre Bras:

> On the 15th (of June) everything appeared so perfectly quiet, that the Duchess of Richmond gave a ball and supper, to which all the world was invited; and it was not till near ten o'clock at night that rumours of an action having taken place between the French and Prussians were circulated through the room in whispers: no credit was to them, however, for some time; but when the General Officers whose corps were in advance began to move, and when orders were given for persons to repair to their regiments, matters then began to be considered in a different light.
>
> At eleven o'clock .the drums beat to arms, and the 5th Division, which garrisoned Brussels, after having bivouacked in the Park until day light, set forward towards the frontiers. On the road we met baggage and sick coming to the rear; but could only learn that the French and Prussians had been fighting the day before, and that another battle was expected when they left the advanced posts.[1]

56

The early hours of 16 June also saw Ney trying to organise his new command so that he could push on to Quatre Bras, but due to the suddenness of his appointment, the Marshal did not know where all his troops were. Consequently, time was lost in the morning before he could gather together what he regarded as sufficient numbers to enable him to attack the Allied forces that were holding the crossroads. This was one of the subjects he referred to in a letter to Joseph Fouché, duc d'Otrante, the hugely influential Minister of Police under Napoleon and King Louis, and who retained power after Napoleon's defeat at Waterloo:

The most false and defamatory reports have been spreading for some days over the public mind, upon the conduct which I have pursued during this short and unfortunate campaign. The journals have reported those odious calumnies, and appear to lend them credit. After having fought for twenty-five years for my country, after having shed my blood for its glory and independence, an attempt is made to accuse me of treason; an attempt is made to mark me out to the people, and the army itself, as the author of the disaster it has just experienced.

Forced to break silence, while it is always painful to speak of oneself, and above all, to answer calumnies, I address myself to you, Sir, as the President of the Provisional Government, for the purpose of laying before you a faithful statement of the events I have witnessed. On the 11th of June, I received an order from the Minister of War to repair to the Imperial presence. I had no command, and no information upon the composition and strength of the army. Neither the Emperor nor his Minister had given me any previous hint, from which I could anticipate that I should be employed in the present campaign. I was consequently taken by surprise, without horse, without accoutrements, and without money, and I was obliged to borrow the necessary expenses of my journey.

Having arrived on the 12th, at Laon, on the 13th at Avesnes, and on the 14th at Beaumont, I purchased, in this last city, two horses from the Duke of Treviso, with which I repaired, on the 15th, to Charleroi, accompanied by my first aide-de-camp, the only officer who attended me. I arrived at the moment when the enemy, attacked by our troops, was retreating upon Fleurus and Gosselies.

The Emperor ordered me immediately to put myself at the head of the 1st and 2d corps of infantry, commanded by Lieutenant-Generals d'Erlon and Reille, of the divisions of light cavalry of Lieutenant-General Piré, of the division of light cavalry of the guards, under the command of Lieutenant-Generals Lefebvre Desnouettes and Colbert, and of two divisions of cavalry of the Count Valmy, forming, in all, eight divisions of infantry, and four of cavalry. With these troops, a part of which only I had as yet under my immediate command, I pursued the enemy, and forced him to evacuate Gosselies, Frasnes, Millet, Heppegnies. There they took up a position for the night, with the exception of the 1st corps, which was still at Marchiennes, and which did not join me till the following day.[2]

The time lost as Ney waited for the rest of his force to arrive at Quatre Bras allowed increasing numbers of Wellington's men to join Bernhard of Saxe Weimar's weak force holding the crossroads and the adjoining Bossu Wood. Now that Wellington had committed his troops to a course of action, the tone of his instructions became more urgent, with simple orders being delivered to his two Corps commanders at 07.00 hours on 16 June. The first part was intended for General Lord Hill:

> The Duke of Wellington requests that you will move the 2d division of infantry upon Braine le Comte immediately. The cavalry has been ordered likewise on Braine le Comte. His Grace is going to Waterloo.

The same message, which was signed by De Lacy Evans, then went to provide the instructions for the Prince of Orange:

> Your Lordship is requested to order Prince Frederick of Orange to move, immediately upon the receipt of this order, the 1st division of the army of the Low Countries, and the Indian brigade, from Sotteghem to Enghien, leaving 500 men, as before directed, in Audenarde.

On the opposing side Marshal Ney may have believed that his earlier orders from Napoleon were imprecise but he was shortly to receive detailed instructions, which were sent from Charleroi on 16 June 1815:

> My Cousin, My Aide-de-Camp, General de Flahault, is directed to deliver this letter to you. The *Major-Général* should have given you orders, but you will receive mine first because my officers travel faster than his. You will receive the operation orders for the day, but I wish to write to you in detail because it is of the highest importance.
>
> I am sending Marshal Grouchy with III and IV Infantry Corps to Sombreffe. I am taking my Guard to Fleurus, and I shall be there myself before midday. I shall attack the enemy if I find him there, and I shall clear the roads as far as Gembloux.

My intention is that, immediately after I have made up my mind, you will be ready to march on Brussels. I shall support you with my Guard, who will be at Fleurus, or at Sombreffe, and I shall wish to reach Brussels tomorrow morning. You will set off with your troops this evening you will cover three or four leagues and reach Brussels by 7 a.m. tomorrow morning.

Therefore you will dispose your troops as follows:-

1 Division 2 leagues in front of Quatre Bras, if it is not inconvenient; 6 Infantry Divisions around Quatre Bras; and a Division at Marbais, in order that I can move it myself to Sombreffe, should I need its assistance, besides it will not delay your march.

The Corps of the Count of Valmy, who has 3,000 Cuirassiers, picked troops, will be placed where the Roman road cuts and crosses the Brussels road, in order that I can call him in to me if necessary. As soon as my course of action has been taken you will order him to move and rejoin you. I should desire to have with me the Division of the Guard commanded by General Lefebvre-Desnoëttes, and I send you two divisions of the Count of Valmy's Corps to replace it. But in my actual scheme I prefer placing the Count of Valmy so that I can recall him if I do not wish to cause General Lefebvre-Desnoëttes to make unnecessary marches, since it is probable that I shall decide to march on Brussels this evening with the Guard. You will cover the Lefebvre Division by the Cavalry Divisions belonging to D'Erlon's and Reille's Corps, in order to spare the Guard. If any fighting occurs with the English, it is preferable that this should fall on the Cavalry of the Line rather than on the Guard.

I have adopted for this campaign the following general principle, to divide my Army into two wings and a reserve. Your Wing will be composed of four divisions of the I Corps, four divisions of the II Corps, two divisions of Light Cavalry, and two divisions of the Corps of the Count of Valmy. This ought not to fall short of 45,000 to 50,000 men.

Marshal Grouchy will have almost the same force, and will command the Right Wing.

The Guard will form the Reserve, and I shall bring it into action on either wing just as the actual circumstances may dictate.

The *Major-Général* issues the most precise orders, so that when you are detached you should not find any difficulty in obeying such orders as you receive. General officers commanding Corps will take orders directly from me when I am present in person.

According to circumstances I shall draw troops from one wing to strengthen my Reserve.

You understand how much importance is attached to the taking of Brussels. From its capture certain things would happen, because such a quick and sudden movement would cut the English Army from Mons, Ostend, etc. I desire that your dispositions may be well conceived, so that at the first order your eight divisions will take the road at once and march rapidly and unhindered to Brussels.[4]

Ney knew that he had to take Quatre Bras and move quickly on Brussels, but he was uncertain as to the strength of the Anglo-Netherlands forces opposing him. Heeding the advice of Reille, who had fought the British in the Peninsular War and who warned that Wellington might have a large body of troops concealed from view, Ney continued to keep the Allied troops at Quatre Bras tied down whilst waiting until more of his men were up before mounting a full-scale attack.

Prince Bernhard of Saxe Weimar was still in position at Quatre Bras and he continued with his description of events in the letter to his father which he wrote from near Waterloo on the 18th.

Towards morning, on the 16th, I was reinforced by a battalion of Dutch Yagers, and a battalion of Militia. Soon after arrived my General of division and the Prince of Orange. With the latter I went to the outposts, and by this order undertook a reconnaissance, with a battalion and two cannon. Towards noon, the Enemy showed strong columns, and began to cannonade us. It is said he had three corps of his army engaged against us on this day. We had only five battalions to oppose to him, and the skirts of a wood to defend to the utmost.

The Duke of Wellington himself was present at the beginning of the action; I kept my ground a long time against an enemy thrice my number, and had only two Belgic cannons to protect myself with. The Enemy took the point of a wood opposite me, and incommoded my left flank. I, without loss of time, took some volunteers, and two companies of Dutch militia, and recovered my wood at the point of the bayonet; I was at the head of the storming parties, and had the honour to be one of the first in the wood.

In cutting away some branches, I wounded myself with my sabre very slightly in the right leg, but was not a moment out of battle: – it is in fact not worthwhile to mention this wound; I write to you about it only that you and my good mother may not be alarmed by exaggerated and foolish reports.[5]

Wellington, in fact, had arrived at Quatre Bras from Brussels just before 10.00 hours. As Ney had still not launched a major assault upon the crossroads, and in the knowledge that Prince Bernhard's small Dutch and Nassau force would, in time, be reinforced with the rest of Wellington's army marching up from Brussels, the Duke felt confident enough to leave his troops and ride over to the east to see what the Prussians were doing. Before he set off, Wellington sent a letter ahead to Blücher. This was addressed from the heights behind Frasnes and was timed at 10.30 hours

> My Dear Prince, My army is disposed as follows: The Prince of Orange's Corps has a division here at Quatre Bras, the remainder are at Nivelles. The Reserve is now marching from Waterloo to Genappe, where it will arrive at midday. At the same hour the English Cavalry will have reached Nivelles. Lord Hill's Corps is at Braine-le-Comte.
>
> I do not see many of the enemy in front of us, and I await the receipt of news from Your Highness, and the arrival of my troops, to decide on my operations for this day. Nothing has been seen in the direction of Binche, nor on our right.[6]

It was at Brye, just to the north of the village of Ligny, beyond which the French army was concentrating, that Wellington met Blücher. It was apparent that Napoleon was going to attack the Prussians and it was equally clear that the Prussians were going to stand and fight.

Blücher's chief of staff, General Gneisenau, asked Wellington to send his troops to support the Prussians, but all that Wellington would commit to was that he would join the Prussians, 'provided I am not attacked myself'. With that he rode back to Quatre Bras to see what was happening there.

What he found was that Ney had begun his attack an hour earlier. Müffling wrote the following in his memoirs:

> On our return to Quatre Bras, we found Marshal Ney fully engaged in the attack, which had begun on the farm of Gemioncourt, occupied by us. The enemy, with their two corps d'armée, displayed such great superiority over Perponcher's division, that it was evidently impossible, unless some extraordinary circumstances intervene, to hold Quatre Bras.[7]

At this point it might be helpful to describe the battlefield. The following was given in a report by Major Carl Jacobi who was the Hanoverian Assistant Quartermaster-General:

> At Quatre Bras, which is comprised by a single farm, [where] the high roads from Brussels to Charleroi and from Nivelles to Namur cross at

right angles. The region is almost completely flat and is traversed by cornfields. Close to Quatre Bras, a few hundred paces to the right of the high road to Chareroi, lies the Bois de Bossu. This wood begins at the farm and runs for a quarter of an hour's march in the same direction as the high road. To the left of the said high road, approximately 2,000 paces from Quatre Bras in the direction of Charleroi, lies the farm of Gémioncourt, and when one takes 2,000 paces along the high road from Quatre Bras to Namur one encounters at 800 paces on the right of the latter the village of Piermont [Piramont]. A wood stretches almost from the high road to the left of this village in the direction of Charleroi. The battle of Quatre Bras took place on this enclosed ground namely, to the left, to the right and behind the Bois de Bossu, and across the high road leading from Nivelles to Namur.[8]

Just as the Netherlands Light Cavalry Brigade trotted up to Quatre Bras to join Prince Bernhard's small force, the French attack increased in ferocity but now the first battalions of the British infantry divisions were marching up to the crossroads.

Wellington, aware that the French pressure was mounting, decided to do what Müffling called 'a resolution worthy of a great commander'. When it might be expected that Wellington would withdraw under the weight of the French onslaught, he did the exact opposite – he attacked.

Wellington ordered the Duke of Brunswick's corps and Picton's 5th Division to advance, with the result that the infantry of General Bachelu's 5th Division of Reille's Corps were pushed backwards. Wellington's plan seemed to be working but then the French 2nd Brigade of Piré's 2nd Cavalry Division (two regiments of Chasseurs and two of Lancers) suddenly struck Picton's 9th Brigade. The following letter was written on 21 June from Brussels by a wounded officer:

> The 9th brigade consisted of 1st, or Royal Scots, 42d, 44th, and 92d one British division and some Brunswickers there before we came up. The 92d took the position in a ditch to cover the guns and the cavalry, being the junior regiment, – while the rest of the division went a little to the left to check the French infantry that were passing on there. We lay in a most disagreeable situation for upwards of an hour, having an excellent view, however, of the fight, but exposed to a most tremendous fire, from their great guns, of shot, shells, grape, &c. which we found great difficulty in keeping clear of. I say keeping clear of, because you can very often see the round shot coming. This heavy fire was maintained against us in consequence of the Duke and his

Staff being only two or three yards in front of the 92d, perfectly seen by the French, and because all the reinforcements which were coming up passed along the road in which we were.

Here I had a remarkable opportunity of witnessing the *sang froid* of the Duke, who, unconcerned at the showers of shot falling on every side of him, and killing and wounding a number of his Staff, stood watching the Enemy and giving orders with as much composed calmness as if he were at a review. The French cavalry were now beginning to advance in front of the 92d, to take the village, and the Brunswick cavalry that were also in our front went on to meet them; but the French putting spurs to their horses to charge, the Brunswickers wheeled about and galloped upon the 92d in the greatest confusion. The French were soon up with their rear men, cutting them down most horribly. The Enemy also dismounted two guns … We did not allow the flying Brunswickers to break through our regiment, but they passed round our right flank, close to the men's bayonets, having the French mingled with them cutting away. We of course could not fire to help them till they had cleared us.

At the same instant, the road from the French lines towards the village, was covered with cavalry at full speed charging. When the Brunswickers cleared our right, we wheeled our grenadiers back on the road, the ditch of which we lined, that they might fire when the first of the French should pass [house] No. 2, the rest were to fire obliquely on the road and on the remains of those that followed the Brunswickers. The volley was decisive.

The front of the French charge was completely separated from the rear by the gap which we made, and nothing was seen but men and horses tumbling on each other. Their rear retreated, and the front dashed through the village cutting down all stragglers. Our assistant-surgeon dressing a man behind a house No. 4, had his bonnet cut in two, and a lance run into his side. Three of them came down the road through the grenadiers at full speed, brandishing their swords, and our rear rank firing at them all the way. Two were brought down, but the third, – (his horse gushing blood from all parts) had just cleared the regiment, when Col. Mitchell made a cut at him with his sabre, which he dexterously parried, but an officer of the Staff cut, with his sword, the hamstrings of the fellow's horse, and he was taken. The rest were likewise taken, and they tell me that eight pursued the Duke a good way. I wonder how he got off, for I saw him in front not five minutes before the charge.

The Enemy's charge repelled, it was now our turn to have our share of charging. The French formed their cavalry again to charge, supported by infantry, and advanced past House No. 2, when Adjutant-General Barnes, our old brigadier in Spain and France, who is doatingly fond of the regiment, came down to the front, and calling out, 'Come on, my old 92d,' the men jumped from the ditch and charged in the finest style, up to the house No. 2. He was then obliged to leave us, as it was not his duty to charge, although he could not resist the impulse.

We were then moved forward from behind the house, with our brave Colonel Cameron at our head. When we jumped from the ditch, the officer with the regimental colour was shot through the heart. The staff of the colour was shattered in six pieces with three balls, and the staff of the King's colour with one. I got the remains of the regimental. When we moved from behind the house, and had passed the corner of the garden parallel to the road, [house] No. 5 we received a volley from a column on the right, which was retreating towards the wood. This fire killed Colonel Cameron and Mr. Becher, and wounded a great many. This column of the Enemy kept us five minutes before we could clear the garden in advance to the wood. The fire here was dreadful. There was an immense slaughter among us at this time, but the French began at last to give way, and retreated up the side of the wood, keeping up, however, a tremendous, fire, and killing a great many of our regiment. We had advanced so far that we were now completely separated from the rest of the line, and scarcely fifty men of those of us who went into action were remaining. A regiment of guards was afterwards sent up to relieve us, but not before thirty of that fifty were hit.

We formed behind the houses after we left the field, with the loss, which you will see by the [London] Gazette, of 23 officers and 270 men.[9]

James Anton was a sergeant with the 42nd Highlanders who would later commit his own account of the action to paper:

A German [King's German Legion] orderly dragoon galloped up exclaiming, 'Franchee! Franchee!' and, wheeling about galloped off. We instantly formed a rallying square; no time for particularity: every man's piece was loaded, and our enemies approaching at full charge; the feet of their horses seemed to tear up the ground. Our skirmishers … fell beneath their lances, a few escaped death or wounds; our brave Colonel [Sir Robert Macara] fell at this time, pierced through the chin until the point reached his brain. Captain [Archibald] Menzies fell covered in wounds.[10]

The Brunswick Corps, which was composed in the main of inexperienced young soldiers, did actually earn great credit at Quatre Bras, though it cost the life of their much-respected Duke. This is an extract from a letter from one of the Duke of Brunswick's officers, dated 29 June:

On the 15th, in the evening, about ten o'clock, a letter was brought from the Duke of Wellington's office, which contained an order, that all the troops might be concentrated at the Allee Verte, near Brussels, on the following morning at day-break. Orders were accordingly given, and sent off as fast as possible: but, the dislocations being rather at a great distance, the troops could not arrive before 5 o'clock; when the Duke, on the instant, marched through Brussels, and so on to the road to Waterloo. Directly afterwards, the Duke of Wellington followed, and, after showing a letter to the Duke, changed his horse; they then set off together, and were as fast as possible followed by their suites. About 10 o'clock, we arrived at Quatre Bras, where we found part of the Nassau troops engaged, and heard that the French advanced very fast, and were exceedingly strong. We then went on a hill to observe their approach; but hardly had they perceived the number of officers, but the rascals fired at us with grenades: so we were obliged to leave the spot, and I narrowly escaped being killed.

About 12 o'clock we returned; and the Duke strongly expressed his wish of having an opportunity of meeting the French in equal force with his troops. To his great satisfaction, the Royal Scotch, the Hanoverians, and his own corps, arrived betwixt one and two o'clock. Tired and hungry as they were, they sang as they passed the Duke, abusing and swearing against Buonaparte, wishing that they might soon meet him, and have an opportunity of setting the soldiers of the Grande Nation to rights. Hardly had we marched half an hour, when we saw the French expecting us on a hill. The Duke of Wellington then ordered to collect the troops as quick as possible, and to prepare for battle. At 2 o'clock all was ready, and the attack began. The battle was very bloody, but we compelled the Enemy to retreat. About half past four the French advanced again, and appeared double the number of the Allied Army; but no fear was shown.

The cannonade began most horribly, which in some respects put the train and baggage in confusion: however, the troops stood, and fought like lions; so the French were again obliged to retreat, and were driven back to their position. Here they had a great advantage, being covered by a little wood, where they had placed all their artillery and riflemen. The Duke of Wellington most likely knew this, and ordered a fresh attack, to get the French out of the wood. The troops advanced, the Brunswick division on the left wing.

When they came near the wood, the French commenced a horrible fire with artillery and case-shot, which occasioned a great loss to our corps. In this attack, which was about 7 o'clock in the evening, the Duke was unfortunately killed on the spot by a case-shot. At this moment I was not far from his highness, and ordered our small carriage, thinking that he was only wounded – when, alas! to my inexpressible sorrow, I found he was dead. My feelings I cannot describe, but you will be able to form to yourself an idea.[11]

As the day progressed increasing numbers of Allied troops reached Quatre Bras, including two batteries of the Royal Artillery, those of Major Cleeves and Major William Lloyd. With Lloyd's battery of 9-pounders, No. 43 Battery, was a young officer who later achieved the rank of major:

> I was with two guns attached to the 69th, Lieutenant-Colonel Morice, and placed myself on their right, when I was directed to follow the four other guns of Major Lloyd's Battery, ordered into action in front of the farm of Quatre Bras, on the Charleroi road to support the Duke of Brunswick. I had hardly quitted the 69th when the Cuirassiers charged from the wood, and before the 69th could get into square they were rode over, broken, and sad havoc made among them, their only Colour taken, the other being 'in the Hospital of Invalides at Paris, taken at Bergen-op-Zoom', but for a battalion of British Guards coming up to their support, and, throwing in one of their destructive fires, compelling the Cuirassiers to return to the wood, not a man save the Colonel and Adjutant would have escaped but for this timely aid.[12]

One of those Guardsmen who helped stabilize the situation, Major S. Rudyard, subsequently described the events of that day:

> On the evening of the 15th, we heard that the French were passing the frontiers, and we received orders to hold ourselves in readiness to march; at two o'clock we received our orders to march, and were off at three. We passed through Braine le Comte, and proceeded to a bivouac near Nivelle. While we were setting ourselves down, an order came to move immediately to the left through Nivelle – having passed it, we heard the firing very close, and soon met many wounded Belgians coming in.

At five o'clock, General Maitland galloped up, and ordered the grenadiers to drive the French out of a wood, and in about half an hour we perfectly cleared it. When we opened at the end of the wood, the enemy threw in a most tremendous fire of round and grape shot, from which we found it necessary to retire. We got out of the wood in another part, and they immediately advanced columns to attack us, which deployed very regularly, and drove us a short way back. However we advanced again, and they gave way, and retired to their guns. They then advanced upon us, and having driven us back a second time, their cavalry attempted to charge; but a square of Black Brunswickers brought them up, while we were nimbly slipt into the wood on our right, lined the ditches, and paid them handsomely. Our loss was very severe, and we found great difficulty in forming our line again.

At last we effected it with the third battalion of our regiment, and then we drove everything before us. We kept possession of the wood all night. The Prussians and French had been engaged from two o'clock in the morning, in the position of Fleurus; and the former had been driven back. The French then tried to get possession of the road to Brussels. They had a severe contest with the Dutch, and one of our divisions, and had succeeded in driving the Dutch out of a wood, (Bossu I think it is called). We arrived at the very moment the French skirmishers were appearing.

We dashed in and cut them up properly, though our loss was severe. Out of 84, I had only 43 left in my company. At night the remains of the battalion bivouacked at the head of the road, and during the night we received a strong reinforcement. They call this the action of Quatre Bras (where two high roads cross).[13]

Having 'marched up towards the Enemy, at each step hearing more clearly the fire of musquetry', another Guards officer recalled:

As we approached the field of action, we met constantly waggons full of men, of all the various nations under the Duke's command, wounded in the most dreadful manner. The sides of the road had a heap of dying and dead, very many of whom were British; such a scene did, indeed, demand every better feeling of the mind to cope with its horrors; and too much cannot be said in praise of the Division of Guards, the very largest part of whom were young soldiers, and volunteers from the Militia, who had never been exposed to the fire of an enemy, or witnessed its effects.

During the period of our advance from Nivelles, I suppose nothing could exceed the anxiety of the moment, with those on the field. The French, who had a large cavalry and artillery, (in both of which arms we were quite destitute, excepting some Belgian and German guns,) had made dreadful havock in our lines, and had succeeded in pushing an immensely strong column of tirailleurs into the wood I have before mentioned, of which they had possessed themselves, and had just began to cross the road, having marched through the wood, and placed affairs in a critical situation, when the Guards luckily came in sight.

The moment we caught a glimpse of them, we halted, formed, and having loaded, and fixed bayonets, advanced; the French immediately retiring; and the very last man who attempted to re-enter the wood, was killed by our grenadiers. At this instant, our men gave three glorious cheers, and, though we had marched fifteen hours without any thing to eat and drink, save the water we procured on the march, we rushed to attack the Enemy. This was done by the 1st brigade, consisting of the 2d and 3d battalions of the first regiment; and the 2d brigade, consisting of the 2d battalion of the Coldstream and third regiment, were formed as a reserve along the chaussée.

As we entered the wood, a few noble fellows, who sunk down overpowered with fatigue, lent their voice to cheer their comrades. The trees were so thick, that it was beyond anything difficult to effect a passage. As we approached, we saw the Enemy behind them, taking aim at us: they contested every bush, and at a small rivulet running through the wood, they attempted a stand but could not resist us, and we at last succeeded in forcing them out of their possessions. The moment we endeavoured to go out of this wood, (which had naturally broken us), the French cavalry charged us; but we at last found the third battalion, who had rather skirted the wood, and formed in front of it, where they afterwards were in hollow square, and repulsed all the attempts of the French cavalry to break them.

Our loss was most tremendous, and nothing could exceed the desperate work of the evening; the French infantry and cavalry fought most desperately; and after a conflict of nearly three hours, (the obstinacy of which could find no parallel, save in the slaughter it occasioned,) we had the happiness to find ourselves complete masters of the road and wood, and that we had at length defeated all the efforts of the French to outflank us, and turn our right, than which nothing could be of greater moment to both parties. General Picton's superb division had been engaged since two o'clock p. m., and was still fighting with the greatest fury; no terms can be found sufficient to explain their exertions. The fine brigade of Highlanders suffered most dreadfully, and so did all the regiments engaged.

The gallant and noble conduct of the Brunswickers was the admiration of every one. I myself saw scarcely any of the Dutch troops; but a regiment of Belgian light cavalry held a long struggle with the famous Cuirassiers, in a way that can never be forgotten; they, poor fellows, were nearly all cut to pieces. These French Cuirassiers charged two German guns, with the intent of taking them, to turn them down the road on our flank. This charge was made along the chaussée running from Charleroi to Brussels; the guns were placed near the farm-houses of Les Quatre Bras, and were loaded, and kept till their close arrival. Two companies, (I think of Highlanders,) posted behind a house and dung-hill, who flanked the Enemy on their approach, and the artillery, received them with such a discharge, and so near, as to lay (within effect like magic) the whole head of the column low; causing it to fly, and be nearly all destroyed.

We had fought till dark; the French became less impetuous, and after a little cannonade they retired from the field. Alas! when we met after the action, how many were wanting among us; how many who were in the full pride of youth and manhood, had gone to that bourn, from whence they could return no more! I shall now close my letter; and in my next, will endeavour to give you some description of the 18th; for, to add to this account now, would be but to harrow up your mind with scenes of misery, of which those only who have been witnesses, can form an adequate idea.[14]

One officer, a Major Oldfield of the Royal Engineers, had a narrow escape when the French cuirassiers charged at the British lines:

A regiment of cuirassiers advancing up this road on the 16th, the Duke *ordered* a Dutch regiment of cavalry to charge them. Colonel Smyth who was sent with the order, put himself at their head to induce them to go on. They were young troops and required encouragement, as soon as they came within a few yards of the enemy, they turned & went off much more rapidly than they had advanced.

Colonel Smyth was in the midst of the melee, his horse came in contact with a large brewing vat that had been thrown out of the public house and was opposite the door. The cuirassiers were cutting & slashing on every side, the horse made an effort & with a leap cleared the tub. The colonel took me down in the morning to look at it, the bodies of the cuirassiers & Dutch dragoons were laying about it on every side.[15]

The following letter was written by a sergeant in the Royal Artillery Drivers, to his father in Edinburgh, from a camp in the Bois de Boulogne, near Paris. It is dated 22 September 1815:

> You ask me to give you a sketch of what fell under my own observation during the late battles, and I shall therefore relate to you such particulars as at present occur to my memory, and such as I know to be true.
>
> On the morning of the 15th June, when we marched from Enghien, we had no idea of being so soon engaged; we expected to march to Mons, and from thence to some place in France. We, however, left Mons on our right, and halted on a height near a town called Nivelle. It was there I heard the first of the firing. The Hollanders were then engaged. We proceeded immediately through Nivelle, on the great road leading from that to Charleroi; we there met several of the Prince of Orange's men leaving the field wounded. When we came nearer the scene of action, we saw the wounded of the brave Highland brigade, whom the surgeons were busy dressing on the north side.
>
> We halted a quarter of an hour, till the guards had formed and charged, when our brigade immediately advanced at a gallop, and came to action near a small village; the enemy's artillery playing very smartly, though without doing much damage, most of the shot going over our heads. There were only four of our brigades in action at this time (six o'clock evening), and none of our cavalry; but they advanced after this in great numbers, by different roads. The action continued till about half past nine o'clock. The enemy seemed superior in numbers, especially in artillery. After the action we lay down by our guns, where I slept as sound as ever I did on a feather bed.

Prince Bernhard of Saxe Weimar continued with his descriptive account of the fighting in the letter he sent to his father:

> While I manfully defended my wood; the Enemy drove back our left wing as far as Quatre Bras. It was on this occasion that the brave Duke of Brunswick was killed by a ball, which entered his breast. Strong columns of infantry turned my right flank; I asked for orders how to act, but received none.
>
> When I saw myself surrounded on all sides, and my people had expended all their ammunition, I retreated in good order through the wood to the neighbourhood of Hautain le Val. The Hanoverian division Alten supported me, and recovered the wood, but lost it again; at last it was forced by the English with great loss, and

maintained through the night. I bivouacked for the night in the wood.[16]

The unidentified officer of the 43rd Light Infantry, whose letter sent from the camp at Clichy near Paris to his friend in Cumberland is quoted at the start of this chapter, also wrote:

At two o'clock we arrived at Genappe, from whence we heard firing very distinctly; half an hour afterwards we saw the French columns advancing, and we had scarcely taken our position when they attacked us. Our front consisted of the 3rd and 5th Divisions, with some Nassau people, and a brigade of cavalry, in all about 13,000 men; while the French forces, according to Ney's account, must have been immense, as his reserve alone consisted of 30,000, which, however, he says, Buonaparte disposed of without having advertised him.

The business was begun by the first battalion of the 95th, which was sent to drive the Enemy out of some corn-fields, and a thick wood, of which they had possession: after sustaining some loss, we succeeded completely; and three companies of Brunswickers were left to keep it, while we acted on another part of the line: they, however, were driven out immediately; and the French also got possession of a village which turned our flanks. We were then obliged to return, and it took us the whole day to retake what had been lost.

While we were employed here, the remainder of the army were in a much more disagreeable situation: for in consequence of our inferiority in cavalry, each regiment was obliged to form a square, in which manner the most desperate attacks of infantry and charges of cavalry were resisted and repelled; and when night put an end to the slaughter, the French not only gave up every attempt on our position, but retired from their own, on which we bivouacked. I will not attempt to describe the sort of night we passed – I will leave you to conceive it. The groans of the wounded and dying, to whom no relief could be afforded, must not be spoken of here, because on the 18th it was fifty thousand times worse. But a handful of men lying in the face of such superior numbers, and being obliged to sleep in squares for fear the Enemy's dragoons, knowing that we were weak in that arm, might make a dash into the camp, was no very pleasant reverie to soothe one to rest.

Exclusive of this, I was annoyed by a wound I had received in the thigh, and which was become excessively painful. I had no greatcoat, and small rain continued falling until late the next day, when it was succeeded by torrents. Boney, however, was determined not to give us much respite, for he attacked our piquets at two in the morning; some companies of the 95th were sent to their support; and we continued skirmishing until eleven o'clock, when the Duke commenced his retreat, which was covered by Lord Uxbridge. The Blues and Life Guards behaved extremely well.[17]

Another description of the fighting was published in the *Caledonian Mercury* on 3 July 1815, having in turn been drawn from a private letter from a soldier of the 42nd Regiment to his father. The letter was written from the General Hospital at Antwerp on 24 June 1815:

After a long silence, I embrace the opportunity of informing you respecting my present situation. On the 15th, about 12 o'clock at night, we turned out, and at two in the morning marched from the city of Brussels, to meet the enemy, who were advancing in great force on that city. About three o'clock in the afternoon of the 16th, we came up with them. Our whole force did not exceed 12,000 men, who were fatigued with a long march of upwards of 20 miles, encumbered with knapsacks and other luggage.

The day was uncommonly warm, and no water was to be had on the road; however, we were brought up, in order of battle. The French being strongly posted in a thick wood, to the number of 40,000 men, including cavalry and lancers, gave us very little time to look round us ere the fight commenced on both sides, in an awful and destructive manner, they having every advantage of us, both as to position and numbers, particularly in cavalry, as the British dragoons had not yet come up. The French cavalry charged the British line of infantry three different times, and did much execution, until we were obliged to form squares of battalions, in order to turn them, which was executed in a most gallant manner, and many hundreds of them never returned. Still they sent up fresh forces, and as often we beat them back.

The battle lasted until it was quite dark, when the enemy began to give way, our poor fellows who were left alive following them as long as they could see, when night put an end to the fatigues of a well fought day. Thousands on both sides lay killed and wounded on the field of battle; and, as the greater part of the action lay in corn fields along a vast track of country, many hundreds must have died for want of assistance through the night, who were not able of themselves to crawl away. I was wounded by a musquet ball, which passed through my right arm and breast, and lodged in my back, from whence it was extracted by a surgeon in the hospital of this place. Captain M. is most severely wounded, having several shots through his body, and the regiment, in general, are mostly cut off.

We have heard, since we came here, that our fine brigade, which entered the field on that eventful day, consisting of the 3d batt. Royal Scots, 42d, 44th, and 92d regiments, are now formed into one battalion, not exceeding in whole 400 men. Lord Wellington retired in the night to wait for reinforcements, and next day our cavalry and the rest of the army arrived ... Nothing can exceed the kindness and attention of the inhabitants of this city to our wounded men: the hospital is constantly filled with ladies and gentlemen, who, although speaking a different language, personally administer to our wants, with the kindest attention, distributing clean shirts, bread, wine, coffee, tea, milk, and fruit of all sorts, with every requisite, for our comfort and accommodation.

Another unidentified officer who was a member of the 3rd Battalion of the 1st Regiment, the Royal Scots, provided the following account:

I have great pleasure in detailing the conduct of the gallant 3rd Battalion of the Royal Scots; and though I have been present with the regiment at the battles of Busaco, Salamanca, Vittoria, Fuentes d'Honor, both stormings of San Sebastian, the passage of the Bidassoa, &c. in all of which they bore a most conspicuous part, and suffered most severely, I can assure you they never evinced more steadiness and determined bravery than at the late battle. About half-past one o'clock on the 16th, the battalion was taken from its place in the centre of the 5th division, by a movement to its own left, by order of Sir Thomas Picton, and instantly by command of that lamented officer brought into action by a charge upon a column of the Enemy: it succeeded beyond our most sanguine expectations in routing this column, who afterwards formed under the protection of their cavalry, and then commenced a most galling fire upon us, which we returned with the utmost steadiness and precision.

The battalion was brought into action under the most trying circumstances imaginable, and continued so for a long time; but they never for one moment lost sight of that character which upon former trials they had so well earned and maintained. The ground through which they moved was planted with corn that took the tallest men up to the shoulders; and the Enemy by this, and the advantage of the rising ground, threw in volley after volley of grape and musketry, which did astonishing execution.

After being engaged for some time in a line, the battalion was formed into a square to resist the Enemy's cavalry, who were then advancing in great force; and I have the pride of stating, that though charged six or seven times by an infinite superiority of numbers, the French cavalry never for an instant made the slightest impression upon the square of the Royal Scots.

The high encomiums given to this battalion on the morning of the 17th, by the General Officers both of Brigade and Division, for its conduct on the 16th, have made me very proud of being a Royal Scot. The Cuirassiers never were able to make the smallest impression upon our squares, nor did we lose one single man by the cavalry. We were at the very commencement of the action sent with Sir James Kempt's brigade, by order of Sir T. Picton, and remained apart from our own brigade the whole day. The 42d and 92d were chiefly engaged near a village, in which the Commander of the Forces remained with the head-quarters for a great part of the afternoon. Our battalion and the 28th formed one square, and it so happened that the Cuirassiers charged that part of the square in which the Royals were posted.[18]

Lloyd's battery was directed to deal with two French batteries on the edge of the Bois de Bossu which were pounding the Brunswick Corps. One of his men, S. Rudyard, later recalled that,

Colonel Kelly, Q.M.G.D., ordered us to take up the position we did under this heavy fire, and before we unlimbered some three or four horses of each Gun and waggon were killed, some wheels disabled, and literally some of our gunners were cut in two, for we were not more than from four to five hundred yards from the Enemy's Batteries.

We succeeded in silencing them, and also in obliging a solid mass of French infantry … to retrograde and return to the wood. Finding ourselves now alone without any support, except a few Lancers of the Brunswickers, and the duty executed that we were ordered upon, we limbered up and walked off towards Quatre Bras and joined our Division.[19]

Ney had actually come very close to success during the day, as Captain Bourdo de Vatry, aide-de-camp to Jérôme Bonaparte, described:

Prince Jérôme was struck on the hip [during the attack upon Bossu Wood], but fortunately the ball hit the big gold scabbard of his sword first and did not penetrate, so he suffered nothing worse than a severe bruise which made him turn pale. Conquering his pain, the Prince remained on horseback at the head of his division, thereby setting an example for us all an example of courage and self-sacrifice. His coolness had an excellent effect. The 8th Cuirassiers, commanded by Colonel Garavaque, were about to launch a strong attack on a Scottish square [*sic*]; the regiment gave the Prince a cheer, and the brave horsemen having broken the square and captured the enemy's colours, presented this trophy to the ex-King [Jérôme was the erstwhile King of Wespphalia]

The position at Quatre Bras had just been taken by Kellermann's cavalry. Marshal Ney was impatiently awaiting the arrival of d'Erlon's corps, when he learnt that the Emperor had altered the direction of this corps and summoned it to join him at Saint-Armand. At the same time an unaccountable panic seized Kellermann's cavalry, which fled back hell for leather after knocking over their commander. Kellermann had the presence of mind to cling to the bits of two of his cuirassier's horses and so avoid being trampled.

As the infantry of the 1st Corps did not come, as it had been called to the battlefield of Ligny, the enemy reoccupied the Quatre Bras position and we were only too happy to prevent the English from going to the aid of the Prussians. This was all we could do in the face of considerable forces then holding Quatre Bras.[20]

Kellermann duly submitted a report to Marshal Ney on his actions that day. Signed 'the count of Valmy (Kellermann, the younger)', it was timed as being complied at about 22.00 hours:

I executed the charge that you have ordered me to do; I encountered the enemy infantry, posted in a small valley beneath their guns. On the spot, without giving the troops time to think, I rushed at the head of the 1st squadron of the 8th ... against the Anglo-Hanoverian infantry, in spite of the extensive fire, from the front and the flanks. Both lines of infantry were knocked over, the greatest disorder was in the enemy line, which we crossed two – three times, the most complete success was ensured if the lancers would have followed us, the cuirassiers, shot upon from all sides, could not exploit the advantage that they had obtained by this most resolute and fearless charge against an infantry which did not let itself be intimidated and which they fired with the greatest coolness as if during an exercise.

We took a flag of the 69th which was taken by the cuirassiers Valgayer and Mourassin. The brigade having taken an enormous loss and seeing that they were not supported, withdrew in the usual disorder as in similar circumstances, my horse was knocked down by two shots, and I fell under it. I was barely able to escape ... I was hurt in the knee and the leg, but nevertheless, I shall be there tomorrow on horseback.[21]

In this way, Kellermann provides a perfectly understandable reason for the precipitate withdrawal of his cuirassiers. The incident regarding d'Erlon's Corps, was far from being easily explained, and was one of the most controversial occurrences of the entire campaign. Ney, possibly with some justification, believed that it cost him victory, as he explained to Fouché:

> On the 16th, I received orders to attack the English in their position at Quatre Bras. We advanced towards the enemy with an enthusiasm difficult to be described. Nothing resisted our impetuosity The battle became general, and victory was no longer doubtful, when, at the moment that I intended to order up the first corps of infantry, which had been left by me in reserve at Frasnes, I learned that the Emperor had disposed of it without adverting me of the circumstance, as well as of the division of Girard of the second corps, on purpose to direct them upon St. Amand, and to strengthen his left wing, which was vigorously engaged with the Prussians. The shock which this intelligence gave me, confounded me.
>
> Having no longer under me more than three divisions, instead of the eight upon which I calculated, I was obliged to renounce the hopes of victory; and, in spite of all my efforts, in spite of the intrepidity and devotion of my troops, my utmost efforts after that could only maintain me in my position till the close of the day. About nine o'clock, the first corps was sent me by the Emperor, to whom it had been of no service. Thus twenty-five or thirty thousand men were, I may say, paralysed, and were idly paraded during the whole of the battle from the right to the left, and the left to the right, without firing a shot.
>
> It is impossible for me, Sir, not to arrest your attention for a moment upon these details, in order to bring before your view all the consequences of this false movement, and, in general, of the bad arrangements during the whole of the day. By what fatality, for example did the Emperor, instead of leading all his forces against Lord Wellington, who would have been attacked unawares, and could not have resisted, consider this attack as secondary? How did the Emperor, after the passage of the Sambre, conceive it possible to fight two battles on the same day? It was to oppose forces double ours, and to do what military men who were witnesses of it can scarcely yet comprehend. Instead of this, had he left a corps of observation to watch the Prussians, and marched with his most

powerful masses to support me, the English army had undoubtedly been destroyed between Quatre Bras, and Genappes; and this position, which separated the two allied armies, being once in our power, would have opened for the Emperor an opportunity of advancing to the right of the Prussians, and of crushing them in their turn. The general opinion in France and especially in the army, was, that the Emperor would have bent his whole efforts to annihilate first the English army; and circumstances were favourable for the accomplishment of such a project: but fate ordered otherwise. On the 17th, the army marched in the direction of Mont St Jean.[22]

Ney made these observations after the end of the campaign. For now, he had to deal with the situation as it presented itself and he reported to Napoleon, via Soult, from Frasnes at 22.00 hours. Nevertheless, he still made a point of referring to the Emperor's decision to divert d'Erlon's Corps away from Quatre Bras:

> Marshal, I have attacked the English position at Quatre Bras with the greatest vigour; but an error of Count D'Erlon's deprived me of a fine victory, for at the very moment when the 5th and 9th Divisions of General Reille's Corps had overthrown everything in front of them, the I Corps marched off to St. Amand to support his Majesty's left; but the fatal thing was that this Corps, having then counter-marched to rejoin my wing, gave no useful assistance on either field.
>
> Prince Jérôme's Division fought with great valour; His Royal Highness has been slightly wounded.
>
> Actually there have been engaged here only 3 Infantry Divisions, a Brigade of Cuirassiers, and General Piré's Cavalry. The Count of Valmy delivered a fine charge. All have done their duty, except the I Corps. The enemy has lost heavily; we have captured some guns and a flag.
>
> We have lost about 2,000 killed and 4,000 wounded. I have called for reports from Generals Reille and D'Erlon, and will forward them to Your Excellency.
>
> Accept, Marshal, the assurance of my deep respect.[23]

Wellington had stabilized his position at Quatre Bras. At Genappe on 16 June, he issued his orders to consolidate all of his forces upon that point the following day in the expectation that Ney would renew his assault upon the crossroads the next morning:

> The 2d division of infantry to move to-morrow morning at daybreak from Nivelles to Quatre Bras. The 4th division of infantry to move at

daybreak to-morrow morning to Nivelles. 16th June, 1815. The reserve artillery to move at daybreak to-morrow morning, the 17th, to Quatre Bras, where it will receive further orders.

These orders then went on to specify the instructions for Major General Sir John Lambert, KCB, who was in charge of the British 10th Brigade:

The brigade of infantry, under the command of Major Gen. Sir J. Lambert, to march from Assche at daybreak to-morrow morning, the 17th inst., to Genappe, on the Namur road, and to remain there until further orders.[24]

Lieutenant General Sir Charles Alten was a Hanoverian in British service, and he reported to his sovereign, His Royal Highness Field Marshal and Governor General the Duke of Cambridge, in a message from Brussels which was dated 20 June 1815. It was delivered by Lieutenant, and Senior Adjutant, Wiegman:

On the evening of the 15th June, the troops broke up from their variously dispersed cantonments. The Duke of Wellington united them with the troops in the neighbourhood of Brussels, near Genappe. The Hereditary Prince of Orange, under whose orders my division was, retreated to Quatre Bras, where the roads from Mons to Namur, and from Brussels to Charleroi, cross each other. The French had divided their army, and attacked the Prussians, the Duke of Wellington, and our corps at the same time. The Hereditary Prince placed us between Quatre Bras and Sarte a Mavelines, with our right wing and our left on the latter village. The troops marched here under a most violent cannonade from the enemy. A wood on the right of Quatre Bras was alternately taken and retaken. The cannonade on both sides was very brisk. The enemy endeavoured several times to force our left. I sent off the field-battalion Lüneburg to drive him from the village of Pierremont in front. The First Lieutenant Von Klenke executed this duty with great courage, took the village, and maintained it against repeated attacks of the enemy.

The enemy's infantry now advanced in columns, against which I detached the battalions, Grupenhagen, Osnabrück, and Bremen. These troops, with the help of the artillery of the Royal German Legion, under Captain Eleves, repulsed the enemy. On the right wing, the enemy's cavalry several times ventured to attack; but the firmness of the troops prevented their being broken. Upon this occasion, the Landwehr battalion Lüneburg particularly distinguished itself under the command of Lieut Col. Ramdohr. These troops allowed the enemy's cavalry to come within thirty paces of them, and then gave a discharge, by which they were driven back with great loss. We were so fortunate as to maintain our position. However, as the Prussian army on our left had received a considerable check, we were obliged to retreat, on the 17th, to Genappe, my division forming the rear-guard. But as the enemy, in the afternoon, appeared there in great force, we marched back on Mont St. Jean, by the road to Brussels.[25]

The Prince of Orange also submitted a report on the day's fighting to his father, the King of the United Netherlands. This was sent from Nivelles at 02.00 hours on the morning of 17 June:

Very early on the morning of the 15th, the Prussian army was attacked in its position, which it quitted in consequence thereof, and retired from Charleroi by Goselies to the neighbourhood of Fleurus. As soon as I was apprized of this attack, I gave orders for the necessary dispositions of the corps d'armee under my command. In consequence of what had occurred with the Prussian army, the battalion of Orange Nassau, which held the village of Frasnes with a battery of mounted artillery, was already attacked on the 15th, at five in the afternoon. These troops remained in possession of their position on the heights of the above-mentioned village not far from the cross road named Les Quatre Bras.

At eight o'clock the skirmishing at this point was at an end. As soon as I was informed of this attack I issued orders to the third division, as also to the cavalry and two English divisions to march to Nivelles, and directed the second division to maintain the position of Les Quatres Bras. Only a part of the second division could immediately proceed thither, as the brigade under the orders of Major General Van Byland could not march from Nivelles until the arrival of the other divisions at Nivelles might be expected. So early as about five o'clock yesterday morning, the fire of the skirmishers commenced at the above-mentioned point, and was kept up till noon without any advantage on either side.

Towards two o'clock, the attack, especially on the part of the cavalry and artillery, became much more violent. As the brigade of light cavalry under the command of Major General Van Merle was not able to come up until about four o'clock. I had till then no cavalry to oppose the enemy. Being sensible of the great importance of maintaining the position on the heights in advance of the intersection of the road at the point called Les Quatres Bras, I had then the good fortune to hold this position against an enemy in all respects, and beyond all comparison, superior in force, since I was attacked by the two *corps d'armee* commanded by Generals D'Erlon and Reille; and as they were not able to succeed in this attack, the Duke of Wellington had time enough to assemble a force to frustrate the designs of the enemy.

The result of this attack was, that after a very severe engagement, which lasted till nine o'clock at night, we not only brought the enemy to a stand, but even drove him back to some extent. The Prussian army having been also attacked yesterday, maintained its main position; and it is beyond doubt that Napoleon directed the attack with a powerful force upon the whole line. Our troops have remained bivouacked on the field of battle, whither I am about to proceed forthwith, as it is highly probable that Napoleon will again endeavour to carry into execution his plans of yesterday.

The Duke of Wellington has caused all the troops that could possibly do so, to assemble at this point. It affords me the highest satisfaction to be able to assure your Majesty that your Majesty's troops fought with much bravery, especially the infantry and artillery. As through circumstances I have not yet been able to receive the reports of the various corps in reference to their loss, it is impossible for me to forward to your Majesty the statement thereof herewith, but which I shall have the honour to do as soon as possible.[26]

Not all the Allied regiments were able to reach Quatre Bras in time to influence the course of the battle as Sergeant Ewart of the 2nd Royal North British Dragoons, the Scots Greys, explained to his brother. This account was reproduced in the *Caledonian Mercury* on 18 September 1815:

All the British cavalry, in fact all the cavalry under the command of Lord Wellington, were lying in quarters round Brussels, and the infantry in camp a little way distant from it, very quietly, until the morning of the 16th, about one o'clock, when the trumpet sounded us to horse, which, I assure you, put us into a bustle; however, we got assembled by five in the morning by regiments; and the whole cavalry met at a place called Ninove, and accordingly we set out to meet our enemy; but, before we had got up, the infantry was engaged for upwards of six hours.

We perfectly heard them, but, alas, could render them not the least assistance, which opportunity the French cavalry embraced, and cut up our infantry most shockingly, particularly the 42d, 79th and 92d regiments, which were almost cut to pieces; however, we got to the field about 11 at night, and before that time the enemy fell back into their intrenchments in a wood in front of us.

The vital crossroads had been held and Wellington's troops still blocked the road to Brussels. What would happen next would depend upon the result of the action between Napoleon and Blücher just a few miles to the west at Ligny.

5

Battle of Ligny

Throughout the morning of 16 June 1815, the Prussian I, II and III Corps had been taking up their positions above the small stream of Ligny. This was part of the Prussian Official Account of the Battle of Ligny written on behalf of Blücher by his Chief of Staff, General Gneisenau:

> The Prussian army was posted on the heights between Brie and Sombref, and beyond the last place, and occupied with a large force the villages of St. Amand and Ligny, situated on its front. Meantime only three corps of the army had joined; the 4th, which was stationed between Liege and Hannut, had been delayed in its march by several circumstances, and was not yet come up. Nevertheless Field Marshal Blucher resolved to give battle, Lord Wellington having already put in motion, to support him, a strong division of his army, as well as his whole reserve, stationed in the environs of Brussels, and the fourth corps of the Prussian army being also on the point of arriving.[1]

Wellington had indeed ridden over to discuss operations with Blücher and offer what support he could, as Colonel von Reiche, Ziethen's Chief of Staff, recalled:

> At one o'clock Blücher appeared on the hill by the mill of Bussy, and not long afterwards the Duke of Wellington rode up. He wore a simple blue overcoat without decorations, an ordinary three-cornered hat with three cockades side by side – one black and two red, the Spanish and Portuguese, with a red and white plume, fastened, as was then the English custom, between the two brims of the hat. Otherwise he was very quietly dressed. For this reason none of our troops recognised him for who or what he was; but as I knew him already … I was able to tell them, and every man standing near turned to look at the famous war hero.

After some discussion he was convinced that the enemy's main force was directed against us and not against Quatre Bras; moreover there could no longer be any uncertainty about the direction of the enemy's attack.

From the hill Wellington could overlook our positions in every direction, and he enquired what measures had been taken or were in hand. At this moment we noticed in the distance a part of the enemy, and Napoleon was clearly distinguishable in the group. Perhaps the eyes of the three greatest military commanders of the age were directed upon each other.

Having promised support and cooperation, Wellington left soon after half past one to his own army. The horse which he rode on this occasion attracted a good deal of attention. A small valise had been strapped to the back of the saddle, and according to one of his staff officers this contained a change of clothes; in addition, a portfolio and pen and ink had been fastened in place of the pistol holder – indications of the way in which English industry knows how to be compendious and practical.[2]

Gneisenau's dispositions for the coming battle were given in brief in the instructions that were issued at 05.00 hours:

> 1st Brigade to occupy the village of St Amand, 3rd Brigade the village of Brye, 4th Brigade Ligny, and 2nd Brigade is to form up in reserve in the centre behind the windmill hill.
>
> I Corps' Reserve cavalry is to deploy behind the village of Ligny, leaving the left of it free for the Reserve Artillery to move into position. To cover this movement, the 12-pounders on the Tombe de Ligny are to remain there until it is completed, and should then depart.[3]

Gneisenau ordered that the two villages should be put in a state of defence, with barricades being formed. Those units not required for the actual defence of St Amand and Ligny were to form up in support behind. These positions were taken up by around 08.00 hours.

Wellington famously disagreed with the manner in which the Prussian army had been deployed, his words having been recorded by the Baron de Ros:

> I told the Prussian officers, in the presence of Hardinge, that according to my judgement, the exposure of the advanced columns, and indeed, of the whole army to cannonade, standing as they did so displayed to the aim of the enemy's fire, was not so prudent.

The marshy banks of the stream made it out of their power to cross and attack the French, while the latter on the other hand, though they could not attack them, had it in their power to cannonade them and shatter them to pieces, after which they might fall upon them by the bridges at the villages. I said that if I were in Blücher's place with English troops, I should withdraw all the columns I saw scattered about in front, and get more of the troops under shelter of the rising ground. However, they seemed to think they knew best, so I came away very shortly.[4]

The Prussian Official Account of the Battle of Ligny, having pointed out that the battle began at 15.00 hours, continues:

The enemy brought up above 150,000 men. The Prussian army was 80,000 strong. The village of St. Amand was the first point attacked by the enemy, who carried it after a vigorous resistance. He then directed his efforts against Ligny; it is a large village, solidly built, situated on a rivulet of the same name. It was there that a contest began which may be considered as one of the most obstinate recorded in history. – Villages have often been taken and retaken, but here the battle continued for five hours in the villages themselves, and the movements forwards or backwards were confined to a very narrow space.

On both sides fresh troops continually came up. Each army had behind the part of the village which it occupied great masses of infantry, which maintained the combat, and were continually renewed by the reinforcements which they received from their rear as well as from the heights on the right and left. About 200 cannon were directed from both sides against the village, which was on fire in several places at once. From time to time the combat extended along the whole line, the enemy having also directed troops against the third corps; however, the main combat was against Ligny.

Things seemed to take a favourable turn for the Prussian troops, a part of the village of St. Amand having been retaken from the French by a battalion commanded by the Field Marshal in person; in consequence of which advantage we had regained the height which had been abandoned, after the loss of St. Amand. Nevertheless the battle continued about Ligny with the same fury.[5]

Major General Baron Willem Benjamin van Panhuys, the Netherlands' Military Commissioner attached to the Prussian headquarters, watched the battle unfold:

One by one great masses of infantry were directed upon Fleurus ... and strong columns of infantry deployed in front of the road from Fleurus parallel with the Ligne stream, which separated the two armies. After being in possession of Fleurus towards two o'clock, he attacked the village of St Amand which was twice taken and retaken, and from that moment until the evening a continuous fire was maintained. The village of Ligny, on which so much seemed to depend the fate of the battle, was taken and retaken three times during a most stubborn contest, during which it was set alight.[6]

Général de Brigade Charles Angélique François Huchet comte de La Bédoyère was one of Napoleon's aides-de-camp:

At three o'clock the 3d corps reached St. Amand, and carried the same, when the Prussians, rallied by Blucher, retook the village. The French, entrenched in the churchyard, defended themselves with obstinacy; but, overpowered by numbers, were about to give way, when General Drouot, who once more decided the fate of battle, galloped up with four batteries of the guard, took the enemy in rear, and arrested his progress.

At the same moment Grouchy was combating successfully at Sombref, while Gerard made an impetuous attack upon the village of Ligny. Its embattled walls, and a long ravine, rendered the approaches no less difficult than dangerous; but those obstacles did not intimidate General Lefol, and the men under his command, who advanced with the bayonet, and in a few minutes the Prussians, repulsed and partly annihilated, quitted the ground. Blucher, conscious that the possession of Ligny must render the French masters of the field, returned to the charge with a body of chosen troops; and there, to use his own words, 'commenced a battle, that may be considered as having been one of the most obstinate recorded in history.'

For five hours, two hundred pieces of ordnance deluged the field with slaughter, blood, and death, during which period the French and Prussians, alternately vanquished and victors, disputed that ensanguined post hand to hand and foot to foot, so that no less than seven times in succession Ligny was taken and lost.[7]

Captain von Reuter commanded a battery of Prussian artillery supporting Ziethen's Corps and was positioned near the Bussy Windmill during the battle:

I suppose it was between two and three o'clock in the afternoon when I received an order to take four guns of my battery and accompany the 4th Regiment in its advance towards St. Amand, while the howitzers and the two remaining guns took up a position opposite Ligny, so as to be able to shell the open ground beyond the village, and the village itself, too, in the event of our not being able to hold it. I halted my guns about six hundred paces from St. Amand, and opened fire on the enemy's artillery in position on the high ground opposite, which at once began to reply with a well-sustained fire of shells, and inflicted heavy losses on us.

Meanwhile the 14th Regiment, without ever thinking of leaving an escort behind for us, pressed gallantly forward to St. Amand, and succeeded in gaining possession of that part of the village. I myself was under the impression that they had been able to occupy the whole of it. The battery had been thus engaged for some hours in its combat with the hostile guns, and were awaiting the order to follow up the movement of the 14th Regiment, when suddenly I became aware of two strong lines of skirmishers which were apparently falling back on us from the village of St. Amand. Imagining that the skirmishers in front of us were our own countrymen, I hastened up the battery and warned my layers not to direct their aim upon them, but to continue to engage the guns opposite. In the meantime the skirmishers in question had got within three hundred paces of the battery.

I had just returned to the right flank of my command, when our surgeon, Zinkernagel, called my attention to the red tufts on the shakos of the sharpshooters. I at once bellowed out the order, 'With grape on the skirmishers!' At the same moment both their lines turned upon us, gave us a volley, and then flung themselves on the ground. By this volley, and the bursting of a shell or two, every horse, except one wheeler, belonging to the gun on my left flank, was either killed or wounded. I ordered the horse to be taken out of one of my ammunition wagons, which had been emptied, and thus intended to make my gun fit to move again, while I meanwhile kept up a slow fire of grape, that had the effect of keeping the marksmen in my front glued to the ground.

But in another moment, all of a sudden, I saw my left flank taken in rear, from the direction of the Ligny brook, by a French staff officer and about fifty horsemen. As these rushed upon us the officer shouted to me in German, 'Surrender, gunners, for you are all prisoners!' With these words he charged down with his men on the flank gun on my left, and dealt a vicious cut at my wheel driver ... who dodged it, however, by flinging himself over on his dead horse. The blow was delivered with such good will that the sabre cut deep into the saddle, and stuck there fast. Gunner Sieberg, however, availing himself of the chance the momentary delay afforded, snatched up the handspike of one of the 12-pounders, and with the words, 'I'll soon show him how to take prisoners!' dealt the officer such a blow on his bearskin that he rolled with a broken skull from the back of his grey charger, which galloped away into the line of skirmishers in our front.

The fifty horsemen, unable to control their horses which bounded after their companion, followed his lead in a moment, rode over the prostrate marksmen, and carried the utmost confusion into the enemy's ranks. I seized the opportunity to limber up all of my guns except the unfortunate one on my left, and to retire on two of our cavalry regiments, which I saw drawn up about two hundred paces to my rear. It was only when I had thus fallen back that the enemy's skirmishers ventured to approach my remaining gun. I could see from a distance how bravely its detachment defended themselves and it with handspikes and their side-arms, and some of them in the end succeeded in regaining the battery. The moment I got near our cavalry I rode up to them and entreated them to endeavour to recapture my gun again from the enemy, but they refused to comply with my request. I, therefore, returned sorrowfully to my battery, which had retired meanwhile behind the hill with the windmill on it near Ligny.

We there replenished our ammunition wagons and limber boxes, and set to rights our guns, and the battery again advanced to come into action on the height. We had, however, hardly reached the crest of the hill when the enemy issued from the village of Ligny in overpowering numbers, and compelled all our troops which were there with us to fall back. The movement was carried with complete steadiness and regularity. It was now about eight o'clock p.m., and the growing darkness was increased by the heavy storm clouds which began to settle all round us.

My battery, in order to avoid capture, had, of course, to conform to this general movement. I now noticed that there was an excellent artillery position about 1,500 paces behind the village of Brye, close to where the Roman road intersects the road to Quatre Bras … I made for this point with all haste, so that I might there place my guns and cover with their fire the retreat of my comrades of the other arms.

A hollow road leading to Sombreffe delayed my progress some minutes. At length I got over this obstacle and attained my goal; but just as I was going to give the word, 'Action rear.' Von Pirch's infantry brigade began to debouch from Brye. The general saw in an instant what he took for a selfish and cowardly movement on my part, dashed his spurs into his horse, and galloped up to me nearly beside himself with passion, amd shouting out, 'My God! Everything is going to the Devil!' 'Truly, sir,' I said, 'matters are not looking very rosy, but the 12-pounder battery No.6, has simply come here to get into a position from whence it thinks it may be able to check the enemy's advance.' 'That then is very brave conduct on your part,' answered the general, at once mollified; 'cling to the position at all hazards, it is of the greatest importance. I will collect a few troops to form an escort to your guns.'

While this short, but animated discussion had been going on his brigade had come up close to where we were. He formed it up to cover us, and sent everyone who was mounted to collect all retreating troops in the neighbourhood for the same purpose, while, as they came up, he called to them, 'Soldiers, there stand your guns; are you not Prussians!'

During the time that a sort of rearguard was thus formed, the battery had opened fire on the enemy's cavalry, which was coming up rather cautiously, and had forced them to fall back again. Later on, a 6-pounder field battery and half a horse artillery battery came up and joined us. The fight then became stationary, and as the darkness came on, fighting gradually ceased on both sides.[8]

The French Official account of the 'Battle of Ligny-under-Fleurus', the name that they gave to the Battle of Ligny, was published in Paris on 21 June 1815:

On the morning of the 16th the army occupied the following position: – The left wing, commanded by the Marshal Duke of Elchingen, and consisting of the 1st and 2d corps of infantry, and the 2d of cavalry, occupied the positions of Frasnes.

The left wing, commanded by Marshal Grouchy, and composed of the 2d and 4th corps of infantry, and the 3d corps of cavalry, occupied the heights in rear of Fleurus.

The Emperor's head-quarters were at Charleroi, where were the Imperial Guard and the 6th corps. The left wing had orders to march upon Quatre Bras, and the right upon Sombref. The Emperor advanced to Fleurus with his reserve.

The columns of Marshal Grouchy being in march, perceived, after having passed Fleurus, the enemy's army, commanded by Field Marshal Blucher, occupying with its left the heights of the mill of Bussy, the village of Sombref, and extending its cavalry a great way forward on the road to Naimur; its right was at St. Amand, and occupied that large village in great force, having before it a ravine which formed its position.

The Emperor reconnoitred the strength and the position of the enemy, and resolved to attack immediately. It became necessary to change front, the right in advance, and pivoting upon Fleurus. General Vandamme marched upon St. Amand, General Girard upon Ligny, and Marshal Grouchy upon Sombref. The 4th division of the 2d corps, commanded by General Girard, marched in reserve behind the corps of General Vandamme. The guard was drawn up on the heights of Fleurus, as well as the cuirassiers of General Milhaud.

At three in the afternoon, these dispositions were finished. The division of General Lefol, forming part of the corps of General Vandamme, was first engaged, and made itself master of St. Amand, whence it drove out the enemy at the point of the bayonet. It kept its ground during the whole of the engagement, at the burial-ground and steeple of St. Amand: but that village, which is very extensive, was the theatre of various combats during the evening; the whole corps of Gen. Vaudamme was there engaged, and the enemy there fought in considerable force.

General Girard, placed as a reserve to the corps of General Vandamme, turned the village by its right, and fought there with his accustomed valour. The respective forces were supported on both sides by about 50 pieces of cannon each.

On the right, General Girard came into action with the 4th corps, at the village of Ligny, which was taken and retaken several times.

Marshal Grouchy, on the extreme right, and General Pajol fought at the village of Sombref. The enemy showed from 80 to 90,000 men, and a great number of cannon.

At seven o'clock we were masters of all the villages situated on the bank of the ravine, which covered the enemy's position; but he still occupied, with all his masses, the heights of the mill of Bussy.[9]

As mentioned in the account of the Battle of Quatre Bras, Napoleon requested the help of d'Erlon's I Corps to strike the right flank of the Prussian positions, which would have turned the Prussian defeat into a disaster. This is the first of these instructions that Soult sent to Ney from Fleurus at 14.00 hours, before the fighting had begun:

Monsieur le Maréchal. The Emperor entrusts me with warning you that the enemy has gathered a corps of troops between Sombreffe and Brye and that at 2.30 p.m., Maréchal de Grouchy will attack them with III and IV Corps. His Majesty's intention is that you should also attack what is before you and that, after you have vigorously pushed the enemy, you should fall back on us to concur in the envelopment of

89

the corps which I have just mentioned. If this corps is burst through before that, then His Majesty will have a manoeuvre made in your direction to hasten your operations also. Instruct the Emperor immediately of your dispositions and of what goes on in your front.[10]

In simpler terms, the message was stating that if Napoleon is successful he will send Ney help and if Ney is successful he should send troops to help the Emperor. Just two and a half hours later Napoleon changed his mind. This order was sent by Soult at 16.30 hours from Ligny:

> Monsieur le Maréchal, I wrote to you an hour ago [sic] that the Emperor would have the enemy attacked at 2 p.m. in the position he had taken between St Amand and Brye. At this moment, the engagement is very pronounced. His Majesty entrusts me with telling you that you must manoeuvre instantly in order to envelop the enemy's right and fall with might and main on his rear. This army is lost if you act vigorously.
>
> The fate of France is in your hands. So do not hesitate for an instant and do operate the movement which the Emperor orders you to make on the heights of Brye and St Amand in order to concur in what will perhaps be decisive victory. The enemy is caught red-handed at the moment when he seeks to re-unite with the English.[11]

Exactly what happened next still remains something of a mystery. All that is known for certain is that an officer from Soult's or Napoleon's staff, usually stated to be General La Bédoyère, rode over to the closest of Ney's formations to Ligny. This was d'Erlon's Corps which, by 16.00 hours, was moving up to Quatre Bras and had reached Gosselies.

D'Erlon rode ahead to tell Ney that he would soon be arriving at the battlefield. During his absence the staff officer from Ligny came across I Corps and with, supposedly, a note written in pencil that he claimed was from Napoleon, persuaded d'Erlon's divisional commanders to turn round and march towards Ligny. When d'Erlon rode back to his corps he found it already in motion eastwards. This note has never been found but it supposedly was as follows, timed at 15.45 hours, though the timing of the message is somewhat suspect.

> In front of Fleurus, Monsieur the Count d'Erlon. The enemy lowers his head into the trap that I intended for him. Bring at once your four divisions of infantry, your division of cavalry, all your artillery, and two divisions of heavy cavalry which I place at your disposal, carry you, say I, with all these forces the height of Saint-Amand and melt

on Ligny. Mister the Count d'Erlon, you will save France and will cover yourself with glory. Napoleon.[12]

So off marched I Corps, coming within sight of the battlefield at Ligny just after 17.00 hours. Ney, however, learnt of d'Erlon's march to Ligny from d'Erlon's chief of staff. He was mad with rage at this movement which he had not been informed of and he sent Delcambre (or d'Elcambre) off with orders for d'Erlon to return immediately to Quatre Bras. D'Erlon wrote the following explanation of the affair in a letter to Marshal Ney's son:

> Towards 11.00 a.m. or midday, Marshal Ney sent me the order to place my army corps under arms and to direct it towards Frasnes and Quatre Bras, where I would receive further orders. Therefore my army corps began to move immediately. After ordering the general in command of the head of the column to make haste, I went on ahead to see what was happening at Quatre Bras, where it seemed to me that General Reille's corps was engaged
>
> Beyond Frasnes, I stopped with some generals of the Guard, where I was joined by General La Bédoyère, who showed me a pencilled note that he was bearing to Marshal Ney and which enjoined the marshal to direct my army corps on Ligny. General La Bédoyère informed me that he had already given the order for this movement by changing the direction of my column, and he indicated to me where I could rejoin it. I immediately took this road and sent my Chief of Staff, General [de Brigade Victor-Joseph] Delcambre, to the Marshal [Ney] to inform him of my new destination.
>
> Marshal Ney sent him back to me ordering me imperatively to return to Quatre Bras, where he was heavily engaged and counted on the cooperation of my army corps. Hence I had to imagine the situation was desperate, since the marshal had taken on it himself to recall me, although he had received the note about which I have spoken above. In consequence, I ordered the column to make a return march. But in spite of all the haste that could be put into this march, my column could not appear to the rear of Quatre Bras until nightfall.
>
> Did General La Bédoyère have the authority to change the direction of my column before having seen the marshal? I do not think so. But in any case, this circumstance alone caused all the marches and counter-marches that paralysed my corps on the 16th June.[13]

I Corps consequently spent the entire day marching forwards and backwards without being able to influence the outcome of either of the battles being fought. D'Erlon's intervention at Ligny or Quatre Bras might well have changed the course of the entire campaign.

Such confusion need not have arisen if Napoleon had deployed his forces differently, according to General Joseph, vicomte de Rogniat, the chief engineer (*commandant du génie*) of *l'armée du Nord*:

> We arrived upon their right flank; reason counceled us to attack this wing; in this way we should have avoided in part the defiles of the brook [the Ligny stream]; we should have approached our own left wing, which was fighting at Quatre Bras, so that both armies could have helped each other, and finally we should have thrown the Prussians far from the English, in forcing them to retire on Namur.

Napoleon later explained in writing the reasons behind his decision not to adopt this seemingly wise course of action:

> The question in this battle was not that of separating the English from the Prussians; we knew that the English could not be ready to act till the next day; but here the point was to hinder that part of the IIId Corps of Blücher which had not joined him by 11. A.M., and which came by way of Namur, and also the IVth Corps, which came from Liége by way of Gembloux, from uniting [with the I and II Corps] on the field of battle. In cutting the enemy's line at Ligny, his whole right wing at St. Amand was turned and compromised; while by simply becoming masters of St Amand, we should have accomplished nothing.[14]

The result of Napoleon's decision was a direct assault upon Ligny, where the fighting was particularly brutal, as Richard Wellmann of the Prussian 29th Regiment experienced:

> In the streets of the village, we fought with clubbed muskets and bayonets. As if overcome by personal hatred, man battled against man. It seemed as if every individual had met his deadliest enemy and rejoiced at the long-awaited opportunity to give expression to this. Pardon was neither asked nor given; the French plunged their bayonets in the chests of those already falling from their wounds; the Prussians swore loudly at their enemies and killed everyone that fell into their hands.[15]

Captain Fritz of the 4th Westphalian Infantry Regiment of *Landwehr* described the condition the troops were in after a day's heavy fighting:

> The light of the long June day was beginning to fail when our very depleted infantry brigade was sent back into reserve ... The men looked terribly worn out after the fighting. In the great heat, gunpowder smoke, sweat and mud had mixed into a crust of dirt, so that their faces looked almost like those of mulattos, and one could hardly distinguish the green collars and facings on their tunics.
>
> Everybody had discarded his stocks; grubby shirts or hairy brown chests stuck out from their open tunics; and many who had been unwilling to leave the ranks on account of a slight wound wore a bandage they had put on themselves. In a number of cases blood was soaking through.
>
> As a result of fighting in the villages for hours on end, and of frequently crawling through hedges, the men's tunics and trousers had got torn, so that they hung in rags and their bare skin showed through.[16]

The French Official account of the 'Battle of Ligny-under-Fleurus' continues its description of the events in this manner:

> The Emperor returned with his Guard to the village of Ligny; General Girard directed General Pecheux to debouch with what remained of the reserve, almost all the troops having been engaged in that village. Eight battalions of the Guard debouched with fixed bayonets, and behind them, four squadrons of the guards, the cuirassiers of General Delort, those of General Milhaud, and the grenadiers of the horse guards.
>
> The Old Guard attacked with the bayonet the enemy's columns, which were on the heights of Bussy, and in an instant covered the field of battle with dead. The squadron of the guard attacked and broke a square, and the cuirassiers repulsed the enemy in all directions. At half past nine o'clock we had forty pieces of cannon, several carriages, colours, and prisoners, and the enemy sought safety in a precipitate retreat. At ten o'clock the battle was finished, and we found ourselves masters of the field of battle.[17]

Gneisenau's official account of the events of the day, predictably, painted a slightly different picture, but accepted that the battle had indeed been lost:

The issue seemed to depend on the arrival of the English troops, or on that of the 4th corps of the Prussian army; in fact, the arrival of this last division would have afforded the Field Marshal the means of making immediately with the right wing an attack, from which great success might be expected. But news arrived that the English division destined to support us was violently attacked by a corps of the French army, and that it was with great difficulty it had maintained itself in its position. – At Quatre Bras, the 4th corps of the army did not appear, so that we were forced to maintain alone the contest with an enemy greatly superior in numbers. – The evening was already much advanced, and the combat about Ligny continued with the same fury and the same equality of success. We invoked, but in vain, the arrival of those succours which were so necessary.

The danger became every hour more and more urgent, all the divisions were engaged or had already been so, and there was not any corps at hand able to support them. Suddenly a division of the enemy's infantry, which, by favour of the night, had made a circuit round the village without being observed, at the same time that some regiments of cuirassiers had forced the passage on the other side, took in the rear the main body of our army, which was posted behind the houses. This surprize on the part of the enemy was decisive, especially at the moment when our cavalry, also posted on a height behind the village, was repulsed by the enemy's cavalry in repeated attacks. Our infantry posted behind Ligny, though forced to retreat, did not suffer itself to be discouraged, either by being surprized by the enemy in the darkness, a circumstance which exaggerates in the mind of man the dangers to which he finds himself exposed, or by the idea of seeing itself surrounded on all sides.

Formed in masses, it coolly repulsed all the attacks of the cavalry, and retreated in good order upon the heights, whence it continued its retrograde movement upon Tilly. In consequence of the sudden irruption of the enemy's cavalry, several of our cannons, in their precipitate retreat, had taken directions which led them to defiles in which they necessarily fell into disorder; in this manner 15 pieces fell into the hands of the enemy.

At the distance of a quarter of a league from the field of battle, the army formed again. The enemy did not venture to pursue it. The village of Brie remained in our possession during the night, as well as Sombref, where General Thielmann had fought with the 3d corps, and where he at day-break slowly began to retreat towards

Gembloux, where the 4th corps, under General Bulow, had at length arrived during the night. The 1st and 2d corps proceeded in the morning behind the defile of Mount St. Guibert. Our losses in killed and wounded was great, the enemy, however, took from us no prisoners, except a part of our wounded.

The battle was lost, but not our honour. Our soldiers had fought with a bravery which equalled every expectation; their fortitude remained unshaken, because everyone retained his confidence in his own strength. On this day Field Marshal Blucher had encountered the greatest dangers. A charge of cavalry, led on by himself, had failed, while that of the enemy was vigorously pursuing. A musket-shot struck the Field Marshal's horse; the animal, far from being stopped in his career by this wound, began to gallop more furiously till it dropped down dead.

The Field Marshal, stunned by the violent fall, lay entangled under the horse. The enemy's cuirassiers following up their advantage, advanced; our last horseman had already passed the Field Marshal; an Adjutant alone remained with him, and had just alighted, resolved to share his fate. The danger was great, but Heaven watched over us. – The enemy pursuing their charge passed rapidly by the Field Marshal without seeing him; the next moment, a second charge of our cavalry having repelled them, they again passed by him with the same precipitation, not perceiving him any more than they had done the first time. Then, but not without difficulty, the Field Marshal was disengaged from under the dead horse, and he immediately mounted a dragoon horse.[18]

The Battle of Ligny was a victory for the French but it was destined to be Napoleon's last triumph. For now, though, the French could celebrate their success, as indicated by the following letter which was written from the French camp at Fleurus on 17 June:

The French armies have again immortalized themselves on the plains of Fleurus. We entered Belgium on the 15th. The Enemy was thrown in a first affair upon every point where he attempted to resist as.

Before Charleroi, several of his squares were broken and taken by some squadrons only: one thousand seven hundred prisoners only could be saved out of five or six thousand men, who composed those squares. Yesterday (the 16th) we encountered the whole of the Enemy's army, in its position near Fleurus; its right, composed of English, under the command of Wellington, was in front of Meller, its centre at St. Amand, and its left at Sombref, a formidable position, covered by the little river Ligny.

The Enemy occupied also the little village of Ligny, in front of this river. Our army debouched in the plain, it's left under Marshal Ney, by Gosselies, the centre where the Emperor was, by Fleurus, and the right under General Girard, upon Sombref. The actions began at two o'clock upon the left and centre. Both sides fought with inconceivable fury. The villages of St. Amand and Ligny were taken and re-taken four times. Our soldiers have all covered themselves with glory. At eight o'clock the Emperor, with his whole guard, had Ligny attacked and carried. Our brave fellows advanced at the first discharge upon the principal position of the Enemy. His army was forced in the centre, and obliged to retreat in the greatest disorder; Blücher, with the Prussians, upon Namur, and Wellington upon Brussels.

Several pieces of cannon were taken by the Guard, who bore down all before them. All marched with cries a thousand times repeated of 'Vive l'Empereur!' These were also the last words of the brave men who fell. Never was such enthusiasm; a British division of five or six thousand Scottish was cut to pieces; we have not seen any of them prisoners. The Noble Lord must be confounded. There were upon the field of battle eight enemies to one Frenchman. Their loss is said to be fifty thousand men. The cannonade was like that at the battle of Moskowa.[19]

Understandably, the author of the official French report on the actions of the 16th adopted an equally triumphant tone:

General Lutzow, a partisan, was taken prisoner. The prisoners assure us, that Field Marshal Blucher was wounded. The flower of the Prussian army was destroyed in this battle. Its loss could not be less than 15,000 men. Our's was 3,000 killed and wounded.

On the left, Marshal Ney had marched on Quatre Bras with a division, which cut to pieces an English division which was stationed there: but being attacked by the Prince of Orange with 25,000 men, partly English, partly Hanoverians in the pay of England, he retired upon his position at Frasnes. There a multiplicity of combats took place; the enemy obstinately endeavoured to force it, but in vain.

The Duke of Elchingen waited for the first corps, which did not arrive till night; he confined himself to maintaining his position. In a square attacked by the 8th regiment of cuirassiers, the colours of the 69th regiment of English infantry fell into our hands. The Duke of Brunswick was killed. The Prince of Orange has been wounded. We are assured that the enemy had many personages and Generals of note killed or wounded; we estimate the loss of the English at from 4 to 5,000 men; ours on this side was very considerable; it amounts to 4,200 killed or wounded. The combat ended with the approach of night. Lord Wellington then evacuated Quatre Bras, and proceeded to Genappes.[20]

News of the French success was relayed to Paris and then at 04.00 hours on the morning of the 17th was transmitted on from the French capital to Lille and then Boulogne:

On the 15th the French army forced the Sambre and entered Charleroi, made 1500 prisoners, took 6 pieces of cannon, and destroyed four Prussian regiments. We have lost very few men.

On the 16th, his Majesty the Emperor gained a complete victory over the English and Prussians united, commanded by Lord Wellington and Prince Blucher.

The Prussians were indeed heavily defeated, and were forced to retreat in some disorder. Everything now depended on the direction of their withdrawal and how quickly Blücher and Gneisenau could regain control of the badly scarred divisions.

Unfortunately, Blücher had been injured and was no longer in contact with his headquarters. How this occurred was related by Major General Baron Willem Benjamin van Panhuys, the Netherlands Military Commissioner attached to Prussian headquarters:

At half past eight the enemy passed the Ligny stream with several columns of cavalry, totalling some 6,000 Cuirassiers. The Feldmarschall acknowledged that he had not half this number of cavalry to oppose the enemy and those at his disposal were for the most part light cavalry, and so the two parties were unevenly matched.

With his usual bravery, he placed himself at the head of one of the squadrons and drove into the enemy, but was taken in the flank by another column; at this moment he fell beneath his horse which had been killed. The enemy passed and re-passed without noticing his person and he returned miraculously from the affair.[21]

Having achieved his strategic aim of separating the two Allied armies with his victory at Ligny, Napoleon then needed to keep Wellington and Blücher apart. This task was handed to Marshal Grouchy, who was given the following instructions:

> My Cousin, I send to you Labédoyère, my aide-de-camp, to carry you the present letter. The major general has to make known to you my intentions; but, as his officers [have] bad mounts, my aide-de-camp will perhaps arrive first.
>
> My intention is that, as commander of the right wing, you take the command of the 3rd corps which is commanded by general Vandamme, the 4th corps which is commanded by General Gerard, the cavalry corps of generals Pajol, Milhaud and Exelmans; that should not make far from 50,000 men. Rendezvous with this right wing at Sombreffe, Make leave consequently, and pursue the corps of Generals Pajol, Milhaud, Exelmans and Vandamme, and, without stopping, continue your movement on Sombreffe. The 4th corps, which is in Chatelet, receives the order directly to go to Sombreffe without passing by Fleurus. This observation is important, because I am posting my headquarters in Fleurus and the [traffic] congestion should be avoided. Send an officer to General Gerard at once to make known to him your movement, and that he executes his own at once.
>
> My intention is that all the Generals take your orders directly; they will take mine only when I am present. I will be in Fleurus between ten and eleven o'clock; I will go to Sombreffe, leaving my Guard, infantry and cavalry in Fleurus; I will lead it to Sombreffe only in case it is necessary. If the enemy is in Sombreffe, I want to attack them; I even want to attack them in Gembloux and to also seize this position, my intention is after having seen these two positions, to leave to night, and to operate with my left wing, commanded by Marshal Ney, towards the English. Do not lose a moment, because the more quickly I make my decision, the better that will apply to the continuation of my operations. I suppose that you are in Fleurus. Communicate constantly with General Gerard, so that he can help you to attack Sombreffe, if it is necessary.
>
> Girard's division is in range of Fleurus; do not dispose of them unless absolutely necessary, because they must march all during the night, also leave my Young Guard and all its artillery at Fleurus.
>
> The count of Valmy, with his two divisions of cuirassiers, will go on the road to Brussels; he is to link up with Marshal Ney, to contribute to this evening's operation on the left wing.

As I said to you, I will be at Fleurus at ten to eleven o'clock, Send me reports on all that you learn. Take care that the road to Fleurus is free. All the data which I have found [says] that the Prussians cannot oppose us with more than 40,000 men.[22]

Everything, it seemed was going almost exactly as Napoleon had planned, despite Ney's disappointing result at Quatre Bras. The Emperor could now concentrate on defeating Wellington whilst Grouchy pursued the Prussians relentlessly to prevent them from rallying.

6

Withdrawal to Mont St Jean

Although Marshal Blücher had maintained his position at Sombref, Wellington wrote to Earl Bathurst in a letter from Waterloo dated 19 June 1815, 'he still found himself much weakened by the severity of the contest in which he had been engaged'. He went on to add,

> As the 4th corps had not arrived, he determined to fall back and to concentrate his army upon Wavre; and he marched in the night, after the action was over. This movement of the Marshal rendered necessary a corresponding one upon my part; and I retired from the farm of Quatre Bras upon Genappe, and thence upon Waterloo, the next morning, the 17th, at ten o'clock.[1]

As Wellington explained, because the Pussians had been forced to retreat, he had to make a corresponding withdrawal or face being cut off from his ally. Wellington, though, did not receive news of Blücher's defeat at Ligny or of the Prussian withdrawal until the morning of the 16th because the aide carrying a message to Müffling was shot off his horse.

It was only when Quartermaster Colonel De Lancey himself actually rode over to the east to find out what was happening that the Duke learnt of the disaster that had befallen the Prussians. The following comments were those that he made to Captain George Bowles:

> Old Blücher has had a damned good licking and gone back to Wavre, eighteen miles. As he has gone back, we must go too. I suppose in England they will say we have been licked. I can't help it; as they are gone back, we must too.[2]

As it happened, Wellington had already made arrangements to withdraw to his chosen position, and quickly decided upon a retreat.

The respective orders, once again signed by De Lacy Evans, were issued at approximately 09.00 hours:

> The 1st division to keep piquets only in the wood on the right of the high road, and to be collected on the road to Nivelles, in rear of the wood.
>
> The 2d division to march from Nivelles to Waterloo, at 10 o'clock.
>
> The 3d division to collect upon the left of the position, holding by its piquets the ground it now occupies.
>
> The 4th brigade 4th division now at Nivelles to march from Nivelles upon Waterloo, at 10 o'clock. The brigades of the 4th division on the road from Braine le Comte, or at Braine le Comte, to collect and halt this day at Braine le Comte.
>
> All the baggage on the road from Braine le Comte to Nivelles to be sent back to Braine le Comte, and to be sent from thence to Hal and Bruxelles.
>
> The 5th division to collect upon the right of the position in three lines, and the 95th regt. to hold the gardens.
>
> The 6th division to be collected in columns of battalions, showing their heads only on the heights on the left of the position of Quatre Bras.
>
> The Brunswick corps to be collected in the wood on the Nivelles road, holding the skirts with their piquets only.
>
> The Nassau troops to be collected in the rear of the wood on the Nivelles road, holding the skirts with their piquets only.
>
> The 2d division of the troops of the Netherlands to march from their present ground on Waterloo, at 10 o'clock (then marching). The march to be in columns of half companies at quarter distance.
>
> The 3d division of the troops of the Netherlands to march from Nivelles at 10 o'clock. The spare musket ammunition to be transported behind Genappe, as well as the reserve artillery. The waggons of the reserve artillery to be parked in the Foret de Soignies.
>
> The British cavalry to be formed at 1 o'clock in three lines in rear of the position at Quatre Bras, to cover the movement of the infantry to the rear, and the retreat of the rear guard.[3]

The following letter was written by a sergeant in the Royal Artillery Drivers, from his camp in the Bois de Boulogne near Paris, to his father in Edinburgh on 22 September 1815.

> We were roused on the morning of the 17th, about three o'clock, by the skirmishing of the out picquets, which continued till about seven,

when we received orders to retire. I was sent off with the spare division of the brigade, and appointed to go to a village called Rhode; but either through ignorance or design, the inhabitants directed us wrong, and it was not till about four in the afternoon that we joined the brigade on the field since called Mount St John and Waterloo.

At that time the enemy's cavalry was following our army close up, harassing the rear. About ten minutes after we had passed, the enemy cut off several detachments with baggage, &c. who were in rear of us.

The withdrawal was also described in a letter from Sergeant Ewart of the Scots Greys to his brother in Ayr, which, written at Rouen, was dated 16 August 1815:

Next morning, 17th, as soon as day, the outposts began to skirmish, and we advanced close upon them. While we shewed ourselves, their cavalry would not come out, which gave our infantry the liberty of forming their line, and braving them out, but all to no purpose.

When Lord Wellington saw that they would not come out of the wood, he made the infantry retreat, and we kept the ground for about three hours, to let the infantry get off before we fell back; but, as soon as we began to retreat, they came out of the wood in clouds; it was about one o'clock of the day when we began our retreat, and the rain and thunder came on most dreadfully, it is impossible to describe the awfulness of it, for in less than five minutes, the whole of us were as wet as if we had come out of a pond.

It continued this way the whole of the afternoon, we all the time falling back and the enemy advancing, until we pressed so close upon our infantry that we were obliged to make a stand to save them, until they formed line upon a height behind us, and had their cannon placed there; we gave them some of our British balls, which silenced them for that night. We lost few men that day, but the enemy must have lost a great number, from the shot firing so fast upon them; this concluded the 17th.[4]

An officer of the Guards, the same individual quoted previously and who is any named as 'a near observer', also corresponded:

Next morning, our men were drawn up in a line of battle fronting the wood where the French had retired [at Quatre Bras]; but they would not venture to attack us. Lord Wellington by a ruse de guerre, however, drew them from the wood, by a rapid retreat, for a few miles, towards Brussels; which brought the French exactly on the spot where he wished to fight them, and where he might bring his cavalry into play.

While retreating, we were overtaken by a most violent thunderstorm and a heavy rain, which rendered us very uncomfortable. During the whole, no man was lost, but the Blues lost three or four; the 1st Life Guards charged some of the French Lancers, and almost cut them to pieces. We were drawn up to give them a second charge, but they would not stand it. This evening, we are bivouacked in a piece of boggy ground, where we were mid-leg up in mud and water.[5]

Though Wellington was retiring on his chosen position near Waterloo, he remained concerned with his right flank, fearing being cut off from his communications with the Channel ports. This had preoccupied him for months before Napoleon had invaded Belgium and it was still a factor in his calculations. With Napoleon close on his heels, Wellington could be certain that he would have to fight at Mont St Jean. Nevertheless, he detached a considerable proportion of his army to Hal (or Halle) to protect that right flank. A 'Memorandum for the Quartermaster-General, 17th June, 1815' stated:

The corps under Prince Frederick of Orange will move from Enghien this evening, and take up a position in front of Hal, occupying the château with two battalions. Colonel Estorff will fall back with his brigade on Hal, and place himself under the orders of Prince Frederick of Orange. Wellington.

On the same day, 'instructions from the Quartermaster-General to Major-General The Hon. Sir Charles Colville, G.C.B.' were issued:

The army retired this day from its position at Quatre-Bras to its present position in front of Waterloo. The brigades of the 4th Division at Braine le Comte are to retire at daylight to-morrow morning upon Hal. Major-General Colville must be guided by the intelligence he receives of the enemy's movements in his march to Hal, whether he moves by the direct route or by Enghien.

Prince Frederick of Orange is to occupy with his corps the position between Hal and Enghien, and is to defend it as long as possible. The army will probably continue in its position in front of Waterloo to-morrow. Lieutenant-Colonel Torrens will inform Major-General Sir Charles Colville of the position and situation of the armies.[6]

An unidentified French soldier wrote the following from Fleurus:

> This morning the (17th) the cavalry of General Pajol is gone in pursuit of the Prussians upon the road to Namur. It is already two leagues and a half in advance; whole bands of prisoners are taken. They do not know what is become of their commanders. The rout is complete on this side, and I hope we shall not so soon hear again of the Prussians, if they should ever be able to rally at all.
>
> As for the English, we shall see now what will become of them. The Emperor is here.
>
> Some private letters from the army give the following particulars: The English are retiring upon Brussels by the forest of Soignies; the Prussians are falling back upon the Meuse in great disorder.
>
> The 17th at 11p.m. the Emperor had his head-quarters at Planchenoit, a village only five leagues from Brussels. The rain fell in torrents. His Majesty was fatigued, but he was very well.
>
> Count Lobau, who was marching with the 6th corps upon Namur, was, with his van-guard, only half a league from the town. Five battalions are gone from Lille to escort the prisoners taken on the 15th and 16th.[7]

The Emperor was obviously disappointed with Ney's failure to either drive Wellington from Quatre Bras or support the force under Napoleon at Ligny. Nevertheless, he evidently felt that the campaign was going well, and that he had succeeded in separating the two allied armies. Marshal Soult wrote to Ney, on Napoleon's behalf, on 17 June 1815:

> General Flahault, who has just reached here, reports that you are in no doubt about the precise result of yesterday's operations on this wing. I thought that I had already acquainted you of the victory which the Emperor gained. The Prussian army has been routed, and General Pajol is now pursuing it along the roads leading to Namur and Liège. We have captured some thousands of prisoners and 30 cannon. Our troops have behaved very well: one charge by six battalions of the guard, and the squadrons of the cavalry division of Delort, pierced the enemy line, caused great disorder and seized the position.
>
> The Emperor is proceeding to the windmill at Bry, past which runs the Namur and Quatre Bras high road; and, as it is possible that the English army will engage your command, then, in such circumstances, the Emperor would march by the Quatre Bras road against the enemy in front of you, whilst you attack them in front with

your divisions, which ought now be concentrated; and in such an eventuality the hostile army would be annihilated immediately.

Yesterday the Emperor remarked with regret that you had not massed your divisions; they acted spasmodically, and consequently, you suffered disproportionate loss.

Not a single Englishman would have escaped if the corps of counts d'Erlon and Reille had been kept together. If count d'Erlon had carried out the movement on St. Amand, prescribed by the Emperor, then the Prussian Army would have been totally destroyed, and we might have captured 30,000 prisoners

The corps of generals Gérand, Vandamme, and the Imperial Guard have been kept together as if they are detached they are exposed to setbacks.

The Emperor hopes and desires that your seven infantry divisions and the cavalry are concentrated, and that they occupy mo more than a league of ground, so as to have the whole force in hand, and ready for immediate action in case of need.

His Majesty's intention is that you will take up a position at Quatre Bras as you were ordered to; but if this is impossible to act in this manner send a detailed report immediately and the Emperor will move there along the road already mentioned; if, on the other hand, you are only confronted with a rear-guard, drive it off, and occupy the position. Today is required for completing this operation, replenishing ammunition, gathering stragglers and detachments. Give orders accordingly, and make sure that all the wounded are transported to the rear.

The well-known partisan leader, Lutzow, who has been taken prisoner, stated that the Prussian army was lost, and that for the second time Blücher has jeopardized the Prussian monarchy.[8]

Just how wrong Napoleon was with his assessment of the state of the Prussian army is made clear in this report by Gneisenau:

On the 17th, in the evening, the Prussian army concentrated itself in the environs of Wavre. Napoleon put himself in motion against Lord Wellington, upon the great road leading from Charleroi to Brussels. An English division maintained, on the same day, near Quartre Bras, a very severe contest with the enemy. Lord Wellington had taken a position on the road to Brussels, having his right wing leaning upon Bruerie la Leu, the centre near Mont St. Jean, and the left wing against La Haye Sainte.

Lord Wellington wrote to the Field Marshal that he was resolved to accept the battle in this position if the Field Marshal would support him with two corps of his army. The Field Marshal proposed to come with his whole army; he even proposed, in case Napoleon should not attack, that the Allies themselves with their whole force united should attack him the next day. This may serve to shew how little the battle of the 16th had disorganized the Prussian army or weakened its moral strength. Thus ended the day of the 17th.[9]

Napoleon spent the morning of the 17th at Ligny, waiting for reports from Ney and Grouchy before committing his reserve force, principally the Imperial Guard, which he had kept under his immediate command, to any particular course of action. Having told Grouchy to 'keep a sword in the backs' of the Prussians, Napoleon decided to concentrate his efforts on Wellington, but Ney, once again appeared to be dragging his feet. Soult wrote this message at midday:

> The Emperor has just placed in position before Marbais a corps of Infantry and the Imperial Guard. His Majesty desires me to tell you that his intention is that you shall attack the enemy at Quatre Bras, and drive them from their position; the corps of Marbais will support your operations. His Majesty is going to Marbais, and awaits impatiently your report.[10]

Ney had actually sent a report (at 06.30 hours), which evidently had not yet arrived at Napoleon's headquarters. In the report, a copy of which has not survived, Ney explained that he was facing a powerful force in a strong position and that he would need the Emperor's support before he could risk attacking again. By the time Napoleon moved up to Quatre Bras, it was already too late, as the Anglo-Netherlands army had spent the morning withdrawing through the forest of Soignes, leaving only a rearguard to face the French. The official French account explains the movements of *l'armée du Nord*:

> In the morning of the 17th, the Emperor repaired to Quatre Bras, whence he marched to attack the English army: he drove it to the entrance of the forest of Soignies, with the left wing and the reserve. The right wing advanced by Sombref, in pursuit of Field Marshal Blucher, who was going towards Wavre, where he appeared to wish to take a position.
> At ten o'clock in the evening, the English army occupied Mount St. Jean with its centre, and was in position before the forest of Soignies: it would have required three hours to attack it; we were therefore obliged to postpone it till the next day. The head-quarters of the

Emperor were established at the farm of Caillou, near Planchenoit. The rain fell in torrents. Thus, on the 17th, the left wing, the right, and the reserve were equally engaged, at a distance of about two leagues.[11]

The Honourable Fred Ponsonby, of the 12th Light Dragoon, who was a cousin of Major General Sir William Ponsonby (who commanded the Union Brigade), described the withdrawal of the Anglo-Netherlands army from Quatre Bras:

> Early in the morning the Duke [of Wellington], having ascertained the retreat and defeat of Blucher, gave orders for all the Infantry to retire to Waterloo. The cavalry with two battalions of the 95th remained as a rear guard to mask the retreat of our infantry. The whole of the Cavalry were drawn up on some rising ground and remained there till after two. It was a most interesting time for the Duke who had every reason to expect that the whole of Bonaparte's army would immediately fall upon him, before he could collect his army on the position of Waterloo.
>
> I was with him, the Duke, just in front of this line of cavalry when we were all observing the preparations and movements of the immense mass of Troops before us. He was occupied reading the newspapers, looking through his glass when anything was observed, and then making observations and laughing at the fashionable news from London.
>
> The French Cavalry were now mounted, it was passed two and the whole of their army were seen getting under arms. We commenced our retreat in three columns. I was with the left column. We had nothing, however, but a skirmish. The centre column had a sharp affair, but we arrived at Waterloo without suffering any material loss. The rain fell in torrents, it was so heavy that my large thick coat was wet thro' in a few minutes. The whole country became almost a swamp.[12]

Captain Cavalie Mercer, in charge of a troop of the Royal Horse Artillery, had helped cover the Allied withdrawal:

> Up came Lord Uxbridge [who had taken charge of the rearguard] ... 'Captain Mercer, are you loaded?' 'Yes, my lord. 'Then give them a round as they rise the hill, and retire as quickly as possible.' ... 'They are coming up the hill,' said Lord Uxbridge. 'Let them get well up before you fire. Do you think you can retire quick enough afterwards?' 'I am sure of it, my lord.' 'Very well, then, keep a good lookout, and point your guns well.'

> I had often longed to see Napoleon, that mighty man of war – that astonishing genius who had filled the world with his renown. Now I saw him.[13]

Mercer was able to see Napoleon because the Emperor of the French was at the forefront of the French pursuit, as Lieutenant Pontécoulant of the Imperial Guard observed:

> It was necessary to have been a witness of the rapid march of this army on the 17th, a march which resembled a steeple chase rather than the pursuit of a retreating enemy … The emperor, mounted on a small and very nimble Arab, galloped at the head of the column; he was always close to the guns, exciting the gunners by his presence and his words, and more than once in the midst of the shells and balls which the enemy artillery showered upon us, was heard to shout to them, in a voice full of hatred, 'Fire, Fire, those are the English!'[14]

It was probably more of anger and frustration than hatred that caused the outburst from Napoleon. He was dismayed by Ney's reluctance to attack the Anglo-Netherlands army which Napoleon saw had been gathered at Quatre Bras but which was now escaping.

The Emperor, realising that the entire campaign plan was in danger, had ridden up to d'Erlon and said to the commander of I Corps,

> In a tone of profound chagrin these words, which have been always graven on my memory:- 'They have ruined France; come, my dear general, put yourself at the head of this cavalry, and vigorously push the English rearguard.' The Emperor never quitted the head of the advance-guard, and was even engaged in a charge of cavalry in debouching from Genappe.[15]

The *Lancaster Gazette* published the following eye-witness account which was dated 22 June and sent from the village of Gommignies:

> Having completed our day's march, I once more take up my pen, and, after giving you some of the leading features of the 17th, shall do my best to relate to you, as far as lies in my power, the most striking incidents of the glorious day of 'Waterloo'.
>
> At day break, on the 17th, we were again under arms, having snatched a hurried repose to our wearied limbs on the ground near which we fought. Uncertain as to the movements of the enemy, or whether they purposed renewing their attack, we were in a state of

anxious suspense: and the skirmishing at intervals in our front made us expect that something was about to be done; during all this time we were employed by parties in bringing in our wounded companions, whom the darkness had the night before prevented our finding, and in doing our best to be ready for anything that might occur, and in assuaging, as well as we could, the sufferings of those around us.

We succeeded in finding the bodies of our four officers, Captains Grose and Brown, Ensigns Lord Hay and Barrington, who were killed; and had the melancholy satisfaction of paying the last tribute of respect to their remains; they were buried near the wood, and one of our officers read the service over them; never did I witness a scene more imposing; those breasts which had a few hours back boldly encountered the greatest perils, did not now disdain to be subdued by pity and affection; and if the ceremony wanted the real clerical solemnity due to its sacred character, it received an ample equivalent in this mark of genuine regard, and the sincerity with which we wished them a more immortal Halo than that which honour could confer.

The whole night was occupied in getting up the cavalry and artillery; and report said, that the Duke of Wellington had it in contemplation to become, in his turn, the assailant; be that as it may, we were ordered to fall back by the Charleroi road through Gemappe, to our position of Waterloo. I will not invite you to accompany us on our march, which was only marked by fatigue, dust, heat, and thirst.

After halting for a short time to ascertain our actual position, we marched to it, and were greeted by one of the very hardest showers of rain I ever remembered to have seen, which lasted nearly half an hour; it then ceased. The whole afternoon was taken up by the various divisions getting to their respective posts, and making active preparations for the expected attack of the morrow.

Jardin Ainé was Napoleon's equerry and was, therefore, responsible for Napoleon's horse. He also had a first-hand view of the momentous events of June 1815:

On the 17th of June, Napoleon left the village where he had slept, and visited the battlefield of the evening before as he always did on the day after a battle. He went very quickly up the hill to Genappes where he remained making observations on the movements of his advance guard; the cavalry attached to which several times charged the British cavalry as it passed out of the town.

At this time a violent storm threw into confusion the whole French army which, owing to their many days of rapid marching, lack of provisions, and want of rest was in a most pitiable state. At last the courage of the French overcame the horrible weather. The troops struggled on with unparalleled valor; in the evening Napoleon visited the outposts in spite of the heavy rain and did his utmost to encourage the men. At seven o'clock, p.m. he took out his watch and said that the troops had need of rest, that they should take up their positions, and that the next day early, they would be under arms.

At this moment shouts were heard from the British army, Napoleon asked what these could be. Marshal Soult (then Chief of Staff) replied 'It is certainly Wellington passing through the ranks that is the cause of the shouting.' At seven o'clock, Napoleon said he wished to bivouac; it was pointed out to him that he was in a ploughed field and in mud up to the knees, he replied to the Marshal, 'Any kind of shelter will suit me for the night' …

Napoleon went into a kind of Inn out of which the troops, who had installed themselves in it, were turned, and here he fixed his General Headquarters, because he did not wish to go to the town of Genappes, which was only a league distant, saying that during the night he would here receive more readily reports from the army. At the same time everyone had found the best available quarters in which to pass the night. Generals Corbineau, La Bedoyere, Flahaut, aides-de-camp on Napoleon's staff, spent the night in riding between the various army corps and returning to him to give an exact account of the movements which were taking place.[16]

The city of Brussels was, of course, almost on the front line and the place was understandably in a state of high alert. One officer, W.A. Scott, provided us with this description:

The news arrived at Brussels that Blucher was defeated, and the English army had retired. '*Cest trop clair – c'est trop clair,*' was repeated on every side. In fact, we were roused, says a correspondent, by a loud knocking at the door, and the cries of '*Les Francois sont ici – Les Francois sont ici.*' Starting up, and the first sight we beheld, was a troop of Belgic cavalry, covered not with glory, but with mud, galloping through the town at full speed, as if the Devil were at their heels; and immediately the heavy baggage waggons, which had been harnessed from the moment of the first alarm, set off full gallop down La Montagne de la Cais, and through every street by which it was possible to effect their escape.

In less than two minutes, the great Square of the Place Royale, which had been crowded with men and horses, carts and baggage waggons, was completely cleared of everything, and entirely deserted. Again were the cries repeated, of *'Les Francois sont ici! – lis s'emparent de la porte de laville!'* The doors of all the bed-rooms were thrown open – the people flew out with their night-caps on, scarcely half dressed, and looking quite distracted, running about pale and trembling, they knew not whither, with packages under their arms – some carrying huge collections of valuable things down to the cellars, and others loaded with their property were flying up to the garrets.

In the yards of the several inns, a scene of the most dreadful confusion ensued; the scuffle that took place to get at the horses and carriages it is impossible to describe; the squabbling of masters and servants, ostlers, chambermaids, coachmen, and gentlemen, all scolding at once, and swearing at each other in French, English, and Flemish; every opprobrious epithet and figure of speech which the three languages contained was exhausted upon each other, and the confusion of tongues we might suppose to resemble the Tower of Babel.

Those who had horses, or means of procuring them, set off with most astonishing expedition, and one carriage after another took the road to Antwerp. The corpse of the Duke of Brunswick had passed through Brussels during the night, and his fate seemed to be much lamented, and to make a great impression upon the people.

Waggons filled with the wounded began to arrive, and the melancholy spectacle of these poor sufferers increased the general despondency. These were streaming with blood, and at every jostle were heard groans or shrieks, which pierced the very heart. The streets were filled with the most pitiable sights. I saw a Belgic soldier dying at the door of his own home, and surrounded by his relatives, who were lamenting over him. Numerous were the sorrowful groups standing round the dead bodies of those who had died of their wounds in the way home. Numbers of wounded who were able to walk, were wandering in every street; their blood-stained clothes and pale haggard countenances looking most dreadful, and giving the idea of sufferings equal to the reality.

In the eagerness to escape, a number of ladies and children, and old men, were crushed to death, and the merchants who had come to barter their goods to strangers, actually left them unprotected, as well as the houses, for a general pillage, by the lower orders of the people. It would be endless to dwell upon every fresh panic. An open town like Brussels, within a few miles of contending armies, its subjects to perpetual alarms, and scarcely an hour passed without some false reports occurring to spread general terror and confusion. Every hour only served to add to the dismay. So great was the alarm in Brussels on Saturday evening, that £100 were offered in vain for a pair of horses to go to Antwerp, a distance of thirty miles! and numbers set off on foot, and embarked in boats upon the canal.[17]

There was at least one person in Brussels who was not immediately alarmed, and that was Lady Frances Wedderburn-Webster, who was, allegedly Wellington's lover. He wrote the following in a letter to her on the evening of the 17th from Waterloo:

We fought a desperate battle on Friday, in which I was successful, though I had but very few troops. The Prussians were very roughly handled, and retired in the night, which obliged me to do the same to this place yesterday. The course of my operations may oblige me to uncover Bruxelles for a moment, and may expose that town to the enemy; for which reason I recommend that you and your family should be prepared to move to Antwerp at a moment's notice.

I will give you the earliest intimation of any danger that may come to my knowledge: at present I know of none.[18]

The Battle of Waterloo: Morning

By 18.00 hours on the 17th, Wellington's wet and muddy force had reached the place that the Duke had ear-marked earlier – the ridge of Mont St Jean to the south of the village of Waterloo. The position was well described by Lieutenant Colonel (later Field Marshal) John Burgoyne of the Royal Engineers:

> It was not that commanding kind of position that is sometimes found, and which strikes the eye at once; on the contrary, the ridge occupied by our army is lower than the heights a mile of two in front, from whence the French army advanced. But it still had many of the essentials of a good fighting position. The flanks were on commanding points, that discovered the ground well all round them, at a fair distance from the main road by which the enemy approached and would have required him to make a considerable detour across country to have turned them ... the whole being about a mile and a half or two miles in extent; it, therefore, was very compact.
>
> In front of the left the ground was well discovered, and with no very favourable points for the enemy's artillery. A road ran along the line in this part with thin hedges along it and a very slight bank, affording some little cover to the infantry if they laid down. This road continued along the centre and right of the position, out of sight of the enemy in those parts, but not affording any cover. The ground in front of the centre and right was more broken ... The whole line was on a ridge, which rounding back to the rear, covered the troops from the sight and from the direct fire of the enemy.[1]

Another description of the battlefield was given by Captain George Ulric Barlow of the 2nd Battalion, 69th Foot in a letter to his father on 7 July 1815:

The position of Waterloo upon which the destinies of Europe was about to be fought, was nothing more than a range of moderate rising ground, touching upon the pavé leading from Nivelles to Brussels & extending on the left to the high road from Genappe & conducting to the same metropolis. Here two routes formed the summit of an angle, meeting near Braine l'Alleud, to which the position of the British army served as the base, or third side, its flanks leaning upon & thus covering either approach.

It was fine commanding open fighting ground, but traversable in all directions by cavalry and cannon. The French artillery lined the whole summit of these heights. The army was drawn up in order of battle behind them a little way down the reverse of the slope so as to be perfectly concealed from the enemy who could by no means get sight of its force or dispositions and according to his own, confirm he was kept in perfect ignorance of its intentions.[2]

We are led to believe that Wellington had earlier reconnoitred the area and, having seen the Mont St Jean position, he allegedly claimed 'I have kept it in my pocket' just in case Napoleon attempted to seize Brussels from the south-east.

Much is made of Wellington's choice of ground at Waterloo. The position of his troops along and in the rear of the Mont St Jean is considered to have been one of the principal reasons for his success on 18 June. However, it would appear that Wellington originally had in mind the ridge to the south of Mont St Jean, where the inn of La Belle Alliance stood. The Duke had sent his Quartermaster-General, Sir William De Lancey, ahead of the retreating army early on the 17th with instructions to mark out the ground for the approaching troops to take up. Wellington arrived in the area later in the afternoon, as FitzRoy Somerset, the Duke's aide, explained:

On arriving near La Belle Alliance he [the Duke] thought it was the position the Qr.M. Genl. would have taken up, being the most commanding ground, but he [De Lancey] had found it too extended to be occupied by our Troops, & so had proceeded further on & marked out a position.[3]

Wellington himself described the position of the Anglo-Netherlands army in his official despatch to Earl Bathurst:

The position which I took up in front of Waterloo crossed the high roads from Charleroi and Nivelles, and had its right thrown back to a ravine near Merke Braine, which was occupied, and its left extended to a height above the hamlet Ter la Haye, which was likewise occupied. In front of the right centre, and near the Nivelles road, we occupied the house and gardens of Hougoumont, which covered the return of that flank; and in front of the left centre we occupied the farm of La Haye Sainte. By our left we communicated with Marshal Prince Blücher at Wavre, through Ohain; and the Marshal had promised me that, in case we should be attacked, he would support me with one or more corps, as might be necessary.[4]

Another soldier who was present on the field of Waterloo described the position of the French, 'which was also a ridge', as being,

immediately opposite to that we occupied, and differing in distances at different parts, but generally, I should say, about 1000 or 1200 yards distant, perhaps a little more. The ground was stronger than that we held, the ascent to it being longer than to ours. The head-quarters of Bonaparte, on the night of the 17th, were at Planchenoit, a farm some little distance in the rear of the French line;- and Mont St. Jean was in the high road, immediately in the line of their advance.[5]

The weather, as much as Ney's reluctance to attack Quatre Bras, considerably helped the successful withdrawal to Waterloo, as Général La Bédoyère recalled:

The night of the 17th was dreadful, and seemed to presage the calamities of the day, as the violent and incessant rains did not allow a moment's rest to the army. The bad state of the roads also prevented the arrival of provisions, and most of the soldiers were without food.[6]

The ferocity of the weather may have helped Wellington but his men suffered just as severely as the French. The following was written by an unnamed officer from the camp at Clichy to his friend in Cumberland:

The whole of the 17th, and indeed until late the next morning, the weather continued dreadful; and we were starving with hunger, no provision having been served out since the march from Brussels. While five officers who composed our mess were looking at each other with the most deplorable faces imaginable, one of the men brought us a fowl he had plundered, and a handful of biscuits, which, though but little, added to some tea we boiled in a camp-kettle, made us rather more comfortable; and we huddled up together, covered ourselves with straw, and were soon as soundly asleep as though reposing on beds of down. I awoke long before day-light, and found myself in a very bad state altogether, being completely wet through in addition to all other ills. Fortunately I soon after this found my way to a shed, of which Sir And. Barnard (our commandant) had taken possession, where there was a fire, and in which with three or four others I remained until the rain abated. About ten o'clock the sun made his appearance, to view the mighty struggle which was to determine the fate of Europe; and about an hour afterwards the French made their dispositions for the attack, which commenced on the right.[7]

The troops had bivouacked overnight close to the positions they were to take up during the battle, though at daybreak there was some re-adjustment as the regiments moved to their assigned places in the line. Following the wet night was a cold morning, as one Highlander recalled:

I never felt colder in my life; everyone of us was shaking like an aspen leaf. An allowance of gin was then served out to each of us which had the effect of infusing warmth into our almost inanimate frames ... We remained on the ground till about six o'clock, when we were ordered to clean ourselves, dry our muskets, try to get forward, and commence cooking.[8]

Another wrote that at dawn,

in the fields of rye along the southern edge of the forest of Soignes, you could hear a murmur like the sea on a distant shore. This was the blended voices of 67,000 men, grumbling, yawning, shivering, stretching cramped limbs, joking as people do when they share discomfort, and arguing about what would happen next.[9]

During the Revolutionary Wars, the territory that is today known as Belgium was overrun by the French and absorbed into the French Republic. The Netherlands was, at that time, the 'United Provinces', a republic with a prince bearing the title of *Stadtholder*. When this was also taken over by the French, the *Stadtholder*, William V of Orange, fled to Britain. The Netherlands was at first called the Batavian Republic under French domination, but, in 1806 this was changed by Napoleon into the Kingdom of Holland, with his brother Louis Bonaparte on the throne. Louis tried to act independently of Napoleon, the result of which was he was forced to abdicate and the territory was incorporated into France. The soldiers of these states fought with the French Army for a number of years and their loyalty to the recently created Kingdom of the United Netherlands was, before the Waterloo campaign, considered questionable – a point raised by Wellington shortly after arriving at Brussels:

> They are completely officered by officers who have been in French service ... It is very well to employ them, but I would not trust one of them out of my sight.[10]

Wellington had therefore decided to integrate the Dutch and Belgian divisions with the British divisions throughout his defensive line. He also arranged many battalions to be formed into what has been described as 'oblongs'. The reason for these oblong formations was explained by Captain James Shaw Kennedy on Wellington's Quartermaster-General staff:

> The French cavalry had, on the 16th, proved itself very formidable at Quatre Bras in its attack ... That cavalry, in immensely augmented numbers, was now forming opposite ... and the ground between them and us presented no obstacle whatever. It was at the same time evident, from the way in which the French guns were taking up their ground, that the [army] would be exposed to a severe artillery fire.
>
> It was therefore of the highest importance that the formation[s] ... should be such that ... [their] passing from line into a formation for resisting cavalry should be as rapid as possible ... To carry these views into effect the strong battalions formed each an oblong on the two centre companies, and when the battalions were weak, two were joined, the right-hand battalion of the two forming left in front, and the left-hand battalion right in front, each in columns of companies.
>
> The fronts of the oblongs were formed by four companies; the rear face of the oblongs by the same strength; and the sides of one company each, which were formed by the outward wheel of the subdivisions. It will be observed that, when a battalion forms oblong in this manner upon two centre companies, the formation is made in less than half the time in which it would form a square on a flank company; and the same applies to deployment.[11]

Amongst the troops in the centre of the Allied line was the 1st Brigade, of Perponcher's 2nd Netherlands Division, commanded by *Generaal-Majoor* Willem Frederik van Bylandt. Much has been written about the deployment of Bylandt's brigade, with most accounts stating that, unlike the rest of the main Anglo-Dutch line, it was posted on the forward slope of the ridge, in a highly exposed position. It was positioned there, states one authority, to keep up a communication between La Haye Sainte and the main allied line.[12]

The scene that morning was described in a graphic account which was published in the *Caledonian Mercury* of 5 October:

> The line being formed about six o'clock, our rear towards Brussels, the artillery in front on a small height, the infantry close columns behind us, with the cavalry in the intervals – (I had every opportunity of seeing the disposition of both armies, having occasion to go with messages from one part of the field to another) – the line of infantry was under cover of the eminence where the artillery was posted – a smart cannonading commenced on both sides, which lasted till dark. It had rained all this day, and at night fell in torrents. I never saw it rain more tremendously. We had not our tents pitched. I lay down for some time under one of the carriages, but was soon forced to rise, being in danger of drowning, as we had retired from the height at the close of the engagement, and lay in a kind of valley all night.
>
> After such an awful night, the morning dawned with gloomy aspect. All over the field, where countless thousands lay, not a whisper was heard. Our fires, which had been long extinguished by the torrents of rain, were rekindled, and we made shift to dry our clothes a little. At day-break the artillery took up the position it had quitted the evening before. About midday the signal gun was fired. Then began that ever memorable battle, so glorious as well as so fatal to the British army.

The actual number of troops taking part in many battles is often hard to ascertain with accuracy. Historians usually act cautiously and use such words as 'approximately' and 'around'. With the Waterloo campaign we have very precise figures from the British Army, and details of the French Army were revealed in the *Hampshire Chronicle* of Monday, 7 August 1815, under the headline 'From French Papers, Paris, July 31':

> The second number of Buonaparte's Portfolio, taken at Charleroi on the 18th of June, has appeared at Brussels. Among the different articles of which it consists, is one entitled, *'Enumeration of some corps of the Army'* it is a paper in the hand-writing of one of Buonaparte's Officers, and exhibits a statement of the force of the corps which fought at Waterloo. The Duke of Wellington was attacked by the 71,000 men comprehended in this statement, viz. 48,000 infantry

118

(including 18,000 of the guard); 16,500 cavalry (including 4000 of the guard); 7000 artillery, and 270 pieces of cannon.

The first and second corps, commanded by Generals Reille and d'Erlon, are comprised in this account. Marshal Grouchy acted on his side with the corps of Vandamme and Gerard, which comprehended together 6000 horse; including infantry, they must have had a force equal to the first and second, that is from 24 to 27,000 men. He had also the 1st and 2d cavalry corps under Excelmans and Pajol, which may be assimilated with the 3d and 4th, stated in the table at 8000 horse each. All this agrees with the numbers that were seen to pass through Namur, and make a general total of 110,000, which, according to the first report, and the accounts of the prisoners, passed the frontiers.

An officer of the 1st Guards, wrote the following in a letter – an account which details both some of the preparations for battle and the dispositions of those involved:

In the morning of the 17th, the Enemy made no further attempt against us; and as the Prussians had retired during the night, we did the same very leisurely, about 11 o'clock, taking up a position in front of a village called Waterloo, at a point where the high road or chaussee to Brussels crosses that from Nivelle to Namur. Here we remained quiet through the night, except that it rained more furiously than I ever experienced, even in Spain. We were quite wet through, and literally up to the ancles in mud. The cavalry were considerably engaged during the day of the 17th, but the Hussars could not make much impression against their heavy-armed opponents. The Life Guards behaved most nobly, and carried everything before them. The morning of the 18th dawned full of expectation of something decisive being done.

But first I must give you some idea of our position. It ran from the Brussels chaussee to the right, about a mile and a half in length, and then turned very sharply to the right and crossed the chaussee from Nivelle to Namur, which two chaussees cross each other, so that we were nearly in a quarter-circle (like an open fan, the two outside sticks being the chaussees.)

At the turn and at the bottom of a slope was a farm and orchards, called Mount St. John. This was the key of our positions, and in front of our centre. On this point the most serious attack was made.

At twelve o'clock the columns of the Enemy moved down from the heights which they had occupied … The British infantry were drawn up in columns under the ridge of the position. We were at the turn or knuckle with two battalions of Brunswickers. The Third Regiment of Guards were in columns in front of the turn, and the Coldstream at the farm-house. The light infantry of the division were to defend the orchard and small wood next to it. The third division were in squares to the left of our squares, and under cover of the ridge.[13]

This French account was actually published in Paris on 21 June 1815 under the heading of *News from the Army*:

At nine in the morning, the rain having somewhat abated, the 1st corps put itself in motion, and placed itself with the left on the road to Brussels, and opposite the village of Mount St. Jean, which appeared the centre of the enemy's position. The second corps leaned its right upon the road to Brussels, and its left upon a small wood within cannon-shot of the English army. The Cuirassiers were in reserve behind, and the Guard in reserve upon the heights. The 6th corps, with the cavalry of General D'Aumont, under the order of Count Lobau, were destined to proceed in rear of our right, to oppose a Prussian corps which appeared to have escaped Marshal Grouchy, and to intend to fall upon our right flank – an intention which had been made known to us by our reports, and by the letter of a Prussian general, inclosing an order of battle, and which was taken by our light troops.

The troops were full of ardour. We estimated the force of the English army at 80,000 men. We supposed that the Prussian corps, which might be in line towards the night, might be 15,000 men. The enemy's force then was upwards of 90,000 men; ours less numerous.[14]

Napoleon could not be certain that Wellington intended to stand and fight at Mont St Jean and so, at 01.00 hours, he walked out with Count Bertrand and his escorting Guards to examine the Anglo-Netherlands' position:

The forest of Soignies looked as if it was on fire; the horizon between this forest, Braine-la-Leud and the farms of La Belle Alliance and La Haye was aglow with bivouac fires; complete silence prevailed ... Several officers who had been sent out on reconnaissance, and some secret agents returning at half-past three, confirmed that the Anglo-Netherlands troops were not making a move ... The day began to dawn. I returned to my headquarters thoroughly satisfied with the great mistake which the enemy general was making.[15]

120

Wellington had made no mistake because he knew that he would not be fighting alone. Müffling had sent a message to Blücher asking the Prussian Field-Marshal what course of action he intended to follow. At around 02.00 hours on the morning of the 18th Müffling received a reply:

> I wish to report to Your Worship that, as a consequence of the news received from the Duke of Wellington that he intends to accept battle tomorrow in the position from Braine l'Alleud to la Haye, that I will set my troops in motion as follows:
>
> At daybreak tomorrow [the 18th] Bülow's Corps will leave Dion-le-Mont, and march through Wavre towards St Lambert to attack the enemy's right flank. II Corps will follow it immediately, and the I and III Corps will hold themselves ready to follow this movement. As the troops are exhausted, and some have yet to arrive, it is impossible to leave earlier. I would request Your Worship to report to me in good time when and how the Duke is attacked, so that I can adjust my measures accordingly.[16]

Sir James Shaw Kennedy, the Third Division's Assistant Quartermaster-General, confirmed the reasons for Wellington's decision to stand and fight at Mont St Jean:

> In order at all to understand the views of the Duke of Wellington as to accepting battle on the field of Waterloo, it is essential to keep this arrangement [with Blücher] fully in view; otherwise the Duke might be justly accused of the utmost temerity and folly in accepting battle, as much of the greater portion of his army consisted of mere Landwehr and of Dutch-Belgian troops.
>
> The latter, from political and other causes, could not be depended upon; which, in fact had already been proved on the 16th. It would be an error to suppose that it was from any want of courage that the Dutch-Belgian troops could not be depended upon; proof enough exists that the people of those countries are capable of the most heroic and persevering exertions when engaged in a cause that they care to support; but under the circumstances in which they were placed on this occasion, they were without confidence, were not acting in a cause which they cordially supported, and showed that it was not one in which they wished to oppose themselves seriously to French troops.[17]

A few hours later Napoleon was alarmed when he received a report saying that Wellington was withdrawing. The vastly experienced d'Erlon, whose corps held the front line, knew this not to be the case. Nevertheless, as d'Erlon later described, Napoleon rode out to see for himself:

> The Emperor came immediately to the advanced posts. I accompanied him; we dismounted in order to get near the enemy's vedettes, and to examine more closely the movements of the English army. He perceived that I was right, and being convinced that the English army was taking position, he said to me: 'Order the men to make their soup, to get their pieces in order, and we will determine what is to be done towards noon.'[18]

After his inspection of the Allied positions, which in truth he could see little of because so many of Wellington's men were out of sight behind Mont St Jean, Napoleon 'reflected' for some time before giving his orders for the attack.

> Once the whole army is ranged in battle order, at about 1 p.m., and when the Emperor gives Marshal Ney the relevant order, the attack will begin in order to capture the village of Mont St Jean, which is the road junction. To this end, the 12-inch [12-pounder] batteries of II Corps and VI Corps will regroup with those of I Corps. These 94 cannon will fire on the troops of Mont St Jean, and Count d'Erlon will begin the attack by bringing forward his left wing division, supporting it, according to the circumstances, by the other I Corps divisions. II Corps will advance so as to keep at the level of Count d'Erlon. The sapper companies of I Corps will be ready to entrench themselves immediately at Mont St Jean.[19]

Napoleon describes the formation of his army which he stated was in eleven columns, as it formed up ready to begin the battle:

> It had been arranged that, of these eleven columns, four were to form the first line, four the second line, and three the third.
> The four columns of the first line were: the first, that on the left, formed by the cavalry of the 2nd Corps; the next, by three infantry divisions of the 2nd Corps; the third, by three infantry divisions of the 1st Corps; and the fourth, by the light cavalry of the 1st Corps.
> The four columns of the second line were: the first, that of the left, formed by Kellermann's corps of cuirassiers; the second, by the two infantry divisions of the 6th Corps; the third, by two light cavalry divisions, one of the 6th Corps, commanded by the divisional General Daumont, the other detached from Pajol's corps and commanded by

the divisional General Subervie; the fourth, by Milhaud's corps of cuirassiers.

The three columns of the third line were: the first, that of the left, formed by the division of mounted grenadiers and the dragoons of the Guard, commanded by General Guyot; the second, by the three divisions of the Old, Middle, and Young Guard, commanded by Lieutenant-Generals Friant, Morand, and Duhesme; the third, by the mounted chasseurs and lancers of the Guard, under Lieutenant-General Lefebvre-Desnouettes. The artillery marched on the flanks of the columns; the parks and the ambulances at the tail.

At 9 o'clock, the heads of the four columns forming the first line arrived at the point where they were to deploy. At the same time the other seven columns could be seen not very far off debouched from the heights. They were on the march, the trumpets and drums summoning them to battle. The music resounded with airs which brought back to the soldiers the memories of a hundred victories. The very soil seemed proud to support so many brave men. This was a magnificent spectacle; and the enemy, who were situated in such a way that every man was visible, must have been struck by it. The army must have seemed twice as big as it really was.[20]

The following was published in the *Lancaster Gazette* of Saturday 21 October under the headline 'BATTLE OF WATERLOO: Faithfully and interestingly detailed, *Village of Gommignies, June 22, 1815*':

Our position was a very compact one, the extreme left resting on La Haye, the left centre on La Haye Sainte, and the right centre on Hougomont, and the extreme right was thrown back to a certain degree in consequence of a ravine which would otherwise have laid it open to the enemy. We were posted near Hougomont, into which the four light companies of the division of Guards, under Colonel McDonald and Lord Saltoun, were thrown. The house had a large garden attached to it, laid out in the Dutch fashion, with parallel walks and high thick hedges, and was surrounded by an orchard. As the army fell back the enemy's cavalry attacked the rear, and there were constant skirmishes and charges of cavalry during the day.

Towards seven o'clock in the evening the French cannonaded Hougomont and our position for near an hour and a half, and were answered by the guns on the top of the hill in our front. We were moved back a little distance to get out of the exact range of the shot, and after continuing during the time I have above mentioned, eagerly awaiting a further development of their attack, the firing ceased, and we continued till the morning in the situation we now held. The weather, which had hitherto been showery, became settled into a decided and heavy rain, which continued in actual torrents the complete night through, accompanied by a gale of wind and constant thunder and lightning.

Such a night few have witnessed, it was one that imagination would point as alone fit for the festival of the demons of death, and for the fates to complete the web of those brave souls whose thread of life was so nearly spun. After such a night of horrors and contending expectations, the dawn of any kind of day was welcome; it seemed however with difficulty to break through the heavy clouds which overhung the earth, and appeared so slowly, that it seemed as if Nature reluctantly lent her light to assist at the scene of carnage and distress, which was to mark the history of this eventful day. Our artillery, which had the night before so admirably answered the fire of the French guns, was all placed on the heights in our front.

It is here necessary for me to remark, that our position comprehended the two roads from Charleroi and Nivelle to Brussels, which united at the village of Mont St. Jean, and formed rather an acute angle. The Prince of Orange's corps composed the first line, with the whole artillery in its front, and Lord Hill's corps the right flank and second line.

Jardin Ainé, was, as mentioned earlier, equerry to the Emperor Napoleon and therefore well placed to detail some of the events that day:

> On the 18th Napoleon having left the bivouac, that is to say the village Caillou on horseback, at half-past nine in the morning came to take up his stand half a league in advance upon a hill where he could discern the movements of the British army.
>
> There he dismounted, and with his field glass endeavoured to discover all the movements in the enemy's line. The chief of the staff suggested that they should begin the attack; he replied that they must wait … Napoleon rode through the lines and gave orders to make certain that every detail was executed with promptitude; he returned often to the spot where in the morning he had started, there he dismounted and, seating himself in a chair which was brought to him, he placed his head between his hands and rested his elbows on his knees.[21]

The Battle of Waterloo was about to begin.

The Struggle for Hougoumont

The Château d'Hougoumont was a key component of Wellington's defensive line and had to be held at all costs. The château complex, a working farm, consisted of the main house surrounded by farm buildings joined by a high wall. Beyond this was a garden, orchard and a not inconsiderable wood.

> The farm is well calculated for defence. The dwelling house in the Centre was a strong square building, with small doors and windows. The barns and granaries formed nearly a square, with one door of communication with the small yard to the South [i.e. facing the French] and from that yard was a door into the garden, a double gate into the wood, under or near the small houses, which I conclude you call the Gardener's house; and another door opening into the lane on the West. There was another carriage gate at the North-West angle of the great yard, leading into the barn, which conducted to the road to Braine-le-Leud.[1]

It is this northern gate which, described above by Lieutenant Colonel (later Lieutenant General) Alexander Woodford of the Coldstream Guards, was to acquire great significance in the battle to come.

Such was the importance of Hougoumont, Wellington placed troops that he could rely upon – the Guards – there. The light company of the 2nd Battalion, Coldstream Guards, was stationed in the farm and château, with the light company of the 2nd Battalion, 3rd Guards, in the garden and grounds, and the two light companies of the 2nd and 3rd Battalions of the 1st Guards in the orchard. The Guards were supported by the 1st Battalion, 2nd Nassau Regiment, with additional detachments of *jägers* and *landwehr* from Kielmansegge's 1st (Hanoverian) Brigade.

Command of Hougoumont was entrusted to Lieutenant Colonel James Macdonnell of the Coldstream Guards. The place had been fortified as much as was possible in the few hours before the first shots of the Battle of Waterloo rang out. The walls had been loopholed, firing platforms had been built and tiles had even been removed from the roof to allow men to fire down upon the attackers.

It was the artillery of General Reille which fired those first shots upon the British positions, marking the start of the assault upon Hougoumont in a contest that would last all day.

Reille gave the job of attacking Hougoumont to Prince Jérôme-Napoléon Bonaparte's 6th Division. Napoleon had no interest in taking such a strong position, all he expected of his younger brother was that he would draw into the struggle for the château as many British troops as possible so that when the Emperor delivered his main assault upon the centre-left of the Anglo-Netherlands line, Wellington would have no reserves to call upon.

The first attack was delivered by General Baron Bauduin's 1st Brigade supported by two batteries of horse artillery. George D. Standen was an Ensign with the 3rd Foot Guards:

> I heard voices, and the drummers beating the *pas de charge*, apparently belonging to Jerome's left Column. I was then in a small field like a crescent on the right flank of the house, adjoining the lane going to Charleroi road from the house, but I am inclined to think they belonged to the right or centre Column. When in turn we retreated, our attacks became more feeble. Although we drove them out, our advances became shorter. They fed an immense force of skirmishers; we had no support.[2]

The French *tirailleurs* ran into the woods with bayonets fixed, but were halted by the fire of three companies from the Nassau regiment and the Hanoverian *jägers*, some 600 men in total. Increasing numbers of French were thrown into the wood and the defenders withdrew, disputing every tree and bush.

It took an hour for the French to clear the wood. They had suffered heavy losses, with Bauduin being just one of many officers being killed or wounded. This was as far as Jérôme's men were supposed to go. With the wood in French hands Reille could bring up the rest of his force hidden by the trees. But the men of the 1st Brigade, seeing themselves only thirty yards from the château and lacking the officers to restrain them, charged across the open ground. They were cut down by heavy fire from the Guards and were driven back into the wood.

This part of the action was watched by Jean-Victor Constantine-Rebècque, Chief of Staff to the Netherlands Army:

The enemy, suffering considerably from the firing coming from the walls, turned his efforts against the 1st Battalion of the 2nd Nassau Regiment which was defending the orchard that flanked the garden. The battalion was overwhelmed and forced to give way; it retreated and the enemy captured the hedge which fronted the orchard, destroying it in several places.[3]

With the allied troops having been forced back into Hougoumont, Sir Augustus Frazer, who commanded the Royal Horse Artillery knew that there were only Jérôme's men still in the wood. This, he believed, gave him a chance to use his troop of howitzers commanded by Major Bull, with their ability to engage in indirect fire:

I ... was rejoiced to hear that his Grace had determined not to lose a wood, 300 yards in front of the part of the line, which was really our weakest point ... Whilst looking around, remarking again that the weak point was our right, and imagining that the enemy, making a demonstration on our centre and left, would forcibly seize the wood, and interpose between us and Braine le Leud, would endeavour to turn the right flank of our second line ... I met Lord Uxbridge, who very handsomely asked me what I thought of the position, and offered me the free use of the Horse artillery.

In a moment Bell [Adjutant of the Horse Artillery] was sent for the Howitzer troop, and I rode up and told the Duke I had done so. By this time the enemy had forced a Belgian battalion [the 2nd Nassau Regiment] out of the orchard to the left of the wood, and there was a hot fire on a battalion (or four companies, I forget which) of the Guards stationed in the buildings and behind the walled garden. The Howitzer troop came up, handsomely; their very appearance encouraged the remainder of the division of the Guards, then lying down to be sheltered from the fire. The Duke said, 'Colonel Frazer, you are going to do a delicate thing; can you depend upon the force of your howitzers? Part of the wood is held by our troops, part by the enemy,' and his Grace calmly explained what I already knew. I answered that I could perfectly depend upon the troop; and after speaking to Major Bull and to all his officers, the troop commenced its fire, and in ten minutes the enemy was driven from the wood.[4]

Jérôme was determined not to be defeated and he fed increasing numbers into the fight. Such was the weight of the French attack, Wellington was compelled to reinforce the defending troops in

Hougoumont, which was exactly what Napoleon wanted, though the Duke did so only sparingly. Lieutenant Colonel Woodford recalled the following:

> At the time I was sent down to Hougoumont (about twelve o'clock or a little after), the Enemy had nearly got into the farmyard. We found them very near the wall, and charged them, upon which they went off, and I took the opportunity of entering the farm by a side door in the lane.
>
> From that time there was much *tiraillerie*, some cannon and howitzer shots, which last I always considered set fire to the barns.
>
> The tirailleurs on the rising ground along the eastern hedge never distinctly showed themselves, though they annoyed us very much by firing at the door which communicated between the courtyard and the garden, and of which they could see the top.
>
> Several cannon shots went into the centre building, where some wounded Officers were lying ... The heat and smoke of the conflagration were very difficult to bear. Several men were burnt, as neither Colonel Macdonell nor myself could penetrate to the stables where the wounded had been carried.[5]

Wellington had seen the fire breaking out inside Hougoumont and sent a note, written on ass or donkey skin, to Lieutenant Colonel Macdonnell:

> I see that the fire has communicated from the hay stack to the Roof of the Chateau. You must however still keep your Men in those parts to which the fire does not reach.
>
> Take care that no Men are lost by the falling in of the Roof or floors. After they will have fallen in occupy the Ruined Walls inside the Garden, particularly if it should be possible for the Enemy to pass through the Embers in the Inside of the House.[6]

According to Lieutenant Colonel Francis Home of the 2nd Battalion, 3rd Foot Guards, the situation of Hougoumont meant that,

> it could not easily be touched by cannon &c, the wood protected it in front and on its right flank they could not bring guns to bear on it without coming close to the edge of the ridge and exposing themselves to our artillery. This in a great degree saved it. Many common shot and grape fell in my direction and perforated the walls in every part, but these reasons prevented it from being steady or effective.

It was this shot, Lieutenant Colonel Home believed, that was the cause of the fire in the buildings at the embattled château:

> About half past one some shot or shells falling amid the stables of the chateau set them and the straw bales on fire, it burst out in an instant in every quarter with an amazing flame and smoke. The confusion at the time was great and many men burned to death or suffocated by the smoke. The Duke of Wellington was at this moment in considerable anxiety. He sent Lt Colonel Hamilton then aide to Sir E. Barnes [Adjutant General] to the chateau with orders to keep it to the last and if that could not be done from the fire as to occupy the strong ground on the right and rear and defend it to extremity. Colonel Hamilton delivered these orders to me and added these words 'Colonel Home, the Duke considers the defence [of] this post of the last consequence to the success of the operations of the day; do you perfectly understand these orders?'
>
> I said, 'Perfectly, and you may assure the Duke from me that his orders shall be punctually obeyed.'
>
> The fire was gradually diminished and about half past two Colonel Hepburn [commanding 3rd Foot Guards] arriving with some fresh troops, things got again into good order.[7]

Amongst those troops of the 3rd Foot Guards who were despatched down to Hougoumont was Ensign Henry Montagu:

> I was attached to the 8th Company of the battalion and remained on the position above Hougoumont till about 2 o'clock, when the 6th, 7th and 8th companies marched down together, to the orchard on our left of the garden. On reaching the left corner of the lower fence, the 6th and 7th companies filed inside the hedge, while the 8th marched in file, up to the gate leading into the grass field beyond the orchard, where there was a road which led through the field, and along the outside of the garden wall.
>
> There we began to form companies, when the French troops, standing in line in a rye field, immediately in our front, commenced firing by sections on us. As we got the company in line we replied as well as we could by file firing, but being much [restricted?] lost many men, and were obliged to retire slowly, firing, to the lower corner, where there was a deep lane.
>
> Here we remained, being shortly afterwards [reinforced] by 2 companies of a Hanoverian regiment [presumably Kielmansegge's men, unless Montagu was referring to the Nassau troops]. I remained

here a considerable time with Colonel Mercer, who was occupied reforming stragglers and men who returned from carrying wounded officers to the rear.[8]

Lieutenant Colonel Daniel Mackinnon, serving in the Coldstream Guards, described his part in the fighting for Hougoumont in a letter from Brussels written on 23 June 1815:

> Our division &c., &c., formed a centre a little above a large farm house (La Belle Alliance) [he actually means Hougoumont] which was the point attacked and occupied by the light company of the division &c., &c. The grenadiers and three other companies of the Coldstreams under my command were ordered to charge the enemy who had surrounded the house. I was wounded in the act, also had a beautiful grey horse shot, however, I did the best that lay in my power and succeeded in repulsing them till relieved by the remainder of the battalion; the whole were then obliged to fortify ourselves in the farm yard which we were ordered to defend, let what would oppose us; in short, we remained in it till night against repeated attacks of the French Army; at last it was demolished and burnt to the ground by the enemy's cannon. My poor dun horse has been almost burnt to death, he lost an eye &c., &c. My servant says he must be shot. The day preceding I also lost a horse, so you will see I have lost all three of my English horses. The ball struck me exactly on the cap of the knee so you may suppose the pain is most excruciating.

Ensign George Standen continues his graphic account:

> A haystack was set fire to in one of the attacks in which our Companies were repulsed, behind which we repeatedly formed and charged; I cannot speak as to time, but think between one and two the French drove the remaining few into the house. After a severe struggle the French forced the rear gate open and came in with us. We flew to the parlour, opened the windows and drove them out, leaving an Officer and some men dead within the wall.
>
> During this time the whole of the barn and cart house were in flames. During the confusion three or four Officers' horses rushed out into the yard from the barn, and in a minute or two rushed back into the flames and were burnt. I mention this as I had always heard horses would never leave fire; perhaps some beam or large piece of wood fell and astonished them.

The ditch at the corner of the wood leading into the orchard was full of dead bodies (we had blocked up the gate), as the French strove repeatedly and gallantly to get through in defiance of the fire from the loopholes so close to them.[9]

An unidentified officer of the 1st Guards replying to Siborne during his quest for information on the various stages of the battle, wrote:

Unfortunately for us, during the cannonade the shot and shells which passed over the artillery, fell into our squares, and I assure you I never was in a more awful situation. Col. Cook (who commanded the battalion) [Major General George Cook actually commanded the Guards Division] was struck with a grape shot as he sat on the ground next to me.

The Enemy now made an attack with infantry and cavalry on the left, in hopes of carrying the chaussee to Brussels; but the artillery guns cut them to pieces every time they advanced. They then attempted to charge the guns with cavalry; but the squares of infantry kept up so smart a fire that they could never reach our guns, though the artillerymen were obliged to leave them to get out of our fire.

When the Enemy found the attempt fail on this point, he ordered an attack on the farm-house, which it was necessary for him to possess in order to turn the right of our position. There it was that the serious struggle commenced. Two companies of light infantry, under Lord Saltoun, disputed the wood and orchard most gallantly, but were at last obliged to retire under cover of the house, when the enemy were charged by the light infantry of the 2d brigade (the Coldstream and 3d), and driven back with great loss. At this period the Coldstream entered the house which the Enemy set on fire by shells, but did not entirely consume it. The Enemy were foiled in two repeated attempts, and were each time severely cut up by the artillery. When they failed in their attacks upon our squares, the cavalry rushed out from between our squares and cut them up most desperately. When he found these efforts vain, he began his attack upon the centre. He first endeavoured to carry the guns with his cavalry, which came up most gallantly; but our squares sent them to the right about three times in great style. I never saw anything so fine, the cavalry rushing out and picking up the deserted cannon.[10]

Major General Cook survived the grape-shot injury but it cost him his arm. The fighting that led to so many suffering such wounds was described in the *Lancaster Gazette* of Saturday, 28 October 1815. This account was written at the village of Gommignies on 22 June:

> About a quarter past eleven o'clock, A.M. the battle commenced, by the French making a most desperate and impetuous attack upon Hougomont; against which, as well as La Haye Sainte, they directed their most furious efforts during the whole day. Hougomont, however, appeared to be the principal object they had in view, since its possession would have uncovered our flank, and have afforded them a most fatal advantage over our line; in a word, had it been lost, nothing short of its being retaken at any rate could have repaired the misfortune. – The French opened upon us a dreadful cross fire from three hundred pieces of artillery, which was answered with a most uncommon precision from our guns; but to be just, we must own that the French batteries were served in a manner that was terrible. – During this period, the enemy pushed his troops into the orchard, &c &c and after its being contested for some hours, he succeeded in reducing our men to nothing but the house itself.
>
> Every tree, every walk, every hedge, every avenue, had been fought for with an obstinacy almost unparalleled, and the French were killed all round, and at the very door of the house, to which, as well as a hay-stack, they succeeded in setting fire; and though all in flames over their heads, our brave fellows never suffered them to penetrate beyond the threshold; the greatest part of the wounded, on both sides, were, alas, here burned to death!
>
> In consequence of this success on the part of the French, the Coldstream, and third regiment, were ordered into the wood, from whence they drove the enemy, and every subsequent struggle they made to re-possess themselves of it, proved abortive. The places of these two battalions of guards were supplied by two of our gallant friends, the black Brunswickers, who seemed, like salamanders, to revel in the smoke and flames. The 2d and 3d battalions of the first regiment were formed with the two battalions of Brunswickers into hollow squares, on the slope and summit of the hill, so as to support each other, and in this situation we all lay down, till between three and four o'clock, P.M. in order to avoid the storm of death, which was flying close over our heads, and at almost every moment carrying destruction among us; and it is, you will allow, a circumstance highly creditable to those men, to have lain so many hours under a fire, which for intensity and precision was never, I believe, equalled; with nothing else to occupy their attention, save watching their companions falling around them, and listening to their mournful cries.

It was about the time I have just named, that the enemy, having gained the orchard, commenced their desperate charges of cavalry, under cover of the smoke which the burning house, &c had caused; the whole of which the wind drifted towards us, and thus prevented our observing their approach.

After the battle, Wellington said that 'the success of the battle of Waterloo turned' upon the following incident, involving the northern gate:

The following details of this soul-stirring incident are gathered from the most reliable French and British sources. The French had ascertained that the defenders received their supplies of ammunition and were being reinforced from time to time by way of the great North Gate. It was therefore determined to make a fierce onslaught on this portion of the line of defence. To this point, accordingly, General Bauduin, the Commander of the first Brigade of Jerome's Division, directed the advance of the 1st Regiment of Léger Infantry. Later, seeing Bauduin fall mortally wounded just before the gateway was reached, the colonel, Cubieres, assumed the direct command, and with loud shouts rode forward towards the one vulnerable spot in the armour of the defence. In order to beat down all opposition he ordered forward a party of Sapeurs, at whose head he placed a brave young officer, the Sous-Lieutenant Legros, but better known among the soldiers as 'L'enfonceur,' who, though at the time an officer of Light Infantry, had served for a period with the Engineers, and was recognised by all as a brave and capable leader for the task in hand.

Seizing a hatchet, and waving his comrades to follow, Legros rushed past the blazing haystack, the dense black smoke from which filled the lane and hid from the defenders the terrible danger which now threatened their position. At this critical moment the group of Guardsmen who had been holding tenaciously to the lane leading to the gateway were compelled by the overwhelming smoke and heat produced by the burning hay, and now by the rapidly increasing pressure of their enemies, to relinquish their post. Seeing themselves about to be outflanked and their retreat cut off by a force now entering the 'friendly hollow way' from the other or east end, the Guards withdrew into the great courtyard of the farm, and hastened to close the great North Gate.

The party now retiring slowly into the courtyard consisted of men from the light companies of the Coldstreams and of the 3rd or Scots Guards. Among them were two brothers, Graham by name, natives of the County Monaghan, also two sergeants of the Scots Guards – Bryce McGregor, a native of Argyleshire, who enlisted at Glasgow in 1799; and Sergeant-Major Ralph Fraser, a veteran who had served with distinction in Egypt in 1801, in Hanover, at Copenhagen, and in the Peninsula, where he was twice badly wounded. Upon these men then fell the brunt of the determined attack of Cubieres' regiment, headed by Legros and his Sapeurs.

A fierce hand-to-hand fight now ensued. Step by step the gallant defenders were forced to give ground. Then, in order to create a diversion, Sergeant Fraser, while his comrades made for the gate, rushed forward into the thickest throng of the enemy, alone and at great personal risk, and attacked the mounted officer whom he saw urging his charger forward with the obvious intention of preventing the heavy gates from being closed. With a powerful thrust of his sergeant's halberd he pulled the officer, who was no other than Cubieres himself, from the saddle; and then, with a swiftness which utterly disconcerted the Frenchmen around him, he rode into the courtyard on the Frenchman's horse before the surprised assailants had realised his daring design. Fraser was, however, closely followed by Legros and about a hundred of the enemy, who, parrying the vigorous bayonet-thrusts of the defenders, threw their combined strength upon the partially closed gate; and, mid the crash of falling timbers and the rattle of crumbling masonry, the great North Gate of Hougoumont was captured.

Only for a moment did victory rest with the Frenchmen. Attracted by the loud shouts of 'Vive l'Empereur!' and the counter-cries for help from the hard-pressed defenders of the gate, Macdonell, calling the three officers near him to follow, made for the courtyard. The sight which met his gaze was sufficient to stagger even the bravest heart. Already a hundred Frenchmen had entered the gateway, and some had penetrated as far as the wicket-gate of the inner yard by which he and his party must pass from the garden to reach the North Gate. Here a dozen Frenchmen of the 1st Leger Regiment had been surrounded by a number of Hanoverian infantrymen, who had been driven into the garden from the orchard by the overwhelming numbers of the enemy. In a few moments the fight here was over, and the intruders hunted down; but not before the Frenchmen had the satisfaction of seeing a young Hanoverian lieutenant, Wilder by name, pursued by another party of Frenchmen towards the farmhouse, and, at the moment when he grasped the handle of the door, cut down by a ferocious Sapeur, who hewed off his hand with an axe.

On entering the courtyard, Macdonell saw that the Guardsmen there were defending themselves at the entrance to the cowhouse and stables which ran eastwards from the gate, and that several of their number were lying wounded at the doorway. Among these latter was one of the brothers Graham of the Coldstreams. From the windows of the parlour, from behind the walls, from the summits of the garrets, from the depths of the cellars, through all the air-holes, through every crack in the stones, the Guards, now in ambush, were firing upon the French in the yard. At the chateau, the defenders, besieged on the staircase and massed on the upper steps, had cut off the lower steps ... Macdonell, as we have said, was a man of giant stature and breadth of frame; and when he rushed like an infuriated lion upon the Frenchmen around the gate they scattered before him. With him were the handful of young officers. They were, like Colonel Macdonell, all officers of the Second Battalion of the Coldstreams ... they were joined by Sergeant John Graham of the light company of their regiment, who, as already described, had, with his now wounded brother and Sergeants Eraser and MacGregor, been holding the enemy in check and preventing them from setting the stables and barn near the great North Gate on fire.

As this small party approached the gate there appeared before them, at the further end of the narrow way, a strong reinforcement of French infantry pouring in from both flanks. The British officers became at once roused to frenzy by the thought of the dire calamity which must befall the whole army if they should fail. With Hougoumont taken Napoleon would entrench himself in the key to the British position, enfilading the right wing and opening the highway by the Nivelles road direct to Brussels.

The little party of officers no sooner burst in fury upon the Frenchmen near the gate than they turned tail and broke up into several parties, some taking refuge in the open cart-shed adjoining the gate, and others making for the barn, where many of the British wounded were lying, and through which there was a direct road to the south or French side of the position. The remainder stood their ground, awaiting the arrival of the reinforcements now in sight. In less time than it takes to relate, Macdonell and Sergeant Graham placed their broad shoulders against the open gates; and, while their comrades engaged and overcame the daring spirits among the enemy who struggled to resist, the heavy doors were swung together, and – Hougoumont was saved!

Immediately stone slabs, broken beams, and the remains or wagons and farm implements were heaped against the gate, and then the storm of baffled and impotent rage burst against the outside. In another instant the heavy cross-bar which held the doors together was fixed by Graham, and the blows of hatchet and bayonet beat unavailingly on the solid planks of which the gate was composed.[11]

Richard MacLaurence was also involved in the fighting inside Hougoumont. He recalled his part in the events there for the *Newcastle Journal* on 12 January 1843:

> Once the French broke into the courtyard, and such a scene of bayonet work I never before or since beheld. It was fairly a trial of strength – the French grenadiers were not to be trifled with and we looked like so many butchers, red with gore.

The struggle for Hougoumont continued all day, and inevitably, its defenders began to run out of ammunition. Staff officer Captain Horace Seymour explained how the Royal Waggon Train kept the defenders supplied, through, of course, that vital northern gate:

> Late in the day of the 18th, I was called to by some Officers of the 3rd Guards defending Hougoumont, to use my best endeavours to send them musket ammunition. Soon afterwards I fell in with a private of the Waggon Train in charge of a tumbrel on the crest of the position. I merely pointed out to him where he was wanted, when he gallantly started his horses, and drove straight down the hill to the Farm, to the gate of which I saw him arrive. He must have lost his horses, as there was a severe fire kept on him. I feel convinced to that man's service the Guards owe their ammunition.[12]

Lieutenant Colonel Francis Home tells of the final hours of the defence of Hougoumont, after the fires had been extinguished:

> After that no very violent attack was made against this post but only a sharp firing kept upon it by light troops until about 6 in the evening when an attack being made along our whole line the enemy turned the left of the orchard and [pushed] the troops there back upon our right.
>
> Things did not remain long in this situation and a general advance from our line won the day and freed the troops in Hougoumont from the fate which they would have met with from the enemy.[13]

9

The French Artillery Bombardment

As the struggle for Hougoumont raged, Napoleon turned his attention to the main Anglo-Netherlands position. A grand battery of eighty-four guns was formed, which unlimbered along a spur about 250 yards from La Haye Sainte. It included the twenty 12-pounders of II and VI Corps, forty 8-pounders of I Corps and twenty-four 12-pounders from the Imperial Guard.[1] These arrangements were noticed by Captain John Kincaid of the 95th Rifles:

> Innumerable black specks were now seen taking post at regular distances in its front, and recognising them as so many pieces of artillery, I knew from experience, although nothing else was yet visible, that they were unerring symptoms of our not being destined to be idle spectators.

Another officer of the 95th Rifles, Captain George Simmons, also recorded his recollections of the events of that morning:

> At daylight the weather cleared. The men commenced cleaning their arms and preparing for the tremendous contest. We were soon convinced the French were forming to give us battle, and had no doubt but Napoleon himself was there. Many old warriors who had fought for years in the Peninsula were proud of being pitted with our gallant chief against Buonaparte and the flower of France.
>   About 11 o'clock in the morning the enemy commenced a heavy cannonade upon our line, which was spiritedly returned from us. The 2nd Brigade of our Division occupied the extreme left of the line, the 1st 95th were upon the chaussee to Charleroi from Bruxeiles; 32nd, 79th, and 28th on the left, under the command of Sir J. Kempt; Sir D. Pack commanded the 2nd Brigade; Sir Thos. Picton commanded this Division. Our Brigade formed column and, from being much exposed

137

to the enemy's guns, suffered severely. About 1 o'clock the enemy's guns were moved nearer. We knew the attack must soon commence.[2]

The 1st Hanoverian Infantry Brigade was part of Major General Carl August von Alten's 3rd Division. This was the strongest British division, with thirteen and a half battalions and a total of 7,676 effectives at the start of the battle:

> From the beginning of the battle, the enemy undertook a massive artillery bombardment against that part of the line that the brigade was covering. The fire ricocheted into the second line, inflicting greater damage on the Nassau Infantry regiment than on the brigade. The two batteries attached to the 3rd Division along with a third which had deployed on the crest of the hill in front of the brigade suffered heavily. Other batteries relieved them several times, but they either quickly ran out of ammunition, or were damaged and left standing. In front of the brigade, several powder wagons blew up.

Lieutenant Colonel James Stanhope was with the 3rd Battalion, 1st Foot Guards, situated to the west of the Charleroi–Brussels road. He wrote in a letter after the battle that because his battalion was placed behind the crest of the hill he was unable to see the whole battlefield. His recollections of that day, in as far as they affected him, nevertheless, were quite clear:

> The hills on which we had seen but small bodies the night before was now black with clustered troops and large masses of infantry … The action began with a cannonade such as I believe never was seen before … Under a most destructive cannonade & having several shells burst in the middle of us, not a man moved from his place …
>
> A number of Staff officers were soon killed & wounded who were at first alone exposed to the cannonade. General Cooke lost his arm, shells began to fall in our squares & though many men were blown up & horribly mangled I never saw such steadiness. As the poor wounded wretches remained in the square it was a horrid sight in cold blood.[3]

Private Clay was with the 3rd Foot Guards. During the night before the battle Clay had fallen up to his neck in a water-filled ditch when taking position behind Hougoumont:

> We remained in a kneeling position under this cover, but annoyed by a most galling fire from our opponent's guns to the left of our position

so near to us, indeed that the spreading of their small shots [from canister] rarely escaped contact with our knapsacks and accoutrements, even the heels of our shoes (whilst kneeling) were struck by them.[4]

The British artillery was not silent though its officers had been instructed not to engage in counter-battery fire but to concentrate their efforts upon the enemy's infantry and cavalry. Several batteries were therefore brought into play against Prince Jérôme's men:

> Jerome's supporting columns had not advanced far when the Duke of Wellington, with his staff, galloped up to the spot on which the Coldstream Guards were formed; and having directed his glass upon the French columns, the guns of Sandham's Foot Battery, attached to Cooke's Division, were ordered to the front. They instantly unlimbered and opened the cannonade from the Anglo-Allied position.
>
> The first discharge was from a howitzer shell which burst over the head of a column moving towards Hougoumont inclosures. The shots from the remaining guns in succession also took effect; and the Battery was soon in full play. It was immediately followed up by an equally well directed fire from Captain Cleeve's Foot Battery of the German legion in front of Alten's Division.[5]

The Allied guns could easily reach the French positions far beyond Hougoumont, as General Foy's *aide-de-camp*, Major Lemonnier-Delafosse, recalled with not a little mischief:

> Behind us in reserve was the brigade of carabineers on which the cannon-balls which passed over us went to fall. To get out of their range, this brigade moved to their left, which provoked General Foy to laugh, 'Ha! Ha! The big boots don't like the rough stuff.' We received the cannon-balls standing firm. They covered us with mud and soaked the ground ... for many of the projectiles buried or muffled themselves whilst rolling along this muddy soil.[6]

Despite Wellington's instructions not to engage in counter-battery fire, one battery commander, Captain Cavalie Mercer of 'G' Troop, Royal Horse Artillery, could not resist the temptation:

> About this time, being impatient of standing idle, and annoyed by the batteries on the Nivelles road, I ventured to commit a folly, for which I should have paid dearly had our Duke chanced to be in our

part of the field. I ventured to disobey orders, and opened a slow deliberate fire at the battery thinking with my 9-pounders soon to silence his 4-pounders.

My astonishment was great, however, when our first gun was responded to by at least half a dozen gentlemen of very superior calibre, whose presence I had not even suspected, and whose superiority we immediately recognised by their rushing noise and long reach, for they flew far beyond us. I instantly saw my folly, and ceased firing, and they did the same – the 4 pounders alone continuing the cannonade as before. But this was not all. The first man of my troop touched was by one of these confounded long shots [Gunner Hunt]. I shall never forget the scream the poor lad gave when struck. It was one of the last they fired, and shattered his left arm to pieces as he stood between the wagons. That scream went to my very soul.[7]

The French guns were therefore able to maintain their bombardment of the Allied positions virtually unchallenged – as experienced by Ensign Wheatley, a Londoner who had joined the 5th Line Battalion of the King's German Legion:

About ten o'clock, the order came to clean out the muskets and fresh load them. Half an allowance of rum was then issued, and we descended into the plain, and took our position in solid Squares. When this was arranged as per order, we were ordered to remain in our position but, if we like, to lay down, which the battalion did [as well as] the officers in the rere [sic].

I took this opportunity of surveying our situation. It was singular to perceive the shoals of Cavalry and artillery suddenly in our rere all arranged in excellent order as if by a magic wand. The whole of the horse Guards stood behind us. For my part I thought they were at Knightsbridge barracks or prancing on St James's Street.

A Ball whizzed in the air. Up we started simultaneously. I looked at my watch. It was just eleven o'clock … In five minutes a stunning noise took place and a shocking havoc commenced.

One could almost feel the undulation of the air from the multitude of cannon shot. The first man who fell was five files on my left. With the utmost distortion of feature he lay on his side shrivelling up every muscle of the body, then dropped lifeless, dying as it's called a death of glory, heaving his last breath on the field of fame. *Dieu m'engarde!*[8]

James Hope of the 92nd Highlanders wrote the following comments on the effects of the French bombardment:

At first we did not mind it much, but in a few minutes it became so terrible, as to strike with awe the oldest veteran in the field. The spirits of the men were very low indeed during the whole of the morning, and although they had been considerably raised before the commencement of the battle, yet there was something wanting to restore their wonton daring, when opposed to the enemies of this country.[9]

Generalmajor Vincke was with the 5th Hanoverian Infantry Brigade in Picton's 5th Division which formed part of the reserve behind the Allied centre:

About noon, two enemy batteries moved up to less than 2,000 paces from the 5th Brigade. They had very heavy guns and the balls fell so far to the rear of us that the dressing station had to be moved further back. The situation soon changed and the enemy artillery severely wounded the commander of a Nassau battalion that was close to the 5th Brigade.[10]

The 40th Regiment, of which Lieutenant Hugh Wray was a member, also formed part of Major General Sir John Lambert's reserve brigade:

We had three companies almost shot to pieces, one shot killed and wounded twenty-five of the 4th Company, another of the same kind killed poor Fisher, my captain and eighteen of our company … another took the 8th [Company] and killed or wounded twenty-three … At the same time poor Fisher was hit I was speaking to him and I got all his brains [over me as] his head was blown to atoms.[11]

Also in the reserve was the 27th (Inniskilling) Regiment which was in the 10th Brigade of the 6th Division which was initially situated behind Mont St Jean farm. The ferocity of the French bombardment was graphically demonstrated by this letter to the *Army and Navy Gazette*:

I have seen many proofs of the intrepidity of the British soldier, but the conduct of the Battalion of the 27th Regiment at Waterloo was the most extraordinary I ever beheld. They were placed in column, under the fire of several batteries, and there, without forming a line or firing a shot in return, the bullets ploughed through their men until nearly two-thirds went down, and the survivors, as fearing their own nerves might give way, but resolved not to go back, pressed their heads and shoulders inwards, forming a solid ring, and thus leaning together, and striving, as it were, to push all to the centre, moved round and round like men in a mill, apparently frantic with horror and excitement, yet firm in the resolution to overcome nature and fall to the last.[12]

As previously mentioned, *Generalmajor* Willem Frederik van Bylandt's 1st Belgian Brigade was at first situated on the forward slope of Mont St Jean and was an easy target for the French artillery, as Harry Ross-Lewin, of the 32nd Regiment, observed:

> As soon as ... the enemy's artillery were in position, the limbers were removed to the rear; a few men remained at each gun, and they began to throw their shot into our columns with great precision. Their practice was undoubtedly very good, and the Belgians adopted a perfectly intelligible although not very soldier-like method of expressing the high opinion they entertained of its excellence; for only one or two shot had passed through them when they faced about, and went in a body to the rear, artillery and all. This little circumstance did not encourage us to place excessive reliance on the support to be expected from our new allies, *les braves Belges*.[13]

Ross-Lewin was actually misinformed. The Prince of Orange had ordered Bylandt to move back from his exposed forward position. There has been much said about the position of Bylandt's Brigade and whether or not it was withdrawn before it suffered unduly from the French guns. Ross-Lewin's account provides us with the answer to this.

Sergeant William Lawrence served with the 40th Foot in Sir Lowry Cole's 6th Division. The battalion, having just returned from America, only reached Waterloo on the morning of the battle:

> Early in the morning of the 18th we were again put on the march to join our lines, our position being in the reserve, which included the Fourth and Twenty-Seventh Regiments, together with a body of Brunswickers and Dutch, and formed a line between Merk Braine and Mont St. Jean on the Brussels road. Our regiment took the left of this road, but did not remain there long, for the French were seen in motion, and on their opening fire from their cannon we soon marched up to action in open column.
>
> During this movement a shell from the enemy cut our deputy-sergeant-major in two, and having passed on to take the head off one of my company of grenadiers named William Hooper, exploded in the rear not more than one yard from me, hurling me at least two yards into the air, but fortunately doing me little injury beyond the shaking and carrying a small piece of skin off the side of my face. It

was indeed another narrow escape, for it burnt the tail of my sash completely off, and turned the handle of my sword perfectly black. I remember remarking to a sergeant who was standing close by me when I fell, 'This is sharp work to begin with, I hope it will end better.'[14]

Ensign Leeke, was with the 52nd Regiment which was in the 3rd Brigade of Lieutenant General Sir Henry Clinton's 2nd Division. This was a light infantry brigade consisting of the 71st (Highland Light Infantry) Regiment as well as the 2nd and 3rd battalions of the 95th Rifles.

The standing to be cannonaded, and having nothing else to do, is about the most unpleasant thing that can happen to soldiers in an engagement ... I do not exactly know the rapidity with which the cannon-balls fly, but I think that two seconds elapsed from the time I saw this shot leave the gun until it struck the front face of the square.

It did not strike the four men in the rear of whom I was standing, but the poor fellows on their right. It was fired with some elevation, and struck the front man about the knees, and coming to the ground under [the] feet of the rear man of the four, whom it severely wounded, it rose and, passing within an inch or two of the Colour pole ... The two men in the first and second rank fell outward, I fear they did not survive; the two others fell within the square. The rear man made a considerable outcry on being wounded.[15]

The 14th Regiment was with the 4th Brigade. This brigade was stationed to the right of Hougoumont with the 51st Regiment spread out along the road to Braine l'Alleud, this line being extended westwards by three companies of the 14th, with the rest of the battalion being held in close support. One of its number was Ensign Keppel:

A round shot took off his head [a bugler] and spattered the whole battalion with his brains, the colours and the ensigns in charge of them coming in for an extra share. One of them, Charles Fraser, a fine gentleman in speech and manner, raised a laugh by drawling out, 'How extremely disgusting!' A second shot carried off six of the men's bayonets, a third broke the breastbone of a Lance-Sergeant, whose piteous cries were anything but encouraging to his youthful comrades.[16]

The following brief note was tucked away in one of the many columns of news published in the *Chester Courant* on Tuesday, 18 July 1815:

Captain Elton, of the Greys, son of Sir Abraham Elton, had two horses shot under him, as he was taking messages from the Earl of Uxbridge to the Duke of Wellington.

Tom Pocock, with the 71st Highland Light Infantry, was initially in reserve behind the right of the Anglo-Netherlands line north of the Nivelles road:

> The artillery had been tearing away, since daybreak, in different parts of the line. About twelve o'clock we received orders to fall in for attack. We then marched up to our position, where we lay on our face of a brae, covering a brigade of guns. – We were so overcome by the fatigue of two day's march, that, scare had we lain down until many of us fell asleep. I slept sound for some time, while the cannon-balls, plunging in amongst us, killed a great many. I was suddenly awakened. A ball struck the ground a little below me, turned me heels-over-head, broke my musket in pieces, and killed a lad at my side. I was stunned and confused, and knew not whether I was wounded or not. I felt a numbness in my arm for some time.
>
> We lay thus, about an hour and a half, under a dreadful fire which cost us about 60 men, while we had never fired a shot. The balls were falling thick amongst us. The young man I lately spoke of lost his legs by a shot at this time. They were cut very close: he soon bled to death.[17]

Even though Napoleon had delayed the start of the battle, the ground was still soft and despite the described effectiveness of the French artillery it was evidently less lethal than it might have under drier conditions. Coupled with Wellington's instructions for the men to remain below the crest of Mont St Jean, casualties were minimised. An officer of the 10th Hussars, wrote that,

> it was the ground that took the effect of the shot, much from its being deep mud, from the rain and trampling of horse and foot – so that often shot did not rise – and shells buried and exploded up and sending up the mud like a fountain. I had mud thrown over me in this way often.[18]

Captain Tomkinson, of the 16th Light Dragoons, had a similar experience, being posted opposite Papelotte and La Haie:

> The ground was so deep that numberless shells burst where they fell, and did little damage or injury from being buried in the ground, and many round shot never rose from the place they first struck the ground,

instead of hopping for half a mile and doing considerable injury. Many lives were saved from this circumstance.[19]

The bombardment by the so-called Grand Battery lasted for around ninety minutes. The French guns fell silent to allow the divisions of d'Erlon's Corps to pass through the line of guns, caissons and limbers and assemble ahead of the artillery for the great attack upon the British left-centre.

10

The Attack Upon the Allied Centre

The Anglo-Netherland's left centre had been subjected to an intense bombardment in preparation for the moment when the infantry of I Corps would crash against the weakened allied line. Now that moment had arrived. Napoleon explained his method of attack:

> I had preferred to turn the enemy's left, rather than his right, first, in order to cut it off from the Prussians who were at Wavres [*sic*], and to oppose their joining up again, if they had intended doing so; and, even if they had not intended doing so, if the attack had been made on the right, the English army, on being repulsed, would have fallen back on the Prussian army; whereas, if made on the left, it would be separated therefrom and thrown back in the direction of the sea; secondly, because the left appeared to be much weaker; thirdly and finally, because I was expecting every moment the arrival of a detachment from Marshal Grouchy on my right, and did not want to run the risks of finding myself separated from it.[1]

Ahead of the French attack was a large body of skirmishers, which was countered by the British light infantry and rifles. Private Thomas Jeremiah of the 95th Rifles recalled:

> About this time the light infantry of all the front line were ordered to the advance and cover the front of the line, this done immediately there appeared coming over the opposite heights a line of *tirailleurs* or French riflemen, both lines were now descending and approaching each other from their respective hills and in the valleys between the 2 armies they met and commenced skirmishing.[2]

Behind the *tirailleurs* and *voltigeurs* came the great bulk of d'Erlon's corps, as noted by George Simmons also with the skirmish line of the 95th:

146

Four columns now made their appearance, amounting to 20,000 men. They moved steadily towards us. We formed a sort of line and commenced a terrible fire upon them, which was returned very spiritedly, they advancing at the same time within a few yards. I had an impression I should not be touched, and was laughing and joking with a young officer about half-past four in the afternoon.

At this time I was a little in front of our line, and hearing the word charge, I looked back at our line, and received a ball, which broke two of my ribs near the backbone, went through my liver, and lodged in my breast. I fell senseless in the mud, and some minutes after found our fellows and the enemy hotly engaged near me. Their skirmishers were beaten back and the column stopped. Two men dragged me away to the farm of Mont St. Jean, a little to the rear, where Mr. Robson extracted a musket-ball from my breast.[3]

Captain Duthilt, was serving in the 45ème *Régiment de Ligne* in *Général de Division* Pierre Marcognet's 3rd Division:

When it was thought that the English had been sufficiently shaken by our cannonade, d'Erlon's four divisions formed up in separate columns. The third, to which my regiment belonged, had to advance like the others in deployed battalions, with only four paces between one and the next – a strange formation and one which was to cost us dear, since we were unable to form square as a defence against cavalry attacks, while the enemy's artillery could plough our formations to a depth of twenty ranks. To whom I Corps owed this unfortunate formation, which proved to be one cause, maybe *the* cause of our failure, nobody knows.

Our turn came eventually. The order to attack was greeted with a frenzied shout of *Vive l'Empereur!* The four columns moved off down the slope, with ported arms and in serried ranks. We were to mount the opposite slope where the English held the ridge and from where their batteries were blasting us. No doubt the distance involved was not great, and an average person on foot would have taken no more than five or six minutes to cover the ground; but the soft and rain-sodden earth and the tall rye slowed up our progress appreciably. As a result the English gunners had plenty of time to work destruction upon us.

However, we did not weaken, and when we were eventually ready to assault the position, the charge was beaten, our pace quickened, and to repeated shouts of *Vive l'Empereur!* we rushed at the batteries. Suddenly our path was blocked: English battalions concealed in a hollow road, stood up and fired at us at close range. We drove them back at the point of the bayonet and climbed higher up the slope and over the stretches of quick hedge which protected their guns. Then we reached the plateau and give a shout of 'Victory!'[4]

Captain Johnny Kincaid, of the 1st Battalion, 95th Rifles, a hardened Peninsular War veteran, wrote that 'the scene at that moment was grand and imposing', going on to add:

> Each regiment ... rent the air with shouts of '*Vive l'Empereur!*', nor did they cease after they had passed; but, backed by the thunder of their artillery, and carrying with them the *rubidub* of drums, and the *tantara* of trumpets, in addition to their increasing shouts, it looked, at first, as if they had some hopes of scaring us off the ground.[5]

Colonel van Zuylen van Nyevelt was chief of staff of the 2nd Netherlands Division. This division was split up with the 1st Brigade posted on the left-centre of the allied line, whilst the 2nd Brigade was located to the east, defending Papelotte and La Haie:

> Three columns advanced to attack our position under the command of Count d'Erlon, with the 105th regiment at their head. The enemy crossed the ravine, where he was outside the range of our fire, and drove back our skirmishers. Having approached us to within fifty paces, not a shot had been fired, but now the impatience of the soldiers could no longer be restrained, and they greeted the enemy with a double row, which caused the firing to be meagre and badly kept up whilst the downfall of some files made an opening to the enemy, through which he forced his way with his columns.
>
> Everything which was immediately in front of him was forced to give way but the pelotons [platoons] on the wings with much cold bloodedness linked up with the adjoining troops. The enemy had now succeeded in passing our first line, and had arrived on the plain. The second line made ready to advance against him.[6]

An officer of the 5th Division wrote from the allied camp at Clichy after the battle, to his friend in Cumberland, stating:

> The Duke's Dispatch will give you a more accurate idea of the ground, and of the grand scale of operations, than I can do; and I shall therefore confine myself to details of less importance which he has passed over.
>
> After having tried the right, and found it strong, Buonaparte manoeuvred until he got 40 pieces of artillery to play on the left,

where the 5th division, a brigade of heavy dragoons, and two companies of artillery, were posted. Our lines were formed behind a hedge, with two companies of the 95th extended in front, to annoy the Enemy's approach.

For some time we saw, that Buonaparte intended to attack us; yet as nothing but cavalry were visible, no one could imagine what were his plans. It was generally supposed, that he would endeavour to turn our flank. But all on a sudden, his cavalry turned to the right and left, and showed large masses of infantry, which advanced up in the most gallant style, to the cries of '*Vive l'Empereur!*' while a most tremendous cannonade was opened to cover their approach. They had arrived at the very hedge behind which we were – the muskets were almost muzzle to muzzle, and a French mounted officer had seized the colours of the 32d regiment.

Appreciating the danger, Lieutenant General Sir Thomas Picton, in command of the British 5th Division in the second line, ordered two of his brigades forward. His 8th Brigade met one of the French columns and halted it with its controlled fire. The 9th Brigade, under Major General Pack also moved forward but unexpectedly found itself facing Marcognet's entire 3rd Division. Robert Winchester was with the 92nd Foot:

> About two or three o'clock in the afternoon a Column between 3,000 to 4,000 men advanced to the hedge at the roadside which leads from the main road near La Haye Saint [to] beyond the left of our position. Previous to this the 92nd had been lying down under cover of the position when they were immediately ordered to stand to their arms, Major General Sir Dennis Pack calling out at the same time '92nd everything has given way on your right and left and you must charge this Column,' upon which he ordered four deep to be formed and closed in to the centre. The Regiment, which was then within about 20 yards of the Column, fired a volley into them. The Enemy on reaching the hedge at the side of the road had ordered arms, and were in the act of shouldering them when they received the volley from the 92nd.[7]

The 92nd was considerably outnumbered and it certainly seemed at this point that the French infantry were on the point of breaking through the Anglo-Netherlands line and, with their cavalry waiting to exploit such a breakthrough, the battle looked to be reaching its climax.

At this point, Lieutenant General Henry Paget, the Earl of Uxbridge, in charge of the Anglo-Dutch Cavalry Corps, made possibly the most important decision of his military career. Under his command were two brigades of heavy cavalry. One was the Household Brigade, which included the Life Guards and the Royal Horse Guards, and the other was called the Union Brigade as it included regiments from England, Ireland and Scotland. Paget ordered the whole of his heavy cavalry to charge.

Involved in the battle with the British infantry the French were unaware that the British dragoons were about to crash into them, as the Captain Duthilt of the 45ème *Régiment de Ligne*, described:

> In the bloody confusion our officers did their duty by trying to establish some sort of order and to reform the platoons, since a disordered group can achieve nothing. Just as I was pushing one of our men back into the ranks I saw him fall at my feet from a sabre slash. I turned instantly – to see English cavalry forcing their way into our midst and hacking us to pieces.
>
> Just as it is difficult, if not impossible, for the best cavalry to break into infantry who are formed up in squares and who defend themselves with coolness and daring, so it is true that once the ranks have been broken and penetrated, then resistance is useless and nothing remains for the cavalry to do but to slaughter at almost no risk to themselves. This is what happened. In vain our poor fellows stood up and stretched out their arms: they could not reach far enough to bayonet those cavalrymen mounted on powerful horses, and the few shots fired in this chaotic mêlée were just as fatal to our own men as to the English. And so we found ourselves defenceless against a relentless enemy who, in the intoxication of battle, sabred even our drummers and fifers without mercy. That is where our eagle was captured; and that is where I saw death close at hand, for best friends fell round me and I was expecting the same fate, all the while wielding my sword mechanically.
>
> When we could offer no further resistance, the mass of the cavalry made ready to cross the valley to seize our guns, while one group of them escorted away what remained of our division.[8]

One notable participant in the charge was Sergeant Ewart as revealed in this account from the *Caledonian Mercury* of Monday, 18 September 1815. It is an extract of a letter dated 16 August 1815, in which Ewart describes his capture of a French eagle to his brother in Ayr:

> Next morning, 18th, the skirmishers began as before, but nothing was done until about twelve o'clock, when Lord Wellington shewed

himself upon the field; we then thought there was something serious to be done. The enemy began forming their lines of battle about nine in the morning; we did not commence till ten. I think it was about eleven when we were ready to receive them; they began upon our right with the most tremendous firing that ever was heard, and I can assure you, they got it as hot as they gave it – then it came down to the left, where they were received by our brave Highlanders; no men could ever behave better!

Our brigade of cavalry covered them. – owing to a column of foreign troops giving way, our brigade was forced to advance to the support of our brave fellows, and which we certainly did in stile; we charged though two of their columns, each about 5000; it was in the first charge I took the eagle from the enemy; he and I had a very hard contest for it; he thrust for my groin, I parried it off, and cut him through the head; after which I was attacked by one of their lancers, who threw his lance at me, but missed the mark, by my throwing it off with my sword by my right side, then I cut him from the chin upwards, which cut went through his teeth; next, I was attacked by a foot soldier, who, after firing at me, charged me with his bayonet, but he very soon lost the combat, for I parried it and cut him down through the head, so that finished the contest for the eagle. After which I presumed to follow my comrades, eagle and all, but was stopped by the General, saying to me, 'You brave fellow, take that to the rear, you have done enough until you get quit of it;' which I was obliged to do, but with great reluctance.

I retired to a height and stood there for upwards of an hour, which gave me a general view of the field, but I cannot express the sight I beheld; the bodies of my brave comrades were lying so thick upon the field that it was scarcely possible to pass, and horses innumerable. I took the eagle into Brussels amidst the acclamations of thousands of the spectators that saw it.

The 1st (Royal) Dragoons experienced similar success. They struck the head of *Général de Brigade* Baron Charles-François Bourgeois', 2nd Brigade. The column, at the front of which was the 105*ème Régiment de Ligne*, was driven back some 200 yards by the Dragoons. Leading one squadron of the Royals was a young captain, A.K. Clark-Kennedy:

When my squadron (the centre one) of the Royal Dragoons had advanced 200 or 300 yards beyond the second hedge, and the first line of infantry had been broke, I perceived a little to my left, an enemy's 'Eagle' amongst the infantry, with which the bearer was making every exertion to get off towards the rear of the column. I immediately rode to the place calling out to 'Secure the colour!' and at the same time, my horse reaching it, I ran my sword into the officer's right side, who carried the 'Eagle', who staggered and fell forwards but I do not think he reached the ground, on account of the pressure of his companions.

I immediately called out a second time 'Secure the Colour, secure the Colour, it belongs to me.' This was addressed to some men who were behind me at the time the officer was in the act of falling. As he fell with the 'Eagle' a little to the left, I was not able to catch the standard so as to be able to hold it. Corporal Stiles and some other men rushed up to my assistance, and the standard was in an instant in the corporal's possession, it falling across him as he came up on my left, before it reached the ground.[9]

The *Caledonian Mercury* also printed the following detailed description in its edition published on 21 August 1817:

Of all the instances of individual suffering and miraculous preservation, which occurred in this tremendous contest, none, perhaps, combined so many interesting features as the situation of the Honourable Colonel Ponsonby, of the 12th Dragoons. The narrative, which is simple and affecting, is drawn up by a friend of the family, from materials occasionally and reluctantly furnished by the gallant but modest officer.

Dear Lady Bessborough, you have often wished for some written account of the adventures and sufferings of your son, Colonel Ponsonby, in the field of Waterloo: the modesty of his nature is, however, no small obstacle in the way. Will the following imperfect sketch supply its place until it comes? The battle was alluded to one morning in the library at A——, and his answers to many of the questions which were put to him are here thrown together, as nearly as I could remember, in his own words:-

The weather cleared up at noon, and the sun shone out a little just as the battle began. – The armies were within eight hundred yards of each other, the videttes, before they were withdrawn, being so near as to be able to converse. At one moment I imagined that I saw Bonaparte, a considerable staff moving rapidly along the front of our line.

I was stationed with my regiment (about three hundred strong) at the extreme of the left wing, and directed to act discretionally; each of the armies was drawn up on a gentle declivity, a small valley lying between them.

At one o'clock, observing, as I thought, unsteadiness in a column of French infantry (fifty by twenty, (one thousand) or thereabouts), which were advancing with an irregular fire, I resolved to charge them. As we were descending in a gallop, we received from our own troops on the right a fire much more destructive than theirs, they having began long before it could take effect, and slackening as we drew nearer; when we were within fifty paces of them, they turned, and much execution was done among them, as we were followed by some Belgians, who had remarked our success.

But we had no sooner passed through them, than we were attacked in our turn, before we could form, by about 300 Polish lancers, who had come down to their relief: the French artillery pouring in among us a heavy fire of grape shot, which , however, for one of our men killed three of their own: in the *melee*, I was disabled almost instantly in both of my arms, and followed by a few of my men, who were presently cut down (no quarter being asked or given), I was carried on by my horse, till receiving a blow on my head from a sabre, I was thrown senseless on my face to the ground. Recovering, I raised myself a little to look round, (being, I believe, at that time in a condition to get up and run away), when a lancer passing by exclaimed, *'Tu n'es pas mort, coquin,'* and struck his lance through my back; my head dropped, the blood gushed into my mouth, a difficulty of breathing came on, and I thought all was over.

Not long afterwards (it was then impossible to measure time, but I must have fallen in less than ten minutes after the charge), a tirailleur came up to plunder me, threatening to take my life. I told him he might search me, directing him to a small side-pocket, in which he found three dollars, being all I had; he unloosed my stock, and tore open my waistcoat, then leaving me in a very uneasy posture, and was no sooner gone, than another came up for the same purpose, but assuring him I had been plundered already, he left me; when an officer, bringing up some troops (to which probably the tirailleurs belonged), and halting where I lay, stooped down and addressed me, saying, he feared I was badly wounded; I replied that I was, and expressed a wish to be removed into the rear; he said it was against the order to remove even their own men; but if they gained the day, as they probably would (for he understood that the Duke of Wellington was killed, and that six of our battalions had surrendered), every possible attention in his power should be shown me. I complained of thirst, and he held his brandy bottle to my lips, directing one of his men to lay me straight on my side, and place a knapsack under my head; he then passed on into the action, and I shall never know to whose generosity I was indebted, as I conceive, for my life: of what rank he was I cannot say, he wore a blue great coat. By and by another tirailleur came and knelt and fired over me, loading and firing many times, and conversing with great gaiety all the while; at last he ran off saying, '*Vous serez bien aisé d'entendre que nous allons retirer; bon jour, mon ami.*'

While the battle continued in that part, several of the wounded men and dead bodies near me were hit with the balls, which came very thick in that place. Towards evening, when the Prussians came, the continued roar of the cannon along theirs and the British line, growing louder and louder as they drew near, was the finest thing I ever heard. It was dusk, when two squadrons of Prussian cavalry, both of them two deep, passed over me in full trot, lifting me from the ground, and tumbling me about cruelly; the clatter of their approach, and the apprehensions it excited, may be easily conceived. – Had a gun come that way, it would have done for me. The battle was then nearly over, or removed to a distance – the cries and groans of the wounded all around me became every instant more and more audible, succeeding to the shouts, imprecations, outcries of '*Vive l'Empereur!*' the discharges of musketry and cannon: now and then intervals of perfect silence, which were worse than the noise – I thought the night would never end. Much about this time, I found a soldier of the Royals lying across my legs, who had probably crawled thither in his agony; his weight, convulsive motions, his noises, and the air issuing through a wound in his side, distressed me greatly, the latter circumstance most of all, as the case was my own. It was not a dark night, and the Prussians were wandering about to plunder, and the scene in Ferdinand Count Fathom came into my mind, though no women, I believe, were there; several of them came and looked at me, and passed on: at length one stopped to examine me. I told him as well as I could (for I could say but little in German) that I was a British officer, and had been plundered already; he did not desist, however, and pulled me about roughly before he left me. About an hour before midnight I saw a soldier in a British uniform coming towards me; he was, I suspect, on the same errand. He came and looked in my face; I spoke instantly, telling him who I was, and assuring him of a reward if he would remain by me. He said he belonged to the 40th regiment, but had missed it. He released me from the dying man; being unarmed, he took up a sword from the ground, and stood over me, pacing backwards and forwards. At eight o'clock in the morning, some English were seen at a distance; he ran to them, and a messenger was sent off to Hervey. A cart came for me. I was placed in it, and carried to a farm-house, about a mile and a half distance, and laid in the bed from which poor Gordon, as I understood afterwards, had been just carried out; the jolting of the cart, and the difficulty of breathing, were very painful. I had received seven wounds; a surgeon slept in my room, and I was saved by continual bleeding, 120 ounces in two days, besides the great loss of blood on the field.

The lances, from their great length and weight, would have struck down my sword long before I lost it, if it had not been bound to my hand. What became of my horse I know not; it was the best I ever had.

The man from the Royals was still breathing when I was removed in the morning, and was soon after taken to the hospital.

Sir Denis Pack said, the greatest risk he run the whole day, was in stopping his men, who were firing on me and my regiment when we began to charge. The French make a great clamour in the action, the English only shout.

Much confusion arose, and many mistakes, from similarity of dress. The Belgians, in particular, suffered greatly from their resemblance to the French, being still in the very same clothes they had served in under Bonaparte.

Colonel Ponsonby mentions the brigade of Denis Pack, amongst which was the 92nd Regiment, which joined in the charge of the Union Brigade and became the subject of Lady Butler's famous painting *Scotland Forever*:

In the afternoon of the 18th, the regiment, which was then reduced to about 200 men, found it necessary to charge a column of the Enemy which came down on them, from 2 to 3000 men: they broke into the centre of the column with the bayonet; and the instant they pierced it, the Scotch Greys dashed in to their support, when they and the 92nd cheered and huzza'd 'Scotland forever.' By the effort which followed, the Enemy to a man were put to the sword or taken prisoners, after which the Greys charged through the Enemy's second line, and took the eagles.

It was perhaps the most destructive battle ever fought. The loss fell almost entirely on our division which, along with the Brunswick troops and some Prussians, was the only one up for the first two hours. The three Scotch regiments are nearly annihilated!! Ours had only six officers who escaped! and some are so dangerously wounded, as to give little hope of their recovery. We were amply revenged, however; and gave the French a lesson, which they will not soon forget.

The devastation of d'Erlon's Corps was remarked on by Lieutenant Robert Winchester. He also served in the 92nd:

> In less than three minutes it was totally destroyed, 2000 ... of them having been made prisoners ... The grass field in which the enemy was formed, which was only an instant before as green and smooth as the fifteen acres in Phoenix Park, was in a few minutes covered with killed and wounded, knapsacks and their contents, arms, accoutrements, &c., literally strewed all over, that to avoid stepping on either one or the other was quite impossible; in fact one could hardly [have] believed, had he not witnessed it, that such complete destruction could have been effected in so short a time.[10]

Sergeant-Major Dickson described the charge of the Scots Greys to E. Bruce Low. Dickson was the regiment's last surviving member of the charge:

> General of the Union Brigade, Sir William Ponsonby, came riding up to us on a small bay hack. I remember that his groom with his chestnut charger could not be found. Beside him was his aide-de-camp, De Lacy Evans. He ordered us forward to within fifty yards of the beech-hedge by the roadside. I can see him now in his long cloak and great cocked hat as he rode up to watch the fighting below. From our new position we could descry the three regiments of Highlanders, only a thousand in all, bravely firing down on the advancing masses of Frenchmen. These numbered thousands, and those on our side of the Brussels road were divided into three solid columns. I have read since that there were fifteen thousand of them under Count D'Erlon spread over the clover, barley, and rye fields in front of our centre, and making straight for us. Then I saw the Brigadier, Sir Denis Pack, turn to the Gordons and shout out with great energy, 'Ninety-second, you must advance! All in front of you have given way.' The Highlanders, who had begun the day by solemnly chanting 'Scots wha hae' as they prepared their morning meal, instantly, with fixed bayonets, began to press forward through the beech and holly hedge to a line of bushes that grew along the face of the slope in front. They uttered loud shouts as they ran forward and fired a volley at twenty yards into the French.
> At this moment our General and his aide-de-camp rode off to the right by the side of the hedge; then suddenly I saw De Lacy Evans wave his hat, and immediately our colonel, Inglis Hamilton, shouted out, 'Now then, Scots Greys, charge!' and, waving his sword in the

air, he rode straight at the hedges in front, which he took in grand style.

At once a great cheer rose from our ranks, and we too waved our swords and followed him. I dug my spur into my brave old Rattler, and we were off like the wind. Just then I saw Major Hankin fall wounded. I felt a strange thrill run through me, and I am sure my noble beast felt the same, for, after rearing for a moment, she sprang forward, uttering loud neighings and snortings, and leapt over the holly-hedge at a terrific speed. It was a grand sight to see the long line of giant grey horses dashing along with flowing manes and heads down, tearing up the turf about them as they went.

The men in their red coats and tall bearskins were cheering loudly, and the trumpeters were sounding the 'Charge.' Beyond the first hedge the road was sunk between high, sloping banks, and it was a very difficult feat to descend without falling; but there were very few accidents, to our surprise.

All of us were greatly excited, and began crying, 'Hurrah, Ninety-Second! Scotland forever!' as we crossed the road. For we heard the Highland pipers playing among the smoke and firing below, and I plainly saw my old friend Pipe-Major Cameron standing apart on a hillock coolly playing 'Johnny Cope, are ye waukin' yet?" in all the din.

At the start of the campaign the Scots Greys numbered just over 350 effectives of all ranks. Together with the 1st Royals and the 6th Inniskillings, the Union Brigade mustered little more than 1,100 bayonets. These, though, were big men on big horses:

Our colonel went on before us, past our guns and down the slope, and we followed; we saw the Royals and Enniskillens clearing the road and hedges at full gallop away to the right. Before me rode young Armour, our rough-rider from Mauchline and Sergeant Ewart on the right, at the end of the line beside our cornet, Kinchant. I rode in the second rank. As we tightened our grip to descend the hillside among the corn, we could make out the feather bonnets of the Highlanders, and heard the officers crying out to them to wheel back by sections. A moment more and we were among them. Poor fellows! some of them had not time to get clear of us, and were knocked down. I remember one lad crying out, 'Eh! But I didna think ye wad ha'e hurt me sae.'

They were all Gordons, and as we passed through them they shouted, 'Go at them, the Greys! Scotland forever!' My blood thrilled at this, and I clutched my sabre tighter. Many of the Highlanders grasped our stirrups, and in the fiercest excitement dashed with us into the fight. The French were uttering loud, discordant yells. Just then I saw the first Frenchman. A young officer of Fusiliers made a slash at me with his sword, but I parried it and broke his arm; the next second we were in the thick of them. We could not see five yards ahead for the smoke. I stuck close by Armour; Ewart was now in front.

The French were fighting like tigers. Some of the wounded were firing at us as we passed; and poor Kinchant, who had spared one of these rascals, was himself shot by the officer he had spared. As we were sweeping down a steep slope on the top of them, they had to give way. Then those in front began to cry out for 'quarter,' throwing down their muskets and taking off their belts. The Gordons at this rushed in and drove the French to the rear. I was now in the front rank, for many of ours had fallen. We now came to an open space covered with bushes, and then I saw Ewart, with five or six infantry men about him, slashing right and left at them. Armour and I dashed up to these half-dozen Frenchmen, who were trying to escape with one of their standards. I cried to Armour to 'Come on!' and we rode at them. Ewart had finished two of them, and was in the act of striking a third man who held the Eagle; next moment I saw Ewart cut him down, and he fell dead. I was just in time to thwart a bayonet-thrust that was aimed at the gallant sergeant's neck. Armour finished another of them. Almost single-handed, Ewart had captured the Imperial Eagle of the 45th 'Invincibles,' which had led them to victory at Austerlitz and Jena ... We cried out, 'Well done, my boy' and as others had come up, we spurred on in search of a like success. Here it was that we came upon two batteries of French guns which had been sent forward to support the infantry. They were now deserted by the gunners and had sunk deep in the mud.

We were saluted with a sharp fire of musketry, and again found ourselves beset by thousands of Frenchmen. We had fallen upon a second column; they were also Fusiliers. Trumpeter Reeves of our troop, who rode by my side, sounded a 'Rally,' and our men came swarming up from all sides, some Enniskillens and Royals being amongst the number. We at once began a furious onslaught on this obstacle, and soon made an impression; the battalions seemed to open out for us to pass through, and so it happened that in five minutes we had cut our way through as many thousands of Frenchmen.

We had now reached the bottom of the slope. There the ground was slippery with deep mud. Urging each other on, we dashed towards the batteries on the ridge above, which had worked such havoc on our ranks. The ground was very difficult, and especially where we crossed the edge of a ploughed field, so that our horses sank to the knees as we struggled on. My brave Rattler was becoming quite exhausted, but we dashed ever onwards.

At this moment Colonel Hamilton rode up to us crying, 'Charge! charge the guns!' and went off like the wind up to the hill towards the terrible battery that had made such deadly work among the Highlanders. It was the last we saw of our colonel, poor fellow! His body was found with both arms cut off. His pockets had been rifled.

Then we got among the guns, and we had our revenge. Such slaughtering! We sabred the gunners, lamed the horses, and cut their traces and harness. I can hear the Frenchmen yet crying 'Diable!' when I struck at them, and the long-drawn hiss through their teeth as my sword went home. Fifteen of their guns could not be fired again that day. The artillery drivers sat on their horses weeping aloud as we went among them; they were mere boys, we thought.

Rattler lost her temper and bit and tore at everything that came in her way. She seemed to have got new strength. I had lost the plume of my bearskin just as we went through the second infantry column; a shot had carried it away. The French infantry were rushing past us in disorder on their way to the rear. Armour shouted to me to dismount, for old Rattler was badly wounded. I did so just in time, for she fell heavily the next second. I caught hold of a French officer's horse and sprang on her back and rode on.

Then we saw a party of horsemen in front of us on the rising ground near a farmhouse. There was 'the Little Corporal' himself, as his veterans called Bonaparte … But the noble beasts were now exhausted and quite blown, so that I began to think it was time to get clear away to our own lines again.

But you can imagine my astonishment when down below, on the very ground we had crossed, appeared at full gallop a couple of regiments of Cuirassiers on the right, and away to the left a regiment of Lancers. I shall never forget the sight. The Cuirassiers, in their sparkling steel breastplates and helmets, mounted on strong black horses, with great blue rugs across the croups, were galloping towards me, tearing up the earth as they went, the trumpets blowing wild notes in the midst of the discharges of grape and canister shot from the heights. Around me there was one continuous noise of clashing arms, shouting of men, neighing and moaning of horses. What were we to do? Behind us we saw masses of French infantry with tall fur hats coming up at the double, and between us and our lines these cavalry. There being no officers about, we saw nothing for it but to go straight at them and trust to Providence to get through. There were half-a-dozen of us Greys and about a dozen of the Royals and Enniskillens on the ridge. We all shouted, 'Come on, lads; that's the road home!' and, dashing our spurs into our horses' sides, set off straight for the Lancers. But we had no chance. I saw the lances rise and fall for a moment, and Sam Tar, the leading man of ours, go down amid the flash of steel. I felt a sudden rage at this, for I knew the poor fellow well; he was a corporal in our troop. The crash as we met was terrible; the horses began to rear and bite and neigh loudly, and then some of our men got down among their feet, and I saw them trying to ward off the lances with their hands.

Cornet Sturges of the Royals came up and was next me on the left, and Armour on the right. 'Stick together, lads!' we cried, and went at it with a will, slashing about us right and left over our horses' necks. The ground around us was very soft, and our horses could hardly drag their feet out of the clay. Here again I came to the ground, for a Lancer finished my new mount, and I thought I was done for. We were returning past the edge of the ploughed field, and then I saw a spectacle I shall never forget. There lay brave old Ponsonby, the General of our Union Brigade, beside his little bay, both dead. His long, fur-lined coat had blown aside, and at his hand I noticed a minature of a lady and his watch; beyond him, our Brigade-Major, Reignolds of the Greys. They had both been pierced by the Lancers a few moments before we came up. Near them was lying a lieutenant of ours, Carruthers of Annandale. My heart was filled with sorrow at this, but I dared not remain for a moment. It was just then I caught sight of a squadron of British Dragoons making straight for us. The Frenchmen at that instant seemed to give way, and in a minute more we were safe! The Dragoons gave us a cheer and rode on after the Lancers. They were the men of our 16th Light Dragoons, of Vandeleur's Brigade, who not only saved us but threw back the Lancers into the hollow.

How I reached our lines I can hardly say, for the next thing I remember is that I was lying with the sole remnants of our brigade in a position far away to the right and rear of our first post, I was told that a third horse that I caught was so wounded that she fell dead as I was mounting her …

There were scarcely half a hundred of the Greys left out of the three hundred who rode off half an hour before. How I escaped is a miracle, for I was through the thick of it all, and received only two slight wounds, one from a bayonet and the other from a lance, and the white plume of my bearskin was shot away. I did not think much of the wounds at the time, and did not report myself.[11]

Dickson said that he scarcely knew how he got back to his lines. This account by Clark-Kennedy, a Scots Greys officer, possibly gives one reason:

> Our infantry which we had passed at the hedge [as the cavalry withdrew], now proved of essential service to us. They had formed small bodies or squares following in the rear of the charge, and not only checked the pursuit [by the French cavalry] but without their support and assistance I am satisfied we should not have got back so well as we did, and certainly could not have secured one-half of the prisoners taken in the charge. Many who had surrendered effected their escape, yet above 2,000 were secured and sent to the rear.[12]

Yet another letter was published in the *Caledonian Mercury*, this time on 3 July 1815. Posted from Brussels on 21 June 1815, it is listed as being a 'copy of a Letter from an Officer of Rank, in the late General Ponsonby's brigade of cavalry, to his Father residing in Scotland':

> MY DEAR FATHER – You will perceive, by this miserable scrawl, that I am wounded in the right hand. The affairs of the 16th and 17th were very sharp, but the battle of the 18th was most obstinately contested, and the most sanguinary ever fought.
>
> Hostilities commenced on the 16th, by an attack on the Prussian advanced posts. Our army was put immediately in motion, and after two affairs we retired to our position, 14 or 15 miles from hence, and covering the great road to this place. Our right rested on a hill, our centre on another more advanced, forming part of the circumference of a circle; the left I did not see.
>
> The attack commenced on the right, but was soon transferred with great fury to the centre. The enemy attacked in three solid columns, of immense depth, supported by cavalry and artillery. Our infantry received them in line. Behind the infantry was General Ponsonby's brigade of cavalry, consisting of the 1st dragoons, the Greys, and Inniskillings. When the infantry had given their fire, we charged through intervals, which the infantry made for us, in open column of half squadrons, and completely upset the enemy's massy columns, not leaving a man. General Ponsonby and Colonel Hamilton of the Greys being killed, the command of the brigade devolved upon me. Nothing could be finer than their conduct, or more successful.
>
> Our strength before the action was 1050, after it about 100, but

many had been sent to escort prisoners. In killed wounded, &c. we lost about two-thirds.

The enemy reiterated his attacks on the centre with fresh troops, but without success. He then made a most desperate attack on the right, where my small brigade of 100 men was called to charge about 400 cavalry, supported by artillery and squares of infantry. I was told that everything depended on our exertions. It was in leading my miserable remains that I received my wound, which, if it does not fester, will not keep me from duty more than eight or ten days. The charge was not successful, indeed almost every man and horse was knocked down. The day was long doubtful, but the fortunate arrival of the Prussians decided it.

The following is an extract from a letter penned after the fighting at Waterloo by an officer in the Light Dragoons:

That previous to the Horse Guards charge, on the 18th, his regiment was ordered to attack a body of Lancers and Cuirassiers, on whom they could make no impression: that numbers of their men having fallen, they were forced to retreat, when the French were ordered to charge in their turn, and from the superior weight of the horses and men, and their species of armour and weapons, he had the mortification to see them cut down numbers of his regiment: that being in the rear, he soon received himself so desperate a shock from one of the lancers as to plunge himself and horse into a deep ditch, with such violence that the horse never got out alive, while he being thrown, fortunately escaped with life, though immersed in, and covered with mud and water: that in his fall, the lancer attempted to run him through, but in the collision luckily missed his aim, and only tore away part of the flesh of the arm: that finding himself in the midst of the enemy, he had offered an officer to surrender, but who declined taking charge of him then, and ordered him to an adjacent field where were several others under similar circumstances: that he had the mortification to witness from thence the over-throw of numbers of the men during their retreat, but at last to his great satisfaction saw the heavy brigade advance to the charge, who in their turn overthrew everything in their way, literally rolling both men and horses of the French over to a considerable distance, by the tremendous force of their charge, and cutting down all before them.

Seeing the face of affairs to be changed, he contemplated upon an escape; and having communicated his idea to a brother officer near him, they together made for another part of the field, and had hardly gained the summit of a steep bank, when looking back, they observed a small French detachment enter the field, and cut down in cold blood all the prisoners there, waiting for the orders of their captors, to the number of 30 or 40, while only himself and companion escaped.[13]

Private Smithies of the 1st Royal Dragoons also recalled the bitter clash with the cuirassiers. The opposing cavalrymen were well matched:

> On we rushed at each other, and when we met the shock was terrific. We wedged ourselves between them as much as possible, to prevent them from cutting, and the noise of the horses, the clashing of swords against armour, can be imagined only by those who have heard it. There were some riders who caught hold of each other's bodies – wrestling fashion – and fighting for life, but the superior physical strength of our regiment soon showed itself.[14]

Napoleon's great attack had failed and there was a lull in the general action whilst d'Erlon re-organised his divisions and Napoleon re-considered his tactics. The Union Brigade, though, had suffered such heavy losses at the hands of the French cavalry it was unable to play any further effective part in the battle. This was the result of indiscipline. Uxbridge had tried to call his men back before they went too far, but in the excitement of the moment, they lost all control. He wrote:

> After the overthrow of the cuirassiers. I had in vain attempted to stop my people by sounding the Rally, but neither voice nor trumpet availed; so I went back to seek the support of the 2nd line, which unhappily had not followed the movements of the heavy cavalry. Had I, when I sounded the Rally, found only four well-formed squadrons coming steadily along at an easy trot, I feel certain the loss the first line suffered when they were finally forced back would have been avoided, and most of these guns might have been secured, for it was obvious the effect of that charge had been prodigious, and for the rest of the day, although the cuirassiers frequently break into our lines, they always did it *mollement* and as if they expected something more behind the curtain.[15]

11

The French Cavalry Charges

After the failure of I Corps, the French artillery resumed its barrage whilst Napoleon decided upon his next move, and for this he turned to his cavalry. The French cavalry was the most effective, and the most feared, in Europe. Used *en masse*, it was capable of changing the course of any battle, and had done so many times in the past. Now might be the moment to throw the cavalry at the Anglo-Allied line.

Wellington's men had suffered repeated bombardment and had been weakened by the assault of d'Erlon's I Corps. Surely they could not hold out much longer under such pressure?

Napoleon ordered Ney to lead the attack. At his disposal were Milhaud's cuirassier corps and the Light Cavalry Division of the Imperial Guard led by Lefèbvre-Desnouettes. In total Ney had a little over 5,000 men. Formidable though this force was, as it moved off with the heavy cavalry in front, waiting on Mont St Jean were 18,000 infantry and fifty-six guns.

Napoleon ordered his Grand Battery to re-double its efforts in advance of the cavalry attack. 'Never had the most veteran soldiers heard such a cannonade,' observed General Count von Alten in command of the 3rd Division.

The French guns, though, subsided as the massed French cavalry moved off. Captain Mercer of the Royal Horse Artillery was stationed to the rear when the attacks began,

> Suddenly a dark mass of cavalry appeared for an instant on the main ridge, then came sweeping down the slope in swarms, reminding me of an enormous surf bursting over the prostrate hull of a stranded vessel, and then running, hissing and foaming up the beach. The hollow space became in a twinkling covered with horsemen, crossing, turning, and riding about in all directions.[1]

164

An Officer of the 5th Division continued the letter to his friend in Cumberland, which we have mentioned before, from the camp at Clichy:

> Now Buonaparte again changed his plan of attack. He sent a great force both on the right and left; but his chief aim was the centre, through which lay the road to Brussels, and to gain this he appeared determined. What we had hitherto seen, was mere 'boys play' in comparison with the 'tug of war' which took place from this time, (3 o'clock) until the day was decided.
>
> All our army was formed in solid squares – the French cuirassiers advanced to the mouth of our cannon – rushed on our bayonets: sometimes walked their horses on all sides of a square to look for an opening, through which they might penetrate, or dashed madly on, thinking to carry everything by desperation. But not a British soldier moved; all personal feeling was forgotten in the enthusiasm of such a moment. Each person seemed to think the day depended on his individual exertions, and both sides vied with each other in acts of gallantry.[2]

Sergeant Morris (who is described as 'a cockney lad of 17 when he enlisted in the 2nd Battalion of the 73rd Regiment in 1813') served with the 71st Regiment:

> A considerable number of the French cuirassiers made their appearance on the rising ground just in our front, took the artillery we had placed there, and came at a gallop down upon us. Their appearance, as an enemy, was certainly enough to inspire a feeling of dread, none of them less than six feet; defended by steel helmets and breastplates, made pigeon-breasted to throw off the balls. Their appearance was of such a formidable nature, that I thought we could not have the slightest chance with them. They came up rapidly until within ten or twelve paces of the square, when our ranks poured into them a well-directed fire, which put them into confusion, and they retired; the two front ranks then discharged their muskets into them.[3]

Ensign Edmund Wheatley was with the 5th Line Battalion, King's German Legion, which was part of the 2nd KGL Brigade of Alten's 3rd Division situated immediately to the west of the Brussels road in the very centre of the Anglo-Netherlands' line:

A black consolidated body was soon seen approaching and we distinguished by sudden flashes of light from the sun's rays, the iron-cased cavalry of the enemy. Shouts of 'Stand firm!' 'Stand firm!' were heard from the little squares around and very quickly these gigantic fellows were upon us.

No words can convey the sensation we felt on seeing these heavy-armed bodies advancing at full gallop against us, flourishing their sabres in the air, striking their armour with the handles, the sun gleaming on the steel. The long horse hair, dishevelled by the wind, bore an appearance confounding the senses to an astonishing disorder. But we dashed them back as coolly as the sturdy rock repels the ocean's foam. The sharp-toothed bayonet bit many an adventurous fool, and on all sides we presented our bristly points like the peevish porcupines assailed by clamorous dogs.[4]

Lieutenant General Rowland Lord Hill, the commander of the British II Corps, also recorded the remarkable French charges:

Four times were our guns in possession of their (French) cavalry, and as often did the bayonets of our infantry rescue them. For upwards of an hour our little squares were surrounded by the elite of the French cavalry; they gallantly stood within forty paces of us, unable to leap over the bristling bayonets, unwilling to retire, and determined never to surrender. Hundreds of them were dropping in all directions from our murderous fire, yet as fast as they dropped others came up to supply their places.

Finding at last it was in vain to attempt to break our determined ranks, they swept round our rear and, rushing into the Nivelles road, attempted to cut their way back to their own lines; but the whole road was lined with our infantry on both sides, and the advanced part of it was an almost impassable barricade of felled trees. Here fell the remainder of these gallant Cuirassiers of whom not one was taken prisoner without first of all being wounded.[5]

Stirring accounts of this series of events eventually began to appear in the British press, a graphic example of which was published in the *Chester Courant* on Tuesday, 4 June 1816:

No part of the field was more fertile in impressive associations, [than] the ground of the 30th, and, I believe, the 73d regiments, brigaded under our gallant countryman, severely wounded in the battle, Sir Colin Halkett. I had already heard much of the firmness of these brave troops, and was to hear still more – To no square did the artillery, and

166

particularly the cuirassiers, pay more frequent and tremendous visits; and never was it shaken for a moment; the almost intimacy of the soldiers with these death-bringing visitants increased so much as the day advanced, that they began to recognise their faces. Their boldness much provoked our men; they galloped up to the bayonet points where of course their horses made a full stop, to the great danger of pitching the riders into the square. They then rode round and round the fearless bulwark of bayonets; and in all the confidence of panoply, often coolly WALKED their horses, to have more time to search for some chasm in the ranks, where they might ride in. The balls absolutely rang upon the mail; and nothing incommoded the rider except bringing down his horse, which at last became the general order. In that event he surrendered himself, and was received into the square, till he could be sent prisoner to the rear; a generosity ill-merited, when it is considered that the French spared but very few lives, which it was in their power to take. Many officers were murdered, after giving up their swords; and when prisoners were collected, cavalry were sent to cut them down, when circumstances at the moment prevented their removal.

The cuirassiers were repeatedly driven off by the 30th, and their comrade regiment, reduced themselves by painful degrees, more and more every attack. – Line was always again formed with unwearied alacrity; no complaint escaped the patient soldier's lips, if we except an occasional cry to be led on. The storm was seen again gathering and rolling on. – The serious command, 're-form square, prepare to receive cavalry,' was promptly and accurately obeyed. The whole were prostrate on their breasts, to let the iron shower of the artillery fly over, and erect in an instant, when the cannon ceased and the cavalry charged. The country do not know one-tenth of the merit of 'the MEN of Waterloo'.

Unable to break in upon the square by open force, a commanding officer of cuirassiers tried a RUSE DE GUERRE; he lowered his sword to General Halkett: several of the officers called out, 'Sir, they surrender.' – 'Be firm and fire,' was the promptly obeyed answer. The General justly suspected an offer of surrender to a body of infantry fixed to the spot in a defensive position, by a body of cavalry, who had the option of galloping off, with all the plain open behind them. – The volley sent the colonel and his cuirassiers, as usual, about, with a laugh of derision from the men he had meant to cut to pieces; and many a ring from their balls, upon the back pieces of the mails.

Ensign Macready was one of those men inside the square of the 30th Regiment. The 30th had lost heavily at Quatre Bras and had to combine with the 73rd Regiment to form this square:

As soon as they quickened their trot into a gallop the Cuirassiers bent their heads so that the peak of their helmets looked like visors and they seemed cased in armour from the plume to the saddle. Not a shot was fired till they were within thirty yards when the word was given ... The effect was magical. Thro' the smoke we could see helmets falling – cavaliers starting from their seats with convulsive springs as they received our balls, horses plunging and rearing in the agonies of fright and pain, and crowds of the soldiery dismounted; part of the squadrons in retreat, but the more daring remainder backing their horses to force them on our bayonets. Our fire soon disposed of these gentlemen.

The main body reformed in our front were reinforced and rapidly and gallantly repeated their attacks. In fact from this time (about four o'clock) till near six we had a constant repetition of these brave but unavailing charges ... The best cavalry is contemptible to a steady and well supplied Infantry regiment – even our men saw this and began to pity the useless perseverance of their assailants and as they advanced would growl 'here come those damned fools again'.[6]

On Friday, 11 August 1815, the *Chester Chronicle* carried this account of the memorable French attacks, it being described as an 'extract of a letter from a native of this city, in the 23d Royal Welsh Fuzileers, at Paris, to his Father, dated Camp, July 24, 1815':

I suppose you have heard of the dreadful battle on the 18th July – it was the most severe battle ever fought! We have lost one Colonel, 1 Major, 8 Captains, 2 Lieutenants, besides a great many men. I believe our Regiment has got the greatest praise of the whole army from the Duke of Wellington, and all the General Officers. Gen. Cole made application to the Duke to get our Regiment attached to his division, and has succeeded. The French fought better than ever on that tremendous day: THEY CHARGED US TEN DIFFERENT TIMES, but, thank God! we made them remember us, for we flanked them in all directions. Their Cavalry was so numerous, that we were *obliged to fight in square the whole day*, altho' fainting for want of a drop of water, but not a drop could be got for fifty guineas!

The cuirassiers in particular attracted much attention in the British press, the following again being published in the *Chester Chronicle*, though this time on Friday, 7 July 1815:

The Cuirassiers of the French Imperial Guards are all arrayed in armour, the front cuirass is in the form of a pigeon's breast, so as to effectually turn off a musket shot, though fired ever so near, owing to its being kept so bright; the back cuirass is made to fit the back; they weigh from 9 to 11lbs. each, according to the size of the man, and are stuffed inside with a pad; they fit on by a kind of fish-scaled clasp, and are put off and on in an instant; they have helmets the same as our Horse Guards, straight long swords, and pistols, but no carbines; and if there is a good horse to be found they are sure to have it. They are all chosen men, must be five feet seven French (above six feet English) have served in three campaigns, been twelve years in the service, and of good character.

Across the United Kingdom, newspapers editors sought or syndicated further accounts. The *Hampshire Telegraph* of Monday, 14 August 1815, for example, contained the following:

The 7th Light Dragoons were first opposed to the Cuirassiers. They broke their swords on the French Cuirassiers and the Frenchmen being large heavy men in armour, on large horses, the Light Dragoons could make no impression – they were obliged to retire. The Heavy Dragoons were then brought up, with instructions to strike only at the limbs. This they did with so much dexterity, the French were astonished, subdued, panic struck; they wavered, and the battle was won.

For its part the *Caledonian Mercury* of Thursday, 27 July 1815, carried this piece under the banner, 'The Battle of Waterloo':

All accounts agree in the great advantage that the French cuirassiers derived from their armour. Their swords were three inches longer than any used by the Allies, and in close action the cuts of our sabres did no execution, except they fortunately came across the neck of the enemy. The latter also, feeling themselves secure in their armour, advanced deliberately and steadily, until they came within about twenty yards of our ranks, as a musket ball could not penetrate their cuirasses at a greater distance. The cuirass, however, was attended with one disadvantage; the wearer, in close action, cannot use his arm with perfect facility in all directions; he chiefly thrusts, but cannot cut with ease.

Wellington had placed much of his artillery on the forward slope of the Mont St Jean ridge. This gave them an uncluttered field of fire up which the French infantry and cavalry had to advance. This forward position, though, placed the gunners in an exposed situation. To solve this, Wellington instructed the artillerymen to continue to fire at the approaching enemy until the last possible moment and then run into the nearest infantry square for protection, leaving their guns where they stood. As the French retreated the gunners could then run back out of the squares and fire at the backs of the enemy.

Lieutenant Colonel William Tomkinson of the 16th Light Dragoons described how well the artillery adapted to this method:

> These attacks were made at intervals for nearly two hours; they were the most singularly daring attempts ever heard of, and in many instances appeared like an inclination to sacrifice themselves sooner than survive the loss of the day. Parties of cuirassiers, from two to three squadrons and frequently less, occasionally supported by a few infantry, and in many instances without infantry, rode up to the hill occupied by our troops.
>
> An officer of cuirassiers rode close up to one of our squares with a detachment of men. He saw he had no chance of success, and by himself alone rode full gallop against the square, was shot and killed. Our men and officers regretted his fate.
>
> The artillerymen at our guns remained at them to the last moment, firing grape on the enemy, by which the cuirassiers suffered. Our infantry got into squares of regiments, and the French Dragoons came riding amongst them, waving their swords and in many instances approaching close to them.
>
> They never attempted in any body to attack the infantry, and after remaining on the position for ten minutes or possibly longer, retired again. The instant they turned their backs, the artillery in the squares of infantry ran to their guns and commenced their fire against them … It was an action in which the artillery suffered greatly and particularly distinguished themselves. Repeatedly they had to leave their guns and take refuge in the squares of infantry, and the instant the French cavalry turned to the rear, they ran to their guns, firing at them in their retreat. They were, too, exposed to the whole fire of the enemy's guns without being suffered to return their fire. They were directed to fire only at the enemy's columns …
>
> I conceive that if any part deserved to be especially named, it was that part of the artillery placed above La Haye Sainte. Captain Ramsay, of the artillery, was killed near this point, his head was carried away by a round shot … During the time the enemy were employed in this attack our guns were in their hands, but without any means on their part of either injuring them or carrying them away. It [the repeated cavalry onslaught] was the most singular, hardy conduct ever heard of, and had such gallantry been properly directed, it must have been

turned to some account. Had it happened immediately after an attack, or been once adopted in the zeal of the moment by any officer foiled in his object, there might be some excuse; but for such a thing to be continued for any length of time, and under officers who had been serving all their lives, is a proceeding quite unaccountable. They made two or three separate attempts from the one just mentioned, all of which ended in the same manner.[7]

Captain Norman Ramsay's untimely death was also reported by the *Liverpool Mercury* of Friday, 10 May 1816:

A brigade of horse-artillery, commanded by the lamented Major Norman Ramsey [*sic*], opened its fire upon the French columns of Cavalry. They retreated repeatedly, but it was only to advance with new fury, and to renew attempts which it seemed impossible for human strength and courage ultimately to withstand. As frequently as the cavalry retreated, our artillery men, rushing out of the squares in which they had found shelter, began again to work their pieces, and made a destructive fire on the retiring squadrons. Two officers of artillery were particularly noticed, who, being in a square which was repeatedly charged, rushed out of it the instant the cavalry retreated, loaded one of the deserted guns which stood near, and fired it upon the horsemen. A French officer observed that this manoeuvre was repeated more than once, and cost his troop many lives.

At the next retreat of his squadron, he stationed himself by the gun, waving his sword, as if defying the British officers again to approach it. He was instantly shot by a grenadier, but prevented, by his self-devotion, a considerable loss to his countrymen. Other French officers and men evinced the same desperate and determined zeal in the cause which they had so rashly and unhappily espoused. One officer of rank, after leading his men as far as they would follow him towards one of the squares of infantry, found himself deserted by them, when the British fire opened, and instantly rode upon the bayonets, throwing open his arms as if to welcome the bullet which should bring him down. He was immediately shot, for the moment admitted of no alternative.

A soldier of the 5th Brigade also wrote of this incident, his account appearing in *Colburn's United Service Magazine* in 1852:

[The cuirassiers] charging with a degree of impetuosity amounting almost to frenzy, they obliged the gunners and men attached to the artillery on our right, to retire for temporary protection to the squares, whilst they furiously passed through the intermediate spaces. Four times the guns were taken and retaken ... In many instances, individuals left their ranks and rode round the squares, with the intention of drawing fire on themselves to enable the cavalry to charge with a greater probability of success.[8]

Lieutenant Colonel Sir Augustus Frazer commanded the Royal Horse Artillery (he was a career soldier who had been admitted as a Gentleman Cadet into the Royal Military Academy, Woolwich, a month before his fourteenth birthday):

The greater part of the action may be called an action of artillery. We had 108 British and 16 Belgic guns in play, the enemy more than 200. The enemy's cavalry behaved nobly, herding us to the very mouth; all our guns were repeatedly abandoned but our gallant infantry formed into squares, never budged, & after each repulse we returned to our guns again ... Our own arm, I speak of the horse artillery, has suffered, but has suffered with honour. I had it in my power to employ it in masses, & it has repaid the confidence placed in its exertions. Bull's Howitzer Troop was brought up against a Wood [Hougoumont] and three times taken & retaken by the enemy.[9]

Lieutenant F. Wells served with Major Lloyd's battery, to the right of which was Major Sandham's battery and on its left was Major Cleeves's King's German Legion battery. These batteries were contiguous with each other along the very crest of Mont St Jean, to the west of the Brussels road:

The Cuirassiers and Cavalry might have charged through the Battery as often as six or seven times, driving us into the Squares, under our Guns, waggons, some defending themselves. In general, a Squadron or two came up the slope on our immediate front, and on their moving off at the appearance of our Cavalry charging, we took advantage [by running out of the squares] to send destruction after them, and when advancing on our fire I have seen four or five men and horses piled upon each other like cards, the men not having even been displaced from the saddle, the effect of canister.[10]

Most of the gunners were able to find shelter in the infantry squares, as arranged, though this did not always happen. Gunner John Edwards was in Ross' troop, Royal Horse Artillery, and he subsequently described to his brother Oliver what happened during one of the charges by the cuirassiers:

> Dressed in steel armour back and breast plates, they weigh about 32 pounds, charged up the main road till they came within 600 yards they extended right and left of the road, we fired case shot at them and swept them off like a swathe of grass before a scythe. The ground was covered with men and horses in 5 minutes, we limbered up but before we could move one yard the French was all around us. Me and four more of our gunners left the gun and formed up with the 1st German Horse [1st Light Dragoons, King's German Legion] and charged the French cavalry, we swept through them four times, with a good horse received 4 cuts as I could not guard my horse and my self at one time.[11]

In another instance, the 42nd Foot (Black Watch) were unable to form square in time before the French cavalry was upon them:

> All day long we had masses of infantry hurled against us, varied by attacks from cavalry, and, as our division [Picton's] held the key of the position, the whole force of the enemy was directed against it. Again and again after receiving the French with a volley, and repelling them with the bayonet, we had scarcely time to form a square before dragoons were upon us.
>
> On one such occasion, being unable to get into a square in time, and seeing a squadron of cavalry bearing down where I and a few men were, ordered them to fling themselves on the ground and allow the horses to pass over. This we did, but it required some nerve to be perfectly still and thus be ridden over. I escaped unhurt, but as the troopers passed back, I got a sword thrust as a sort of query whether I was as dead as I looked! However, I lay motionless, and the bullets whizzing about did not allow my inquisitive friend to prolong his enquiries.[12]

Another account, originally written at the village of Gommignies on 22 June was published in the *Lancaster Gazette* of Saturday, 28 October 1815:

> At this period the battle assumed a character beyond description interesting, and anxiously awful. Bonaparte was about to use against us an arm which he had never yet wielded but with success. Confidently relying upon the issue of this attack, he charged our

artillery and infantry, hoping to capture the one, and break the other, and by instantly establishing his own infantry on the heights to carry the Brussels road, and throw our line into confusion. These cavalry, selected for their tried gallantry and skill (not their height or mustachios) who were the terror of Northern Europe, and had never yet been foiled, were first brought up by the 3d battalion of the 1st regiment. Never was British valour and discipline so pre-eminent as on this occasion, the steady appearance of this battalion caused the famous cuirassiers to pull up, and a few of them, with a courage worthy of a better cause, rode out of the ranks and fired at our people, and mounted officers, with their pistols, hoping to make the face of the square throw its fire upon them, and thus become an easy prey; but our men, with a steadiness no language can do justice to, defied their efforts and did not pull a single trigger. –

The French then made a sudden rush, but were received in such a manner, and with a volley so well directed, as at once to turn them; they then made an attempt on the 2d battalion, and the Brunswickers, with similar success, and astonished at their own failure, the cool intrepidity of their opponents, and the British cheers, they faced about. This same game was played in succession by the Imperial Horse Guards, and Polish Lancers, none of whom could at all succeed in breaking our squares, or making the least impression upon them whatever. – During their attacks, our cavalry rushed out from between the squares, and carried havoc through the enemy's ranks, which were nearly all destroyed. I cannot here resist relating an anecdote of Major Lloyd, of the artillery, who, with another officer, (whose name I could not learn) was obliged to take refuge in our square at the time these charges were made, being unable to continue longer at their posts. There was a gun between our battalion and the Brunswickers, which had been drawn back; this, Major L. with his friend, discharged five or six times at the French cavalry, alternately loading it and retiring to the square, as circumstances required. We could see the French knocked off their horses as fast as they came up, and one cannot refuse to call them men of singular gallantry; one of them, indeed, an officer of the Imperial Guards, seeing a gun about to be discharged at his companions, rode at it, and never suffered its fire to be repeated while he lived. He was at length killed by a Brunswick rifleman, and certainly saved a large part of his regiment by this act of self devotion.

Thus discomfited, Buonaparte renewed his cannonade, which was destructive to a degree, preparatory to an attack of his whole infantry. I constantly saw the noble Duke of Wellington riding backwards and forwards, like the Genius of the Storm, who, borne upon its wings, directed its thunders where to burst. He was everywhere to be found, encouraging, directing, animating. He was in a blue coat, with a plain cocked hat; his telescope in his hand, there was nothing that escaped him, nothing he did not take advantage of, and his lynx's eyes seemed to penetrate the smoke, and forestall the movements of the foe. How he escaped, that merciful Power alone can tell, who vouchsafed to the allied arms the issue of this pre eminent contest, for such it is, whether considered as an action by itself, or with regard to the results which it has brought about.

One spot that Wellington was positioned at in the battle was in a square of the 1st Foot Guards during one of the cavalry charges, as Ensign Rees Howell Gronow of the 1st Guards recalled:

About four p.m. the enemy's artillery in front of us ceased firing all of a sudden, and we saw large masses of cavalry advance: not a man present who survived could have forgotten in after life the awful grandeur of that charge. You perceived at a distance what appeared to be an overwhelming, long moving line, which, ever advancing, glittered like a stormy wave of the sea when it catches the sunlight. On came the mounted host until they got near enough, whilst the very earth seemed to vibrate beneath their thundering tramp. One might suppose that nothing could have resisted the shock of this terrible moving mass.

They were the famous cuirassiers, almost all old soldiers, who had distinguished themselves on most of the battlefields of Europe. In an almost incredibly short period they were within twenty yards of us, shouting 'Vive l'Empereur!' The word of command, 'Prepare to receive cavalry,' had been given, every man in the front ranks knelt, and a wall bristling with steel, held together by steady hands, presented itself to the infuriated cuirassiers. I should observe that just before this charge the duke entered by one of the angles of the square, accompanied only by one aide-de-camp; all the rest of his staff being either killed or wounded.

Our commander-in-chief, as far as I could judge, appeared perfectly composed; but looked very thoughtful and pale. He was dressed in a grey great-coat with a cape, white cravat, leather pantaloons, Hessian boots, and a large cocked hat a la Russe. The charge of the French cavalry was gallantly executed; but our well-directed fire brought men and horses down, and ere long the utmost confusion arose in their ranks. The officers were exceedingly brave, and by their gestures and fearless bearing did all in their power to encourage their men to form again and renew the attack. The Duke sat unmoved, mounted on his favourite charger. I recollect his asking Colonel Stanhope what o'clock it was, upon which Stanhope took out his watch, and said it was twenty minutes past four. The Duke replied, 'The battle is mine; and if the Prussians arrive soon, there will be an end of the war.'...

Again and again various cavalry regiments, heavy dragoons, lancers, hussars, carabineers of the Guard, endeavoured to break our walls of steel. The enemy's cavalry had to advance over ground which was so heavy that they could not reach us except at a trot; they therefore came upon us in a much more compact mass than they probably would have done if the ground had been more favourable. When they got within ten or fifteen yards they discharged their carbines, to the cry of '*Vive I'Empereur!*' but their fire produced little effect, as is generally the case with the fire of cavalry. Our men had orders not to fire unless they could do so on a near mass; the object being to economize our ammunition, and not to waste it on scattered soldiers. The result was, that when the cavalry had discharged their carbines and were still far off, we occasionally stood face to face, looking at each other inactively, not knowing what the next move might be. The lancers were particularly troublesome, and approached us with the utmost daring.

On one occasion I remember, the enemy's artillery having made a gap in the square, the lancers were evidently waiting to avail themselves of it, to rush among us, when Colonel Staples at once observing their intention, with the utmost promptness filled up the gap, and thus again completed our impregnable steel wall; but in this act he fell mortally wounded. The cavalry seeing this, made no attempt to carry out their original intentions, and observing that we had entirely regained our square, confined themselves to hovering round us. I must not forget to mention that the lancers in particular never failed to despatch our wounded whenever they had an opportunity of doing so.

When we received cavalry, the order was to fire low; so that on the first discharge of musketry the ground was strewed with the fallen horses and their riders, which impeded the advance of those behind them and broke the shock of the charge. It was pitiable to witness the agony of the poor horses, who really seemed conscious of the dangers that surrounded them: we often saw a poor wounded animal raise its head, as if looking for its rider to afford him aid. There is nothing perhaps amongst the episodes of a great battle more striking than the

Napoleon's landing at Golfe Juan. (Anne S.K. Brown Military Collection, Brown University Library)

Napoleon at the distribution of the Eagles at the Champ de Mars.
(Anne S.K. Brown Military Collection, Brown University Library)

The 28th Regiment at Quatre Bras by Elizabeth Thompson. The artist choose to portray the moment at 17.00 hours on 16 June 1815, "when the gallant 28th braced itself for one massive, final charge of terrifying Polish Lancers and cuirassier veterans led by Marshal Ney".

The Battle of Ligny. (Anne S.K. Brown Military Collection, Brown University Library)

The fatal wounding of the Duke of Brunswick at Quatre Bras.
(Anne S.K. Brown Military Collection, Brown University Library)

The Prince of Orange leading the Netherlands troops at Quatre Bras.
(Anne S.K. Brown Military Collection, Brown University Library)

The interior of Hougoumont during the battle. On the right is the chapel and on the far right is the entrance to the orchard and wood.
(Anne S.K. Brown Military Collection, Brown University Library)

The interior of Hougoumont after the battle.
(Anne S.K. Brown Military Collection, Brown University Library)

The Duke of Wellington.
(Anne S.K. Brown Military
Collection, Brown University
Library)

The guns of Napoleon's
Grand Battery open fire
on the Anglo-Allied line.
(Anne S.K. Brown Military
Collection, Brown University
Library)

The 2nd Light Battalion, King's German Legion was posted in La Haye Sainte from the outset of the battle.
(Anne S.K. Brown Military Collection, Brown University Library)

Men of the Household Cavalry Regiments, the 1st and 2nd Life Guards and the Royal Horse Guards.
(Anne S.K. Brown Military Collection, Brown University Library)

French cavalry charging a British square. The abandoned British artillery pieces can be seen in front of the square.
(Anne S.K. Brown Military Collection, Brown University Library)

The Earl of Uxbridge commanded the Anglo-Allied cavalry, and was nominally Wellington's second-in-command.
(Anne S.K. Brown Military Collection, Brown University Library)

The Life Guards crashing into the French I Corps.
(Anne S.K. Brown Military Collection, Brown University Library)

The 2nd (Royal North British) Dragoons were all mounted on white horses and therefore acquired the name the Scots Greys.
(Anne S.K. Brown Military Collection, Brown University Library)

The 2nd Life Guards charging French Cuirassiers.
(Anne S.K. Brown Military Collection, Brown University Library)

The taking of the Eagle of the French 45th Line.
(Anne S.K. Brown Military Collection, Brown University Library)

The 6th (Inniskilling) Dragoons
formed part of Major General Sir
William Ponsonby's Union Brigade.
(Anne S.K. Brown Military Collection, Brown
University Library)

Men of the Coldstream Guards
(Battalion Company and Grenadier
Company).
(Anne S.K. Brown Military Collection, Brown
University Library)

1st (Royal) Dragoon Guards were
brigaded with the Life Guards and
the Royal Horse Guards to form the
Household Brigade.
(Anne S.K. Brown Military Collection, Brown
University Library)

Corporal John Shaw of the 2nd
Lifeguards.
(Anne S.K. Brown Military Collection, Brown
University Library)

A British infantry square being attacked by cuirassiers and lancers.

(Anne S.K. Brown Military Collection, Brown University Library)

Sergeant Burg, Grenadière de la Garde, 1815.

(Anne S.K. Brown Military Collection, Brown University Library)

Last stand of the Old Guard.
(Anne S.K. Brown Military Collection,
Brown University Library)

Field Marshal Blücher
portrayed at La Belle Alliance
as the British and Prussian
troops join up at the moment
of victory on the evening of 18
June 1815.
(Anne S.K. Brown Military Collection,
Brown University Library)

Napoleon leaves the battlefield to escape in his carriage.

The capture of Napoleon's carriage at Genappe by Prussian cavalry.

The field of waterloo as it appeared the morning after the battle.
(Anne S.K. Brown Military Collection, Brown University Library)

Napoleon's final abdication.
(Anne S.K. Brown Military Collection, Brown University Library)

Marshal Ney's execution on 6 December 1815.
(Anne S.K. Brown Military Collection, Brown University Library)

Napoleon on board HMS *Bellerophon* on his final voyage to exile on St Helena.
(Anne S.K. Brown Military Collection, Brown University Library)

debris of a cavalry charge, where men and horses are seen scattered and wounded on the ground in every variety of painful attitude. Many a time the heart sickened at the moaning tones of agony which came from man and scarcely less intelligent horse, as they lay in fearful agony upon the field of battle.[13]

Wellington was undoubtedly in the thick of the action throughout the fighting on that fateful summer's day in 1815:

The great danger to which the Duke of Wellington was exposed in the late battle, is shewn by two circumstances that have reached us from good authority. His aide-de-camp, Colonel Sir A. Gordon, respectfully remonstrated with him on his remaining so far within the range of a very destructive fire. The Duke said, he would take one more view of that part of the field, and go. Having employed his telescope for two or three minutes, his Grace was turning his horse, when Colonel Gordon, who was accompanying him, was killed by his side. Another aide-de-camp, Colonel Canning, had put his hand upon the saddle of the Duke's horse, while receiving orders. As he withdrew it, his hand was shattered by a ball.[14]

Ironically, the cavalry charges were to some degree welcomed by the allied infantry as it meant that the French guns had to cease firing, as Ensign William Leeke of the 52nd explained. Until a little after 15.00 hours the 52nd had been held in reserve in front of Merbe Braine but was moved forward after the first of the cavalry charges had been repulsed:

Immediately, on descending the slope of the position towards the enemy, the regiment, almost concealed by the tall rye, which was then for the first time trampled down, formed two squares. I remember we were not far from the north-eastern point of the Hougoumont inclosure, and on the narrow white road which, passing within 100 yards of that point, crosses the interval between the British and French positions in the direction of La Belle Alliance … The old soldiers, who had served during the whole of the Peninsula war, stated that they were never exposed to such a cannonade as that which the 52nd squares had to undergo on this occasion for two hours and a half, from the French artillery planted about half a mile in their front. Our own artillery, on, or just under the crest of our position, were also firing over our heads the whole time, either at the enemy's troops or at their guns. Some shrapnel-shells burst short, and wounded some of the 52nd men; but the firing of these shells was discontinued, on our notice of what they were doing to the artillery above us.

In the right square of the 52nd, and I suppose it was the same in all the squares of our brigade [Adam's], there was one incessant roar of round-shot and shells passing over or close to us on either flank; occasionally they made gaps in the square. The only interval that occurred in the cannonade was when we were charged by the French cavalry, for they, of course, could not fire upon our squares for fear of injuring their own squadrons, so that the charges of cavalry were a great relief to us all I believe; at least, I know they were so to me.[15]

The 27th (Inniskilling) Regiment, was part of Major General Sir John Lambert's 10th Brigade and was initially placed in reserve behind Mont St Jean farm. Later in the afternoon it was moved up to the crossroads and suffered heavily at the hands of the French gunners, as Major Mill of the 40th Regiment testified:

A very tremendous cannonade was commenced by the French on our lines, and uninterruptedly continued. We lay down in square to escape as far as possible its destructive effects. Half the Inniskillings were mowed down in a similar position, without having power or opportunity to return a shot.

At one time the officer commanding the Twenty-Seventh, when there was temporary cessation from artillery, rode up to our major, and announced the fact of having barely an officer left to command each company. Major Browne offered to lend him some of the Fortieth. This, however, was imperatively declined. 'The sergeants of the regiment,' he said, 'liked to command the companies, and he would be loathe to deprive them of the honour.' Whenever there was an intermission in this fire, it was to find ourselves surrounded and beset by hordes of horsemen, who were slashing and cutting at our kneeling ranks. The file firing of our standing ranks, being concentrated and constant, was very effectual against their attacks, and both horse and rider were to be constantly discerned rolling over on to the plain, and the remainder flying back in disorder to their own lines.[16]

An officer wrote to his father from Quatre Bras on 19th June:

At noon on the 18th the French made the most desperate attack with artillery, cavalry, and tirailleurs, ever witnessed. Our defence was equally terrible. The whole line was formed in squares and battalions;

not one man fell back; the whole stood firm. The French cavalry repeatedly attacked echelon of squares after echelon, and were repulsed ten or eleven times with immense loss. Our squares stood in the face of shot, shells, and everything else; which caused great destruction, without our being able to return a shot.[17]

The French cavalry had been repulsed with very heavy losses and there was simply no point in throwing the brave horsemen against the Anglo-Netherlands squares again. This did not mean that Ney was going to give up his attempt at breaking the Anglo-Allied line, far from it, but his next effort would be a combined infantry and cavalry attack. Still standing in Ney's path, however, was the farm of La Haye Sainte.

12

The Fall of La Haye Sainte

One of the reasons for the failure of d'Erlon's corps to break through the Anglo-Dutch line was the farmhouse of La Haye Sainte which stood at the foot of Mont St Jean. The massed columns had to divert around the farm complex, causing them to lose momentum. Every subsequent advance directly upon the centre of the Allied positions meant having to negotiate or deviate around this obstacle which was initially held by Major Baring, with between 380 and 400 men of the 2nd Light Battalion, King's German Legion, though later reinforced with other units. It was clear that La Haye Sainte had to be taken at all costs.

Major Konrad Ludwig Georg Baring survived the battle to leave a detailed account of the stubborn defence of this key position:

> The dwelling-house, barn, and stables were surrounded by a rectangular wall, forming a court in the interior. Towards the enemy's side was an orchard, surrounded by a hedge, and in rear was a kitchen-garden, bounded by a small wall towards the road, but on the other sides by a hedge. Two doors and three large gates led from the court to the exterior; but of these, that of the bam had been unfortunately broken and burned by the troops.
>
> The battalion consisted of six companies, which did not number four hundred men; I posted three companies in the orchard, two in the buildings, and one in the garden. Important as the possession of this farm apparently was, the means of defending it were very insufficient, and besides, I was ordered, immediately on arriving there, to send off the pioneers of the battalion to Hougoumont, so that I had not even a hatchet; for unfortunately the mule that carried the entrenching tools was lost the day before.[1]

Lieutenant G.D. Graeme, who was serving in the 2nd Light Battalion of the King's German Legion, explained the situation further:

We had no loopholes excepting three great apertures, which we made with difficulty when we were told in the morning that we were to defend the farm. We had no scaffolding, nor means of making any, having burnt the carts, etc. [for firewood]. Our loopholes, if they may be thus termed, were on a level with the road on the outside.[2]

An abatis[3] was also placed across the road a little in the front of the farm's main gate, behind which the defenders could stand and which would further hinder the French advance. Baring continued with his story:

Shortly after noon, some skirmishers commenced the attack. I made the men lie down and forbade all firing until the enemy were quite near. The first shot broke the bridle of my horse close to my hand, and the second killed major Bosewiel, who was standing near me. The enemy did not stop long skirmishing, but immediately advanced over the height, with two close columns, one of which attacked the buildings, and the other threw itself in mass into the orchard, shewing the greatest contempt for our fire. It was not possible for our small disjointed numbers fully to withstand this furious attack of such a superior force, and we retired upon the barn, in a more united position, in order to continue the defence: my horse's leg was broken, and I was obliged to take that of the adjutant.

The farm complex was soon all but surrounded by the 2,000 men of the 1st Brigade of d'Erlon's 1st Division. It seemed that at any minute the little garrison of the farm would be overcome. Seeing Baring's predicament, Count Kielmansegge, in command of the 1st Hanoverian Brigade, sent the Light Battalion Lüneburg under Colonel von Klencke down to help. The Lüneburgers moved down to La Haye Sainte in line. Now reinforced, Baring tried to recover the orchard, and the Germans charged the French at bayonet point (more accurately at sword point as the Baker rifles with which they were armed carried short swords, or hangers, in place of bayonets).

At this juncture Dubois' cuirassier brigade of the IV Cavalry Corps rode up in support of d'Erlon's infantry. The Lüneburgers were taken by surprise by the sudden appearance of the cavalry and instead of forming square they ran back up the ridge from where they had come, taking with them some of the KGL including Baring himself. Three companies of the 95th, now completely isolated, and seeing the Germans running back to the main Allied position also abandoned the sandpit where they were posted and rushed up the ridge.

Fortunately, the charge of the Household and Union brigades drove the cuirassiers away from La Haye Sainte and, as he recalled, Baring and his men were able to recover the farm:

> About half an hour's respite was now given us by the enemy, and we employed the time in preparing ourselves against a new attack; this followed in the same force as before; namely, from two sides by two close columns, which, with the greatest rapidity, nearly surrounded us, and, despising danger, fought with a degree of courage which I had never before witnessed in Frenchmen.
>
> Favoured by their advancing in masses, every bullet of ours hit, and seldom were the effects limited to one assailant; this did not, however, prevent them from throwing themselves against the walls, and endeavouring to wrest the arms from the hands of my men, through the loop-holes; many lives were sacrificed to the defence of the doors and gates; the most obstinate contest was carried on where the gate was wanting, and where the enemy seemed determined to enter. On this spot seventeen Frenchmen already lay dead, and their bodies served as a protection to those who pressed after them to the same spot.
>
> Meantime four lines of French cavalry had formed on the right front of the farm: the first cuirassiers, second lancers, third dragoons, and fourth hussars, and it was clear to me that their intention was to attack the squares of our division in position, in order by destroying them to break the whole line. This was a critical moment, for what would be our fate if they succeeded! As they marched upon the position by the farm, I brought all the fire possible to bear upon them; many men and horses were overthrown, but they were not discouraged. Without in the least troubling themselves about our fire, they advanced with the greatest intrepidity, and attacked the infantry. All this I could see, and confess freely that now and then I felt some apprehension.

Napoleon, if we are to believe the claims in his memoirs, had ordered Ney to seize La Haye Sainte when d'Erlon had mounted his first great assault. Yet it was only after the repulse of the massed cavalry that Napoleon told Ney to concentrate again on capturing the farm. This was most likely because Ney was so heavily involved with the cavalry charges that La Haye Sainte was temporarily forgotten. Nevertheless, the day was slipping away with no sign that the Anglo-Netherlands army was going to break. Defeat stared Napoleon in the face, yet there was still time for one last big attack; but before that could be mounted, the farm had to be captured. Colonel Heymes, Ney's senior aide-de-camp recalled this incident:

> It was six o'clock, the emperor gave the order to renew the attack in the centre that had drawn to a halt; but it needed fresh infantry to do this and the Marshal had none available. Half of the soldiers that had been committed to it were dead or wounded, the other half, exhausted, lacked ammunition. The Marshal sent his senior ADC to inform the emperor and to ask for new troops.
>
> The emperor replied, 'Where do you want me to get them from? Do you want me to make them? ...' this was reported *verbatim* to the Marshal who could then see that the battle was far from being won.[4]

So the task of taking the farm was handed to Colonel Charlet who commanded the 1st Brigade of the 1st Division of d'Erlon's Corps. It is believed that the attack was actually undertaken by the 13*ème Légère* supported by a detachment of the 1st Engineers. Baring recalled that,

> Our small position was soon again attacked with the same fury, and defended with the same courage as before. Captain von Wurmb was sent to my assistance with the skirmishers of the fifth line battalion, and I placed them in the court; but welcome as this reinforcement was, it could not compensate for the want of ammunition, which every moment increased, so that after half an hour more of uninterrupted fighting, I sent off an officer with the same request. This was as fruitless as the other two applications; however, two hundred Nassau troops were sent me.

Baring refers to the 5th Line Battalion, King's German Legion, but he does not tell the full story of what happened to this battalion. Lieutenant Colonel Wilhelm von Linsingen, who commanded the battalion did, however, provide some details:

> In the afternoon I received the order to advance in line with the 5th Line Battalion and to push the enemy who had surrounded la Haie Sainte back with tthe bayonet. The 5th Battalion was fortunate to achieve this, and the enemy, consisting of around a single regiment, withdrew as we advanced. But before the battalion had the chance to pass on the right of la Haie Sainte, and before I was able to issue the order to form square, the enemy cavalry consisting of between five and six squadrons of cuirassiers, who were covered by the

undulations in the hollow ground … launched an unexpected attack and the 5th Line Battalion was almost completely annihilated in this charge … I afterwards assembled the remnants of the battalion in the hollow, which consisted of only 19 serviceable men.[5]

Amongst those lost by the 5th Line Battalion was Ensign Wheatley who had been wounded and was taken prisoner:

Colonel Ompteda ordered us instantly into line to charge, with a strong injunction to 'walk' forward, until he gave the word. When within sixty yards he cried 'Charge', we ran forward huzzaring. The trumpet sounded and no-one but a soldier can describe the thrill one instantly feels in such an awful moment. At the bugle sound the French stood until we just reached them. I ran by Colonel Ompteda who cried out, 'That's right, Wheatley!'

I found myself in contact with a French officer but 'ere we could decide, he fell by an unknown hand. I then ran at a drummer, but he leaped over a ditch through a hedge in which he stuck fast. I heard a cry of, 'The Cavalry! The Cavalry!' But so eager was I that I did not mind it at the moment, and when on the eve of dragging the Frenchman back (his iron-bound hat having saved him from a cut) I recollect no more. On recovering my senses, I look'd up and found myself, bare-headed, in a clay ditch, with a violent headache. Close by me lay Colonel Ompteda [who commanded the 2nd King's German Legion Brigade] on his back, his head stretched back with his mouth open, and a hole in his throat.[6]

Ompteda's death was recorded by Captain Charles Berger, another officer serving in the King's German Legion:

I saw that the French had their muskets pointed at the Colonel, but they did not fire. The officers struck the men's barrels up with their swords. They seemed astonished at the extraordinary calm approach of the solitary horseman whose white plume showed him to be an officer of high rank. He soon reached the enemy's line of infantry before the garden hedge. He jumped in, and I clearly saw his sword strikes smite the shakos off. The nearest French officer looked on with admiration without attempting to check the attack.

When I looked round for my company I found I was alone. Turning my eyes again to the enemy, I saw Colonel Ompteda, in the midmost throng of the enemy's infantry, sink from his horse and vanish.[7]

No more reinforcements were to reach the farm, surrounded as it was by French infantry and cavalry, and with ammunition running desperately low, it could only be a matter of time before the remarkable defence of La Haye Sainte came to an end. In his account Baring recalled the following:

> The principal contest was now carried on at the open entrance to the barn. At length the enemy, not being able to succeed by open force, resorted to the expedient of setting the place on fire, and soon a thick smoke was seen rising from the barn! Our alarm was now extreme, for although there was water in the court, all means of drawing it, and carrying it were wanting, – every vessel having been broken up. Luckily the Nassau troops carried large field cooking kettles; I tore a kettle from the back of one of the men; several officers followed my example, and filling the kettles with water, they carried them, facing almost certain death, to the fire. The men did the same, and soon not one of the Nassauers was left with his kettle, and the fire was thus luckily extinguished; – but alas! with the blood of many a brave man! Many of the men, although covered with wounds, could not be brought to retire. 'So long as our officers fight, and we can stand,' was their constant reply, 'we will not stir from the spot.'
>
> It would be injustice to a skirmisher named Frederick Lindau, if I did not mention him: Bleeding from two wounds in the head and carrying in his pocket a considerable bag of gold which he had taken from an enemy's officer, he stood at the small back barn door, and from thence defended the main entrance in his front. I told him to go back, as the cloth about his head was not sufficient to stop the strong flow of blood; he, however, as regardless of his wounds as of his gold, answered: 'He would be a scoundrel that deserted you, so long as his head is on his shoulders'.

With every new attack Baring became more and more convinced of the importance of holding the post. 'With every attack also, the weight of the responsibility that devolved upon me increased,' he wrote, adding:

> In battles, as is well known, trifles, apparently of little importance, have often incalculable influence. What must have been my feelings, therefore, when, on counting the cartridges, I found that, on an average, there was not more than from three to four each! The men made nothing of the diminished physical strength which their excessive exertions had caused, and immediately filled up the holes that had been made in the walls by the enemy's guns, but they could

185

not remain insensible to the position in which they were placed by the want of ammunition, and made the most reasonable remonstrances to me on the subject. These were not wanting to make me renew the most urgent representations, and finally to report specifically that I was not capable of sustaining another attack in the present condition. All was in vain! With what uneasiness did I now see two enemy's columns again in march against us! At this moment I would have blessed the ball that came to deprive me of life. – But more than life was at stake, and the extraordinary danger required extraordinary exertion and firmness ...

The enemy gave me no time for thought; they were already close by our weak walls, and now, irritated by the opposition which they had experienced, attacked with renewed fury. The contest commenced at the barn, which they again succeeded in setting on fire. It was extinguished, ammunition was sent me. This was also without effect.

Our fire gradually diminished, and in the same proportion did our perplexity increase; already I heard many voices calling out for ammunition ... Even the officers, who, during the whole day, had shewn the greatest courage, represented to me the impossibility of retaining the post under such circumstances. The enemy, who too soon observed our wants, now boldly broke in one of the doors; however, as only a few could come in at a time, these were instantly bayonetted, and the rear hesitated to follow. They now mounted the roof and walls, from which my unfortunate men were certain marks; at the same time they pressed in through the open barn, which could no longer be defended. Inexpressibly painful as the decision was to me of giving up the place, my feeling of duty as a man overcame that of honour, and I gave the order to retire through the house into the garden. How much these words cost me, and by what feelings they wore accompanied, he only can judge who has been placed in a similar situation!

Baring refers to the heroics of Friedrich Lindau, who also wrote an account of the defence and fall of La Haye Sainte. Here he described its eventual capture by the French:

Soon after this the farm was stormed again and my captain ordered me to remain by the gateway. This time the battle lasted longer as ever more columns advanced. We soon ran short of cartridges, so that as soon as one of our men fell we immediately went through his pockets. At the same time Major Baring, who constantly rode round the farm,

[was] reassuring us that fresh ammunition would soon arrive. Soon afterwards I got a bullet through the back of my head, which I informed my captain about as he stood above me on the platform. He ordered me to go back. 'No,' I answered, 'So long as I can stand I stay at my post.'

Meanwhile I undid my scarf, wet it with rum and asked one of my comrades to pour rum into the wound and tie the scarf round my head. I attached my hat firmly to my pack and reloaded my rifle ...

Soon after that I heard a cry at the door of the barn: 'The enemy mean to get through here.' I went there and had scarcely fired a few shots down into the barn when I noticed thick smoke under the beam. Major Baring and Sergeant Reese from Tündern and Poppe immediately hurried in with kettles that they had filled at a pond to empty in the barn. The loopholes behind us were now weakly manned and the French maintained heavy fire on us through them, but it became weaker and I and some of my comrades went back in front of the loopholes.

Then just as I had fired, a Frenchman, seized my rifle to snatch it away. I said to my neighbour, 'Look, the dog has seized my rifle.'

'Wait,' he said, 'I have a bullet,' and at once the Frenchman fell. At the same moment another seized my rifle, but my next man on the right stabbed him in the face. I needed to draw my rifle back to load it, but a mass of bullets flew by me, rattling on the stone of the wall. One took the worsted tuft from my shoulder. Another shattered the cock on my rifle ...

I looked for another – there were plenty around – and took my place again at my loophole. I had soon fired my shots, though, and before I could shoot again I had to search the pockets of my fallen comrades for ammunition, but they were mostly empty by now. Thus our fire became weaker and the pressure of the French grew.[8]

Baring concludes his narrative with a description of the events that led to the capture of the farmhouse of La Haye Sainte:

Fearing the bad impression which retiring from the house into the garden would make upon the men, and wishing to see whether it was possible still to hold any part of the place, I left to ... three officers the honour of being the last. The passage through the house being very narrow, many of the men were overtaken by the enemy, who vented their fury upon them in the lowest abuse, and the most brutal treatment. Among the sufferers here was ensign Frank, who had already been wounded: the first man that attacked him, he ran through with his sabre, but at the same moment, his arm was broken by a ball from another; nevertheless he reached a bed room, and succeeded in concealing himself behind a bed. Two of the men also took refuge in the same place, but the French followed close at their heels, crying *'Pas de pardon à ces B—verds'*, and shot them before his face: Frank had himself the good luck to remain undiscovered until the place again fell into our hands. As I was now fully convinced, and the officers agreed with me, that the garden was not to be maintained when the enemy were in possession of the dwelling house, I made the men retire singly to the main position. The French, pleased, perhaps, with their success, did not molest us in retreat.

Not all the defenders got away so easily, including Lieutenant Graeme – as described in a letter he wrote in June 1815 shortly after the battle:

We had all to pass through a narrow passage. We wanted to halt the men and make one more charge, but it was impossible; the fellows were firing down the passage. An Officer of our Company called to me, 'Take care,' but I was too busy stopping the men, and answered, 'Never mind, let the blackguard fire.' He was about five yards off, and levelling his piece just at me, when this Officer stabbed him in the mouth and out through his neck; he fell immediately.

But now they flocked in; this Officer got two shots, and ran into a room, where he lay behind a bed all the time they had possession of the house; sometimes the room was full of them, and some wounded soldiers of ours who lay there and cried out 'pardon' were shot, the monsters saying, 'Take that for the fine defence you have made.'

An Officer and four men came first in; the Officer got me by the collar, and said to his men, *'C'est ce coquin.'* Immediately the fellows had their bayonets down, and made a dead stick at me, which I parried with my sword, the Officer always running about and then coming to me again and shaking me by the collar; but they all looked so frightened and pale as ashes, I thought, 'You shan't keep me,' and I bolted off, through the lobby; they fired two shots after me, and cried out *'Coquin,'* but did not follow me. I rejoined the remnant of my Regiment.[9]

La Haye Sainte had been lost and the Anglo-Netherlands centre was finally exposed. Though the day was well advanced, there was still ample time for one final French attack – one last chance for Napoleon.

13

The Arrival of the Prussians

La Haye Sainte was at last in French hands, and the Anglo-Netherlands' centre was now exposed, but Napoleon could not use all his remaining strength to attack Wellington as the Prussians had appeared on the battlefield. It may be recalled that Grouchy had been told to pursue the Prussians 'without stopping'. So what had gone wrong? And where was Grouchy with the rest of *l'armée du Nord*?

Further instructions had been sent to Grouchy at 11.00 hours on the morning of the 17th:

> Proceed to Gembloux with the cavalry corps of Generals Pajol and Exelmans, the light cavalry of IV Corps (Gérard), the Teste infantry division and the III (Vandamme) and IV Infantry Corps. You will reconnoitre in the direction of Namur and Maastricht and you will pursue the enemy. Scout out his march and inform me of his movements to enable me to penetrate his intentions. I am transferring my headquarters to Quatre-Bras, where the English still were this morning. Our communications will therefore be by the paved road of Namur.
>
> If the enemy has evacuated Namur, write to the General commanding the 2nd Military Division at Charlemont in order to have this town occupied by a few battalions of the National Guard. It is important to penetrate Blücher's and Wellington's intentions and to know whether they propose to re-unite their armies to cover Brussels and Liége by tempting fate in a battle. In any case, keep your two infantry corps constantly together in two and a half miles of ground with several retreat exits; post intermediary cavalry detachments to communicate with General Headquarters.[1]

Though fairly detailed, nothing in these instructions actually stated that Grouchy must make sure the Prussians should be prevented from joining

Wellington. Furthermore, quite how Grouchy was expected to penetrate Blücher's and Wellington's intentions is a mystery.

Nevertheless, Grouchy set off in pursuit of Blücher with around 30,000 men, Napoleon having reduced his force by subtracting a division of infantry and one of cavalry. At 22.00 hours on the 17th, Grouchy sent his first report from Gembloux, though it was not received at Napoleon's headquarters until 04.00 hours on the 18th:

> Sire, the enemy, 30,000 strong, continue to retreat. It seems from all reports that, from Sauvenières, the Prussians have divided into two columns. One must have taken the road to Wavre through Sart-a-Walhain, the other seems to have taken the direction of Perwès [Liége]. A third one, with artillery, is retreating on Namur. One can infer that a portion is going to join Wellington and that the centre, which is Blücher's army, retreats on Liége. If the Prussians' mass retires on Wavre, I shall follow it in this direction to prevent it from reaching Brussels and to separate it from Wellington. If on the contrary, their principal forces have marched on Perwès I shall follow them in pursuit through this town.[2]

Though the Prussians had undoubtedly been badly beaten at Ligny, and in the chaos of battle Blücher was nowhere to be found, the various divisions were still organised and under the control of their officers, as can be seen from the assesment of *Oberstleutnant* Ludwig-August-Friedrich-Karl von Reiche. At the end of the Battle of Ligny, he states:

> the village of Brye was still held by troops of I and II Corps, and III Corps remained unaffected in its position at Sombreffe, while the troops ejected from Ligny, mainly from I Corps and II Corps, had been forced back to the cobbled road running from Nivelles to Namur and, from there farther back to the old Roman road. As the IV Corps was not going to arrive in time for the battle, it had been sent orders to leave the Orneau valley and Gembloux to its left and to move to the plateau Artelle.
>
> With the exception of those units that had just come from the combats around Ligny, the troops were in good order, and still capable of fighting. This was not the case for those who had fought around Ligny, but that was to be expected.[3]

There were many crucial moments during the Waterloo campaign and none was of greater significance than the decision that was taken by General Gneisenau as his army fell back from Ligny. The natural line of retreat for the Prussian army, and the safest one, was back along its communications eastwards towards Namur. This, however, would have taken it away from Wellington.

Gneisenau decided, in his commander's absence, to withdraw towards Brussels where, he hoped, he would be able to make contact with the Anglo-Dutch army. When Blücher eventually resurfaced, after being roughly handled during the latter stages of the Battle of Ligny, he confirmed Gneisenau's decision.

Whether or not the Prussians would be able to join forces with Wellington's army depended on Grouchy. Napoleon had been unusually slow to put the two wings of his army into motion on the 17th. As a result Grouchy was left far behind when the Prussians retreated from Ligny. It was not until the early morning of the 18th that Grouchy was able to provide accurate information concerning the direction in which the Prussians were moving, and it was not good news for Napoleon to whom he submitted the following report at 06.00 hours:

> Sire, All my reports and information confirm that the enemy is retiring on Brussels to concentrate there or to give battle after joining Wellington. I and II Corps of Blücher's army seem to be marching, the first on Corbais, the second on Chaumont. They must have started yesterday evening (17 June) at 8 p.m. from Tourinnes and marched all night; fortunately the weather was so bad that they cannot have gone very far. I am leaving this instant for Sart-a-Walhain and from there to Corbais and Wavre.[4]

Though Grouchy said that the Prussians had not gone far, they were, though, well ahead of him and Blücher had already set in motion the arrangements for his army to join Wellington at Waterloo, after the Duke had informed the Prussian field marshal that he intended to give battle on Mont St Jean. Confirmation of this was sent to Müffling just before midnight on the 17th:

> I have the honour to report to Your Excellency that, following upon information I have received that the Duke of Wellington intends tomorrow to meet an attack in his positions from Braine L'Alleud to La Haye, I have arranged to dispose my troops as follows: von Bülow's [IV] Corps will march tomorrow at daybreak from Dion-le-Mont, through Wavre towards St Lambert, in order to attack the enemy right flank. II Corps will follow him immediately, while I and III will hold themselves in readiness to follow up this movement.

The exhaustion of the troops, some of whom have not arrived [i.e. the last of IV Corps], makes it impossible to move any earlier. I beg your Excellency, however, to let me know in good time when and how the Duke is being attacked so that I may make my dispositions accordingly.[5]

Grouchy would have to move very quickly if he was to prevent the Allied armies from joining forces. He did not and has been roundly condemned by many for this, including Napoleon. Yet there may still have been time for Grouchy to march directly to Waterloo and thus play a part in the battle if he was instructed to do so. This is Napoleon's reply to Grouchy from his post at Caillou, timed at 10.00 hours on the morning of the 18th, written by Soult, as Napoleon was preparing to attack Wellington at Waterloo:

Marshal – The Emperor has received your last report dated from Gembloux. You talk to His Majesty of two Prussian columns which have passed at Sauvenières and Sart-a-Walhain. However, some reports say a third column, quite a strong one, passed through Géry and Gentinnes marching towards Wavre. The Emperor enjoins me to warn you that at this moment he is about to have the English army attacked at Waterloo near the Forest of Soignes where it has taken up position. His Majesty therefore desires that you should direct your movements on Wavre so as to come nearer to us, to establish operational and liaison contact with us, pushing in front of you the Prussian army corps who have taken this direction and who might have stopped at Wavre, where you must arrive as soon as possible.

You will have the Prussian army corps who have taken to your right followed by some light corps so as to observe their movements and to gather their stragglers. Instruct me immediately of your dispositions and of your march as well as of the information you possess on the enemy, and do not neglect to bind your communications with us. The Emperor desires to have news of you very often.[6]

Grouchy, therefore, drove his troops on towards Wavre to face General Johann von Thielmann whose Prussian III Corps had been handed the task of delaying the right wing of *l'armée du Nord*. Meanwhile Bülow's corps was nearing Waterloo. Just as Napoleon was anticipating the start of d'Erlon's great attack upon the Anglo-Netherlands' centre, troops were spotted in the distance on the French right. Fearing that these might be Prussians, Napoleon immediately told Soult to write the following to Grouchy:

At 6 o'clock this morning, you wrote to the Emperor that you were marching on Sart-a-Walhain. Thus, it was your plan to move to Corbais and Wavre. This movement conforms with His Majesty's dispositions which have been communicated to you. However, the Emperor orders me to tell you that you must always manoeuvre in our direction and seek to come closer to us in order to join us before any corps can come between us. I do not indicate any direction to you. It is for you to see the point where we are, to regulate yourself in consequence and bind our communications, as well as always to be in a position to fall upon any enemy troops which would seek to worry our right flank, and to crush them. At this time, the battle is engaged on the line at Waterloo in front of the forest of Soignes. The enemy centre is at Mont St Jean, so do manoeuvre to join our right.[7]

Before the message could be sent, the following incident occurred – an event later described by *Pharmacien Aide-Major* Fée:

It was then that a gendarme d'élite brought in a Prussian officer as a prisoner. I noticed his shortness and undistinguished face. The cavalryman [who had brought him to Napoleon], to make him arrive more quickly, lifted him off the ground for five or six paces and, with a strong arm, pushed him forward. The emperor had him questioned.[8]

Napoleon himself would later write of this unusual meeting:

This hussar was the bearer of a letter. He was extremely intelligent and gave by word of mouth all the information that could be desired. The column which was to be seen at Saint Lambert was the advance guard of the Prussian General Bülow, who was arriving with 30,000 men; it was the 4th Prussian Corps which had not been engaged at Ligny.[9]

Napoleon responded quickly by adding the following note to Grouchy's message:

A letter has just been intercepted states that General Bülow is about to attack our right flank. We believe that we notice this corps now on the heights of St Lambert. Do not lose a moment in drawing near to us, and effecting a junction with us, in order to crush Bülow whom you will catch in the very act of concentrating [with Wellington].[10]

Colonel Marbot had been detached with his regiment of the 7th Hussars plus a battalion of infantry at the start of the battle to the right to watch for the arrival of Grouchy. His instructions 'prescribed to me to leave the bulk of my command always in view of the field of battle, to post 200 infantry in the Wood of Frishermont, one squadron at Lasne, having the outposts as far as St Lambert'.

Marbot learnt from some of the locals that Grouchy's force was likely to cross the Dyle at Limale, Limelette and Wavre. He passed this information on to Napoleon who ordered Marbot to reconnoitre in those directions:

> I proceeded to St. Lambert with a squadron to reinforce the troops there. I saw in the distance a strong column, approaching St. Lambert. I sent an officer in all haste to forewarn the Emperor.

Napoleon did not want to his men to know that the Prussian army was breathing down their necks, so he told Marbot

> … to advance boldly, that this body of troops could be nothing else than the corps of Marshal Grouchy, coming from Limale, and pushing before it some stray Prussians of whom the prisoners I had just taken were a part.[11]

Bülow's men had struggled along narrow roads entirely unsuited to the passage of an army, as Reiche subsequently described:

> The march to the battlefield was extremely difficult. Bottomless paths, cut into deep defiles, had to be followed. The ground on both sides was almost all wooded, so that there could be no question of evasive action, and the march was very slow, particularly since at many places men and horses could move only in single file and the artillery could be brought up only with the greatest difficulty. As a result the columns became very stretched … any attempt to keep them closed up had to be abandoned and we had to be content if only the brigades and regiments just remained together as units.[12]

Napoleon needed to hold back Bülow until Grouchy could arrive. To accomplish this he despatched the light cavalry divisions of Domon and Subervie and Lobau's VI Corps. He also moved part of the Imperial Guard infantry to La Belle Alliance to show a solid front to Wellington. As Ney was leading the masses cavalry charges at the Anglo-Netherlands squares Lobau came under fire from the leading units of Bülow's corps, as *Chef d'escadron* Dupy of the 7th Hussars of the 1st Cavalry Brigade, 1st Cavalry Division described:

Until towards 4 pm, we remained peaceful spectators of the battle. At this time, General Domon came to me; the fire of the English had almost ceased. He told me that the battle was won, that the enemy army was in retreat, that we were there to make a junction with Marshal Grouchy's corps and that by evening we would be in Brussels. He left.

A few moments later, instead of meeting Marshal Grouchy's troops, we received the attack of a regiment of Prussian uhlans. We repulsed them vigorously and chased after them. But we were forced to retreat by case shot fired by six guns, behind which the uhlans retired.[13]

Throughout the battle, Müffling sent despatch officers in 'continual succession' to keep Blücher informed of the progress of the battle. He wrote:

After 3 o'clock the Duke's situation became critical, unless the succour of the Prussian army arrived soon. On the receipt of my reports, it was resolved not to await the arrival of the whole of Bülow's corps on the plateau, but to advance out of the wood as soon as the two twelve-pounder batteries arrived.

At four o'clock the Field Marshal began his cannonade, as well as his advance against Planchenois [Plancenoit] ... and as the advance guard of the 1st corps (General von Ziethen) had already appeared in the position on the nearest height, I begged Generals Vandeleur and Vivian to hasten immediately with their six regiments of English cavalry to the assistance of the distressed [Anglo-Netherlands] centre, on account of the arrival of the Prussian corps they were no longer wanted on the left wing.[14]

Lieutenant Henry Duperier was with the 18th Hussars, which formed part of Major General Sir Hussey Vivian's 6th Cavalry Brigade:

All the light cavalry and hussars were withdrawn and put for a very few minutes under a hill considerable on our right and entirely under the position of our army, being as we wise creatures usually do, our left flank open ... it was to make place for 5,000 of Prussian cavalry.[15]

Müffling continued with his narrative:

Almost simultaneously with the movement of these regiments [Vandeleur's and Vivian's Hussars], the enemy advanced with infantry against the left wing at Papelotte.

195

General Ziethen's advanced guard, which I was expecting with the utmost impatience, suddenly turned round, and disappeared from the height just as the enemy took possession of Papelotte with his Guards. I hastened after this advanced guard on the other side of the height, from whence I saw them in full retreat.[16]

What had caused Ziethen to retreat at this vital stage of the battle? 'By this retrograde movement of General von Ziethen,' Müffling wrote, 'the battle might have been lost'.

The man responsible for this near disaster was Ziethen's chief of staff, Lieutenant Colonel von Reiche. He had been told by von Müffling that Ziethen should 'link up' with Wellington's left wing:

> With these instructions I hurried back to the column and having decided not to waste time by first looking for General Ziethen, who was further back, I gave the advance-guard the appropriate direction in the light of Müffling's instructions ... I was hurrying back towards the corps in order to report to General Ziethen, when Captain von Scharnhorst ... on Prince Blücher's staff, dashed up to me, shouting that the 1st Army Corps must push on immediately to Blücher beyond Frichermont, because things were beginning to go badly there ...
>
> Never in my life have I found myself in such a difficult situation. On the one hand Blücher's order ... and the thought that our troops were perhaps in danger there and could not hold out any longer. On the other hand the certainty that Wellington was counting on our arrival ... General Steinmetz, who commanded the advance-guard, came up to the halted troops at this very moment, stormed at me in his usual violent manner, and insisted upon an advance ... My embarrassment increased not a little when General Steinmetz let the head of the column resume its march and himself went past the point where the road to Frichermont branches off.[17]

This is what Müffling had witnessed – what appeared to be Ziethen's Corps retreating, though it was actually marching away from Wellington's left wing towards Frichermont. At that moment Ziethen appeared and Müffling was able to help clarify the situation. I Corps turned back and marched to link up with Wellington's left. 'Nobody,' wrote Reiche, 'could have been more pleased than I was'. The official Prussian account continued:

> It was half-past four o'clock. The excessive difficulties of the passage by the defile of St. Lambert had considerably retarded the march of the Prussian columns, so that only two brigades of the 4th corps had arrived

at the covered position which was assigned to them. The decisive moment was come; there was not an instant to be lost. The generals did not suffer it to escape. They resolved immediately to begin the attack with the troops which they had at hand. Gen. Bulow, therefore, with two brigades and a corps of cavalry, advanced rapidly upon the rear of the enemy's right wing. The enemy did not lose his presence of mind; he instantly turned his reserve against us, and a murderous conflict began on that side. The combat remained long uncertain.[18]

Jardin Ainé, equerry to the Emperor Napoleon, was a spectator to the dramatic events of that fateful afternoon and left an insightful eyewitness account:

> At three o'clock [sic] an aide-de-camp from the right wing came to tell him that they were repulsed and that the artillery was insufficient. Napoleon immediately called General Drouet in order to direct him to hasten to reinforce this army corps which was suffering so heavily, but one saw on Napoleon's face a look of disquietude instead of the joy which it had shown on the great day of Fleurus. The whole morning he showed extreme depression.[19]

The fighting on the French right flank centred around the village of Plancenoit and, with Prussian pressure mounting, Napoleon sent in his Young Guard, which counter-attacked and seized the village. The Prussians, though, were not to be stopped, as Colonel von Hillier described:

> In the second assault two battalions of the 14th Brigade also took part [as well as the 15th Brigade], while I kept the 1st Silesian Militia regiment in reserve. This attack was also repelled, but the troops did not lose their morale. Lieutenant General Gneisenau was also here. With his influence and that of the officers of the 15th regiment it was possible to lead up the columns for a third time and with great success.[20]

Behind Bülow the Prussian I Corps and II Corps were moving towards the French right flank and rear. Unless Napoleon could do something spectacular, he would soon be swept away by the Prussians. With his cavalry weakened and exhausted by their attacks upon the British squares, Napoleon had only one body of men left – the infantry of the Middle and Old Guard.

The Attack of the
Imperial Guard

With the Prussians bearing down on his flank and with his cavalry weakened and exhausted by its attacks upon the British squares, Napoleon had only one body of men left – the infantry of the Imperial Guard.

Napoleon's Guard was like no other. At its peak it had reached a total of 35,000 infantry, 8,000 cavalry and 200 guns. Not all of its component regiments were considered elite, indeed many of the regiments that formed what was termed the Young Guard were often new recruits.

The next in seniority were those regiments that formed the Middle Guard, with the Old Guard being the most prodigious in the Army. Very high entry standards had to be met for entry into the Old Guard. When he returned to power in 1815, Napoleon maintained these high standards. A minimum of twelve years' service was required for the infantry of the Old Guard, and eight for the cavalry and artillery. All had to have served in several campaigns. Such was the quality of *l'armée du Nord*, for the Waterloo campaign that even those that sought to serve in the Young Guard needed to have had a minimum of four years' service.[1]

The Imperial Guard's reputation was second to none. Though Napoleon held the Old Guard back, only using it when necessary, everyone knew that when the Old Guard was called into the attack, it spelt the end for the enemy. That time had now come.

He sent four battalions of the Old Guard – three of Grenadiers and one of Chasseurs to support the Young Guard and stabilise the situation on the right flank. Then, with the rest of the Old and Middle Guard infantry, Napoleon launched his final attack upon Wellington's thinning line.

The problem was that the sound of gunfire could be heard to the east. If the French troops knew that the Prussians were about to fall on their flank they might well refuse to commit themselves to an attack against the British. Napoleon knew this only too well but he decided to use this to his advantage, by telling his men that the gunfire heralded the arrival not of Blücher, but Grouchy!

He sent one of his aides to inform Ney of the appearance of Grouchy. '*Moniseur le Maréchal*,' exclaimed General Dejean, '*Vive l'Empereur! Voilà Grouchy!*' This ruse worked, as Ney explained, albeit temporarily:

> About seven o'clock in the evening, after the most frightful carnage which I have ever witnessed, General Labedoyere came to me with a message from the Emperor, that Marshal Grouchy had arrived on our right, and attacked the left of the English and Prussians united. This General Officer, in riding along the lines, spread this intelligence among the soldiers, whose courage and devotion remained unshaken, and who gave new proofs of them at that moment, in spite of the fatigue which they experienced. Immediately after, what was my astonishment, I should rather say indignation, when I learned that so far from Marshal Grouchy having arrived to support us, as the whole army had been assured, between forty and fifty thousand Prussians attacked our extreme right, and forced it to retire!
>
> Whether the Emperor was deceived with regard to the time when the Marshal could support him, or whether the march of the Marshal was retarded by the efforts of the enemy longer than was calculated upon, the fact is, that at the moment when his arrival was announced to us, he was only at Wavre upon the Dyle, which to us was the same as if he had been 800 leagues from the field of battle.
>
> A short time afterwards, I saw four regiments of the middle guard, conducted by the Emperor, arriving. With these troops he wished to renew the attack, and to penetrate the centre of the enemy. He ordered me to lead them on; Generals, officers, and soldiers, all displayed the greatest intrepidity.[2]

This was unquestionably the 'crisis' point of the battle, as Shaw-Kennedy, the Quartermaster-General of the Third Division, explains:

> La Haye Sainte was in the hands of the enemy; also the knoll on the opposite side of the road; also the garden and ground on the Anglo-Allied side of it; Ompteda's brigade was nearly annihilated, and Kielmansegge's so thinned, that those two brigades could not hold their position. That part of the field of battle, therefore, which was between Halkett's left and Kempt's right, was unprotected; and being the very centre of the Duke's line of battle, was consequently that point above all others, which the enemy wished to gain. The danger

was imminent; and at no other period of the action was the result so precarious as at that moment.[3]

Spearheading the attack of the Guard were five battalions, about 3,000 men, in battalion squares, formed in columns. These were the regiments of the Middle Guard, the 3rd and 4th Chasseurs and the 3rd and 4th Grenadiers. Baron Duchard's horse artillery had placed a two-gun team between each battalion. Behind the Middle Guard were about 1,500 men of the Old Guard, the 2nd Battalions of the 1st and 2nd Chasseurs and the 2nd Grenadiers. Naploeon's most precious regiment, the two battalions of the 1st Grenadiers, remained in reserve.

The course of the battle now hung in the balance, as the officer whose letter from the Camp of Clichy to his friend in Cumberland we have already perused, described:

> Buonaparte charged with his Imperial Guards. The Duke of Wellington led on a brigade consisting of the 52nd and 95th regiments. Lord Uxbridge was with every squadron of cavalry which was ordered forward. Poor Picton was killed at the head of our Division, while advancing. But in short, look through the list engaged on that day, and it would be difficult to point out one who had not distinguished himself as much as another. Until eight o'clock, the contest raged without intermission, and a feather seemed only wanting in either scale to turn the balance.
>
> At this hour, our situation on the left centre was desperate. The 5th Division, having borne the brunt of the battle, was reduced from 6000 to 1800. The 6th Division; at least the British part of it, consisting of four regiments, formed in our rear as a reserve, was almost destroyed, without having tired a shot, by the terrible play of artillery, and the fire of the light troops. The 27th had 400 men, and every officer but one subaltern, knocked down in square, without moving an inch, or discharging one musket; and at that time I mention, both divisions could not oppose a sufficient front to the Enemy, who was rapidly advancing with crowds of fresh troops. We had not a single company for support, and the men were so completely worn out, that it required the greatest exertion on the part of the officers to keep up their spirits. Not a soldier thought of giving ground; but victory seemed hopeless, and they gave themselves up to death with perfect indifference. A last effort was our only chance.[4]

Having watched the drama unfold at close quarters, Napoleon's aide was ideally placed to provide this first-hand account:

200

Buonaparte himself could not see from the lateral point which he occupied, although it is very true that he was close enough to the enemy's batteries. As the corps passed him, he smiled, and addressed to them expressions of confidence and encouragement.

The march of these old warriors was very firm and there was something solemn in it. Their appearance was very fierce. A kind of savage silence reigned among them. There was in their looks a mixture of surprise and discontent occasioned by their unexpected meeting with Buonaparte who as they thought, was at their head. In proportion as they ranged up the eminence and darted forward on the squares which occupied its summit the artillery vomited death upon them, and killed them in batches.

This part of the scene came directly under Buonaparte's eye, without his being able to see what passed on the height itself as he still kept himself, as it were, enveloped in the corner of the ravine. It was then precisely a quarter of an hour from seven o'clock and it was at this very moment that the decisive crisis of the battle commenced.

Buonaparte had then six persons close to him: these were, his brother Jerome, Generals Bertrand, Drouot, Bernard, Colbert, and Labedoyere. At every step which he took, or seemed to take to put his own person in front Generals Bertrand and Drouot threw themselves before his horse's head, and exclaimed in a pathetic accent: 'Ah! Sire, what are you going to do? Consider that the safety of France and of the army depends entirely upon you; all is lost if any accident happen to you'. Buonaparte yielded to their entreaties with a real or apparent effort by which he seemed to gain control over himself.[5]

The following description is an extract taken from a letter written by a British staff officer in Paris on 15 July 1815:

Such was the state of affairs at about seven o'clock. Our loss had been immense, that of the enemy considerably greater; but their determination to carry our position appeared undiminished. The Prussians, who since about four o'clock had been seen, at a distance advancing, had about half past five sent forward a small body of troops, which the light troops of the enemy soon obliged to fall back; and the French advanced a force which nearly possessed themselves of the village of Ter la Haye, before which, they, prior to this, contented themselves with skirmishing only.

An anxiety for the arrival of the Prussian army was now to be seen in the countenance of every one, that can better be imagined than described. At length, however, the event so long expected and so much required took place: the Prussians, whose march had been delayed by bad roads and the passage of a defile, began to deploy in very considerable force, and move directly against the right flank of the enemy, whilst the fire of their artillery was soon seen extending even towards their rear.

Those who had witnessed the enormous masses by which we had during the day been attacked, were much surprised at seeing the very numerous artillery and infantry. that Bonaparte opposed to this advance; and they then, if possible, felt more strongly than ever, how happy for us was the diversion thus given by our allies, to so considerable a body of apparently fresh troops, who might otherwise, in spite of the resistance with which the attacks had been hitherto met, have eventually deprived us of victory, by overwhelming numbers. As if, however, in a fit of desperation, it was the moment I have just described that Bonaparte chose for his last, I may almost say, most desperate effort: it was soon evident that (to use, if I recollect rightly, his own words employed on a former occasion) 'the enemy no longer fought for victory, but for retreat and safety.' Yet, such was the impetuosity with which this attack was made, so great were the losses we had experienced, that success again appeared almost within his grasp.[6]

Lieutenant Edward Macready was serving with the British 30th Regiment:

It was near seven o'clock, and our front had sustained three attacks from fresh troops, when the Imperial Guard was seen ascending our position in as correct order as at a review. As they rose step by step before us, and crossed the ridge, their red epaulettes and cross-belts put on over their blue great-coats, gave them a gigantic appearance, which was increased by their high hairy caps and long red feathers, which waved with the nod of their heads as they kept time to a drum in the centre of their column. 'Now for a clawing,' I muttered, and I confess, when I saw the imposing advance of these men, and thought of the character they had gained, I looked for nothing but a bayonet in my body, and I half breathed a confident sort of wish that it might not touch my vitals.

While we were moving up the slope, [Lieutenant Colonel Hugh] Halkett, as well as the noise permitted us to hear, addressed us and said, 'My boys, you have done everything I could have wished, and more than I could expect, but much remains to be done; at this moment we have nothing for it but a charge.' Our brave fellows replied by three cheers. The enemy halted, carried arms about 40 paces from us, and fired a volley. We returned it, and giving our 'Hurrah!' brought down the bayonets. Our surprise was inexpressible, when, pushing through the clearing smoke, we saw the back of the Imperial Grenadiers; we halted and stared at each other as if mistrusting our eyesight. Some 9-pounders from the rear of our right poured in the grape amongst them, and the slaughter was dreadful. In no part of the field did I see carcases so heaped upon each other.[7]

Captain H.W. Powell, of the 1st Foot Guards recalled that the 1st Brigade of Guards was ordered by Wellington to take ground to its left and form line four deep:

This brought the Brigade precisely on the spot the Emperor had chosen for his attack. There ran along this part of the position a cart road, on one side of which was a ditch and bank, in and under which the Brigade sheltered themselves during the cannonade, which might have lasted three-quarters of an hour. Without the protection of this bank every creature must have perished.

The Emperor probably calculated on this effect, for suddenly the firing ceased, and as the smoke cleared away a most superb sight opened upon us. A close Column of Grenadiers (about seventies in front) of la Moyenne [Middle] Garde, about 6,000 strong, led, as we have since heard, by Marshal Ney, were seen ascending the rise *au pas de charge* shouting '*Vive l'Empereur*'. They continued to advance till within fifty or sixty paces of our front, when the Brigade were ordered to stand up. Whether it was from the sudden appearance of a Corps so near to them, which must have seemed as starting out of the ground, or the tremendously heavy fire we threw into them, *La Garde*, who had never before failed in an attack *suddenly* stopped. Those who from a distance and more on the flank could see the affair, tell us that the effect of our fire seemed to force the head of the Column bodily back.

In less than a minute above 300 were down. They now wavered, and several of the rear divisions began to draw out as if to deploy, whilst some of the men in their rear beginning to fire over the heads of those in front was so evident proof of their confusion, that Lord Saltoun … holloa out, '*Now's the time, my boys*'. Immediately the Brigade sprang forward. La Garde turned and gave us little opportunity of trying the steel. We charged down the hill till we had passed the end of the orchard of Hougoumont, when our right flank became exposed to another heavy Column (as we afterwards understood of the Chasseurs of the Garde) who were advancing in support of the former Column. This circumstance, besides that our charge was isolated, obliged the Brigade to retire towards their original position.[8]

The attack was described by an officer in the Guards in a letter written shortly after the battle:

After these failures he brought up his *Garde Imperiale*, just opposite to our brigade, which had formed in line on their advancing. We were all lying under shelter of a small bank, as they covered their advance with a most terrible fire of grape and musketry. Buonaparte led them himself to the rise of the hill, and told them that was the way to Brussels.

We allowed them to approach very near – when we opened so destructive a fire that there were soon above 300 of them upon the ground, and they began to waver. We instantly charged, but they ran as fast as possible. The Duke of Wellington observing this crisis, brought up the 42d and 95th, taking the enemy in flank, and leading them himself quite close up. The enemy's column was entirely dispersed. After this, we were again annoyed with grape and musketry, which obliged us to retire. On fronting, we saw another heavy column of the Chasseurs de la Garde Imperiale.[9]

It was this second Imperial Guard column of the Chasseurs that now had to be countered, as Lieutenant Colonel John Cross, at the time a captain in the 52nd Regiment, explained. He takes up his story after a French cuirassier officer had deserted and ridden up to the 52nd pointing at the direction the French attack was about to be made:

The 52nd halted in two lines ten yards behind the cross road where the ground sloped towards our position ... the 52nd wheeled, the left company nearly a quarter circle to the left, and formed ... the remainder were formed into two lines, not four deep ... A strong company of the 52nd was sent to skirmish in front, and to fire into the Imperial column. At this moment General Adam came to the 52nd from the 71st, and desired the 52nd to move on ... The 52nd still moved on passing the entire front of Byng's [2nd] brigade of British Guards, who were stationary and not firing, about three hundred yards or so to their front, and forming possibly a right angle or perhaps an obtuse angle with the line of the Guards. At the moment the 52nd commenced the movement, Lord Hill was near the British Guards commanded by Maitland, and no movement on their part had taken place. Therefore it is imagined, when the 52nd commenced the movement, they were shortly followed by the 71st and the whole of General Clinton's division, the Imperial troops saw their flank and rear were menaced by a mass of troops marching on their flank, they halted …

The 52nd in the mean time had proceeded within a short distance of the rising ground on which the French were formed, when a body of British cavalry were perceived in full speed approaching the front of the left company of the 52nd. The officers of the company gave the order to fire, supposing they had come from the enemy's column. The three adjoining companies wheeled back to form square. The Battalion at this time was under a heavy fire from the Imperal Guards and the Regiment was halted for a few moments to enable the three companies to rectify their line. At this moment, while the three companies were forming up, the Duke was close to the rear, and said, 'Well, never mind, go on, go on.' This halt brought the 71st close on the right of the 52nd … The 52nd then advanced at full speed, the greater part of the French gave way in confusion.[10]

This small tribute to the contribution made by the 71st was printed in the *Chester Courant* on Tuesday, 8 August 1815:

COMPLIMENT. – A letter from an officer of the 71st, speaking of the conduct of that corps on the 18th ult. observes – 'O!' by the bye, *our piper was in play again!* When the imperial guards made their last charge upon us, and when retiring owing to the gallant fire kept up in the square, the piper played up the 71st quick march followed with the charge. Major-General Adam being in the square exclaimed, *'well done 71st, you are all lions together; and for you piper, you are an honour to your country – forward my lads, and give them the charge in style, as I know and see you can do!'* This was the critical moment that turned the scale of the action, and I do assure you we made them scamper.

Later that same year, on Friday, 17 November 1815, the pages of the *Chester Chronicle* carried the following account:

It was near seven o'clock when Bonaparte, who had till then remained on the hill, from which he clearly saw all that was passing, contemplated with a look of ferocity the hideous scene of butchery beneath him. The more numerous the difficulties which occurred, the more obstinate did he appear. He was indignant at obstacles which he had so little foreseen, and far from thinking that it was wrong to sacrifice an army, which placed unbounded confidence in him, he incessantly sent fresh troops, with orders to charge and force their way in spite of every resistance. He was several times told, that appearances were bad, and that the troops were exhausted; but his only answer was, 'Forward, forward!'

A General sent information, that he could not maintain his position, on account of being dreadfully annoyed by a battery, and asked what he was to do? 'To *take* the battery,' said Bonaparte, turning his back on the aide-de-camp!

An English officer, who was wounded and made a prisoner, was brought to him. He made several inquiries, and among the rest, what was the strength of the English army. The officer told him that it was very strong, and would almost immediately be reinforced by sixty thousand men. 'So much the better,' said he; 'the more we meet, the more we shall conquer.' He dispatched several messengers with dispatches, which he dictated to a secretary, and repeated many times, in a tone of distraction. 'The victory is mine – remember to say that.' It was at this period, when all his attempts had been abortive, that information was brought to him of Prussian columns debouching on his right flank, and threatening his rear; but he would not believe these reports, and constantly answered, that these pretended Prussian troops were no other than those of General Grouchy. It was not long, however, before he was undeceived by the violence of the enemy's attack. Part of the 6th corps was sent to sustain this new shock, until Grouchy's corps arrived, which was every minute expected. The Prussian corps which now appeared in the field at so critical a juncture, was that of General Bulow.

Bonaparte, without altering his resolution in any degree, was of opinion that the moment was come to decide the day. He formed, for this purpose, a fourth column, almost entirely composed of the guards, and directed it at the pas de-charge on Mont Saint Jean, after having dispatched instructions to every point, that the movement, on which he thought victory to depend, might be seconded. The veterans marched up the hill with the intrepidity which might be expected of them. The whole army resumed its vigour, and the conduct was resumed throughout the line. The guards made repeated charges, and were as often repulsed. Overpowered by an irresistible discharge of artillery, which seemed every moment to increase, these invincible grenadiers saw their ranks constantly thinned; but they closed together with perfect coolness, and advanced into the heat of the fray without intimidation.

Nothing arrested their progress but death, or the severest wounds.

The hour of their defeat, however, was come. Enormous masses of infantry, supported by an immense force of cavalry, to which the French could oppose no resistance, as their own was entirely destroyed, poured down upon them from all sides with a degree of fury which made all idea of quarter, on either part, out of the question.

On Saturday, 28 October 1815, the *Lancaster Gazette* contained this account:

Upon the cavalry being repulsed, the Duke himself ordered our second battalion to form line with the third battalion [of the 1st Guards], and after advancing to the brow of the hill, to lie down and shelter ourselves from the fire. Here we remained, I imagine, near an hour. It was now about seven o'clock. The French infantry had in vain been brought up against our line, and as a last resource, Buonaparte resolved upon attacking our part of the position with his Veteran Imperial Guard, promising them the plunder of Brussels. Their artillery covered them, and they advanced in solid column to where we lay. The Duke, who was riding behind us, watched their approach, and at length, when within an hundred yards of us, exclaimed 'Up, Guards, and at them again!' Never was there a prouder moment than this for our country or ourselves.

The household troops of both nations were now, for the first time, brought in contact, and on the issue of their struggle the greatest of stakes was placed. The enemy did not expect to meet us so soon; we suffered them to approach still nearer, and then delivered a fire into them, which made them halt; a second, like the first, carried hundreds of deaths into their mass, and without suffering them to deploy, we gave them three British cheers, and a British charge of the bayonet. This was too much for their nerves, and they fled in disorder.

The situation was repeated over at Plancenoit:

Despite their great courage and stamina, the French Guards fighting in the village began to show signs of wavering. The church was already on fire with columns of red flame coming out of the windows, aisles and doors. In the village itself, still the scene of bitter house-to-house fighting, everything was burning, adding to the confusion. However, once Major von Witzleben's manoeuvre was accomplished and the French Guards saw their flank and rear threatened, they began to withdraw.[11]

The Imperial Guard infantry did indeed break and fall back in disorder. Seeing this someone shouted the chilling words *'La Garde recule'*. The Guard had never been beaten before. No-one in the French army could ever imagine such a situation and the effect it had upon them was catastrophic. They knew it was the end.

15

The End of the Battle

The news that the Guard had been defeated tore through the French ranks in moments and, despite their best efforts, the French generals could not keep their men in formation. As one French officer noted, panic spread like lightning.

> The guard, that immoveable phalanx, which, in the greatest disasters, had always been the rallying point of the army, and had served it as a rampart, the guard, in fine, the terror of the enemy, had been appalled, and was flying, dispersed among the multitude.
>
> Every one now prepared to save himself as he could; they pushed, they crowded; groups, more or less numerous, formed, and passively followed those by which they were preceded. Some not daring to deviate from the high road, attempted to force themselves a passage through the carriages, with which it was covered: others directed their course to the right or left, as fancy guided; fear exaggerates every danger, and night, which was now gaining upon them, without being very dark, contributed greatly to increase the disorder.[1]

With the sudden disintegration of the enemy, Wellington knew that the moment had come to finish them off. Standing up on his stirrups he took off his hat and waved his men forward. For the first time that day, the Anglo-Netherlands army took the offensive. That attack was ordered at around 19.30 hours, Wellington later explained,

> … when I saw the confusion in their position upon the repulse of the last attack of their infantry, and when I rallied and brought up again into the first line the Brunswick infantry. The whole of the British and Allied cavalry of our army was collected in rear of our centre; that is, between Hougoumont and La Haye Sainte.

The infantry was advanced in line. I halted them for a moment in the bottom, that they might be in order to attack some battalions of the enemy still on the heights. The cavalry halted likewise. The whole moved forward again in very few moments. The enemy did not stand the attack. Some had fled before we halted. The whole abandoned their position. The cavalry was then ordered to charge, and moved round the flanks of the battalions of infantry. The infantry was formed into columns, and moved in pursuit of battalions.[2]

Johnny Kincaid of the 95th, recalled that 'presently a cheer, which we knew to be British, commenced far to the right', adding:

Every one pricked up his ears; – it was Lord Wellington's long wished-for orders to advance; it gradually approached, growing louder as it grew near; – we took it up by instinct, charged through the hedge down upon the old knoll, sending our adversaries flying at the point of the bayonet. Lord Wellington galloped up to us at the instant, and our men began to cheer him; but he called out, 'No cheering, my lads, but forward and complete your victory!'[3]

An unidentified soldier wrote the following graphic description which was printed in the *Lancaster Gazette* of Saturday, 28 October 1815:

The shape of their column was tracked by their dying and dead, and not less than three hundred of them had fallen in two minutes, to rise no more. Seeing the fate of their companions, a regiment of tirailleurs of the guard attempted to attack our flank; we instantly charged them, and our cheers rendered anything further unnecessary, for they never waited our approach. The French now formed solid squares in their rear, to resist our advance, which, however, our cavalry cut to pieces. The Duke now ordered the whole line to move forward: nothing could be more beautiful.

The sun, which had hitherto been veiled, at this instant shed upon us its departing rays, as if to smile upon the efforts we were making, and bless them with success. As we proceeded in line down the slope, the regiments on the high ground on our flanks were formed into hollow squares, in which manner they accompanied us, in order to protect us from cavalry – the blow was now struck, the victory was complete, and the enemy fled in every direction: his *deroute* was the most perfect ever known; in the space of a mile and a half along the road, we found more than thirty guns, besides ammunition waggons, &c. &c.

Our noble and brave coadjutors, the Prussians, who had some time since been dealing out havoc in the rear of the enemy, now falling in with our line of march, we halted, and let them continue the pursuit. Bonaparte fled the field on the advance of the Prussians, and the annihilation of his Imperial Guard, with whose overthrow all his hopes perished. Thus ended the day of 'Waterloo'.

The skill and courage of our artillery could not be exceeded. The brigade of Guards, in Hougomont, suffered nothing to rob them of their post: every regiment eclipses its former deeds by the glories of today; and I cannot better close this than by informing you, that when we halted for the night, which we did close to where Bonaparte had been during a great portion of the battle, and were preparing our bivouac by the road side, a regiment of Prussian lancers coming by, halted and played '*God save the King*,' than which nothing could be more appropriate or grateful to our feelings; and I am sure I need scarcely add, that we gave them three heartfelt cheers, as the only return we could then offer.

As *l'armée du Nord* began to disintegrate Ziethen's I Corps reached the battlefield, as Gneisenau later described:

At this moment, the enemy was broken in three places; he abandoned his positions. Our troops rushed forward at the *pas de charge*, and attacked him on all sides, while, at the same time, the whole English line advanced. Circumstances were extremely favourable to the attack formed by the Prussian army; the ground rose in an amphitheatre, so that our artillery could freely open its fire from the summit of a great many heights which rose gradually above each other, and in the intervals of which the troops descended into the plain, formed into brigades, and in the greatest order; while fresh corps continually unfolded themselves, issuing from the forest on the height behind us.[4]

Guards officer Colonel James Hamilton Stanhope, who, in the years after the Napoleonic Wars, became a Member of Parliament, recalled:

The arrival of the Prussian cavalry sweeping round the right flank of the enemy, in masses with columns as far as the eye could reach, was a magnificent spectacle. The French were beat before but this was a very pretty finale. The Prussians pursued all night and gave no quarter and took most of the artillery which had not fallen into our hands before.[5]

211

Wellington duly acknowledged the important, if not vital, part played by the Prussians troops in his official despatch:

> I should not do justice to my own feelings, or to Marshal Blücher and the Prussian Army, if I did not attribute the successful result of this arduous day to the cordial and timely assistance I received from them. The operation of General Bülow upon the enemy's flank was a most decisive one; and, even if I had not found myself in a situation to make the attack which produced the final result, it would have forced the enemy to retire if his attacks should have failed, and would have prevented him from taking advantage of them if they should unfortunately have succeeded.[6]

An extract from a letter by an officer in the Household Cavalry relates this period of the battle from his perspective:

> At the conclusion of the battle, we were masters of the field; and only one officer of the 2nd Life Guards, with two corporals and forty privates remained. There was no officer of the 1st Regiment, all, or most of them having been dismounted. The command of the two regiments for the night was given by Lord Somerset to the remaining officer of the 2d. Col. Lygon had one horse shot under him, towards the conclusion of the battle, and the horses of several of our officers were wounded.
>
> Lord Wellington was with the brigade the greater part of the day, during which time I saw him repeatedly. He seemed much pleased and was heard to observe, towards the evening, to the general officer near him, that it was the hardest battle he had ever fought, and that he had seen many charges, but never any to equal the charges of the Heavy Brigades, particularly the Household. We made in all four charges: viz., two against cavalry, and two against the Imperial Guards.[7]

An Allied staff officer wrote about the last stages of the battle in a letter sent from Paris and which was dated 15 July:

> The eagle eye of our noble Duke soon ... discovered the purpose for which those that remained of the Imperial guards, were now led to sacrifice; he observed, that both infantry and artillery were moving off from the rear of the position which the French had during the day occupied; and with that decision which he has before so often evinced, he directed an immediate advance of the whole line, and an

attack of those troops of the enemy who stood formed to cover this retreat. The order was no sooner given, than executed with that spirit which the British are so well known to possess on these occasions; and those soldiers who might well be supposed to be harassed and fatigued with the severity and duration of the battle, rushed on against the enemy's ranks apparently as fresh, and with as much vigour, as though the action had but just commenced.

The most opportune arrival, shortly prior to this, of the two brigades of cavalry from the left, commanded by Major-generals Vandeleur and Vivian, had materially contributed to give confidence to our troops during the most trying part of the preceding attack. And when the advance was ordered, Major-general Vivian's brigade (on which occasion the 10th and 18th Hussars particularly distinguished themselves), passing the infantry, charged, and totally defeated the bodies of the enemy's cavalry which stood formed in their centre and on their left; and at the same time driving their artillery from their guns, left only opposed to our infantry, squares of the Imperial guards, who, from their steady countenance to the last, sustained that high character they had acquired during so many years of war, under the immediate command of that extraordinary man for whom such great numbers of them had already devoted themselves.

Nothing, however, could check the advance of the troops who were rapidly moving against them. Those distinguished regiments, the 52d and 71st, part of General Adam's brigade, soon put to flight that part of the enemy formed more immediately on the high road. On all other points also our attacks were equally successful; and the two brigades of cavalry last mentioned, advancing at the same time, their rout was completed, and in an instant the whole were in retreat and confusion; and this was, if possible, increased by the success of the Prussians, who had about this time entered the high road in the rear of the French position.[8]

George Woodberry was with the 18th Hussars in the charge made by Vivian's cavalry brigade mentioned above by the Allied staff officer:

> Vivian's brigade had passed the whole day on the extreme left flank of the army; it had not been engaged before half past seven when the Prussians arrived. We then had to cross over to the right and charged the Imperial Guard, the cuirassiers, the lancers and the artillery, blazing a trail through the middle of the whole of this mass until we came up to the farm of la Belle-Alliance, where we were ordered to halt, and where we gave three cheers at the fleeing enemy.[9]

Charging along with the hussars was the 11th Light Dragoons, a member of which was George Farmer, who became caught up in the drama and excitement, and inevitable confusion:

> There was a heart-stirring cheer begun, I know not where, but very soon audible over the whole of our front; and we, too, were ordered to leap into the saddle and move forward. On we went at a gallop, dashing past the weary yet gallant footmen, and, shouting as we went, drove fiercely and without check up to the muzzles of a hostile battery. A furious discharge of grape met us, and thinned our ranks. Before it man and horse went down; but the survivors, never pulling back or pausing to look back, scattered the gunners to the winds, and the cannon were our own.
>
> Just at this moment, Sergeant Emmet of the 11th, whom I covered, received a shot in the groin, which made him reel in the saddle, from which he would have fallen, had I not caught him; while at the same time a ball struck me on the knee, the bone of which was saved by the interposition of my unrolled cloak ... then I plied my spurs into my horse's sides, and flew to the front. But by this time it was too dark to distinguish one corps from another. I therefore attached myself to the first body of horse which I overtook, and in three minutes found myself in the middle of the enemy.
>
> There was a momentary check, during which the men demanded one of another, what regiment this was. I do not know how the discovery of their own absolute intermingling might have operated, had not an officer called aloud, 'Never mind your regiments, men, but follow me.' In an instant I sprang to his side, and, seeing a mass of infantry close upon us, who, by the blaze of musketry, we at once recognised to be French, he shouted out, 'Charge!' and nobly led the way. We rushed on; the enemy fired, and eight of our number fell, among whom was our gallant. A musket-ball pierced his heart; he sprang out of his saddle and fell dead to the ground.[10]

An officer wrote to his father from Quatre Bras on 19 June. His letter included the following interesting description:

> At eight o'clock, the Enemy moved forward his old guard, who were received by the first brigade of Guards, and a Dutch brigade, with Saltoun at their head, with such a fire, that they took to their heels – their whole army fled in the greatest disorder, and was followed in sweeping lines, as fast as the lines could move. Our cavalry cut them to pieces. The abandoned guns, carriages, knap sacks and muskets,

choked up the ground, and for five miles, in which we followed them last night, the field was covered with the bodies of Frenchmen only.[11]

The French official account written after the battle presents a somewhat different version of events, ascribing Napoleon's defeat to mistaken identity and 'ill disposed persons':

> At half-after eight o'clock, the four battalions of the middle Guard, who had been sent to the ridge on the other side of Mount St. Jean, in order to support the Cuirassiers, being greatly annoyed by the grape-shot, endeavoured to carry the batteries with the bayonet. At the end of the day, a charge directed against their flank by several English squadrons put them in disorder. The fugitives recrossed the ravine. Several regiments near at hand seeing some troops belonging to the Guard in confusion, believed it was the Old Guard, and in consequence, were thrown into disorder. Cries of 'All is lost! the Guard is driven back!' were heard on every side. The soldiers pretend, even, that on many points, ill disposed persons, placed for the purpose, called out, '*Sauve qui pent.*'
>
> However this may be, a panic at once spread itself throughout the whole field of battle, and they threw themselves in the greatest disorder on the line of communication: soldiers, cannoneers, caissons, all pressed to this point; the Old Guard, which was in reserve, was infected, and was itself hurried along.
>
> In an instant, the army was nothing but a confused mass; all the soldiers of all arms were mixed, and it was utterly impossible to rally a single corps. The enemy, who perceived this astonishing confusion, attacked with their cavalry. The disorder increased; and such was the confusion, owing to night coming on, that it was impossible to rally the troops, and point out to them the error.
>
> Thus a battle terminated – a day of false manoeuvres rectified, still greater successes insured for the next day – all was lost by a moment of panic terror. Even the squadrons of service, drawn up by the side of the Emperor, were overthrown and disorganised by these tumultuous waves, and there was then nothing else to be done but to follow the torrent. The parks of reserve, the baggage which had not repassed the Sambre – in short, everything that was on the field of battle remained in the power of the enemy. It was impossible to wait for our troops on our right; everyone knows what the bravest army in the world is when thus confusedly mixed, and when its organisation no longer exists.[12]

The following is an extract of a letter from an unnamed Guards officer:

We got about two miles that evening, taking ourselves 30 pieces of cannon. Nothing could be more complete and decisive. Most fortunately the Prussians came on the field at this moment, and pursued the Enemy through the night.

The following account was published by the *Chester Chronicle* in its edition published on Friday, 17 November 1815:

It was in vain that Bonaparte attempted to make a final effort by bringing into action some battalions of the guards, which had not yet been employed, and which he himself headed. All was useless. Intimidated by what passed around them, and overpowered by numbers, this feeble reserve soon yielded, and with the rest fled back like a torrent. The artillerymen abandoned their cannon; the soldiers of the waggon-train cut the traces of their horses; the infantry, the cavalry, and every other species of soldiery, formed one confused intermingled mass, partly flying along roads, and partly across the fields. The Generals were lost in this crowd; the corps had no longer any regular commander, and not a single battalion existed, behind which the rest could attempt to rally. Even the guards, who had hitherto been the very bulwark of the army, and the terror of the enemy, were dispersed among the multitude, the disorder of which was increased by the darkness of the night.

The fugitives, painfully pressed by an overwhelming foe, ran rapidly over the two leagues which separate Genappe from the field of battle, and at length reached this small place, where the greater number trusted that they should be able to pass the night. In order to oppose some obstacles to the enemy, they collected carriages on the road, and barricaded the entrance to the principal street. A few cannon were collected in the form of a battery; bivouacs were formed in the town and its environs, and the soldiers went into the houses for the purpose of finding an asylum and food; but scarcely were these dispositions made, when the enemy appeared. The discharge of cannon, on their part, spread universal alarm among their downcast enemies. All fled again, and the retreat became more disorderly than ever!

At this time everyone was ignorant of Bonaparte's fate, for he had suddenly disappeared. The general report was that he had fallen in the heat of battle. This intelligence being conveyed to a well known General, he replied in the words of Megret, after the death of Charles XII, at Friederickstadt: 'Then the tragedy is ended.' (*Voilà le pièce finie.*) Others said, that while making a charge at the head of his guards, he

216

had been dismounted and taken prisoner. The same uncertainty prevailed as to Marshall Ney, and most of the principal officers.

A great number of persons affirmed that they had seen Bonaparte pass through the crowd, and that they knew him by his grey great coat and horse. This proved to be the fact. When the last battalions of the guards, which he led into action, were overthrown, he was carried away with them, and surrounded on all sides by the enemy. He then sought refuge in an orchard adjoining to the farm of Cailon [Caillou], where he was afterwards met by two officers of the guards, who were, like him, endeavouring to elude the enemy. To them he made himself known, and he passed together over the plain, upon which were scattered various Prussian parties. These, however, luckily for the fugitives, were employed in plundering the captured equipage. Bonaparte was recognised on several occasions, in spite of the darkness of night, and the soldiers whispered to each other as he passed – 'Look! There is the Emperor!' These words seemed almost to alarm him, and he hurried forward through the multitude. Where were now the acclamations, which used to greet his ear the moment he appeared in the midst of his troops?

Général de division Jean-Martin, Baron Petit, commanded the *1er Régiment des Grenadiers à pied*, the senior regiment of the French Army and he was with Napoleon as *l'armée du Nord* collapsed. He writes here in the third person:

The Emperor galloped back and placed himself inside the square of the 1st Battalion of Grenadiers. The whole army was in the most appalling disorder. Infantry, cavalry, artillery – everybody was fleeing in all directions. Soon no unit retained any order except the two squares formed by this regiment's two battalions posted to the right and left of the main road. On orders from the Emperor, their commander, General Petit, had the *grenadière* sounded to rally those guardsmen who had been caught up in the torrent of fugitives. The enemy was close at our heels, and, fearing that he might penetrate the squares, we were obliged to fire at the men who were being pursued and who threw themselves wildly at the squares ...

It was now almost dark. The Emperor himself gave the order for us to leave our positions, which were no longer tenable, being entirely outflanked to left and right. The two squares withdrew in good order, the 1st Battalion across country, the second along the road. A halt had to be made every few minutes so as to maintain the lines of the squares and to give time for the *tirailleurs* and the fugitives to catch up.[13]

217

Jardin Ainé also described his master's last moments on the battlefield:

'Let us go forward,' Napoleon replied. 'We must do better still. *Courage mes braves*: Let us advance!' Having said this he rode off at a gallop close to the ranks encouraging the soldiers, who did not keep their position long, for a hail of artillery falling on their left ruined all. In addition to this, the strong line of British cavalry made a great onslaught on the squares of the guard and put all to rout.

It was at this moment that the Duke of Wellington sent to summon the Guard to surrender. General Kembraune [Cambronne] replied that the Guard knew how to fight, to die, but not to surrender. Our right was crushed by the corps of Bülow who with his artillery had not appeared during the day but who now sought to cut off all retreat.

Napoleon towards eight o'clock in the evening, seeing that his army was almost beaten, commenced to despair of the success which two hours before he believed to be assured. He remained on the battlefield until half-past nine when it was absolutely necessary to leave. Assured of a good guide, we passed to the right of Genappes and through the fields; we marched all the night without knowing too well where we were going until the morning. Towards four o'clock in the morning we came to Charleroi where Napoleon, owing to the onrush of the army in beating a retreat, had much difficulty in proceeding. At last after he had left the town, he found in a little meadow on the right a small bivouac fire made by some soldiers. He stopped by it to warm himself and said to General Corbineau, 'Et bien Monsieur, we have done a fine thing.' General Corbineau saluted him and replied, 'Sire, it is the utter ruin of France.' Napoleon turned round, shrugged his shoulders and remained absorbed for some moments.

He was at this time extremely pale and haggard and much changed. He took a small glass of wine and a morsel of bread which one of his equerries had in his pocket, and some moments later mounted, asking if the horse galloped well. He went as far as Philippeville where he arrived at mid-day and took some wine to revive himself. He again set out at two o'clock in a mail carriage towards Paris where he arrived on the 21st at 7 a.m. at the Elysée whence he departed on the 12th, in the same month.[14]

The British troops were exhausted after the long pounding they had endured, and with the Prussians taking up the pursuit most of Wellington's men bivouacked in the vicinity of the battlefield. Captain Mercer of the Royal Horse Artillery, despite his tiredness, could not sleep and he looked out across the battlefield which was illuminated by moonlight:

Here and there some poor wretch, sitting up amidst the countless dead, busied himself in endeavours to staunch the flowing stream with which his life was fast ebbing away. Many whom I saw so employed that night were, when morning dawned, lying stiff and tranquil ... From time to time a figure would half rise itself from the ground, and then, with a desperate groan, fall back again. Others, slowly and painfully rising, stronger, or having less deadly hurt, would stagger away with uncertain steps across the field in search of succour. Many of these I followed with my gaze until lost in the obscurity of the distance; but many, alas! after staggering a few paces, would sink again on the ground, probably to rise no more. It was heart-rending – and yet I gazed![15]

An experienced officer described the scene after the battle in a letter that was sent 'from the Bivouac' near Landrécies:

After our bivouac of the 18th after the battle, we marched to Nivelles, over the terrible field so horrible a scene, scarcely any man ever witnessed; the ground, for the space of a league, was covered with bodies absolutely lying in ranks, and horses grouped in heaps, with their riders. Towards our right was a chateau, which during the battle, took fire from the Enemy's shells; and in that state was heroically defended by Saltoun, and afterwards by the 2nd brigade of Guards. The appearance brought to my mind St. Sebastian; it was equally horrid, though on a smaller scale.[16]

A similar gruesome picture was subsequently painted by Captain Johnny Kincaid of the 95th Rifles:

The field of battle next morning presented a frightful scene of carnage; it seemed as if the world had tumbled to pieces, and three-fourths of everything destroyed in the wreck. The ground running parallel to the front of where we had stood was so thickly strewed with fallen men and horses that it was difficult to step clear of their bodies – many of the former still alive, and imploring assistance which it was not in our power to bestow.

The usual salutation on meeting an acquaintance of another regiment after an action was to ask who had been hit, but on this occasion it was 'Who's alive?'[17]

Another Rifles veteran, Major Harry Smith, was equally moved by what he witnessed on the Waterloo battlefield:

I had been over many a field of battle, but with the exception of one spot at New Orleans, and the breach of Badjoz, I had never seen anything to be compared with what I saw. At Waterloo, the *whole* field from right to left was a mass of dead bodies. In one spot, to the right of La Haye Sainte, the French Cuirassiers were literally piled on each other; many soldiers not wounded lying under their horses; others fearfully wounded, occasionally with their horses struggling upon their wounded bodies. The sight was sickening, and I had no means to assist them.[18]

Under the headline, 'Battle of Waterloo' the *Caledonian Mercury* of 5 October 1815 provided its readers with this description of the aftermath of the fighting:

What pen can describe the scenes which presented themselves on the morning of the 19th, on the field of battle? – Nature shudders at the idea. I never think upon it but with horror. Death had reaped a plentiful harvest, and displayed his ravages in their ugliest forms. Poor mutilated wretches still lay in the agonies of death, calling or making signs for a drop of water. There was none to be had.

The ground being of a sandy nature, had soaked up all the rain which fell on the 17th – even the blood which was shed had disappeared. Here a dead man served for a pillar to his dying companion – others lay, as it were, holding each other in a last embrace. I was at first afraid to look upon such an awful spectacle; but at length I walked to a considerable distance from our brigade, from curiosity.

The rifle corps and cavalry seemed to have suffered most in the battle; at least, I observed most of them lying on the ground over which I went. I saw several men and women from the adjacent villages stripping the dead; and I am told that these wretches plundered many of the wounded. As we marched off the ground, we passed by a farm-house, which seemed to have been obstinately defended. An immense number of dead bodies lay here, both French and English. The house had been set on fire by a shell, during the time that a party of both armies were charging each other in the farm-yard.

I recollect of no other incidents which I was witness to, than what is related above. I could easily have made up a better story, by giving you a romantic account of personal skirmishes and hair-breadth escapes; but I have stated nothing but what you may depend upon as fact.

The officer who wrote to his friend in Cumberland from the camp at Clichy, ends his story of the battle:

> I will not attempt to describe the scene of slaughter which the fields presented, or what any person possessed of the least spark of humanity must have felt, while we viewed the dreadful situation of some thousands of wounded wretches who remained without assistance through a bitter cold night, succeeded by a day of most scorching heat; English and French were dying by the side of each other; and I have no doubt, hundreds who were not discovered when the dead were buried, and who were unable to crawl to any habitation, must have perished by famine.
>
> For my own part, when we halted for the night, I sunk down almost insensible from fatigue; my spirits and strength were completely exhausted. I was so weak, and the wound in my thigh so painful, from want of attention, and in consequence of severe exercise, that after I got to Nivelles, and secured quarters, I did not awake regularly for 36 hours.[19]

A jubilant Gebhard Leberecht von Blücher wrote to his wife from Genappe the day after the battle:

> My friend Wellington and I have put an end to Bonaparte's dancing. His army is in utter rout. All his artillery, his baggage, his wagons and his coaches are in my hands. The insignia of all the orders to which he belonged, which were found in his carriage, have just been brought to me in a casket. I had two horses killed under me yesterday. We shall be finished with Bonaparte shortly.[20]

Wellington described the battle to his old comrade in arms, Marshal Lord Beresford, when he wrote from Gonesse on 2 July:

> You will have heard of our battle on the 18th. Never did I see such a pounding match. Both sides were what the boxers call gluttons. Napoleon did not manoeuvre at all. He just moved forward in the old style, and was driven off in the old style. The only difference was that he mixed cavalry with his infantry, and supported both with an enormous quantity of artillery. I had the infantry for some time in squares, and we had the French cavalry walking about us as if they had been our own. I never saw the British infantry behave so well.[21]

To his brother Wellington noted that 'It was the most desperate business I was ever in', adding 'I never took so much trouble about any battle, and never was so near to being beat.'[22] As for Napoleon, the Emperor declared that,

> The Anglo-Dutch army was saved twice during the day by the Prussians; the first time, before three o'clock, by the arrival of General Bülow, with 30,000 men; and the second time, by the arrival of Marshal Blücher, with 31,000 men. During that day, 69,000 Frenchmen defeated 120,000. Victory was snatched from them between eight and nine o'clock, by 150,000 men.[23]

Wellington all but agreed: 'It has been a damned nice thing – the nearest run thing you ever saw in your life.'[24]

16

The Battle of Wavre

We have seen that Grouchy played no part in the Battle of Waterloo. So what happened to the Marshal and the right wing of *l'armée du Nord*? We know that he had allowed the Prussians to escape during the evening of the 17th, though he still seems to have believed that his forces could block the Prussians attempting to move beyond Wavre. After riding up to his III Corps to check on its progress, he sat down to a late breakfast, a little after 11.00 hours, after writing the following despatch:

> The I, II, and III Prussian Corps, under Blücher, are marching towards Brussels. Two of these corps marched through Sart-à-Walhain, or passed just to the right of the place; they marched in three columns roughly keeping abreast of each other … One Corps coming from Liège [Bülow's IV] effected its concentration with those that had fought at Fleurus … It would seem as though they intend to give battle to their pursuers [Grouchy's force], or finally to join hands with Wellington; such was the reports spread by their officers, who, in their usual boasting spirit, pretend that they only left the field of battle on June 16 [Battle of Ligny] in order to ensure their junction with the English army at Brussels. This evening I shall have massed my troops at Wavre and thus shall find myself between the Prussian Army and Wellington, who, I presume, is retreating before Your Majesty.[1]

Around this time the cannons opened fire at Waterloo and their roar could be heard by Grouchy and his men. General Gérard immediately urged the Marshal to cancel his current arrangements and march without delay to the sound of the guns. 'Marshal, it is your duty to march to the cannon,' he insisted. Grouchy was not impressed at being told by a subordinate what his duty was and replied:

My duty is to execute the Emperor's orders, which direct me to follow the Prussian. It would be infringing his commands to pursue the course of action which you recommend.[2]

Another source provides a slightly longer explanation from Grouchy:

The Emperor told me yesterday that he intended to attack the English Army if Wellington accepted battle. I am therefore not at all surprised by the present engagement. Had the Emperor wished me to take part in it, he would not have kept me away from him at the very time he was marching against the English Army. Anyway, if I take my Army corps along country lanes, soaked by yesterday's and this morning's rain, I shall not arrive in time at the place of combat.[3]

Though, seemingly, he felt he was doing the right thing, Grouchy was conscious that his conduct needed explaining and he wrote the following to Soult on the 19th:

My honour makes it a matter of duty to explain myself in regard to my dispositions of yesterday. The instructions which I received from the Emperor, left me free to manoeuvre in no other direction than Wavre. I was obliged, therefore, to refuse the advice which Count Gérard thought he had a right to offer me. I do ample justice to General Gérard's talents and brilliant vigour; but you are doubtless as surprised as I was, that a general officer, ignorant of the Emperor's orders, and the data which inspired the Marshal of France, under whose orders he was placed, should have presumed publicly to dictate to the latter, his line of conduct. The advanced hour of the day, the distance from the point where the cannonading was heard, the condition of the roads, made it impossible to arrive in time to share in the action which was taking place. At any rate, whatever the subsequent events may have been, the Emperor's orders, the substance of which I have just disclosed to you, did not permit of me acting otherwise than I have done.[4]

After their defeat at Ligny, Blücher's men had withdrawn to the town of Wavre on the River Dyle. At around 13.00 hours on the 18th the advance units of General Exelmans' II Cavalry Corps made contact with the Prussian rearguard but Grouchy was not in a position to engage the Prussians with all his force until 15.00 hours.

With the bulk of the Prussian army marching as fast as it could towards Waterloo to join Wellington, General Johann von Thielmann with III

Corps was given the task of holding back Grouchy. The French Marshal had around 33,000 men and eighty guns. Thielmann had just 17,000 men and forty-eight guns but his position was a strong one.

The Dyle, normally a shallow stream at this time of the year and easily fordable, was in flood because of the torrential rain of the previous day. The town of Wavre extended for about half a mile along the left, or west, bank of the Dyle. It was connected with a few buildings, effectively a suburb of the town, on the eastern bank by two stone bridges, the larger of which carried the main Brussels–Namur road.

About three-quarters of a mile up-stream, on the Wavre side of the river, was the Mill of Bierges, which was destined to be the scene of the fiercest fighting. Here there was a wooden bridge, carrying a narrow country road. At Limale, a village two-and-a-half miles upstream from Wavre and at Limelette, another village a mile further on, there were wooden bridges across the Dyle. All the buildings along the river had been hastily loopholed by Thielmann's men and the two stone bridges had been strongly barricaded. Behind Wavre was a hill which could afford good cover for reserves and there were numerous lateral lanes along which troops could easily be moved to any threatened sector.

Thielmann placed his 10th Division and 11th Division behind Wavre, with the 12th Division posted at Bierges, behind the village. The 9th Division was supposed to be the general reserve, but its commander, General Borcke, believing that III Corps was marching with Blücher, had set off to join the main army. By the time Thielmann was aware of Borcke's departure it was too late to call him back. The loss of Borcke's nine battalions and accompanying artillery meant that Thielmann now had less than half as many men as Grouchy.[5]

Pushing ahead in front of Exelmans's cavalry was General Vandamme with the French III Corps. He arrived in front of Wavre some time between 15.00 hours and 16.00 hours. Anxious to prevent the Prussians from joining Wellington, Vandamme attacked Wavre without waiting either for the rest of the right wing to arrive and without even waiting for Grouchy.

'Wavre was occupied by the Prussians,' wrote General Baron Pierre Berthezène, who saw that that Grouchy had adopted the wrong course of action and that attacking Wavre was a pointless waste of life:

> Its houses were garrisoned by skirmishers. Its bridge was barricaded and swept by the fire of numerous guns which were established on the heights dominating the left bank of the Dyle. General Vandamme attacked the town as soon as he arrived before it, without taking any

measure to ensure success. He simply ordered Habert's division to enter it in column. In spite of the murderous fire of the enemy, this column reached the bridge but when Habert was wounded, it retired in disorder and came to reform at the entrance of the town. This stupid attack cost us five or six hundred men ... Besides, the occupation of Wavre could have no influence on the outcome of the campaign.[6]

Captain Charles François of the 30ème *Infanterie de Ligne*, who had served in the French Army since volunteering in 1792, had a similar opinion of the battle:

> The attack was general and directed against Thielmann's troops. The infantry and cavalry performed prodigies of valour which served only to kill and wound many men ... This action had little use and cost us 1100 men. It hardly honours our generals, who seem to be groping their way forward and we heard gunfire all day on our left, in the direction of Waterloo. Unlike my usual self, I was depressed and low in spirits, I was furious.[7]

Grouchy sent a report on the battle to Napoleon from Dinant on 20 June 1815:

> It was not until after seven in the evening of the 18th of June, that I received the letter of the Duke of Dalmatia, which directed me to march on St. Lambert, and to attack General Bulow. I fell in with the enemy as I was marching on Wavre. He was immediately driven into Wavre, and General Vandamme's corps attacked that town, and was warmly engaged. The portion of Wavre, on the right of the Dyle, was carried, but much difficulty was experienced in debouching on the other side. General Girard was wounded by a ball in the breast while endeavouring to carry the mill of Bielge [*sic*] in order to pass the river, but in which he did not succeed, and Lieutenant General Aix had been killed in the attack on the town.
>
> In this state of things, being impatient to co-operate with your Majesty's army on that important day, I detached several corps to force the passage of the Dyle and march against Bulow. The corps of Vandamme, in the meantime, maintained the attack on Wavre, and on the mill, whence the enemy showed an intention to debouch, but which I did not conceive he was capable of effecting. I arrived at Limale, passed the river, and the heights were carried by the division of Vichery and the cavalry. Night did not permit us to advance farther, and I no longer heard the cannon on the side where your Majesty was engaged.[8]

Hulot's Division of Gérard's IV Corps was ordered to force a passage of the Dyle at the Mill of Bierges, led by Gérard himself. The attack was beaten back, with Gérard being badly wounded. All, though, was not lost, because General Pajol's I Cavalry Corps had seized the bridge at Limale. The bridge was defended by three battalions of infantry and three squadrons of cavalry, but the bridge, quite unaccountably, had not been barricaded. Pajol sent a regiment of hussars charging across the bridge. So narrow was the bridge, the hussars could only gallop three abreast. They charged directly into the guns of the Prussian infantry and captured the vital bridge. At last the French were across the Dyle.

As soon as he realised that the river had been crossed, Thielmann sent all the troops he could spare to try and drive the French back over the Dyle. It was now dark, but the situation was so critical that neither side could afford to stop fighting. General Stülpnagel led the Prussian counter-attack. The ground, though, was unfamiliar to the Prussians and the darkness was intense and the attack soon lost cohesion and stuttered to a halt.

The difficulty of fighting in the dark was graphically portrayed by Second Lieutenant Mannkopff, who was in charge of the skirmish platoon of the 4th Company of the Prussian 31st Regiment:

> We advanced with our skirmishers out in front and a long and determined battle broke out with the enemy voltigeurs in the darkness and amid the man-high corn that covered the fields. This soon became chaotically confused, with man fighting man. In this, my men and I had to face enemy voltigeurs and cavalry sometimes to our front, sometimes to our rear. About midnight, where possible, our skirmishers pulled back to the columns and a bayonet attack was made at the charge. However, because of the darkness and high corn, it was impossible to see and keep order …
>
> Meanwhile, my skirmishers had rejoined the battalion and during this attack suddenly stumbled into a deep sunken road or ditch. At that moment, a volley of small arms fire from the opposite side struck us. However, probably because the other side of the sunken road was higher, the shots mostly went over the heads of our soldiers and un-mounted officers, some of them making a loud rattling sound on hitting our bayonets. All our mounted officers were hit, though, including the regimental commander, Major von Kesteloot, and the battalion commander … Shortly after this bayonet charge, we broke off the battle and, without the enemy following up, withdrew to a pine forest close behind us.[9]

As he continued his narrative, Grouchy described the events of the 19th:

> I halted in this situation until day-light. Wavre and Bielge were occupied by the Prussians, who, at three in the morning of the 19th, attacked in their turn, wishing to take advantage of the difficult position in which I was, and expecting to drive me into the defile, and take the artillery which had debouched, and make me repass the Dyle. Their efforts were fruitless. The Prussians were repulsed, and the village of Bielge taken. The brave General Penny was killed.
>
> General Vandamme then passed one of his divisions by Bielge, and carried with ease the heights of Wavre, and along the whole of my line the success was complete. I was in front of Rozierne, preparing to march on Brussels, when I received the sad intelligence of the loss of the battle of Waterloo. The officer who brought it informed me, that your Majesty was retreating on the Sambre, without being able to indicate any particular point on which I should direct my march. I ceased to pursue, and began my retrograde movement.[10]

Grouchy now had to try to save his corps. He successfully disentangled himself from Thielmann and marched south to Philippeville and then to Mézières, all the time heading for Paris. Whilst this might seem the most obvious and sensible strategy, one of his subordinates, General Vandamme, believed this was the wrong course of action:

> In the morning of the 19th when the *Maréchal* received through a superior officer of the Emperor's General Staff the news of the loss of the battle of Waterloo, the *Maréchal* lost his head and asked for advice from his generals on what to do next. General Vandamme certifies that he gave advice to leave the weak Prussian corps of General Thielemann, which had been beaten and which was out of action, behind and to march with two united corps towards Bruxelles, to cross that city and to rest the troops on the heights behind the city near the road to Assche, where the townspeople were supposed to have brought food to them.
>
> From there the march was to have gone on through Alost to Ghent, and then the corps would have directed themselves through Courtrai towards Lille where, protected by the fortresses of the northern department, they would have been able to reform so as to start a new campaign. It is obvious that this march could not have been undertaken without encountering many obstacles, that the continuation of the campaign would have taken a completely

different turn by preventing a victorious army from marching towards Paris, and perhaps fixing the theatre of war in Belgium.[11]

Grouchy may not have changed the course of the campaign, but he had kept his wing of the army intact, which gave Napoleon hope. The Emperor may have lost a battle, but the war might still be won.

17

The Pursuit

The Allies may have indeed won the Battle of Waterloo, but there was still a chance that Napoleon could rally his troops. What was needed now was a vigorous pursuit to make sure that the broken *l'armée du Nord* was unable to reform. A contemporary account of the pursuit was published shortly after the battle:

> The pursuit was continued on the part of the British, as long as the light would admit; and even until some mistakes had occurred from the mixture of Prussian, and British troops it was then relinquished to our brave Allies; the Prussian army, who, from having had less to do during the day, were more equal to it, and whose commander, Marshal Blucher, had promised our Field-marshal, when they happily met at the farm of La Belle Alliance after it became dark, that it should be continued without intermission throughout the night; a promise he most faithfully kept.[1]

Wellington later told Earl Stanhope of that memorable meeting between the two victorious commanders, which inspired the so-often reproduced painting by Daniel Maclise that hangs in the Palace of Westminster:

> Blücher and I met near *La Belle Alliance*; we were both on horseback; but he embraced and kissed me, exclaiming, *Mein lieber Kamerad*, and then *quelle affaire!* Which was pretty much all he knew of French.[2]

Wellington wrote the following in his official despatch to Earl Bathurst from Waterloo on 19 June:

> I continued the pursuit till long after dark, and then discontinued it only on account of the fatigue of our troops, who had been engaged

during twelve hours, and because I found myself on the same road with Marshal Blücher, who assured me of his intention to follow the enemy throughout the night. He has sent me word this morning that he had taken 60 pieces of cannon belonging to the Imperial Guard, and several carriages, baggage, &c., belonging to Buonaparte, in Genappe. I propose to move this morning upon Nivelles, and not to discontinue my operations.[3]

This was followed by another despatch later that day, which was printed in the *Norfolk Chronicle* of Saturday, 1 July 1815:

MY LORD – I have to inform your Lordship, in addition to my dispatch of this morning, that we have already got here five thousand prisoners taken in the action of yesterday, and that there are above two thousand more coming tomorrow: there will probably be many more. Among the prisoners are the Count Loubau, who commanded the 6th corps, and General Cambrone, who commanded a division of the guards. I propose to send the whole to England by Ostend. I have the honour to be, &c, WELLINGTON

Wellington did indeed send the prisoners back to the United Kingdom, as was reported in the *Hampshire Chronicle* of Monday, 3 July 1815:

Upwards of 2000 prisoners, taken at the battle of Waterloo, arrived at this port on Tuesday night, in the Cumberland and Ramillies, of 74 guns, the Grampus, of 50, and the Castor frigate. Wednesday morning the same ships sailed with them to Plymouth, for the purpose of lodging them in Dartmoor Prison.

Two thousand eight hundred and forty-five French prisoners were brought over by the Erebus and Foxhound's convoy. There were 3000 more ready to embark, and 3000 wounded English and French prisoners on their way to Ostend.

The reinforcements destined for our gallant cavalry in Belgium, embarked at Ramsgate yesterday; they consist of detachments from the 7th, 10th, and 18th Hussars, and 11th, 12th, 16th, and 23d Light Dragoons. Besides these, detachments of the Life Guards and Blues marched into Canterbury yesterday, and proceeded this day also for embarkation at Ramsgate.

The declaration of war against France arrived here on Saturday, and occasioned a general bustle in the Dock-yard and among the naval officers. Several ships of war have sailed, and others are expected to sail hourly, with orders to take, sink, burn or destroy all

French vessels, whether under the white or tri-coloured flag, and to protect our trade from privateers.

A remarkably detailed account of the pursuit of the French forces was published in the *Hull Packet* of 28 November 1815:

> A very interesting publication has just issued from the French press under the above title ['Battle of Waterloo'], from which we give the following extract. Several accounts of this memorable engagement have appeared, all of them substantially agreeing as to the fighting part, but the present French account supplies us with a relation of what took place in the retreat, which is not to be found in any other publication; it is therefore, in this respect, very interesting – anything relating to this memorable and decisive battle must be ever so to all true Britons.
>
> The English and Prussians having completely effected a junction, the two Commanders-in-Chief, Wellington and Blucher, met at the farm of La Belle Alliance, and concerted measures for following up their success. The former had suffered very considerably during the action; their cavalry, in particular, being very much fatigued, would find great difficulty in pushing the French in such a lively manner, as to prevent them from rallying: but the Prussian cavalry being fresh, hastened to take the advanced posts, and pressed upon us too closely to allow one minute's repose.
>
> The mass of fugitives thus crowded together, rapidly passed over the space of two leagues, between the field of battle and Genappe, and at length arrived in that small town, where the greatest part of them thought of stopping, in order to pass the night. With the intention of opposing some obstacles to the enemies' progress, every exertion was made to accumulate carriages on the road, and to barricade the entrance of the principal street; some pieces were placed in battery, and bivouacs were established in the town and the environs; the soldiers scattered themselves through the houses, for the purpose of seeking for an asylum and food; but hardly were these dispositions made, when the enemy presented himself: a few cannon shot fired upon the cavalry, which were debouching, threw everything into confusion – the camp is immediately in motion, an universal flight takes place, and a disorderly retreat recommences, with more irregularity and confusion than ever.

In the midst of this 'clearing away', noted the author of the *Hull Packet*'s account, 'no one knew what was become of Buonaparte, who had

232

disappeared. It was confidently asserted that he had fallen in the engagement':

> When this news was announced to a certain General Officer, very well known, he replied, in the words of Megret, after the fall of Charles XII at Frederickstadt – *Well! The play is over.* – Others asserted, that having charged several times at the head of the guard, he had been dismounted and made prisoner. The same uncertainty prevailed as to the fate of Marshal Ney, the Major-General, and of most of the principal Generals.
>
> Very many persons affirmed that they saw Buonaparte passing on, solely attentive to his own personal safety, in the midst of the crowd, and that they recognised him perfectly well from his grey great coat, and his dappled charger. This last was the true version. Buonaparte, at the moment when the last remaining battalions of the guard which he had led were routed, forced along by them, and enveloped on all sides by the enemy, had thrown himself into an orchard belonging to the farm of La Belle Alliance. It was in that place that he was met by two horsemen of the guard, wanderers like himself, to whom he made himself known, and who became his conductors, opening a passage for him through the parties of Prussian soldiers scattered over the plain; but the greater number of whom, happily for him, were busily employed in seizing upon and plundering his equipages and baggage. Notwithstanding the darkness of the night, he was perceived and recognized in many places, where his presence was noted by the soldiers, who called to one another, in a low voice, '*The Emperor! The Emperor!*' – These words appeared an alarming cry to him, and he immediately took himself off as quick as the confusion of the multitude, in the midst of which he was entangled, would permit. What were become of those obstreperous acclamations which used to accompany him in the midst of his army, as soon as he appeared?
>
> The French army continued their disastrous march during the entire night, covering their route with the wrecks of their misfortune, and assailed every moment by fresh charges of the enemy, which completed their disorder. The degree of terror which prevailed at this discomfiture was such that numerous groups of cavalry and of infantry, well armed, suffered themselves to be attacked without attempting to defend themselves against some wretched lancers, whom it would have been quite sufficient to have turned round upon, in order to put them to flight.
>
> At day break, the wretched remains of our army arrived, partly at Charleroi, partly at Marchienne, when they made haste to cross the

Sambre. That unfortunate army, lately so brilliant, now in the most ruined condition, and harassed with fatigue, presented an aspect so much the more hideous, as it was followed by a great number of wounded, some on foot, others mounted on train horses, and who, pale, exhausted, and with their wounds wrapped up with rags covered with blood, and promiscuously marching in the midst of a confused column, which filled the entire breadth of the road, recalled to memory, in the most affecting manner, the scenes of carnage which had taken place.

The carriages of various kinds, which, in proportion as they approached the Sambre, found themselves retarded in their march by the passing of those which happened to be foremost, were crowded on each other on the roads which lead to the bridges of Charleroi and of Marchienne. The enemies' cavalry did not fail to make their appearance, and surprised them in the midst of this confusion; no man then thought of any thing but of making his escape; the drivers, in their flight, cut the harness of their horses, and followed by all that were about them, run in disorder towards the bridges, or along the banks of the river, endeavouring to find a passage. Thus all the remaining artillery and *materiel* of every kind, fell into the hands of the enemy, who also, on that occasion made a great number of prisoners.

That portion of the army which, after having placed the Sambre between them and the Prussians, thought they could stop there, and who had established bivouacs in the orchards and the meadows, which lie on the right bank of that river broke up in all haste when informed of the approach of the enemy, by the extreme confusion which his appearance had excited. Without waiting for orders – without making any attempt to cut down the bridge, and without time to recover themselves, a disorderly flight is again renewed; every man sets off at the same time, and each takes his own measures without knowing what was to happen.

At a little distance from Charleroi, two different routes present themselves, one leads to Avesnes, and the other to Philipeville. Having had no instructions as to the route which they should take, and not seeing any of their chiefs, the army divides into two divisions; the most numerous body follows the route which they had taken in advancing, and direct marches towards Avesnes; the other keeps to the left and marches upon Philipeville. A great number of individuals detached themselves from the rest, without any other object than to avoid the pursuit of the cavalry, throwing themselves into the great surrounding woods; thus the army dispersed themselves more and more every step, and almost totally disappeared.

It was by this last mentioned route that Buonaparte had chosen to make his retreat. Deserting from his army once more, he abandoned it without making any effort to rally it, in the midst of dangers, which it seemed to please him to aggravate still more, by giving it up to anarchy and total dissolution. Thousands of soldiers, in scattered parties, wandering as chance might direct, and issuing from the woods, spread themselves over the country, carrying alarm wherever they go. The wretched inhabitants are struck with astonishment at hearing, almost at the same moment of the success, the irreparable defeat of the French army, and at finding themselves a prey to an enemy, whom a victory, purchased with their blood, must have rendered more cruel, at the very moment when they were rejoicing at finding the theatre of war removed at a distance from them. All the strong places immediately shut their gates; and repel by force the fugitives that endeavoured to enter, oblige them to fall back upon the adjoining communes, where they practised all kinds of excesses.

It was under this description of a fugitive, and in the midst of a terror-struck multitude of them, that Buonaparte, confounded with dismay, and less assured than any of those who accompanied him, came to demand, in a suppliant manner, an entrance into Philipeville: he stood in need of the protection of the ramparts of that town to conceal him from the active pursuit of the Prussians, who were following close upon his heels, with the utmost vigilance, and who had already sent off, in that direction, numerous parties, into which he was apprehensive of falling. When arrived at the city gates, he had to bear the humiliation of seeing himself interrogated by a guard, before whom he declared his Imperial dignity, and who did not suffer him to pass till that was recognised by the Governor, who was called upon to ascertain his identity. He himself then entered, with some persons constituting a more humble suite, and the barriers were forthwith closed.

A short time after an order was given to disperse the crowds of soldiers which every moment were increasing about and before the entrances to the town. The report having spread among them that their illustrious Emperor was at length found, and that he was in that place, they esteemed it their duty to establish their camp about his person, and besides, reckoned it as certain, for the means of protecting him, that the fortress would be at length opened for them. But the prudence of Buonaparte was here discernible. He judged that such a collection of soldiers might attract the enemy to that point, and cause his place of refuge to be discovered, consequently he sent them an order to continue their route; but as he had, like a General, profoundly analyzed the means of acting upon the *moral* of his troops after a defeat, in order to insure the full and prompt execution of his orders, he made use of a little stratagem, the success of which was infallible. Some emissaries proceeding from the town ran towards the camp in a great fright, crying: – 'Ho! Save your lives, here are the Cossacks! Quick, quick! The Cossacks! The Cossacks!' We may readily imagine that nothing more was necessary, and that everything disappeared in an instant.

Wellington's despatches during the pursuit were quoted in whole or in part in most of the British provincial newspapers such as in the *Cambridge Chronicle and Journal* of Friday, 7 July 1815. This account appeared under the announcement, 'Dispatches, of which the following are extracts, have been this day [29 June 1815, Downing Street] received by Earl Bathurst, from Field Marshal his Grace the Duke of Wellington':

We have continued in march on the left of the Sambre since I wrote to you. Marshal Blucher crossed that river on the 19th, in pursuit of the enemy, and both armies entered the French territories yesterday; the Prussians by Beaumont, and the Allied Army under my command, by Bavay. – The remains of the French army have retired upon Laon. All accounts agree in stating, that it is in a very wretched state, and that, in addition to its losses in battle and in prisoners, it is losing vast numbers of men by desertion.

The soldiers quit their regiments in parties, and return to their homes; those of the cavalry and artillery selling their horses to the people of the country. The 3d corps, which in my dispatch of the 19th I informed your Lordship had been detached to observe the Prussian army, remained in the neighbourhood of Wavre, till the 20th – it then made good its retreat by Namur and Dinant. This corps is the only one remaining entire. – I am not yet able to transmit your Lordship returns of the killed and wounded in the army in the late actions. It gives me the greatest satisfaction to inform you, that Colonel Delancey is not dead; he is badly wounded, but his recovery is not doubted, and I hope will be early.

Colonel De Lancey did not in fact recover. For his part, Ensign Wheatley, who had been captured at La Haye Sainte, was forced to march with the retreating French army:

The roads and ditches were crammed with groaning wounded, and really I felt for them as if they were English for military hatred is never felt for the helpless but against the daring and the Capable ... we entered Genappe where the day before I was free as air, carrying terror and dismay among beef carts and biscuit wagons [but now] a poor, cast down captive, exposed to the insults and bravado of thousands of intoxicated, insolent enemies.

I entered the town alongside a foot soldier on horseback, his right leg [so] shattered at the knee that his leg hung down by one single piece of sinew, and my stomach sickened as it dangled backwards and forwards splashing his horse with gore and marrow. The fellow pale and aghast, chewing dry biscuit to allay his scorching thirst. '*Voila, un français!*' said an officer to me, pointing at him as I passed, proud of the fellow's fortitude, not envious of his situation.[4]

A Prussian officer called Julius was also a prisoner of the French. He described the state of the French troops on 19 June:

The things I witnessed exceeded anything I had expected, and were beyond belief. Had I not actually seen it all, I should have considered it impossible for a disciplined army – an army such as the French was – to melt away to such an extent. Not only the main road [from Beaumont] as far as one could see in either direction, but also every side road and footpath was covered with soldiers of every rank, of every arm of the service, in the most complete and utter confusion. Generals, officers, wounded men – and these included some who had just had limbs amputated: everybody walked or rode in disorder. The entire army had disintegrated.

There was no longer anyone to give orders, or anyone to obey. Each man appeared bent on nothing but saving his own skin. Like a turbulent forest stream this chaotic mass surged around the waggon in which I was sitting with several companions in misfortune. Jostled by the crowd, hampered by the bottomless lane, this waggon could hardly be dragged forward ...

Very occasionally someone would shout to us: '*Sauvez-vous!* We are lost! Thank God we shall have peace at long last! We shall be going home!' Several times the cry came up from the rear: 'He's coming! The enemy's coming! *Sauve qui peut!*' and then everyone ran in desperate haste. Some threw down their weapons, others their knapsacks, and they took refuge in the corn or behind hedges until the reassuring shout of 'No, no, it's all right! They're our own men!' calmed down the panic.

A single cavalry regiment could have taken many thousands of prisoners here, because there was no question of offering resistance or of sticking together.[5]

Another involved in the retreat was Captain Coignet who was baggage-master-general at Napoleon's headquarters:

> We had the greatest difficulty in getting away. We could not make way through the panic-stricken multitude, and it was still worse when we arrived at Jemmapes. The Emperor tried to re-establish some kind of order among the retreating troops, but his efforts were in vain. Men of all units from every corps struggled and fought their way along the streets of the little town, with no-one in command of them, panic-stricken, flying before the Prussian cavalry, which hurrah'd continually in rear of them. The one thought uppermost in the minds of all was to get across the little bridge which had been thrown over the Dyle. Nothing could stand in the way of them.[6]

Even though the French had been defeated at Waterloo, the result of the campaign against Napoleon remained uncertain for many days and any snippet of information found its way into the newspapers, such as this brief note which was published in the *Chester Chronicle* on Friday, 7 July:

> A letter from an Officer of the Guards, in the advanced division, dated the 20th, states, that on the 19th, while in progress of following up the victory of the 18th, they were attacked by a party of the French, issuing from a wood, with great fury, and that the assailants were received with great firmness and repulsed with considerable loss.
>
> The chief loss of our cavalry arose from the different mode of arming them from the enemy. The cuirassiers, whose bodies are protected by armour, and the lancers, whose arms are much more powerful than the sabre, possessed from these circumstances great advantage.

Before the Allies could advance into France and complete their victory, they had to contend with the triple chain of border fortresses. The ones blocking Wellington's line of advance were at Valenciennes, Cambrai and Peronne.

Sir Charles Colville, with the 4th Division, was given the task of dealing with Cambrai. The place was summoned to surrender but this was rejected. Colville responded by bombarding the fortress but as he possessed only field artillery, this had little effect. Colville, therefore, decided to assault the place on the night of 24 June. William Wheeler of the 51st later recalled the attack:

> We had collected what ladders and ropes we could find in the farm houses, then we began splicing to enable us to scale the walls if

238

necessary. A flag of truce was sent to the Town but they were fired at, which caused them to return, and a ball had passed through the trumpeter's cap. We were now ready for storming and were only waiting the order to advance. In a short time our field pieces opened when a shell. I believe the first thrown from the howitzer, set a large building on fire. We now pushed on to the works near the gate, got into the trenches, fixed our ladders and were soon in possession of the top of the wall. The opposition was trifling, the regular soldiers fled to the citadel, and the shop-keepers to their shops.[7]

Wellington sent the following despatch from Joncourt the day after the assault:

FINDING that the garrison of Cambray was not very strong, and that the place was not very well supplied with what was wanting for its defence, I sent Lieutenant-General Sir Charles Colville there, on the day before yesterday, with one brigade of the 4th division, and Sir C. Grant's brigade of cavalry; and upon his report of the strength of the place, I sent the whole division yesterday morning.

I have now the satisfaction of reporting that Sir Charles Colville took the town by Escalade yesterday evening, with trifling loss, and from the communications which he has since had with the Governor of the citadel, I have every reason to hope that that post will have been surrendered to a Governor sent there by the King of France, to take possession of it, in the course of this day.

St Quentin has been abandoned by the enemy, and is in possession of Marshal Prince Blucher, and the castle of Guise surrendered last night.

All accounts concur in stating, that it is impossible for the enemy to collect an army to make head against us.

It appears that the French corps which was opposed to the Prussians on the 18th instant, and had been at Wavre, suffered considerably in its retreat, and lost some of its cannon.[8]

The Prussians had a far more difficult task ahead, with the fortresses of Maubeuge, Landrecies, Mariembourg, Philippeville, Rocroi, Givet and Mézières all to be tackled. For the siege of Maubeuge, the most formidable of these fortresses, the British siege train, of thirty-eight heavy guns was brought up from Mons and a regular siege was undertaken. After a punishing bombardment, the place surrendered on the evening of 11 July.[9]

The following two vignettes relating to Waterloo were subsequently published in the *Chester Chronicle* of Friday, 7 July 1815:

After the battle of the 16th, the French, with their usual insolence and barbarity, cut off the ears of a number of Prussian soldiers, and sent them in this mutilated state to Prince Blucher's head-quarters. It is to be hoped that the pursuing Prussian army will take most ample vengeance on those inhuman scoundrels.

Evidently the Prussians did take their revenge:

The war, it is mentioned, had taken a most savage character between the French and Prussians from the very beginning. Before the opening of the campaign, the 1st and 2d corps of the rebels had confederated and hoisted the *black* flag. They openly avowed, that they would give no quarter to the Prussians, and in general they kept their word. The Prussian loss, in all the affairs together, is calculated at near 20,000 men. The Prussians, however, most amply revenged themselves on the flying French, whom they butchered without mercy; and as the cavalry of Bulow's corps were numerous, fresh, and unbroken, they did incredible execution.

Such reprisals by the Prussians were also witnessed by James Gibney of the 15th Hussars:

These gentlemen literally ransacked many houses, and we coming after them as we did, were uncommonly bad off. They were like a swarm of locusts, making all barren around them. Indeed, for miles around they seem to have wantonly destroyed all they could lay their hands on. If revenge for the French occupation of Berlin a short time previously was their object, they certainly obtained it.[10]

Revenge was certainly a factor in the way the Prussians treated the French, as was explained to Sergeant Wheeler:

You English know nothing of the sufferings of war as we do. England has never been overrun by French Armies as our country has, or you would act as we do. The French acted a cruel part in Prussia, destroyed our houses violated our Mothers, our wives, our daughters, and sisters, and murdered them afterwards, they taught us a lesson we are now come to France to put into practice.[11]

Such sights may have shocked the British troops, but they themselves were not blameless and took advantage of the situation that presented itself. Private Farmer of the 11th Light Dragoons wrote:

240

As the foolish people had left all their effects behind them, we saw no reason why we should not ... appropriate them to our own use. The consequence was that our meals were not only abundant but sumptuous: – fowls, geese, turkeys, ducks, pigs, rabbits, and flour and garden-stuff in abundance, furnished forth, with wine and beer, our daily tables.[12]

Napoleon, meanwhile, had seen that there was little he could accomplish by remaining with his disorganised army and, leaving Soult to try and re-establish some kind of control, the Emperor rushed on to Paris, appreciating that his presence there was necessary to maintain public order. He reached the capital on 21 June. 'All is not lost,' he wrote to his brother Joseph. 'There is still time to retrieve the situation.'[13] That remained to be seen.

18

The March on Paris

Napoleon had lost a battle, but he did not accept that he had lost the war or the support of his people. In a letter to Joseph on 19 June, he set out his defensive plans:

> I suppose that, when I reassemble my forces, I shall have 150,000 men. The *fédérés* and National Guards (such of them as are fit to fight) will provide 100,000 men, and the regimental depots a further 50,000. Thus I shall have 300,000 soldiers ready immediately to bring against the enemy. I shall use carriage horses to drag the guns; raise 100,000 men by conscription; arm them with muskets taken from Royalists and from National Guards unfit for service; organise a mass levy in Dauphiné , the district of Lyons, Burgundy, Lorraine, Champagne; and overwhelm the enemy ... I have heard nothing of Grouchy. If he has not been captured, as I rather fear, that will give me 50,000 men within three days – plenty to keep the enemy occupied, as to allow time for Paris and France to do their duty. The Austrians are slow marchers; the Prussians fear the peasantry and dare not advance too far. There is still time to retrieve the situation.[1]

It was evident that Napoleon was determined to fight on and, as can be seen, if given time to recover, might well raise a very considerable force. Wellington, therefore, had no choice but to join the Prussians in invading France and defeating Napoleon before he could put his plans into place. The following proclamation was issued from Wellington's headquarters at Malplaquet on 21 June 1815:

> I announce to the French, that I enter their territory at the head of an army already victorious, not as an enemy (except of the usurper, the enemy of the human race, with whom there can be neither peace nor truce), but to aid them to shake off the iron yoke by which they are

oppressed. I therefore give to my army the subjoined orders, and I desire that every one who violates them may be made known to me.

The French know, however, that I have a right to require, that they conduct themselves in such a manner that I may be able to protect them against those who seek to do them evil.

They must, then, furnish the requisitions that will be made them by persons authorised to make them, taking receipts in due form and order; that they remain quietly at their homes, and have no correspondence or communication with the Usurper, or with his adherents.

All those who shall absent themselves from their homes, after the entrance of the army into France, and all those who shall be absent in the service of the Usurper, shall be considered as enemies and his adherents, and their property shall be appropriated to the subsistence of the army.

Alongside the above announcement was an Order of the Day which was issued by Wellington's Acting Adjutant-General, J. Waters, on 20 June, extracts from which are as follows:

As the army is going to enter the French territory, the troops of different nations now under the command of Field-Marshal the Duke of Wellington are desired to remember, that their respective Sovereigns are the allies of his Majesty the King of France, and that France must therefore be considered as a friendly country.

It is ordered, that nothing be taken either by the officers or soldiers without payment.

The Commissaries of the army will provide for the wants of the troops in the usual manner, and it is not permitted to the officers and soldiers of the army to make requisitions.

The Commissaries will be authorised by the Field Marshal, or by the Generals who command the troops of the respective nations (that is to say, in case their provisions are not regulated by an English Commissary) to make the necessary requisitions, for which they shall give regular receipts, and they must perfectly understand that they will be responsible for all that they receive by requisitions, from the inhabitants of France, in the same manner as if they made purchases for the account of their Government in their own country.

The fortress of Sedan was bombarded into surrender by *Generalleutenant* von Engelhardt with the North German Federal Army Corps on 27 June, whilst the fortress of Mézières was besieged the following day. Charleville was stormed on 29 June by Engelhardt's men. Reims and

Mohon were occupied, leaving only two small fortresses on the border, those at Montmédy, still to be taken.

The follwing information was printed in the *Hague Currant* of 28 June. It is interesting to read at the end of this item, that two of Napoleon's former marshals were now turning against him:

> The advanced posts of the Allies are near Compeigne. General Ziethen, commanding the 1st corps of Prince Blucher's army, received in writing an invitation from the French General Morand, to put an end to hostilities, 'because Napoleon, the only pretext for them, sacrificing himself a second time for the happiness of France, had abdicated the throne'.
>
> This letter, far from stopping the progress, did not even receive an answer.
>
> Bonaparte's abdication in favour of his son, or his stepson, or the Duke of Orleans, having been rejected by the Peers, the Provisional Government, Cambaceres, Fouche, and Carnot, was formed; from this Bonaparte seemed to find protection against the popular spirit at Paris, as well as [*illegible*] the declaration of one of the Chambers, that he was [*illegible*] of the law.
>
> The substance of these accounts is confirmed by Colonel O[u]dinot, who arrived on the 26th at Bergen, in Hainault, in order to offer to his Majesty the King of France, the services of his father the Duke of Reggio, and those of the Duke of Taranto (Macdonald).[2]

Though the army under Wellington had received strict orders concerning their conduct whilst in France, the Prussians, it would appear, had no such inhibitions, as Gronow, of the 1st Guards, observed:

> We perceived, on entering France, that our allies the Prussians had committed fearful atrocities on the defenceless inhabitants of the villages and farms which lay in their line of march ... Whenever we arrived at towns or villages through which the Prussians had passed, we found that every article of furniture in the houses had been destroyed in the most wanton manner: looking glasses, mahogany bedsteads, pictures, beds and mattresses, had been hacked, cut, half-burned, and scattered about in every direction; and, on the slightest remonstrance of the wretched inhabitants, they were beaten in a most shameful manner, and sometimes shot.[3]

There was a reason for this difference in discipline between the Prussians and the British which was explained to Wellington by Müffling:

On the march to Paris, the Prussian army made longer marches than the English; and when in the morning [of the 20th] I made my daily communications to the Duke, I took the liberty of respectfully calling his attention to this, and suggesting that it would be better if he kept the same pace as his ally. He was silent at first, but on my urging him again to move more rapidly, he said to me: 'Do not press me on this point, for I tell you, it won't do. If you were better acquainted with the English army, its composition and habits, you would say the same. I cannot separate from my tents and supplies. My troops must be well kept and well supplied in camp, if order and discipline are to be maintained. It is better that I should arrive two days later in Paris than discipline should be relaxed.'[4]

There were, though, acts of ill-discipline amongst the British troops, sometimes with fatal consequences. Private Wheeler wrote the following concerning an incident at Cambrai:

A Ser[geant] Corporal and four men fell in with a barrel of gunpowder. They being drunk took it for brandy and [the] Corporal ... fired into it, as he said to make a bung hole, while the others were waiting with their tin canteens to catch the supposed liquor, but it blew up and all the [would be] brandy merchants were dreadfully mutilated ... so dreadfully scorched as it is feared that four cannot recover, and the other two will not be fit for service again.[5]

Blücher had reached Compiègne by 27 June 1815. From there he found a moment to write a letter to his wife:

Here I sit in a room where Marie-Louise [Napoleon's second wife] celebrated her wedding night. Nothing could be more beautiful, more agreeable than Compiègne. The only pity is that I have to leave again early tomorrow, as I must reach Paris in three days. It is possible and highly likely that Bonaparte will be handed over to me and to Lord Wellington. I shall probably not be able to do better than to have him shot, which would be a service to mankind. In Paris everyone has deserted him and he is hated and scorned.[6]

Like many publications throughout the land, the *Hampshire Chronicle* of Monday, 3 July 1815 summarised Wellington's latest despatch:

Dispatches from the Duke of Wellington, brought by Mr. Cline, the Messenger, were received last evening. They are dated, the 27th, from

Joucourt, at which place his Grace's head-quarters remained since the 25th. This pause is not attributed to any obstruction which he had met with, but to a desire to await the co-operation of the Austrians and Russians. It appears from the German Papers, that they are crossing the Rhine in great force. The French fortresses, on the Flemish frontier, had been summoned, in the name of the King of France, and the speedy surrender of several of them was expected.

In the Brussels Papers is inserted a Proclamation to the people of France by Prince Schwartzenburgh – The expectation of the entrance of the Duke of Wellington into Paris to-day was general in the Netherlands. The inhabitants of Lisle are said to have risen in favour of Louis XVIII; and throughout the department of the North the white cockade is general.

All the Newspapers in Paris are stopped printing for the present; those of Tuesday were the last printed; and the Exchange has risen 5 per cent. in favour of England since the last accounts.

A Royalist Officer employed in conducting the correspondence between Jersey and Brittany, has brought official intelligence of Rennes being in the possession of the Royalists and that several small towns of that province have hoisted the white flag. By the same Officer a confirmation had been received of the taking of General Travot, and the rout of his army in La Vendée.

The same newspaper was able to make the following announcement, on the progress of the allied advance, a week later, on 7 July:

The Allied British and Prussian army continues its uninterrupted advance to Paris. On the 29th, the Duke of Wellington was at Orville, a village about 50 miles from Paris; and thence his Grace dates the dispatch, and accompanies it with the list of those brave men who have bled in the cause of European liberty and civilization. The British army that morning was between St. Just, on the Clermont road, and La Taube, on the road of Senlis.

It was to advance in the course of the day, and the head-quarters were expected to be fixed in the evening at Le Plessis Longeau, a country seat belonging to Madame Villette, the niece of Voltaire, situated near Pont St. Maxence, on the Oise. Marshal Blucher with the Prussians, was in advance of the English on the Senlis road; and it was calculated, that in the course of the day his light troops would reach St. Dennis, only 6 miles from Paris! At this point the Prussian army were to halt to await the coming of the Duke of Wellington, who was proceeding by forced marches from Compiegne. The junction

246

was expected to be formed on the 30th, in which case the triumphal entry into Paris would take place on Saturday last, the 1st of July.

The London Gazette was, and remains, the official government publication and Wellington's despatches were first revealed to the public in that paper. The following extract from Wellington's despatch, describing the advance upon Paris, was published in its pages on Friday, 7 July 1815:

> The enemy have fortified the heights of Montmartre and the town of St. Denis strongly; and by means of the little rivers Rouillon and la Vielle Mar, they have inundated the ground on the north side of that town, and water having been introduced into the canal de l'Ourcq, and the bank formed into a parapet and batteries, they have a strong position on this side of Paris.
>
> The heights of Belleville are likewise strongly fortified, but I am not aware that any defensive works have been thrown up on the left of the Seine.
>
> Having collected in Paris all the troops remaining after the battle of the 18th, and all the depôts of the whole army, it is supposed the enemy have there about 40 or 50,000 troops of the line and guards, besides the national guards, a new levy called Les Tirailleurs de la Garde, and the Federés.

It certainly appeared that Marshal Davout, the Minister of War and Governor of Paris, was going to fight to defend the French capital. With the troops that Grouchy had managed to extricate from Belgium, Davout had at least 90,000 men to oppose the combined weight of the Prussian and Anglo-Netherlands force which was approximately 120,000 strong.

John Cam Hobhouse, later Lord Broughton, was in Paris and he described the nervousness of the Parisians fearing a terrible battle in their streets:

> It was commonly reported early in the afternoon that a general action was on the point of being fought. The throng and the silence, and the eager looks of the multitudes in the gardens and boulevards, the groups collected round, and trailing after two or three straggling dragoons leading their wounded horses, or carrying orders to the headquarters ... the dead, unsocial solemnity of the heavy patrols parading the streets without music; the doors of the houses and courts all shut; the upper windows opened every now and then, and occupied by female faces, as the clattering horse of a gendarme announced the expectation of

247

intelligence – every appearance of anxiety and apprehension, unusual even since the commencement of the siege, was to be recognised at the first glance for an hour or two after it was known that the two armies were in presence. More than once crowds rushed towards the elevated spots of the gardens and squares at the exclamation of individuals who announced the opening cannonade.[7]

Davout was persuaded not to bring death and destruction to the beautiful boulevards of the capital and a convention was signed at St Cloud on 3 July by which the French army was to evacuate Paris within three days, prior to it being disbanded. The *Chester Courant* of 11 July 1815, stated:

After waiting during the whole week in anxious expectation of the arrival of Dispatches, we are this day most fortunately enabled to announce the receipt of official information of this most important event which may be considered as putting the seal to our late triumphs, and as bringing this afflicting war to a happy and unexpectedly speedy conclusion. We cannot but congratulate the country that this final triumph has been accomplished without any further loss on our part. The British troops have not been engaged since the 18th. A full proportion of their valuable blood was then contributed to the general cause. – The gallant Prussians too have bled freely; but we trust no more sacrifice of life will be necessary.

All the preparations made for the defence of Paris were found to be of no avail, from the plan of attack formed by the Allied Commanders. There was a considerable force in the place; but no works having been thrown up on the south side to stop the progress of the assailants, any attempt at resistance could have only tended to a wanton destruction of life and property, the odium of which must have fallen upon the Provisional Government, and the military faction which supports them. The policy, on the other hand, of allowing them to withdraw beyond the Loire, is obvious. As the Allies have uniformly disclaimed all intention of dictating a government to France, it was right that the Duke of Wellington and Marshal Blucher should not carry their pretensions beyond the attainment of an important military advantage, yielded up without any sacrifice on their part; leaving the claims of the Provisional Government, or of Napoleon II, to be decided between the French Plenipotentiaries and the Ministers of the Allied Sovereigns.

In the mean time, the possession of Paris will lead to an event rendering this question very easy of solution. Louis XVIII, will return to his capital amidst the acclamations of thousands of his subjects. He will re-assemble his Chamber of Peers and Deputies, and proceed to exercise all the functions of Government. He was universally recognized by the Powers of Europe; when absent from his territory, they did not retract that recognition. Will they, when they find him again seated on his Throne, refuse to acknowledge him, and espouse the claims of Napoleon II, or leave the question of the sovereignty of France for a time, in abeyance? It would be absurd to suppose that they will. We are persuaded that the ruling parties in France view the consequences of the surrender of Paris in the same light; and though they may put on 'a swashing and a martial outside' their genuine object is to make the best terms they can for their personal safety.

19

The Fall of Napoleon

After handing over control of the wreckage of *l'armée du Nord* to Soult and taking a brief rest, Napoleon spent the night of the 18th at Laon. He then pressed on to Paris, arriving at the Élysée Palace on 21 June. What subsequently occurred was reported in the *Norfolk Chronicle* of Saturday, 1 July 1815:

> Napoleon returned to Paris from the army on the 21st – on that day there were very tumultuous debates in the two Houses of Representatives on the necessity of Buonaparte's Abdication. On the 22d he sent in his Abdication in favour of his Son, and a Provisional Executive Government was appointed, consisting of Carnot, Fouche, Caulaincourt, Grenier, and Quinette, (a junta of Jacobins, Regicides, and Buonapartists.) – It was attempted in debate, by the Minister of the Interior (Carnot) to shew that Soult had rallied 60,000 men on the Northern Frontier; but this was denied by Marshal Ney, with great warmth, who asserted that 20,000 men was the utmost number that could be mustered, and that the Allies had passed the frontiers, and could be in Paris in six or seven days.

The document detailing Napoleon's abdication on 22 June 1815, was entitled 'Declaration to the French People':

> In the beginning the war to maintain our national independence, I was counting on the union of all our efforts, but since then the circumstances appear to have changed, and I offer to sacrifice myself to the hatred of the enemies of France … My political life is over and I proclaim my son, under the title of Napoleon II, Emperor of France.[1]

There was not the slightest chance of Napoleon's son being declared emperor, and this was immediately rejected. The story continued in the

Hampshire Telegraph of Monday, 14 August 1815, under the headline 'Conduct of Bonaparte After the Battle of Waterloo (Said to be written by himself)':

> The Emperor, though far from being convinced, came to a speedy decision: – 'The honour and glory of France have been the objects of my life,' said he; 'you know it; it shall not be said that my personal interests shall ever stand in the way of their accomplishment; may you succeed without me; I abdicate; may the Allies have been really sincere in their communication.' The Emperor was then at the Elysée. The acclamations of the public were heard round the Palace; as a simple citizen he wished to avoid them, and departed for Malmaison.
>
> Still they followed him. On the morning even of the same day on which he set out, troops, which were marching upon a high road, made the air resound with their favourite cries, and accompanied him to his retreat, at which he was much affected ...
>
> In the mean time the enemy approached rapidly, and arrived at the gates of the city – the cannon were heard.
>
> On the 29th, at the moment of ascending his carriage, Napoleon sent a confidential person to the Provisional Government with this message: – 'I know the position of the enemy, their advanced corps is not numerous. – There is only occasion to shew the moral force of our army, the hope of the soldiers would revive on seeing their old General. In abdicating the power, I have not renounced the glorious title of every citizen – that of defending his country. If it is required, I answer for beating the enemy, and inspiring the army with dispositions which shall procure you more favourable negociations. This object gained, I engage on my word to re-ascend my carriage, and to pursue the route to the place which I have chosen.'
>
> An answer was returned, that it was too late, and that negociations were already commenced.

Fouché, who was determined to be rid of Napoleon, suggested to the Emperor that, for his safety, he should leave the country. In fact Fouché was quite correct in warning Napoleon that his life was in danger, as Blücher announced that Napoleon was to be seized *dead or alive*!

Wellington, however, wanted nothing to do with arresting or killing Napoleon, as the Prussians did. Consequently General Gneisenau wrote to Müffling on 27 June:

> Bonaparte has been declared under outlawry by the Allied powers. The Duke of Wellington may possibly (from parliamentary

251

considerations) hesitate to fulfil the declaration of the Powers. Therefore Your Excellency will direct negotiations to the effect that Bonaparte may be surrendered to us, with a view to his execution.[2]

Napoleon needed to get out of France quickly and he seems to have favoured the United States for his place of exile. The Provisional Government asked Wellington for the necessary passport and two French frigates were made available for the voyage from Rochefort-sur-Loire. Napoleon and his party travelled down to that port, arriving there on 3 July.

Meanwhile, Louis XVIII returned to Paris and the Provisional Government was abolished. Nothing now stood in the way of the royalists, or the Allied Powers, from getting their hands on the erstwhile Emperor. In desperation Napoleon contacted the British Royal Navy commander at Rocheford, Captain Maitland of HMS *Bellerophon*, asking if his passports had arrived. They never would. The Allies had no intention of letting Napoleon live in either the UK or the USA. This was made clear by Lord Liverpool in a letter to Castlereagh on 15 July:

> I am desirous of apprising you of our sentiments respecting Bonaparte. If you should succeed in getting possession of his person, and the King of France does not feel sufficiently strong to bring him to justice as a rebel, we are ready to take upon ourselves the custody of his person, on the part of the Allied powers … We incline at present strongly to the opinion that the best place of custody would be at a distance from Europe. And that the Cape of Good Hope or St. Helena would be the proper stations for that purpose. [3]

Ships of the Royal Navy had blockaded Rochefort and, though Napoleon did try to arrange passage to the United States, there was no real possibility of him escaping. The next moves were reported, in a somewhat disjointed fashion, in the *Caledonian Mercury* on Monday, 24 July 1815. This account began with the introduction, 'Letters from Rochefort, dated the 12th, contain the following particulars, on the authenticity of which we have reason to rely':

> Since the beginning of the present month, eleven English ships have blockaded the port of Rochefort with such vigilance, as to render it difficult for the smallest vessel to escape. Napoleon, to satisfy himself as to the disposition of the English fleet, embarked on the 8th on board the Saale, one of the frigates which were to convey him to North America. Next day he sent General Bertrand in a boat to the English

Admiral to ask a free passage for his frigates; but the Admiral, so far from granting his request, declared that he would attack the moment they should attempt to leave the port. He added, however, that if Napoleon Bonaparte should be inclined to come on board his ship, he would receive him with every respect; that he would answer for his personal safety; that he would sail with him for England; and that he had no doubt but that the British Government would afterwards convey him (Napoleon) wherever he might intimate his desire to go.

Though this reply did not perfectly square with the projects of the Ex-Emperor, he immediately declared that he, above all things, preferred relying upon English honour; and that, besides, he would not risk the lives of the crews of the two frigates in endeavouring to effect a passage in spite of the vigilance of the cruizing squadron. Soon after, he embarked in a small flag of truce, and went on board the English Admiral. He has not since been seen to return. It is merely known that the ship was to sail on the 12th, and in fact we have lost sight of her since day-break.

The extensive entry in the *Caledonian Mercury* also contained this snaphot:

SURRENDER OF BONAPARTE. The political career of Bonaparte is at length closed. The following communication, containing the important intelligence of his surrender to Captain Maitland, of the *Bellerophon*, has been received from Lord Castlereagh, and has been published in an Extraordinary Gazette; to which various other particulars are added from the French papers.

There was also a translation of an extract from a letter written by the Maritime Prefect of Rochefort, a *Monsieur* Bonnefoux, to the French Minister of the Marine:

In execution of your Excellency's orders, I embarked in my boat, accompanied by Baron Ricard, Prefect of the Lower Charente. The reports from the Roads for the 14th had not then reached me, but I was informed by Captain Philibert, commanding the Amphitrite frigate, that Bonaparte had embarked on board the Epervier brig, as a flag of truce, determined to proceed to the English cruizing station.

Accordingly, at day-break, we saw him manoeuvring to make the English ship Bellerophon, commanded by Captain Maitland, who, on perceiving that Bonaparte was steering towards him, had hoisted the white flag at the mizzen.

Bonaparte, and the persons in his suite, were received on board the English ship. The officer whom I had left to make observations, communicated to me this important news, and General Becker, who arrived soon after, confirmed it.

Thus at last, under the protection of the white flag, and on board the English ship Bellerophon, has Bonaparte terminated the enterprise which he planned and executed.

Captain Frederick Maitland described the moment when Napoleon arrived on board HMS *Bellerophon*, an event which had been arranged for 06.00 hours. Maitland chose this early time for a reason:

On coming on board the *Bellerophon*, he was received without any of the honours generally paid to persons of high rank; the guard was drawn out on the break of the poop, but did not present arms. His Majesty's Government had merely given directions, in the event of him being captured, for his being removed into any one of His Majesty's ships that might fall in with him; but no instructions had been given as to the light in which he was to be viewed.

As it is not customary, however, on board a British ship of war, to pay any such honours before the colours are hoisted at eight o'clock in the morning, or after sunset, I made the early hour an excuse for withholding them upon this occasion.[4]

Maitland set sail for Britain on the 16th, as this newspaper report indicates:

Contrary winds or calms made the voyage long and tedious. They made Torbay only on the 25th, where *orders were found to have no communication with the land*. But all the boats of the country, on the news of Napoleon's arrival surrounded the ship. On the morrow the whole population of the country were there, without distinction of rank or sex.

Napoleon, who was principally occupied in reading, in conversation at intervals with some of his suite, and taking a walk regularly several times a day upon the poop, looked at all these curious people with the same countenance he would have done from the windows of the Tuileries. One of the ship's officers inquired if he was not indignant at beholding such a multitude of gazers around him, and, without waiting for an answer added, but, indeed, if he was, he might thank himself for it, since he had made himself so great and celebrated.

He had the English Papers to read to him, which caricatured, in the most ridiculous manner, his coming on board, the reception he had met with, and the conversation he had entered into. Some English Officers, reprobating all these follies as insults to him – 'The multitude,' said he, 'only judge from such *Blue Beard* tales – grave historians, who write for posterity, characterise men solely by their actions, and I leave my defence to them.'

On the third day they were ordered round to Plymouth – there the ship seemed condemned to a more rigorous captivity.[5]

By the time HMS *Bellerophon* had reached Plymouth, news of Napoleon's arrival in the UK had spread and thousands descended upon Devonport amid unprecedented scenes:

On Thursday and Friday last the curiosity of immense numbers of persons in Plymouth Sound was gratified by the most ample view of Buonaparte. On the last-mentioned day there were, at four *p.m.* upwards of 1000 boats in the Sound. The scene at this time beggared all description. The guard boats, strongly manned, dashed through the water, running against every boat that happened to be too near. The centinels of the Bellerophon, and of the guard frigates, the Eurotas and Liffy, were every moment presenting their pieces to intimidate the curious multitude. At last a movement was observed on board the Bellerophon – the seamen were seen pressing to the forecastle, the booms became covered, and with unsatisfactory curiosity, they pressed so closely on the centinels, that they were obliged to clear the gangways.

The marines were now also noticed on the poop, and the officers and seamen, by a simultaneous movement, uncovered, without orders, so completely had he ingratiated himself with all hearts. A moment after, to gratify the people in the boats, as well as to view the sublime spectacle before him, the object of boundless curiosity advanced to the starboard gangway: the mass of boats endeavoured to precipitate themselves on the ship – the guard boats dashed furiously through the water – some boats were struck, persons overturned into the sea – the centinels presented their pieces, all in vain, the force was overwhelming – screams and curses were alternately heard – the next moment all was calm – 'the Emperor' was bowing to the multitude – he stood before them six or seven minutes, and retired for a short time.

In this manner was the time spent during the whole of Friday, till eight in the evening. Buonaparte certainly is endeavouring to gratify the spectators as much as possible, and he will have enough to do, for the country is precipitating itself into Plymouth Dock. – Boats are arriving every moment from the ports in Devonshire, Cornwall, and even from Dorsetshire. The people in the large pleasure-boats, however, have but a small chance of seeing him, as the mass of small boats prevent access to the ship. Saturday was a very unfavourable day as it rained hard. Hitherto none have boarded the ship but Lord Keith and Mr. Penn, the Pilot, of Cawsand. The time when Buonaparte is most seen is from three o'clock until eight P.M. The boats got near enough to view his features distinctly, and even to hear him speak.[6]

The British press was eager to publish any little piece of information they could about Napoleon, as exemplified by this note in the *Hull Packet* of Tuesday, 22 August 1815:

Some of Buonaparte's linen, sent ashore to be washed, has been held in such esteem, that many individuals at Plymouth have temporarily put on one of his shirts, waistcoats, or neckcloths, merely for the purpose of saying that they had worn his clothes!

The Parisian newspaper *La Quotidienne* was clearly behind the restoration of Louis and glad to see the back of Napoleon:

The last remaining subject of disquiet for Europe has just disappeared: Buonaparte is held prisoner. The man who banished peace and tranquillity from the world for so many years has finally been condemned to perpetual rest. That same energy which upset and ravaged the universe is now enchained forever.[7]

It had been indicated to Napoleon that he was to be exiled at St Helena in the South Atlantic, the prospect of which appalled him and he submitted frequent appeals to be allowed to live freely in Britain:

I would rather die than go to St. Helena, or be confined in some fortress. I desire to live in England, a free man, protected by and subject to its laws, and bound by any promises or arrangements which may be desirable …[8]

It was not to be. Napoleon would never be allowed to remain anywhere in or near Europe. This was revealed in the *Bury and Norwich Post* of 2 August 1815:

On Sunday morning Sir Henry Bunbury, Under Secretary of State for the War Department, set off for Plymouth to communicate to Bonaparte the resolution of the Cabinet, in concurrence with their Allies, as to his future fate. He is accompanied by the son of Earl Bathurst, and Mr. Guy, the King's Messenger. It is believed that all the property which he may have on board the Bellerophon will be strictly taken an account of, and such things only as may be necessary to his comfort in the Island of St. Helena be put on board the Northumberland. Some servants will only be permitted to accompany him. Sir H. Lowe will succeed Col. Mark Wilks, as Governor of the Island; and it is said that a residence, with a plot of 25 acres, will be allotted near the Governor's house on the high lands for this extraordinary man, to whom the Empire of the West, as he said himself, was too circumscribed.

It would be on St Helena where the great man would spend his final years. His departure on HMS *Northumberland* brought to an end the era that will forever bear his name. Watching him transfer to *Northumberland* was Lady Charlotte Fitzgerald, a daughter of the 1st Earl of Moira:

Napoleon was received on board the *Northumberland* only as a lieut.-general! He touched his hat to the sentry as he passed the gangway, he desired Lord Keith to introduce the officers of the *N.* to him, and if he felt his situation concealed it. You will be curious to know if I think he has abandoned hope. Oh no, I never saw a man look less hopeless – so far from it he gave the impression of planning his future vengeance on his enemies – others may suppose his career finished but I am sure he does not – he appears most to resemble a bust of marble or bronze as *cold* and as *fixed*, he seems quite inaccessible to human tenderness or human distress – still he is wonderful!

20

The Occupation of Paris

Much of France was taken over by the victorious armies which included troops from most of the fifteen countries that had formed the Seventh Coalition against Napoleon. This 'extract of a Dispatch from Lieutenant Colonel Leake to Viscount Castlereagh, dated Pontarlier, July 12', was published in the *Cambridge Chronicle and Journal* on Friday, 28 July 1815:

> I profit of the opportunity to inform your Lordship that the Swiss forces, now amounting to twenty-one thousand, and daily increasing, still occupy the position from Morteau to Pontarlier, with light corps, advanced on the right and left towards St. Hypolite and Salins. The head-quarters are still at Neuchatel.
>
> An aid du champ, sent here from Marshal Jourdan, at Besancon, announced yesterday the submission of the garrison of that place to the King's orders, and requested, in consequence, a suspension of arms on the part of the Swiss army. General de Castela, Chief of the Swiss Staff, who is now here, gives me to understand that the request will be granted, upon condition that a corps of the enemy, now at Salins, shall be removed, in order to allow the Swiss troops to move forward.
>
> The Gazette also contains a dispatch from Mr. Fielding, attached to the head quarters of the Piedmontese Contingent, stating that the positions of Aiguebelle, Conflans and l'Hopital, have been taken from the French. In consequence of the abdication of Bonaparte, an armistice was soon after proposed by the French and accepted by General Trink, an Austrian General.

The armistice meant the cessation of hostilities, but there was still considerable uncertainty as to how the Parisians would react and in particular the armed forces in and around the capital which had shown such support for Napoleon and contempt for King Louis. However, it would seem from the following private correspondence in the *Caledonian Mercury* of Saturday, 22 July 1815, that the French people had accepted defeat:

> Major Barlow, the brother of the late governor of Madras of that name, arrived in town this morning from the head quarters of the British army at Paris. Through this channel of information we learn, that all the stories that have been so industriously circulated, of commotions at the French capital, are unfounded, and that the city is in a state of perfect repose. The contributions exacted were the only circumstance that seemed at all to have awakened the sensibility of the Parisians, but the burthens were not to be imposed on Paris alone, and were already extended through the reach of forty miles to the neighbouring country. It is also presumed that the same expedient will be adopted for the subsistence and pay of the allies occupying France, and military governors are to be appointed in several of the eastern provinces, to remove any obstacle from the paternal feelings of the Sovereign to the execution of such a purpose.
>
> The British army in the immediate vicinity of Paris, and composed exclusively of native troops, is to consist of 20,000 men, and other detachments are to be stationed permanently in several of the fortresses. The total number now under orders for embarkation, or in progress on the voyage to France, are 12,000, the greater portion of which were in the Downs this morning when Major Barlow landed.

After the initial acceptance, or resignation to the fact, of occupation in Paris and the departure of Napoleon, the mood soon changed:

> The Paris papers received in the course of the week, as well as private letters, continue to describe France and its capital as in the highest state of discontent and anarchy, produced, no doubt, by the evils naturally attendant on such an immense military force of the Allies being burthened on the country; the intrigues of the partisans inimical to the Bourbons; and the apparent irresolution and want of firmness exhibited in all the measures of the Government.[1]

The British, at least, made every effort to curb pillaging amongst the occupying forces. Edward Costello of the 95th Rifles, was assigned to the Provost Guard responsible for keeping order in and around the French capital:

259

We were under the command of the Provost Marshal, named Stanway, whose instructions were to take all whom he found marauding about the gardens in the neighbourhood of Paris, and to march them down to his guard-house for punishment.

The Provost was a keen fellow, and sometimes would pounce on as many as eighteen or twenty in the course of a morning; these were immediately flogged, according to the amount of their offence, or the resistance they made, and instantly liberated.

The depredations, however, became so universal that the inhabitants of Paris complained to the generals of divisions, and we, in consequence, received orders to keep a stricter look-out, and take into custody and flog every man we caught in the act of plunder ...

We had a deal of trouble with the Belgians especially. These fellows would go forth in sections, and lay everything waste before them. This was not for want, as they were well supplied with regular rations from Paris ...

One morning we brought in sixteen of them, and the Provost as usual, marched them into the little yard where the punishments were generally inflicted. The triangles [upon which they would be tied whilst being flogged] stared them in the face from the centre of the ground, and the culprits one and all, as soon as they rolled their eyes on it, gave a bellow of horror, fell on their knees, and commenced praying and crossing themselves, and other symptoms of repentance; but Stanway was inexorable.

Our men had the greatest difficulty in unbreeching them, and getting them tied to the halberds. The first stripped, I recollect, was a short, stumpy, fat, desperate looking fellow ... The first whistle of the cat, even before it reached him, appeared to have verified the assumption, for he roared to such a degree, and his fellow culprits sympathised so loudly, and with such a crash of Belgic, that it set the whole vicinity by the ears, and actually aroused their whole regiment quartered in the village, and the place became an uproar. The Belgians flew to arms and instantly surrounded the guard-house; Stanway nevertheless was determined not to relax his duty, and ordered every man of us to load, and placed us in different parts of the building, barricading the doorways, prepared for every resistance, and during intervals, continued the flagellation.[2]

Though such efforts were made to prevent looting, the Allied generals evidently had little regard for Parisian sensitivities, as they were only too pleased to arrange displays of their military might, in numerous victory parades. One such, called a 'Grand Review', took place in Paris and was reported on by the *Chester Chronicle* of Friday, 18 August 1815:

Some very interesting particulars of the Grand Review which took place at Paris, of the British and other troops, under the command of the Duke of Wellington, have been published. – A British army reviewed at PARIS! only let us fancy to ourselves a French victorious army reviewed in HYDE PARK, and our sensibility as to the disgrace of such a catastrophe, will make us feel the value of the triumph we have gained.

At about ten o'clock in the morning, the Duke came, in full uniform, with all his stars, ribbons, &c. having the Emperor of Russia on his right, and the Emperor of Austria on his left, followed by an immense retinue; they passed the whole grand line amidst a cloud of dust, that absolutely obscured the Sun, and took their post of salute in the Place de Louis XVth, on the spot where Louis the XVIth was murdered – a crime that has led to the infinite misery and humiliation of the French nation.

The cavalry and artillery are said to have *darted up* to from half squadrons near the point of salute, in a style which confounded the poor Parisians, and made the ground quake beneath their feet! Their appearance was most admirable. The columns of British infantry moved on with a beautiful solidity, their caps ornamented with oak, laurel, &c.

As a Fit of military exultation, after their dangers and labours, they marched past the saluting point to the air of the '*Downfall of Paris*'. This all the bands had before played when marching through St. Denis. The Duke feeling with that delicacy which he was often envinced, sent an Aid-de-Camp to say, that he was hurt at the circumstances; the next regiment therefore discounted the air in question, but in the true humour of soldiers, struck up '*Nong tong paw*,' the first lines of which song are apposite enough-

'John Bull for pastime took a prance,

'Some time ago, to peep at France!'

The Nassau troops, it is said, were so beautifully equipped, that they appeared soldiers rather for the stage than the field; the British were a striking and admired contrast. They had nothing for shew, but in the essential equipment of soldiers were more perfect than any of the others. All they had that was USEFUL, bore signs that it had been USED, and their tattered colours on their broken poles flew in the faces of the French, to shew that they had fought their way to the spot of their triumph, and had well carved a right to exult. The greatest contrast of all, in the eyes of the Parisians, was between the Belgians and the Highlanders, the latter immediately followed the former.

The Belgians had neither the appearance nor the discipline of soldiers – the division of Guards and Scotch, that trod on their heels, was the most perfect specimen of a serious, practised, well trained, body of brave men, representing at once the strength and virtues of their grateful and exalted country. All the French spectators were anxious to see them, and were delighted with them when they came; but the Belgians had been greeted with a profusion of *sacres, diables, abominations!* One does not know how they deserved this. Our artillery and cavalry were beyond all comparison superior to those of other nations. The Review was directed to the Emperor of Russia, who received and returned the salutes.

This was far from being the only review, as a similar event took place on 22 September, as described in the *Hereford Journal* of Wednesday, 4 October 1815:

Extract of a private letter, dated Paris, Sept. 23. – 'The whole of the English army, including the continental troops in British pay, were reviewed yesterday in the extensive plain between Paris and St. Denis; the troops began to move at seven in the morning: at first they formed one vast line, the Duke of Wellington, with the Emperors of Russia and Austria, the King of Prussia, Prince Schwartzenberg, the Archduke Constantine, and several other Austrian, Russian, and Prussian Princes, rode with great rapidity along this line; they suddenly halted about the centre, and almost instantly the whole was formed into separate columns, moving in different lines towards a point at a considerable distance in front, where they again formed a line of close column, and in that form passed in review before his Grace and the Allied Sovereigns.

The appearance of the troops was greatly admired; they performed various evolutions with wonderful rapidity and precision. They moved in precisely the same order as at the battle of Waterloo, in close columns; in this form the British troops are found absolutely impenetrable. The number of cavalry was very small, only a regiment of the guards and some German horse. The colours of almost every regiment were quite tattered, from the shots that passed through them during the campaigns of the Peninsula and France.

The dress of the Duke of Wellington was remarkably plain, a scarlet coat without epaulets, and a cocked hat without a feather, he did not even wear a sash; he was, however, decorated with several stars and crosses. The Emperor of Russia was on his right during a great part of the day; he appeared to make observations upon several regiments as they passed. The King of Prussia went over the field with his nephew and his two sons, on foot, for several hours, and conversed with several French ladies whom they met, and by whom they probably were not recognised, from the plainness of their dress. Lord Stewart rode with the Emperor of Austria and Prince Schwartzenberg during the whole review. His Lordship was dressed in a rich hussar uniform, and mounted upon one of the most beautiful horses I have ever seen.

The deep animosity shown by the Prussians towards the French civilians had softened by August 1815, as revealed in the *Hampshire Chronicle* of 7 August:

It was stated a few days ago in the French Papers, that Marshal Blucher had given permission to his troops to assist the farmers in gathering in the harvest. The Duke of Wellington has written a letter to the Prefect of Police to the same effect, and offered besides, the waggons of the army to convey the corn. This measure is a most humane one, as the events of the war have reduced very much the number of horses in France, and the regulations respecting the National Guard removed a number of labourers from their ordinary occupations. This arrangement will furnish employment to our troops, and remove them from the dissipations of Paris. They are to receive the customary wages of the country, at least the Prussians do.

There was also widespread fraternisation between the British and the French, of which Ensign Bakewell of the 27th (Inniskilling) Regiment took advantage.

I went into one of the milliner's shops, apparently as respectable as any one of those in the square, where I bought a few pairs of gloves. The owner, a pert young lady, had another in her company, whom I assumed was a customer and with whom I flirted, saying '*Vol a vous*' [*Voulez-vous*] to which she replied 'We [Oui] *Monsieur*'. Says I: '*la cushie*' [*se coucher*], Mademoiselle', and she repeated 'We [Oui] *Monsieur*'. Then, with the mistress of the shop, she accompanied me into an adjoining street, where she lived when not otherwise engaged, and where we amused ourselves. This pursuit was frequently repeated.[3]

Throughout the Napoleonic Wars looting was commonplace, particularly by the French armies when they invaded enemy territory. The occupation of Paris gave the Prussians the opportunity to take back some of the items that had been stolen by the French. This report entitled, 'Restitution of works of art carried off by the French' and dated

Aix-la-Chapelle, 25 July 1815, was signed by the President of the Prussian Provinces of the Rhine:

By an official letter from the Counsellor of State, M. Ribbentrop, Intendant-General of the army of the Lower Rhine, dated Paris, July 15, I have received information, that his Excellency Field Marshal Prince Blucher of Wahlstadt, immediately after the taking of Paris, ordered that all the works of art and literature which are there, and which had been previously carried off by the French from the States of his Prussian Majesty, should be seized and restored to the places from which they were taken. For the execution of this order, a Special Committee has been appointed at Paris, under the direction of an Intendant-General, and at the same time a line of conveyances from Paris to the Rhine.

The first convoy left Paris on the 16th; among the articles which it brings, is the invaluable picture of St. Peter, which Rubens presented to Cologne, his native city, and which the audacious hands of our enemies ravished from the sacred and classic soil. Orders have also been given, that the beautiful columns of granite and porphyry, carried off by the same sacrilegious hands from the sanctuary of our Cathedral at Aix-la-Chapelle, and placed afterwards to support the arched roof of the Hall of Antiquities at Paris, shall be pulled down, and brought back to Aix-la-Chapelle. I had particularly requested our illustrious Field Marshal, immediately upon the taking of Paris, to cause these two articles to be restored; he has immediately complied with this desire, and has thus acquired a particular right to the gratitude of the cities of Cologne and Aix-la-Chapelle.

You see, Prussians of the Rhine, that the State of which you are the youngest children, has not forgotten to seize the first opportunity to make you participate in the fruits of its victories. Your cities will celebrate with grateful joy, the day on which the property plundered from your ancestors, re-taken from a rapacious enemy, by the powerful hand of your King and his warriors, shall re-enter your walls, &c.[4]

By a coincidental juxtaposition, the following day, 26 July, witnessed French property being removed by her enemies. This report was written that day from Brussels. No doubt these were seen as the spoils of war rather than looted treasure:

The French cannon brought from La Belle Alliance are placed here upon the Esplanade, without the gate Du Rivage, till they shall be embarked for England. They are 87 in number, as well cannon as howitzers. Some have the cypher Louis XIV, others have the words 'liberty, equality,' and the greater number the cypher of Napoleon; fifty others are expected in a short time.

France would suffer severely for its support of Napoleon, with considerable reparations being demanded. The *Cheltenham Chronicle* of Thursday, 29 February 1816 stated that,

> Philippeville, Marienburgh, Landau, Thionville, and perhaps some other fortresses, are to be taken permanently from France – not less than twelve more to be held for three or four years, by the Allies, who, commanded by Wellington, will amount to 150,000 men. Seven hundred millions of livres will be raised as contributions.

21

The Fallen

The 'butcher's bill' for Waterloo was high indeed. The French, as might be expected, suffered the heaviest casualties, amounting to approximately 25,000 killed and wounded on the 18th. Grouchy lost another 2,600 at Wavre. The Anglo-Dutch casualties numbered some 15,000, of which 10,000 were British, with the Netherlands army losing more than 4,000, and the Brunswick and Nassau contingents around 1,300. Prussian casualties numbered 7,000 at Waterloo and a further 2,500 were killed or wounded at Wavre.[1]

Ensign Gronow of the Guards was one of those who walked round the battlefield on the morning after the battle. He went on to record the following:

> I visited Hougoumont, in order to witness with my own eyes the traces of one of the most hotly contested spots of the field of battle. I first came upon the orchard, and there discovered heaps of dead men, in various uniforms: those of the Guards in their usual red jackets, the German Legion in green, and the French dressed in blue, mingled together.
>
> The dead and the wounded positively covered the whole area of the orchard; not less than two thousand men had there fallen. The apple-trees presented a singular appearance; shattered branches were seen hanging about their mother trunks in such profusion, that one might almost suppose the stiff-growing and stunted tree had been converted into the willow: every tree was riddled and smashed in a manner which told that the showers of shot had been incessant.[2]

Lieutenant Colonel William Scott, in his account of the Battle of Waterloo, provided his readers with a graphic description of the aftermath of the battle:

Scarce had the news of the victory reached Brussels, and the adjoining parts, before women lost to every sense of shame, and men, as callous in their hearts as these, on Sunday night repaired to the field of battle. The groans of death resounded on every side, and screams of agony, and many, who had been before enjoying all the luxuries of life, would have given at this moment all they possessed, for a cup of cold water, to touch their quivering lips. But instead of that, wretches were everywhere spread over the field, knocking out the brains of those who were disabled, of all nations, not from motives of humanity, but to rob them of what they might have about them. After this they would tear off the epaulets and lace from the clothes, and decorations of honour smeared with blood, made more dismal by the glimmering light of the moon; with weary steps they stole from body to body, and some of the common soldiers were also engaged in the same acts.

The fields were made slippery with blood, and here and there were seen horses limping, and seeking to find a blade of uncontaminated grass, but in vain. All the waters were tinged with blood, which still expressive of horror and ferocity, would in any other hearts have inspired an awful dread. – Everywhere were seen the fragments of guns, broken swords covered with blood and human hair, parts severed from the human body, here a carcase without an head, there a body without an arm, a leg, or jaw.

Death in all varieties of shapes stalked over the field. All distinctions had now ceased, and in promiscuous heaps lay the victors and the vanquished, German, Englishman, Dutch, Hanoverian, Belgian, Prussian, and Frenchman, all near each other silent as the grave, but before full of animosity, and desire of slaughter. The brave man and the coward lay side by side, the implorer for mercy, and he who refused it, the man who braved God and devil, and he, who had his prayer-book in his pocket, and uttered many a fervent ejaculation to his God and Saviour, the men who volunteered in such a business, and those, who were forced into the service, not from will, but through power.

In one short day, 60,000 persons were in the vigour and pride of youth, made mute forever, and their souls gone to that bourn, whence no traveller returns. Here also were found many who, forgetting the weakness and tenderness of their nature, were hunting over the dead, to have a last farewell look, of their slaughtered husbands, or if they could be happy enough to bind up their wounds, and save them, for themselves and family.

When the morning dawned what were the frightful appearances of those who had been murdering and robbing the dying, begrimed

267

with blood, and carrying away a soldier's coat filled with the treasure they had taken. As the numbers became augmented, the search was more eager – fingers and ears were cut off for the rings – some of these poor wretches were then alive and unable to carry off a sufficient number of heavy firelocks found in the field, you saw the women, laden with the ramrods, thinking them more valuable, and these were collected into piles. The clothes were now stripped from their naked bodies, and a new scene of horror displayed itself to those who had humanity to feel. But the wretch, the cause of all this slaughter was unmoved at such, or a worse sight; for in one Bulletin, he dares to say, 'that the crimson blood contrasted with snow on the ground, had a beautiful effect,' and 'the battle of Ligny was like the representation of a Drama or play.'

How frightful became the scene, when a week after, the bodies began to turn black and putrify, and no longer could any features be recognized. A cadaverous smell issued from every part, and wounded horses fed upon the barks of trees. Here and there a head and arm appeared amidst the tumuli, and at that late period even many were found, who still moved upon the field of battle, when touched.[3]

This robbing of the dead was also noted by a reporter for the *Caledonian Mercury*, the edition in question being published on Monday, 27 July 1815:

With every possible diligence and care that could be used, many of the wounded lay two days upon the field of battle, before their wounds were dressed and they could be removed. The preference was, of course, given to our own gallant heroes, and a peremptory order was issued to that effect. Many days after the battle the fields of Waterloo continued to present great numbers of poor persons, particularly females, seeking for plunder. Every rag was searched, in expectation it could produce gold or silver, lace, or money.

Among the most common spoils were the eagles worn on the fronts of the caps of some of the French regiments. These, when broken off, were sold at Brussels for about two francs each. Among the French killed and wounded, were observed an immense number of letters from friends, relatives, and lovers, who have to lament their loss.

The number of deaths in the hospitals at Brussels was last week estimated at about thirty a day.

There was another side to this scene, where care and compassion for the wounded was foremost, but the vast number of severely wounded men was too great for the Belgian capital to handle and they were just left in the streets unattended:

> We then saw humanity exerting herself, and the wounded of all nations placed into waggons, and conveyed to Brussels. Some few had crawled so far from the field of battle. But the numbers were so great, that neither the hospitals nor private houses, were sufficient to receive the wretched victims. The French too often were denied, admittance, and were seen perishing in the streets from hunger. The majority even of the English could not be received into houses, and lay in the open air. The hospitals were so crowded, that the legs, and arms, as they were taken off were thrown under the bed, and lay in putrified heaps.
>
> In the same bed were seen the dying and the dead, and the same waggons were employed to bring in the wounded from the field of battle, and in carrying away for Christian burial the dead. Here was a man with a locke'd jaw, hungry, but incapable of eating, then a wound opened afresh, and the poor wretch was seen bleeding to death for the want of medical aid, otherwise employed. These wounds had been festering for many hours unattended.
>
> Each countenance looked pale and ghastly, and the wretch who caused all this misery and anguish was himself without a scratch, nor did he ever receive a wound ... Wives who came to attend upon their wounded husbands, who were then too ill to be seen, and died at the first sight of their beloved partners. Lovers who deplored the deaths of those, whom they were engaged to marry. The field of battle was strewed with affectionate letters of this sort. Brothers, who possessed the strongest affections, came to weep over their dead brother's body. Some had lost five sons, in short, the feelings of distress, no one can picture. It was the flower of the human race cut off in the bud, leaving disconsolated mourners upon the earth.[4]

As with every conflict, many families sought to retrieve the bodies of their loved ones and return them to the UK. These efforts produced some moving stories, such as that in the *Hampshire Chronicle* of 7 August 1815:

> The whole afflicted family of the Earl of Carlisle were so anxious to redeem, if possible, the remains of their relative, the Hon. Major Howard, who fell so gallantly in the battle of Waterloo, that the Duke of York most humanely wrote over to the Duke of Wellington, requesting that every endeavour might be made to effect it.

On inquiry, it was found that two serjeants of the 10th Hussars had interred him on the field, who said, they believed that they could trace out the spot. They were in consequence dispatched from Paris for this purpose, and on traversing this wide field of slaughter, were fortunate enough to discover the place of sepulchre, from which they immediately dug up the remains of their heroic officer, enclosed them in a leaden shell, with which they were provided, and took them to Brussels, from whence they were removed to Ostend, and conveyed to England.

Most of the dead were not recovered by their families, but were gathered up from the battlefield by large groups of local peasants:

Entirely to clear the ground of dead men and horses occupied a period of ten or twelve days, and this disgusting duty was performed entirely by the peasantry. The human bodies were for the most part thrown into large holes, fifteen or twenty feet square; while those of the animals were generally honoured with a funeral pile and burned. To drag the large carcasses, some of which were inflated to an enormous bulk, was a work of great labour.[5]

The actual burial process was described by a one individual:

The general burying was truly horrible – large square holes were dug about six feet deep, and thirty or forty young fellows, stripped to their skins were thrown into each, pell mell, and then covered over in so slovenly a manner that sometimes a hand or a foot peeped through the earth.[6]

Miss Charlotte Eaton, who was on a family visit to Brussels when the campaign abruptly began, rode out to Waterloo some weeks after the battle and saw more that she bargained for:

On top of the ridge in front of the British position, on the left of the road, we traced a long line of graves, or rather pits, into which hundreds of dead had been thrown as they had fallen in their ranks ... The effluvia which arose from them, even beneath the open canopy of heaven, was horrible; and the pure west wind of summer, as it passed us, seemed pestiferous, so deadly was the smell that in many places [it] pervaded the field.[7]

On 22 June 1815, Captain William Fyre, who was on furlough from service in Celyon, wrote the following:

This morning [22 June] I went to visit the field of the battle, but on arrival there the sight was too horrible to behold. I felt sick in the stomach and was obliged to return. The multitude of carcases, the heaps of wounded men with mangled limbs unable to move, and perishing from not having their wounds dressed or from hunger, as the Allies were, of course, obliged to take their surgeons and wagons with them, formed a spectacle I shall never forget.[8]

In the weeks after the battle the newspapers printed many tributes to those that had been killed. The following was published in the *Cambridge Chronicle and Journal* of 28 July 1815:

Amongst the gallant heroes who have been fallen in the defence of their country, on the ever-memorable 18th of June, on the plains of Waterloo, few are more lamented than Lieutenant-Colonel Currie, of Dalebank, in Annandale, Assistant Adjutant-General on Lord Hill's Staff. This excellent and valuable officer received his commission at the early age of 15, from the Duke of York, in consequence of the meritorious conduct of his father in the army, and, for a period of above 20 years, had been constantly distinguishing himself in actual service.

He fought bravely, and was severely wounded, under Sir Ralph Abercromby, in Egypt; and served for several years in the West Indies, by which his health was greatly impaired. – He was also actively employed as an Aide-de-Camp to Lord Hill, the whole of the war in the Peninsula and in France, where he conducted himself with such ability and bravery, as repeatedly on the field of battle to receive the thanks of the Commander in Chief; and particularly at Talavera, at the passage of the Douro, Almaraz, and Aroyo de Molinos.

It is melancholy, although glorious, to record, that Lieutenant-Colonel Currie was the tenth of this gallant and amiable family who have nobly sacrificed their lives in defence of their King and Country, six of whom have died on the field of battle.

In a letter dated 12 July 1815, Lieutenant Colonel Leake noted the following:

Lieutenant-Colonel Charles Fox Canning, who fell in the late tremendous conflict at Waterloo, had served with the Duke of Wellington as his Aide-de-Camp during the whole of the Peninsular war, and was with him in every action and siege from the battle of Talavera to that of Orthes. At the termination of the war he went to

Brussels, where his regiment was quartered, and was preparing to go into the field with it, when the Duke accidently met him in the street, when he was received with the usual cordiality, and the next day he had the inexpressible gratification of finding himself restored, without solicitation, to the honourable situation he had held through so many campaigns.

The affecting particulars of his last moments we cannot help repeating, as a proof, that among many other splendid qualities, the Duke of Wellington eminently possesses the power of engaging the affections of his officers, whose most anxious thoughts seem always directed toward the safety of their Commander. –

Towards the close of the action of the 18th, Lieutenant-Colonel Canning received orders from the Duke to carry a message of importance to a distant part of the line: he had delivered it and was returning, when a grape-shot struck him in the stomach. He fell, and his friend Lord March immediately rode up to his assistance. As he approached him the Colonel raised himself up, and with eagerness demanded if the Duke was safe? Being assured that he was, he seemed satisfied, and said, 'God bless him!' then taking the hand of the Nobleman who had so kindly come to his assistance, he had just strength to say – 'God bless you!' and expired.[9]

Another sad tale was that of Gunner Butterworth of Mercer's troop:

He had just finished ramming down the shot, and was stepping back outside the wheel, when his foot struck in the miry soil, pulling him forward the moment the gun was fired. As a man naturally does when falling, he threw out both arms before him, and they were blown off at the elbows. He raised himself a little on his two stumps, and looked up most piteously in my face.

To assist him was impossible – the safety of all, everything, depended upon not slackening our fire, and I was obliged to turn from him … I afterwards learned that he had succeeded in rising and was gone to the rear; but on inquiring for him next day some of my people who had been sent to Waterloo told me that they saw his body by the roadside near the farm of Mont St Jean – bled to death![10]

There were also funerals for the fallen, including that of the most senior Allied commander to die in the campaign, the Duke of Brunswick. The ceremony was reported in the *Cheltenham Chronicle* of Thursday, 17 August 1815, in an extract of a letter from an unnamed officer written at Hanover on 6 July:

We have been engaged here in the mournful occupation of attending the funeral of the Duke of Brunswick, who was killed at the battle of Waterloo, and whose body was sent to Brunswick for interment. It is 40 miles off, so that we were obliged to make two days of it; the poor Brunswick people are in great distress, and even the peasants are all in mourning.

The ceremony of the funeral was extremely fine, it was at night, and the whole town was illuminated, in addition, some thousands of servants, all in mourning, with wax flambeaux. The whole palace and church were completely hung with black cloth; a magnificent canopy of black velvet and silver was placed over a simple bust of the Duke in white marble, crowned with laurel; the coffin was as fine as it was possible, and upon it all his military decorations, fastened together by a wreath of laurel; the procession began at midnight. We walked about a mile through the town, from the place to the church; the streets were all gravelled on purpose.

The body was carried on a magnificent funeral car, drawn by eight horses all in black velvet and feathers. His eldest son (12 years old) the present Duke, was chief mourner; the Duke of Cambridge led him by the hand, immediately after the coffin. The second son, 11 years old, followed next, led by his uncle, the Duke Augustus. They are both very fine boys, and were much affected; they were dressed in long black clothes, with white ruffs and weepers. The funeral service at church is not near so fine as ours, nor so impressive. The body was laid in the centre of the church; the galleries were hung with black drapery, and were filled with ladies, all in black. Minute guns were fired all the time of the ceremony; and when the body was carried into the vault, vollies of musketry. The whole was magnificent and impressive.

A similar scene was played out on Saturday, 1 July at Ostend. It was reported in the *Chester Chronicle* six days later as the body of the most senior British officer to lose his life was embarked on a ship for England:

On Saturday morning the Garrison Battalion, of 1400 men, lined the streets of Ostend, and the remains of General Picton were followed by the Governor of the town, Admiral Malcolm, all the principal inhabitants, the officers of the army and navy, and detachments from several regiments, the band playing the *Dead March in Saul*, and the garrison firing minute guns until the coffin was put into a launch, towed by a boat, with the crews properly dressed, and an officer in each from every ship there, and then the *Wrangler*, which brought the corpse over, fired minute guns until it was received on board her in the outer roads. – The sight was grand and solemn.

'Jack' Shaw was a well-known pugilist who had joined the Lifeguards when he was eighteen. He was an impressive six feet in his stockings and weighed fifteen stones. He used dumbbells to strengthen his arms which 'added to regular sword' practice had 'given him a wrist strong and flexible as a bar of steel'. His death at Waterloo, was reported in more than one newspaper, including the *Chester Courant* of Tuesday, 11 July 1815:

> Shaw, the pugilistic Life-Guardsman, fell in the battle of Waterloo. The Life Guards were in the heat of the action. Shaw was wounded in many places, but at length fell from his horse, after having dealt out death to the enemy by wholesale.
>
> The action had nearly ceased when the wound in his abdomen deprived him of the power of pursuing his career of glory. In the heat of the battle, in the village, an old woman had secreted herself in her cottage, and the corporal was conveyed by some faithful comrades to her abode. After stripping off the gold lace on the dress which distinguished him as a corporal, his body was decently interred.

Finally, the *Chester Courant* of Tuesday, 8 August 1815, recorded that 'Major General Sir William Ponsonby, it may be recalled, led the Union Brigade in its charge against d'Erlon's I Corps, but he did not survive that charge'. The following explanation of his death was repeated in a number of newspapers, including that day's *Chester Courant*:

> The following particulars, on the truth of which we perfectly rely, have been communicated to us respecting the fall of this lamented Officer, on the glorious day of the 18th of June. It has been mentioned, that his death was to be attributed to his being badly mounted; and this is perfectly correct. He led his brigade against the Polish Lancers, and checked at once their destructive charges against the British Infantry; but having pushed on at some distance from his troops, accompanied only by one aide-de-camp, he entered a newly ploughed field, where the ground was excessively soft. – Here his horse struck, and was utterly incapable of extricating himself.
>
> At this instant a body of Lancers approached at full speed. Sir William saw that his fate was decided. He took out a picture and his watch, and was in the act of giving them to his aide-de-camp to deliver to his wife and family when the Lancers came up. They were

both killed on the spot. His body was found, as we mentioned some time ago, laying beside his horse, pierced with seven lance wounds. Before the day was ended, the Polish Lancers were almost entirely cut to pieces by the brigade which this brave Officer had led against them.

There were also a number of reports of the bodies of women being found on the battlefield in French uniforms, indicating that they were fighting in the regiments alongside the men. Captain Henry Ross-Lewin of the 32nd Foot, claimed that he saw two such women:

> I saw one of them … she was dressed in a nankeen jacket and trousers and had been killed by a ball which had passed through her head. One can only wonder – were these women fighting for their men, or for France?[11]

22

The Survivors' Stories

There were many remarkable stories both about and from those who survived the battles of the Waterloo campaign. Amongst those was what was described as 'Sufferings of a Wounded Officer':

> An officer, who was wounded on the 18th, walked to Brussels, in a state almost too dreadful to be described. The rain descended in torrents; the roads were deep and miry; he was in severe agony with his wound; he was unable to bear the motion of a carriage; and his strength scarcely sufficed for him to crawl along. He was repeatedly forced out of the road, to avoid being crushed to death, and compelled to proceed through the deep wet grass and entangling briers of the forest of Soignes. Once, a Brunswick soldier ran violently against his wounded arm, and gave him excruciating pain; – he threw off the man, who lifted his sabre to cut him down; but, on seeing his wound, the fellow showed signs of commiseration, and passed on.[1]

George Simmons of the 95th Rifles was wounded at Waterloo after enduring the French artillery bombardment for around four hours:

> I received the dangerous wound which laid me amongst many others in the mud. Most of the men with me were killed, so it was some time before any officer noticed me, and not until I had been trampled over many times. The next place I found myself in was where the men and officers had been collected for the surgeon. A good surgeon, a friend of mine, instantly came to examine my wound. My breast was dreadfully swelled. He made a deep cut under the right pap, and dislodged from the breast-bone a musket-ball.
>
> I was suffocating with the injury my lungs had sustained. He took a quart of blood from my arm. I now began to feel my miseries. Sergeant Fairfoot was also here wounded in the arm. He got me

everything he could, and said he would go and knock some French prisoner off his horse for me in order to get me off. The balls were riddling the house we were in. He got me a horse. They tried to lift me upon it, but I fainted; some other officer took it.

In consequence of a movement the French made with all their forces, our people were obliged to retire. If I stayed I must be a prisoner, and being a prisoner was the same as being lost. Poor Fairfoot was in great agitation. He came with another horse. I remember some Life Guardsmen helped me on. Oh what I suffered! I had to ride twelve miles. I forgot to tell you the ball went through my ribs, and also through my body. The motion of it made the blood pump out, and the bones cut the flesh to a jelly.

I made my way to the house I had been billeted on – very respectable people. I arrived about 10 o'clock on that doleful night. The whole family came out to receive me. The good man and his wife were extremely grieved. I had everything possible got for me, a surgeon sent for, a quart of blood taken from me, wrapped up in poultices, and a most excellent nurse. In four days I had six quarts of blood taken from me, the inflammation ran so high in my lungs. At present everything is going on well.[2]

Another rifleman, Edward Costello made the following comments about the treatment of the wounded whilst he was in Brussels:

The French I have ever found to be brave, yet I cannot say they will undergo a surgical operation with the cool, unflinching spirit of a British soldier. An incident here which came under my notice may in some measure show the difference of the two nations.

An English soldier belonging to, if I recollect rightly, the 1st Royal Dragoons, evidently an old weather-beaten warfarer, while undergoing the amputation of an arm below the elbow, held the injured limb with his other hand without betraying the slightest emotion, save occasionally helping out his pain by spitting forth the proceeds of a large plug of tobacco, which he chewed unmercifully while under the operation.

Near to him was a Frenchman, bellowing lustily, while a surgeon was probing for a ball near the shoulder. This seemed to annoy the Englishman more than anything else, and so much so, that as soon as his arm was amputated, he struck the Frenchman a smart blow across the breech with the severed limb, holding it at the wrist, saying, 'Here, take that, and stuff it down your throat, and stop your damned bellowing!'[3]

Amongst the early reports from the battle was that the Earl of Uxbridge's wound had proved fatal. This piece of news was corrected in the *Chester Chronicle* of Friday, 7 July 1815:

> The report of the death the Earl of Uxbridge is unfounded. – Letters have been received from his Lady, (who left town, accompanied by her eldest child, about three years of age, immediately on receiving the information of his Lordship's situation) which state, that the gallant Hero is so far recovered as to be enabled to accompany her Ladyship to England in the course of a few days. His Lordship's leg was struck by a grape shot, and after he fell, he was carried to a distance of more than eight miles, before any assistance could be procured; some time elapsed before he would allow himself to be dressed. – This noble family have suffered severely, as there are four of his Lordship's cousins among the killed and wounded.

It may be recalled that Colonel Fred Ponsonby had been stabbed in the back by a French Lancer. He continues with his story after the *tirailleur* had left him:

> A squadron of Prussian Cavalry passed over me. I was a good deal hurt by the Horses – in general Horses will avoid treading upon men but the Field was so covered, that they had no spare space for their feet.
>
> Night now came on. I knew the Battle was won. I had felt little anxiety about myself during the day as I considered my case desperate, but now the night air relieved my breathing, and I had a hope of seeing somebody I knew. I was plundered again by the Prussians. Soon after an English Soldier examined me. I persuaded him to stay with me. I suffered but little pain from my wounds, but I had a most dreadful thirst and there were no means of getting a drop of water. I thought the night would never end.
>
> At last Morning came, the Soldier saw a Dragoon, he was fortunately of the 11th in the same Brigade with me. He came and they tried to get me on his Horse, but not being able to do so, he rode in to Head Quarters, and a wagon was sent for me. Young Vandeleur of my Reg came with it, he brought a Canteen of Water. It is impossible to describe the gratification I felt in drinking it. I was of course very much exhausted having lost a great deal of blood from five wounds. I had been on the ground for near 18 hours. I was taken to the Inn in Waterloo, it had been the Duke's Quarters. Hume dressed my wounds. I remained about a week in this Village and was then carried into Brussels.[4]

Under the headline 'THE WATERLOO SUFFERERS' the *Morning Post* of Saturday, 2 September 1815 printed the following report from Brussels:

> Assistance afforded to the Waterloo Sufferers, at the Ho. 5 Section, No. 929, Rue de la Fourche, at Brussels. – This medical repository of Le Sieur Vander S.S. Kerckhore, was converted into a temporary hospital, for the reception and cure of the sick and wounded after the memorable battle of Waterloo, 19th June, 1815.
>
> The proprietor of the said residence, and his partner, Le Sieur S. Railens, both Members of the Medical and Surgical College at Brussels, commenced their exertions in behalf of the wounded, at nine o'clock in the morning. The sick and wounded who presented themselves, met with every assistance and relief required in consequence of their wounds; those deprived of means and friends, were humanely supplied with clothing, nourishment, lodging, and every attention paid to their several surgical and medical wants.
>
> One of the rooms in this said residence was solely appropriated by the Lady of the house, and her children, for the preparation of lint and bandages, which were daily carefully washed and aired. Within, and in the environs of the town, the afflicted, who were of all nations, presented themselves to the numbers of 200 to 250 per day; extracting from some pieces of iron, bullets, stones, and otherwise performing the most serious operations. These glorious sufferers are now happily restored to health. Every necessary supply was gratuitously supplied from this medical repository.
>
> These two young practitioners were, by special appointment, in attendance near the field of battle during the 16th, 17th, and 18th of June, affording great assistance in dressing of the wounded. On the 17th they happily succeeded in saving two waggons of wounded English guards, our brave allies, these vehicles being much dilapidated and totally forsaken. These worthy members, assisted by a quarter-master, conveyed, or rather dragged these suffering veterans to the outskirts; after having refreshed them and dressed their wounds, procured safe conveyance, and carefully lodged them in the town, in a house prepared for their reception.
>
> These humane exertions are still, and will be continued in this course of laudable suffering. The number of the afflicted happily daily decrease, being reduced to 80 from 100 per day.

Not everyone who was wounded during the Waterloo campaign received such sympathetic reporting as those Waterloo sufferers, as this piece of investigative journalism in the *Northampton Mercury* of Saturday, 25 November 1815 shows:

> It is certainly true (says a Morning Paper) that the Prince of Orange applied to our Government for *a year's pay*, on account of the slight wound that he received in the battle of Waterloo, to the astonishment of all the British army. The answer of his Royal Highness the Commander in Chief, was admirable. He said, 'Certainly, his Serene Highness is entitled to the money – but he must conform to the regulations of the service. He must come over and submit himself to *inspection* by the Board.' The office has heard no more of the Prince's application.

There were many remarkable stories of soldiers surviving terrible injuries, such as this one from the *Leeds Intelligencer* of Monday, 18 March 1816:

> Among the wounded survivors of the Inniskilling Dragoons now in Exeter, there is a serjeant who received in the battle of Waterloo, *thirteen* sabre wounds in his body, a musket-ball passed through his thigh, and both his arms were broken. In this state he lay on the field of battle (amidst a heap of slain), from Sunday to the Tuesday evening following, when the persons employed to bury the dead observing some signs of life in him, he was conveyed to an hospital, and recovered.

A similar story of survival against the odds was recounted in the *Cambridge Chronicle and Journal* of Friday, 4 August 1815:

> At the Battle of Waterloo, an officer belonging to one of the Highland Regiments was wounded and lay for a long time apparently dead; he at length so far recovered so as to raise up his head to see if any assistance was near. Just at that instant three Frenchmen came up, and one of the cowardly scoundrels fired at him, but the ball fortunately passed betwixt his arm and his body.
>
> A private soldier, of the same regiment, hearing the report, snatched up a broad sword, and ran at the Frenchmen, who fled precipitately, and the noble fellow took his wounded Officer on his shoulders and carried him to hospital.

None of these stories, however, could compare with the very sad tale described by Edward Costello of the 95th Rifles:

A young fellow, a German, one of the drivers to the German artillery, had lost both his legs by a round-shot, which passing through the horse's belly, had carried away both limbs; while on the ground in this mangled state, he received a dreadful gash in one of his arms, from a French cuirassier, and a ball in the other; through these he was also obliged to undergo the amputation of both arms, one below the elbow and the other above; here the unfortunate youth (for he was not more than nineteen) lay a branchless trunk, and up to the moment I left, though numbers died from lesser wounds, survived.[5]

A story concerning Napoleon's carriage driver published in the *Cambridge Chronicle and Journal* of Friday, 1 March 1816 was reproduced in a number of newspapers, indicating how great the interest in Waterloo still was:

The coachman who drove Bonaparte's carriage, who was stated to have been killed in taking it after the battle of Waterloo, is, it seems, alive, and is now in London. His name is John Horne, a native of Holland; he received no less than twelve wounds, and was left for dead. He remained near the road side all night. The following morning he crawled towards Jemappe, and remained six days without his wounds being dressed, when he was met by an English officer, who very humanely conveyed him to Brussels, where his wounds were dressed by an English surgeon, and his right arm amputated close to his shoulder.

Such enduring interest is exemplified by the two following newspaper reports. The first was in the *Morning Post* of 27 March 1899:

In the village of Rolvenden, in the Weald of Kent, there is living an old woman named Moon, who was present at the battles of Quatre Bras and Waterloo. Her father, a colour-sergeant of the 3rd Battalion the Rifle Brigade, served throughout the Peninsular War, and took part in the battles of Badajoz, Salamanca and other conflicts. He died of wounds received at Waterloo some months after the battle and before he had received his pension. Mrs Moon was born in the Peninsula, her mother doing work for the forces when operating there. Though Mrs Moon is now infirm, her intellect is clear and her memory good.

It was later reported that Mrs Moon died in October 1903. She was four years old at the time of the battle and had ridden in a wagon over the field on the evening of 18 June 1815. The second of these reports comes from the *New York Times* of 16 July 1905:

> Last Saturday we announced that there was a survivor of Waterloo but a little while ago. John Vaughan is still alive, and he was a bugler in the great fight. 'I saw him at Walsall Railway Station two months ago,' writes a correspondent, 'and had a conversation with him, in the course of which he told me he was born at Aldershot, March, 1801.' He can walk well enough, but two wounds in the left leg make help necessary when it comes to getting into a railway carriage. He sells bootlaces, as we said, for the veteran finds he cannot live on his country's gratitude, which comes to seven shillings a week. Surely we might do a little better than that for John Vaughan!

23

Recriminations

Almost immediately after the restoration of Louis XVIII, it was announced in *Le Moniteur* that those senior individuals in France who were seen as having helped Napoleon regain power were going to be dealt with:

> All those officers who betrayed the King before March 20th [i.e. before Napoleon had become de facto head of state] or attacked France and the government with armed force, as well as those who seized power by violence, will be arrested and brought before competent courts-martial in their respective military districts.[1]

This led to a few high-profile arrests, trials, suicides and executions. The most notable of these was the trial of Marshal Ney, who at one time was arguably the most influential man in the French Army. After Napoleon's first abdication, Ney had decided to accept a position in the Bourbon army but then became the highest ranking officer to join Napoleon as he advanced on Paris in March 1815.

Exactly what fate awaited him after Napoleon had abdicated for a second time was the subject of much speculation, as shown in the note in the *Hampshire Chronicle* of Monday, 3 July 1815:

> It has been rumoured that Marshall Ney, in attempting to escape to America, has been taken in a schooner belonging to the United States.

This was soon found to be false information. 'Several of the partisans of Bonaparte, who have been in the late revolution', ran a piece in the *Caledonian Mercury* of Saturday, 22 July 1815,

> ... have, it is said, been invited to quit France. Ney has received passports for Switzerland. Maret is to proceed to Saxe Weimar, and

Murat is at Toulon, hesitating whether he shall join his family at Prague, or whether he shall go to England.

It was very apparent to many of Napoleon's supporters that their lives were in danger all the time they remained in France. The following report, from the *Morning Post* of 15 August 1815, concerns Marshal Guillaume Marie Anne Brune who was the commander of the Army of the Var, and as such was responsible for the defence of the south of France against the Austrian army:

> After Marshal Brune had quitted Toulon, he proceeded with passports from M. De Riviere; he was recognised by the populace at Avignon, and a commotion immediately ensued. M. Brune quitted the carriage, and sought refuge in one of the inns. The Prefect who had previously seen him, and advised him to continue his route without delay, was much perplexed. During four hours and a half, at the peril of his own life, he defended that of M. Brune.
>
> All his efforts, however, were insufficient to allay the fury of the populace – There was no armed force in the town. At length, when the Marshal deemed it certain the gate of his asylum would be forced, he put an end to his existence with a pistol. The Prefect of the Vaucluse has given orders for the prosecution of the principal authors of the above tumult.

Whether or not he killed himself or was killed by the Royalists is uncertain. His body was thrown into the River Rhône but later recovered.

Fearing a similar end Ney went into hiding, but such a well-known and distinctive individual could not remain out of sight for long. His arrest was detailed in many newspapers, including the *Morning Post* of 15 August 1815, which quoted a report from Paris dated 11 August:

> Marshal Ney has been discovered in the Canton de Figeac, near the bounds of the department du Cantal. He was forthwith arrested and conveyed to Aurillac. This important event may be attributed to the vigilance of M. Locard, Prefect of du Cantal. The Captain of the Gendarmerie executed the orders of M. Locard, with the greatest zeal and activity.
>
> The following circumstances respecting Ney are extracted from a letter from Riam, dated the 9th.
>
> Marshal Ney had retired with much secrecy to the chateau of one of his friends near Aurillac. His presence prevented the reception of much company in the house. An individual of the town dining there

284

one day, remarked a sabre, which appeared to him to be exceedingly curious and valuable.

On his return to Aurillac, the Gentleman spoke of the circumstance to several of his friends as very remarkable. One of these observed, 'That sabre can only belong to Murat or Ney – no one but these had a sabre of that kind. On this information being conveyed to the Sub-Prefect, steps were taken for the arrestation of the Marshal.'

Marshal Soult, who had acted as Napoleon's Chief of Staff during the Hundred Days campaign, was also arrested, as reported in the *Chester Courant* on Tuesday, 25 July 1815:

Marshal Soult has been arrested at Mende, by the National Guards, who lodged him in the prefecture, where he waits the orders of Government. The Prefect and Commandant of this Department have been also arrested, and imprisoned in the steeple of the Cathedral.

Soult faced trail and was banished from France. He returned in 1819 and eventually became the French Prime Minister.

Murat, the former King of Naples who had disobeyed Napoleon by launching his premature offensive, tried to regain his throne. However, he was captured in Naples, brought before a tribunal and sentenced to death, as related by his widow:

The prisoner listened to his sentence with coolness and contempt. He was then led into a little court of the castle, where he found a party of soldiers drawn up in two files. Upon these preparations he looked calmly, and refused to permit his eyes to be covered. Then advancing in front of the party, and, placing himself in an attitude to meet the bullets, he called out to the soldiers, 'Spare my face – aim at the heart.' No sooner had he uttered these words than the party fired, and he, who had been so lately King of the Two Sicilies, fell dead, holding fast with his hands the portraits of his family.[2]

The trial of Marshal Ney was reported in most of the British newspapers, including the *Cambridge Chronicle and Journal* of Friday, 24 November 1815, which detailed the appeal of Ney to the Allied Powers concerning the legality of the charge laid against him. His argument was as follows:

Victory soon decided in favour of the English and Prussian arms on the plains of Waterloo, and brought them under the walls of Paris.

There remained, to oppose their ulterior progress, a corps of the French army, which might have sold their lives dearly. A negociation took place, and on the 3d of July, a convention between the two parties was signed. The 12th article of which, says:

'Shall be equally respected, persons and private property; the inhabitants, and, in general, all the individuals who are in the capital, shall continue to enjoy their rights and liberty, without being disturbed or sought after for any thing relating to the functions they occupy, or shall have occupied, *their conduct and their political opinions.*' The Convention has been since ratified by each of the Allied Sovereigns.

Ney might seem here to have a good case. However, this was the reply sent to him, from Paris on 15 November 1815, by the Allied supreme commander, the Duke of Wellington:

I have had the honour of receiving the note which you addressed to me on the 13th instant, relative to the operation of the Capitulation of Paris in your case.

The Capitulation of Paris of the 3d July last, was made between the Commander-in-Chief of the Allied and Parisian Armies on the one part, and the Prince d'Eckmuhl [Marshal Davout] Commander-in-Chief of the French Army, on the other, and related *exclusively* to the *military occupation of Paris.*

The object of the twelfth article was to prevent any measure of severity under the *military authority of those who made it towards any persons in Paris*, on account of any offices they had filled, or any conduct or political opinions of theirs : but it never was intended, and never could be intended, to prevent either the existing French Government, under whose authority the French Commander in Chief must have acted, or any French Government which might succeed to it, from acting in this respect as it might seem fit.

This, it would seem, sealed Ney's fate. Further details concerning Ney's trial appeared in the *Caledonian Mercury* of 25 November 1815. The first report was dated 18 November:

Generals Grouchy, Lefebvre, Desnouettes, Gilly, and Michaud, have been arrested. Talleyrand, de Jaucourt, and Gouvion St Cyr, have refused to sit upon the trial of Ney, upon the grounds of their being members of the Administration under which he was arrested, and consequently his accusers. Augereau has also declined sitting upon his trial.

The second part of the *Caledonian Mercury*'s account was dated the next day, 19 November. It, too, had been sent from Paris:

> I am told that Ney betrays great fears for the result of his trial, and that his courage has forsaken him. His confessor is constantly with him, and he is frequently found in tears. He is to be transferred to-morrow to the Luxemburg, where he is to remain in a place of security near the Chamber of Peers. His trial is definitely fixed for Tuesday next, and it is expected his fate will be decided on the Thursday following.

The decision of the court was that Ney was guilty of 'having maintained intelligence with Buonaparte in order to second the progress of his arms against French territory on the night of 13–14 March [when he went over to Napoleon's side]; having aided him with troops and men; by speeches in public places, broadsheets, posters and printed material, of having directly incited the citizens to fight one another; of having encouraged soldiers to pass over to the enemy.'[3] The death sentence was pronounced.

The following report in the *Sussex Advertiser* of 18 December 1815, carried the headline 'Further Particulars of the Last Moments of Marshal Ney':

> When the judgment was announced to him, he said, 'it would have been more military to have said, you are to bite the dust.' At the execution, he endeavoured to protest against the iniquity of the sentence, and appealed to God and posterity. The Officer, commanding the veterans attempting to give the word, appeared struck dumb. L'Espinois (the commander of the military division) then said, 'Officer, if you cannot command, I will,' the latter remaining silent, the Marshal himself said, 'Soldiers, do your duty,' upon which the platoon ordered for the purpose, fired at random, only five out of sixteen balls fired struck the Marshal, who fell upon his knees, and died instantly. The officer recovering himself said, 'There is still a platoon, let them shoot me also.' The officer is put under arrest.
>
> Marshal Ney was buried yesterday at the cemetery of La Chaise. Madame Ney was accompanied to the Thulleries by her four children and sister, she remained in the salon de la paix some time before the Duc de Duras came to inform her that she could not be received by the king, and leading her down the grand staircase, acquainted her with the mournful execution; she fainted, and was with difficulty removed to her carriage amidst the cries of her children, and the lamentations of the spectators of this distressing scene. She had several times

endeavoured to see the Duchess d'Angouleme, near to whose person she had been brought up when a child; the Duchess however, as well as the Princess, constantly refused to see her.

Not every trial resulted in the death sentence. General Pierre-Jacques-Etienne Michel Cambronne commanded the 1st Chasseurs of the Old Guard. A dedicated supporter of Napoleon, he had followed him to Elba and returned with the Emperor to overthrow Louis. The story of the results of his trial were published in the *Liverpool Mercury* of Friday, 10 May 1816:

> During the deliberation of the Court, which lasted very long in Cambronne's case, that General having withdrawn, called for a dinner, of which he eat most composedly and plentifully. – Suspecting that a fatal sentence awaited him, and his mind being fully made up to that event, he occupied himself afterwards in making some last arrangements, and in preparing the following letter to the Commander of the 1st military division.
>
> 'M. de Lespinois – I am condemned to death. I address you this letter to apprise you that I positively disclaim all applications for pardon that may be made for me, either by my family, my friends, or my counsel. The only favour which I solicit of those who are competent to grant it, is that my sentence be executed immediately.'
>
> When his cousin, a most interesting young Lady, ran up to him to inform him of his acquittal, he said – 'Well then, my letters will be useless;' and he was going to destroy them, when she snatched up the one in question and preserved it. My translation of it is literal.

It was not only French officers that faced inquests into their conduct. The Duke of Cumberland's Hussars, which formed part of the 1st Hanoverian Cavalry Brigade, was posted behind the main Anglo-Netherlands line at Waterloo. After the charge by the British heavy cavalry, Colonel Hake was asked to move his regiment further forward. The Hussars did not move.

Unlike the British cavalry regiments which had dismounted to reduce casualties from the French artillery, the Cumberland Hussars remained in their saddles and suffered accordingly. Uxbridge saw that the Hussars were wavering under the bombardment and were beginning to fall back. He sent his aide over to see what was happening. Colonel von Hake apparently explained that since his men were volunteers and their horses were their own property, he did not believe that he could order them to remain under fire. Despite Seymour's insistence, the Hussars left the field and rode all the way back to Brussels declaring that the battle was lost and that the French would be in the Belgian capital within hours. As a consequence, Hake faced a court-martial. This was reported in the *Cambridge Chronicle and Journal* on Friday, 1 March 1816:

Advices from Hanover state, that the court martial ordered to enquire into the conduct of Colonel Hake, formerly commanding the Cumberland hussars, as well as of the regiment accused of having failed in its duty, in leaving the field of battle at Waterloo, on the 18th of June, has condemned Colonel Hake to be cashiered and degraded, but acquitted the regiment of the charge of having disordered the ranks of the army. Major Mellzing, the second in command, is severely reprimanded for not having opposed the retreat of his corps.

The following extract from 'Paul's Letters to his Kinsfolks,' will explain the foregoing paragraph:-

'In another part of the field, the Hanoverian hussars of Cumberland, as they were called, a corps distinguished for their handsome appearance and complete equipment, were ordered to support a charge made by the British. Their gallant commanding officer showed no alacrity in obeying this order, and indeed observed so much ceremony, that, after having been once and again ordered to advance, an aide-de-camp of the Duke of Wellington informed him of his Grace's command that he should either advance or draw off his men entirely, and not remain there to show a bad example, and discourage others. The gallant officer of hussars, considering this as a serious option submitted to his own decision, was not long in making his choice; and having expressed to the aide-de-camp his sense of the Duke's kindness, and of the consideration which he had for raw troops under a fire of such unexampled severity, said he would embrace the alternative of drawing his men off, and posting them behind the hamlet of St. John. This he accordingly did, in spite of the reproaches of the aide-de-camp, who loaded him with every epithet that is most disgraceful to a soldier.

'The incident, although sufficiently mortifying in itself, and attended, as may be supposed, with no little inconvenience at such a moment, had something in it so comic, that neither the General nor any of his attendants were able to resist laughing when it was communicated by the incensed aide-de-camp. I have been told that many of the officers and soldiers of this unlucky regiment left it in shame, joined themselves to other bodies of cavalry, and behaved well in the action. But the valiant commander, not finding himself comfortable in the place of refuge which he had himself chosen, fled to Brussels, and alarmed the town with a report that the French were at his heels. His regiment was afterwards in a manner disbanded, or attached to the service of the commissariat.'

Hake was not the only Allied officer that was brought before a court-martial, as reported in the *Hereford Journal* of Wednesday, 27 September 1815:

Ramsgate, Sept 21. – We regret to announce the landing here of a British Officer from Ostend, under arrest and in irons, said to have entered the French army, and taken at the battle of Waterloo. He is a fine looking young man, and appeared indifferent as to his disgraceful situation. The cause assigned for his traitorous conduct is from having, when in the Peninsula with the immortal Wellington, undergone a Court Martial, the sentence of which inflicted a severe, though merited, wound upon his honour as an Officer and a Gentleman. The offence he has now been guilty of, we are happy to reflect, is of a rare and almost unheard of description in the British Army.

24

Travellers' Tales

As Wellington had observed, many people travelled from the United Kingdom to Waterloo after the battle. Unlike the sites of the great engagements in Portugal and Spain, Waterloo was an easy and safe place to visit and many of those that did felt compelled to write about their experiences. Amongst the early visitors was a Reverend Rudge:

> Every part of the field of battle was strewed with different articles belonging to those who had fought and bled. Every thing around attested the horrors of war, and the march of devastation. On every side were scattered the arms and clothing of the slain; shoes, caps and belts, and every other military appendage, either stained with blood, or covered with dirt. In the corn fields, which had been completely ploughed up by trampling of the horses, and the movement of the soldiers, a number of books, cards, and letters were seen.

Rudge then made his way across to Hougoumont where one of the mass graves was located:

> The smell here was particularly offensive, and in some places, parts of the human body were distinctly to be recognised. The earth with which they had been covered, had sunk in, and exhibited here and there an arm and a human face, the flesh nearly wasted away, and the features of the countenance hardly distinguishable from the change they had undergone.[1]

Miss Charlotte Eaton painted an equally graphic picture of the Waterloo battlefield in the aftermath of the fighting:

> In many places the excavations made by the shells had thrown up the earth all around them; the marks of horses' hoofs, that had plunged

291

ankle deep in clay, were hardened in the sun; and the feet of men deeply stamped in the ground left traces of where many a deadly struggle had been. The ground was ploughed up in several places with the charge of the cavalry and the whole field was literally covered with soldiers' caps, shoes, gloves, belts, and scabbards, broken feathers battered into the mud, remnants of tattered scarlet cloth, bits of fur and leather, black stocks and haversacks belonging to French soldiers, buckles, packs of cards, books, and innumerable papers of every description ... printed French military returns, muster rolls, love-letters and washing bills; illegible songs, scattered sheets of military music, epistles without number in praise of 'l'Empereur, le Grand Napoléon' ... The quantities of letters and of blank sheets of dirty writing paper were so great that they literally whitened the face of the earth.[2]

The following extract of a private letter posted in Ghent was published in the *Chester Chronicle* on 17 November 1815:

Before closing my letter, I must beg your indulgence for a superfluous word or two, on a subject, which is every traveller's theme, the present situation of the plains of Waterloo. I was there yesterday, and remained several hours on the illustrious field, where my heart beat high at the recollection of the country I belonged to. The eye embraces at a glance the whole eventful scene, and with the preliminary notions every Englishman possesses, it is impossible not to comprehend immediately the grand manoeuvres of that memorable day.

Here the audacious enemy advanced even to *La Haye Sainte*, but were arrested in their furious career by our immortal Chief in person, who, at the head of his intrepid soldiers, retook that blood stained spot. The cottage has been entirely new roofed, though its shattered walls and doors still testify the obstinate combat it gave rise to. On the left wing behind and before the hedge, but especially near the spot where the gallant Picton fell, a multitude of little mounds cover the ashes of the British and Allied Soldiers, who were intered in heaps together.

It was not without unfeigned emotion we cast a regard of gratitude and admiration on those heroes' graves, over which the grass and some wild flowers are just beginning to spring! At the extremity of the right wing, we recognized the brush, where the Prince of Orange, emulating his forefathers, was wounded; and then reached the too famous chateau of Hougoumont, where destruction dealt its most deadly blows. The interior of the edifice, consumed by fire, and demolished by the cannon, presents a melancholy mass of ruins; the trees in the neighbourhood are pierced with balls, though their foliage and growth appear a little more injured than what might be expected in this unusually fine season. We next crossed the fatal field where our artillery crushed eleven hundred intrepid Frenchmen, who, with a gallantry worthy of a better cause, persevered in the desperate attack. It was in contemplating this spot, the morning after the battle, that a British Officer observed, that the heaps of [*illegible*] dead of all nations amassed together, presented to his mind '*an immense army in a profound sleep.*'

The plains around it towards *La Belle Alliance*, are yet deeply imprinted with the hoofs of horses, all taking a direction from which but few were doomed to return. In some parts the slain are interred so near the surface of the earth that black portions of the human frame piercing their tenements, strike the spectator with horror!

We had now reached *La Belle Alliance*, and reposed ourselves in the chamber, wherein Blucher and Wellington embraced each other amidst the exulting shouts of victory, and the more distant roar of the cannon pursuing and exterminating the flying foe. A more interesting spectacle I never witnessed. Honour to those heroes who devoted themselves to certain death for their country's cause with Spartan inflexibility! – that grateful country has already consecrated to them a crown of well-earned laurels, of which not a leaf will ever lose its verdure.

We found dispersed over the field of battle, fragments of shells and other engines of destruction, while in the cottage of Lacoste, Napoleon's guide, the credulous Englishman was purchasing sabres, and buttons, and cuirasses, and other relics, of which, in all probability, the greater part was concealed at Brussels for this express purpose. Many of the adjoining villages have been enriched by the plunder of the dying and the dead, and M. Lacoste still draws deeply on the curiosity of the traveller, whom he adroitly satisfies, with narratives and anecdotes, fashioned to the political party he is presumed to support.

Another extract from a letter, this time coming from a German officer and which was dated 16 July 1815, states the following:

I have visited the field of battle. The sleep of the dead is sound. On the spot where this day month thousands thronged and fought, where thousands sank and bled, and groaned and died, there is now not a living soul, and over all hovers the stillness of the grave.

293

In Ligny 2000 dead were buried. Here fought the Westphalian and Berg regiments. Ligny is a village built of stone and thatched with straw, on a small stream which flows through flat meadows. In the village are several farm-houses, inclosed with walls and gates. Every farm-house the Prussians had converted into a fortress. The French endeavoured to penetrate through the village by means of superior numbers. Four times were they driven out. At last they set on fire the farm-houses in the upper end of the village with their howitzers; but the Prussians still kept their ground at the lower end. A whole company of Westphalian troops fell in the court-yard at the church; on the terrace before the church lay 50 dead.

In the evening the French surrounded the village. The Prussians retired half a league: the position was lost; and it is incomprehensible why the French did not follow up the advantage they had obtained, and again attack the Prussians in the night.

This was on the 16th.[3]

This brief note was published in the *Caledonian Mercury* of 27 July 1815, once again under the oft-used headline 'The Battle of Waterloo':

La Belle Alliance, the little place from which, with a silly and unmeaning conceit, some of the papers would denominate the grand battle of the 18th, consists of not more than three or four wretched houses, one of which is nearly destroyed by the cannon shot. The plain of Waterloo is a magnificent scene, and a prize-fighting ground worthy of such a battle.

The position of the French was woody; that of the Allies chiefly covered with grain. Rye was the prevailing species. It grows so high, that a Scotch regiment, in advancing through a field of it on the 16th, was nearly cut to pieces without seeing an enemy. The French observed its approach by the tops of its muskets shining in the corn, and took their aim accordingly, while our troops could only fire at random.

As the following article in the *Leicester Journal* of Friday, 26 January 1816 states, any stories or visits to Waterloo were newsworthy:

So deep is the interest in the immortal battle of Waterloo, that whatever relates to it is eagerly perused by the public; and, notwithstanding the lapse of time, and the quantity of information already before them, their thirst is as yet unalloyed.

Our Author left Brussels, and proceeded to the field of battle, whither our readers must attend him.

'With that conflict of feelings which the expectation of soon seeing the scene of such a battle as Waterloo naturally occasioned, our party consisting of three, was in readiness by six in the morning on the 31st July. When we had mounted our carriage, we called to the postilion – *"Waterloo!"* – *"Oui, Monsieur l'Anglois,"* he answered, with a smack of his whip, and an emphasis which showed that he felt that conducting Englishmen *thither*, was conducting them to their own proper domain. There had been rain during the night, and the morning was gloomy; having, as we are told, the same appearance as that of the 18th of June: of course we would not have exchanged it for the brightest sunshine – The ground would be wet, but so it was on the day of the battle; and further, in point of time, we should just arrive about the hour it commenced.

'After driving three or four miles, we entered the awful forest of Soigné. It covers an immense extent of country from east to west, but is only about six or seven miles broad, where the road passes through it to Waterloo.

'Our postilion pointed out the little mounds where men and horses had been interred; they were apparent every hundred yards. The sepulture had been hurried and imperfect, especially of the horses; occasional hoofs, and even limbs, showing themselves. Often bayonet scabbards stuck out; and caps, shoes, and pieces of cloth, scarcely in the gloom distinguishable from the mud in which they lay, gave indication of the spots where many a soldier, after bleeding in the field, and toiling along the road to expected aid and comfort, unassisted, almost unpitied, by the self engaged sufferers who saw him fall, had sunk to rise no more. Some rain fell as we were bestowing a passing survey upon these affecting monuments of the brave, in a situation the most dismal we had ever beheld.

'Waterloo's village, and small neat church, with its brick built dome, was now in our view, situated in a recess of the wood, evidently cleared for it. The road was now quite out of the forest; which, however, blackened the whole region to east and west as far as the eye could reach. In this poor hamlet, which history is to name with veneration as long as time endures, the peasants have been at pains to preserve the chalking on the doors; on which we recognised the well known names of celebrated officers, or the officers of the several departments at head quarters.

'We were immediately surrounded by the people offering for sale, with great importunity, the relics of the field; particularly the eagles which the French soldiers wore as cap plates. A few cuirasses, both the back and the breast pieces, were likewise held up to us, as well as sabres, bayonets, and other spoils.

'We drove a mile forward to the still smaller hamlet of Mount St. John, by a gradual ascent of the road; to right and left of which the British army bivouacked on the eve of the battle; having advanced over the high ground in the morning, to the southern slope facing the enemy, on fair open ground, without an advantage, to decide the fate of the world.

'Mount St. John is quite behind the British line; and had its name given by Bonaparte to what was properly the farm house of La Haye Sainte, which he did succeed in carrying; but certainly he never was so far advanced as Mont St. John; indeed he never did, for more than a few minutes, at any time succeed in penetrating the English line.

'We left our carriage at this last hamlet, and walked on to the field with nervous anticipation. To the right and left were the multiplied marks of the artillery wheels, as rivalling 'lightning's course in ruin and in speed,' they had careered to their enemies in the memorable line. Whole tracks were marked by the feet of the cavalry, often fetlock deep in mud. The last homes of the brave began to appear, with the larger tumuli of their horses, more frequent as we approached the scene of contest. Keeping still the great road, we came to a tree which formed the precise centre of the British line; the well chosen station of the Duke of Wellington, when not occasionally visiting other parts of the position to confirm the unflinching spirit of his gallant comrades. It commanded a full view of the intermediate plain, and the whole of the enemy's vast force upon the adverse slope and country beyond it, with every movement made or threatened by him.

'Nothing is more false than the French apology (added to their never-failing pretence of being overpowered by numbers), that the British position was naturally strong, and carefully fortified. *Un-entrenched* stood the British army, along its whole position, on a slope so gentle, that a coach driving up would not slacken pace; and to the ridge of which the French cavalry found no difficulty in galloping at full speed to the very bayonets of their opponents, who threw themselves into squares, their only entrenchments, to receive the charge. It was, to use a favourite English phrase, just the place for "*a fair set to; a clear field, and no favour.*"

'We had the good fortune to meet with a very intelligent English officer, who had been in the action, and who had that day paid his first visit to the field, after recovering of his wound.

'From Lord Wellington's station, we stood and gazed on the whole scene: not daring to break silence for some minutes. And deep was now the silence of the vast sepulchre of 20,000 men, contrasted with the roar and the carnage of the battle. The gloomy weather still lasted; and was valued by us, as peculiarly suitable to the scene we were contemplating. The imagination is incalculably aided by viewing the scene of a memorable battle. The actors being generally familiar to us, we can easily people the field with them; and become thereby actually present, in conception, at the moment of the event. Indeed, so very simple is the field of Waterloo, that a conception of very ordinary power may quite take it from description alone. Although here and there varied by inequalities and indulations, it will serve all popular purposes to say, that at the distance from each other of about a mile, the contending armies occupied parallel high grounds, sloping with almost equal declivity, to a plain of about half a mile broad which intervened.

'The English line, or rather two lines, extended about a mile and a half – the French masses something more than two miles. The Brussels road ran at right angles through both armies; forming the centre of each. On this road, in one line, are the villages of Waterloo, and Mont St. John, and the farm houses of La Haye Sante, and La Belle Alliance; and the only other place which requires to be referred to is the memorable *Chateau* of Hougomont, advanced a short way in front of nearly the right of the British position.

'The road from Brussels to Nivelles, which branches off at Waterloo from the great road already described, passed the right of the army; which last being thrown back into a curve, crossed the angle formed by the two roads, like the scale of a quadrant. A number of smaller roads and foot-paths intersected the field in all directions, none of them of any importance in the affair, excepting always those which admitted the brave Prussians to their share of the glory of delivering the world.'

Even two years after the battle, interest had not waned, as this report printed in the *Chester Courant* of Tuesday, 29 July 1817 demonstrates:

The following particulars have been communicated by a person of Liverpool, just returned from a tour through the Netherlands:-

The village of Waterloo and its environs are at this moment, perhaps, more interesting to an English visitor than at any period since the battle. The most affecting testimonials to the memory of different illustrious individuals who fell in that terrible conflict meet the eye in almost every direction. The interior of the church of Waterloo, a small, but very neat structure, is nearly covered with monuments to the memory of British officers. All of these are written in such a strain of manly and modest simplicity, and some of them under circumstances of such affecting tenderness, that every English reader, while his heart is touched with the deepest sympathy, must feel himself elated in belonging to a country which has produced instances of such unparalleled heroism.

In the church-yard, among many other monuments, appears the mausoleum of the Marquess of Anglesey's leg, with an inscription that reflects the highest honour on that distinguished nobleman.

To the wall of La Haye Sainte, next the high road, is affixed a plain mural monument, with a short, but most sublime and touching inscription, to the honour of those officers of the German Legion who fell in the arduous task of defending this farm against an entire division of the French army. It is erected by the surviving officers of that distinguished regiment, to the memory of their departed brethren.

The celebrated chateau of Hougoumont remains in the state in which it was left after the battle, – a heap of ruins. The marks of the shot still remain on the trees and garden wall, where the English guards fought with such persevering and unsubdued energy.

A splendid monument is now erecting in the open field, on the very spot where the hero fell, to the memory of Sir Alexander Gordon, of whom such distinguished mention was made in the House of Commons and by the Duke of Wellington. The inscription, which, like all the others, is admirably written, states, that it is dedicated to the memory of the deceased, by his seven surviving brothers and sisters. The same inscription appears in the French language on the opposite side of the pedestal.

But of all the testimonials which have been erected on this most interesting occasion, there is none more deeply affecting than a plain black stone, which appears in the centre of the church of Waterloo, the inscription of which is written in Latin, and signed Henry Cuppage; after stating that the conduct and gallantry of the deceased had been such as to attract the notice even of their great Commander-in-Chief, it concludes with these affecting expressions: – 'His only surviving brother, who fought by his side during that long and arduous day, and at night received his last breath whilst supporting him in his arms, has erected this simple stone to the memory of one who was endeared to him by the strongest ties that can bind two human beings to each other.'

It is painful to conclude this account with an instance of the behaviour of the ungrateful Belgians on a late occasion, which can never be forgotten. The inhabitants of Brussels and its neighbourhood, including many distinguished personages, public functionaries, &c. celebrated the anniversary of the battle of Waterloo on the 18th ult. by a splendid fête champétre given on the field itself. The Brussels papers of the following day gave a minute account of this brilliant commemoration, with all the toasts, speeches, &c. which were delivered on so striking an occasion. Would it be believed, that neither the name of the Duke of Wellington, nor the English army is once mentioned in the narration?

The following account was also published in 1817, mentioning that 'La Belle Alliance is a farm-house, situate on the plains of Waterloo, about three-quarters of a mile from La Haye Sainte, on the road to Gemappe':

> The house, which is very small, is kept by M. Decase; and the writer of this article visited the place in May, 1816, together with several military gentlemen, who explained to him most minutely the situation of the contending armies on the glorious 18th of June, 1815. The outbuildings of La Belle Alliance are in ruins. At a short distance from this house is the cottage which formerly belonged to the peasant, who was detained by Buonaparte, as his guide and interpreter. This cottager attended me and my companions over the plains of Waterloo, and spoke in high terms of the bravery of the British troops, and the determined resolution of the enemy.
>
> At this place, as well as in other parts of the country about Waterloo, the peasants offer to travellers innumerable relics of the dreadful conflict. Helmets, cuirasses, sabres, medals, eagles, buttons, and various other articles, are here to be purchased on easy terms. I purchased, for twelve francs, (ten shillings English), a very handsome sword, which belonged to a grenadier of Napoleon's imperial guard.[4]

According to Edward Cotton of the 7th Hussars, who had written his account having visited the battlefield some years later,

> The most interesting objects now at Hougoumont, for visitors to see are the north gateway facing our position, by which the enemy entered, its burnt beams, the small barn where many of the wounded were burnt, the cannon-ball hole in the east gable of the building attached to the present farm-house ... The cannon-ball [which] entered the west end of the large building [is] still in existence; consequently [it] must have passed through four, if not five walls, before it came out at the east end looking into the garden, or park.[5]

Amongst the most famous travellers to write about the battlefield in the years following the battle was Victor Hugo, who wrote the following passage in his famous book *Les Misérables*:

The field of Waterloo to-day has that calm which belongs to the earth, impassive support of man; it resembles any other plain.

At night, however, a sort of visionary mist arises from it, and if some traveller be walking there, if he looks, if he listens, if he dreams ... The terrible 18th of June is again before him ... the lines of infantry undulate in the plain, furious gallops traverse the horizon; the bewildered dreamer sees the flash of sabres, the glistening of bayonets, the bursting of shells, the awful intermingling of the thunders; he hears, like the death-rattle from the depths of a tomb, the vague clamour of the phantom battle; these shadows are grenadiers; these gleams are cuirassiers ... and the ravines run red, and the trees shiver, and there is fury even in the clouds, and, in the darkness, all those savage heights. Mont Saint Jean, Hougoumont, Frischermonte, Papelotte, Plachenoit, appear confusedly crowned with whirlwinds of spectres exterminating each other.[6]

25

Honouring the Brave

Victory brings with it rewards and a proud nation sought to honour its heroes. Though the award of Prize Money was a well-established principle in the Royal Navy, it was also applied to the victories of the British Army. Though generally distributed at the instigation of Commanders-in-Chief, in some instances the funds were controlled by local commanders. The Waterloo Prize Money was, however, granted by Parliament and was divided as follows:[1]

	£	s.	d.
Commander-in-Chief	61,000	0	0
General Officers	1,274	10	10 ¾
Field officers and colonels	433	2	4 ½
Captains	90	7	3 ¾
Subalterns	34	14	9 ½
Sergeants	19	4	4
Corporals, drummers and privates	2	11	4

The *Chester Chronicle* on 4 June 1819, took a moment to point out to its readers that 'by the above scale' the Duke of Wellington,

> Gains a share nearly equal to 50 General Officers, 113 Field Officers, 666 Captains, 1,818 Subalterns, 3,158 Serjeants, [and] 24,000 Rank and File.

The distribution of the Prize Money was not without controversy. The matter was raised in Parliament on 7 May 1819 by Henry Bennet, the MP for Shrewsbury:

> Whether it was from the vague and unsatisfactory regulations made for the distribution of this money, or from what other cause he knew not, but the effect was, that numbers of those who were entitled to it

301

had been refused, while it was foisted upon those who had no claim whatever to receive it. The troops not actually engaged had been deprived of this money, though they were employed as beneficially, in protecting the flanks of the army and guarding the baggage, &c. as they otherwise could be: yet those troops who were on their passage from America, and those who had been lounging in St. James's-street, when the battle was fought, and who had travelled over to Paris, en bourgeois, in their gigs, were allowed to participate in it.

The whole of the medical department, who had the care of the wounded of all countries, were also excluded from any share of this money. Was this fair or equitable? The whole of the Hanoverian corps, who had sustained great injury in the action, had also been excluded, with the exception (and it was rather a curious sort of exception), of those officers who had run away from their regiments, either before or during the action. Those officers who had so ran away, having joined the army before it reached Paris, were allowed prize money, while those who had remained at their posts were, according to some new-fangled rule, refused it.

Some more fair and liberal division of this prize-money ought to be made, and he hoped the noble lord would take the subject into consideration.

In addition to the generous prize money, the Duke of Wellington received other rewards, as the *Norfolk Chronicle* of Saturday, 1 July 1815 reported:

On FRIDAY, the THANKS of PARLIAMENT were voted to the DUKE of WELLINGTON for the consummate ability, unexampled exertion, and irresistible ardour which he displayed in the command of the allied army, in his conflict with, and splendid victory over Buonaparte in person. Thanks were also voted to the Officers and Troops respectively, who shared in the glory of the day, as well as to Marshal Blucher, and the Prussian Army, for their important assistance, which so materially contributed to the success.

In compliance with a Message from the Prince Regent, the sum of 200,000 *l* was likewise voted (in addition to sums already granted to his Grace) for the purpose of building and furnishing a house fit for the residence of the Duke of Wellington. While on this topic, the Earl of *Liverpool* remarked, that he never knew a more disinterested man than the Duke. Since his appointment to high command, there were several occasions when he must have been in difficult and even distressed circumstances, and yet he had never made any application for money.

Wellington may have been a duke in the British aristocracy, but in August 1815 he became a prince in the United Netherlands:

> The Secretary of State to the King of the Netherlands has officially announced that his Majesty has conferred the title of Prince of Waterloo upon the Duke of Wellington, and the title of Marquis of Heusden upon the Earl of Clancarty.[2]

Field Marshal Blücher was already a Prince, and all he received from King Frederick William, the King of Prussia, was a medal. The order conferred 'was accompanied with the following very gracious note in the King's own hand writing' (the note being dated 26 July 1815):

> As a memorial of your late victories, I wish you to wear the insignia which you will receive with this note, in the place of the Iron Cross of the first class. I know that no golden ornament can heighten the splendour of your merits; but it is a delightful task for me to announce, by suitable external distinctions, how fully I acknowledge them, reserving to myself for more peaceful times the pleasure of giving you still further marks of my continued gratitude.[3]

Wellington was indeed amply rewarded for his services, but the ordinary solders were not forgotten. As the announcement in the *Morning Post* of Monday, 31 July 1815 reveals, the men received more than just their prize money:

> We are rejoiced to hear that his Royal Highness the Prince Regent is about to testify his sense of the conduct of the British army in the battle of Waterloo, by increasing the pension of wounded Officers, and to allow Subalterns, Non-commissioned Officers, and Soldiers, to count two years' service in virtue of that victory, and to be honourably distinguished as 'Waterloo Men.'

It was also decided that every man that had taken part in the Waterloo campaign, whether they had actually been involved in any of the fighting or not, would be issued with a medal. The issue of the medal was announced in *The London Gazette* of 23 April 1816, the memorandum being dated 'Horse-Guards, March 10, 1816':

> The Prince Regent, has been graciously pleased, in the name and on the behalf of His Majesty, to command, that, in commemoration of the brilliant and decisive victory of Waterloo, a medal shall be

conferred upon every Officer, Non-Commissioned Officer, and Soldier of the British Army present upon that memorable occasion.

His Royal Highness has further been pleased to command, that the ribband issued with the medal shall never be worn, but with the medal suspended to it.

About 39,000 medals were struck, (6,000 to the cavalry, 4,000 to the Guards, 16,000 to the infantry, 5,000 to the Artillery, 6,500 to the King's German Legion and 1,500 to miscellaneous units, attachments and others) and the first instalment was reported by the Mint as being ready for delivery on 4 March 1816. They were issued throughout 1816 and 1817.

Not only was the Waterloo Medal the first campaign medal awarded to all ranks, it was also the first medal awarded to the next-of-kin of men killed in action. As well as the award of the medal, recipients were also credited with two extra years' service and pay.

The distribution of the medals to the Scots Greys was recorded in the *Caledonian Mercury* of 22 April 1816. The medals were handed out by Colonel Clarke, who made the following speech:

> I have the pleasure this day to deliver these medals to the regiment, which is the most gratifying duty that has fallen to my lot since I had the honour of commanding one of the finest, I was most tempted to say, the finest regiment of cavalry in the British service, whose well-known valour needs no comment from an humble individual like myself. Its fame is registered in the hearts of all men, and its name will live revered and respected as long as history remains.
>
> May happiness be yours, and may you all long live to enjoy these honourable marks of your country's applause. May they stimulate those who wear them to further acts of bravery, wherever their services may be required, and may the bright example stimulate the young recruit.
>
> At this moment I feel but one regret, that it is not in my power to present every man in the regiment with a medal; but let not those who are excluded from the honour feel the slightest uneasiness. I now allude to those who were serving at the depot. We all know, that their hearts panted to share the glories of the day; but the various duties on which they were employed at home were of the highest magnitude; and it must also be recollected, that many of them were actually engaged in providing comforts for their comrades on service.
>
> It remains for me only to urge one request, that every man will most religiously treasure the medal given to him by the Prince Regent,

in the name and on behalf of his Majesty, as a testimony of his most gracious approbation of their well earned fame; – let them guard the precious gift to the latest hour of their lives; and, when summoned from this to a better world, let them bequeath it to their children, who will proudly exclaim, 'This was my father's – who gained immortal honour at the battle of Waterloo! This was my father's – who gloriously assisted in giving peace to Europe! This was my father's – who helped to hurl the tyrant Bonaparte from the throne of France to the rock of St. Helena.'

A few days later, it was the turn of the men of the 23rd Light Dragoons. This account of the presentation ceremony, written by a reporter for the *Morning Post*, was published on Friday, 30 May 1816:

Last Sunday [30 April], we witnessed a grand, interesting and gratifying Military Spectacle, at Radspole Barracks, that imposed on the feelings of every one present the most reverential awe. It being the period appointed that Lieut.-Colonel CUTCLIFFE read the commands of his Royal Highness the Commander-in-Chief, previous to his distributing the honourable Medals to that part of the 23d Regiment of Light Dragoons which so nobly distinguished itself at the ever-memorable Battle of Waterloo, on the 18th of last June ...

In the morning the troops paraded as usual for Divine Service; after which, the ranks were opened to receive those inestimable badges of distinction.

The guard, which formed on the right of the regiment, wheeled to the left; the Standard-bearers, together with the Troop Sergeant-Majors, formed in their front; the latter for the purpose of carrying the Medals of their respective Troops, which were laid on separate silver salvers ...

Their distribution being completed, Lieut.-Colonel CUTCLIFFE addressed the Regiment in very eloquent, animated, and appropriate terms; at the conclusion of which, the vociferations and heartfelt acclamations of the whole Regiment were heard at a great distance, and repeated by a very respectable assemblage of visitants and inhabitants.

The myth that it was the Grenadiers of the Old Guard who in the 1st Guards defeated in the last French attack at Waterloo became firmly established almost immediately after the battle, and indeed is still widely believed today. This received official recognition in a note from the War Office on 29 July, which was reproduced in the *Cambridge Chronicle* of Friday, 4 August 1815:

The Prince Regent, as a mark of his Royal approbation of the distinguished gallantry of the Brigade of Foot Guards in the Victory of Waterloo, has been pleased, in the name and on behalf of his Majesty, to approve of all the Ensigns of the three Regiments of Foot Guards having the rank of Lieutenants, and that such rank shall be attached to all the future appointments to Ensigncies in the Foot Guards in the same manner as the Lieutenants of those Regiments obtain the rank of Captain. – His Royal Highness has also been pleased to approve of the 1st Regiment of Foot Guards being made a Regiment of Grenadiers, and styled 'The 1st or Grenadier Regiment of Foot Guards,' in commemoration of their having defeated the Grenadiers of the French Imperial Guards upon this occasion.

Another of the Household regiments to be honoured was the Life Guards, who, it was announced, would be granted the same ranks as those referred to above in the Foot Guards.[4]

The Prince Regent then went one step further, as the *Lancaster Gazette* of Saturday, 29 July 1815, duly reported:

The Prince Regent, as a mark of his high approbation of the distinguished bravery and good conduct of the 1st and 2d Life Guards at the battle of Waterloo, on the 18th ult. is pleased to declare himself Colonel in Chief of both the Regiments of Life Guards.

His Royal Highness the Regent has been pleased, in the name and on the behalf of his Majesty, to approve of all the British regiments of cavalry and infantry which were engaged in the battle of Waterloo, being permitted to bear on their colours and appointments, in addition to any other badges or devices that may have heretofore been granted to those regiments, 'Waterloo', in commemoration of their distinguished services, on the 18th of June, 1815.

A more significant gesture was made when a 'Great Patriotic Meeting' was held in London at the City of London Tavern by the Merchants, Bankers 'and others' to 'consider opening a subscription for the relief of the Widows of those who fell in the Battle of Waterloo'. The Chairman was the banker Mr Alexander Baring. Another banker, by the name of Fuller, opened the subscription by promising the sum of 200 guineas and at the same time hoping that 'gentlemen of Bond-street would lay off buying baubles and nonsense, and a pack of fooleries' and urging them instead to 'spend their money more laudably' – not only for the good of their fellow-men but also their soul. The meeting ended with £500 having been subscribed.

The idea was quickly seized upon by towns and cities around the United Kingdom, an example of which was reported in the *Leeds Intelligencer* of Monday, 31 July 1815:

> At a MEETING of the INHABITANTS of the Town and Neighbourhood of Huddersfield, convened by the Constable, and held on the 24th of July, 1815, for the Purpose of cheerfully co-operating with their Fellow-Subjects, on a Case so interesting to the Feelings of Britons, by manifesting their Support in pecuniary Aid, to the WIDOWS and CHILDREN of those who have so nobly fallen, and to those who return Disabled, from the same glorious Struggles at Waterloo, &c.

The Chairman was one Mr. W. M. Rhodes. The meeting passed the following resolution, as the same edition of the *Leeds Intelligencer* noted:

> *Resolved*. That a subscription be now opened, for the Benefit of the Families of the Brave Men Killed, and of the Wounded Sufferers of the British Army, under the command of the Illustrious Wellington, in the signal Victory of Waterloo, and in the several Battles which preceded or may succeed during the present Campaign; and that all Persons be invited to join in this Expression of National Gratitude: – They are reminded, that the Army most nobly did their Duty to their Country, – and they called upon, *to do their Duty to the Army*.

Such subscriptions were soon to adopt a more formal and official status after this announcement by the Prince Regent:

> WATERLOO SUBSCRIPTION. – The Prince Regent has written a Mandatory Letter to the Archbishops of Canterbury and York, requesting the benevolent interposition of the Church in aid of the Waterloo Subscription; and in consequence of this humane recommendation, there will be a collection made for that patriotic fund throughout all the parishes of the Empire. The official letter directs, that 'the ministers do effectually excite their parishioners to a liberal contribution, which shall be collected the week following the Sermon, at their respective dwellings, by the churchwardens and overseers of the poor, in each parish.'[5]

In the end, the Waterloo Subscription fund managed to raise sufficient funds for the widows to receive £10 per year – but only if they remained unmarried!

26

After the Battle Anecdotes

The Battle of Waterloo ended a generation of warfare and throughout the early decades of the nineteenth century it continued to be the subject of books, memoirs and occasionally newspaper articles. Such articles and recollections were as random as the selection presented here.

On Friday, 17 May 1816, for example, the *Chester Chronicle* published the following account under the title, 'Memorable Anecdote':

At the Battle of Waterloo, Major Dick, of the 42d Highlanders, preferring to fight on foot in front of his men, had given his horse to hold to a little drummer-boy of the regiment. After some hard fighting with the French horse cuirassiers and lancers, and receiving several severe wounds, he fell, from loss of blood, near a brave private (Donald Mackintosh) of his corps, who was mortally wounded at the same instant. The little drummer had left the horse to assist poor Donald; a lancer seeing the horse, thought him a fair prize, and made a dash at him; this did not escape the watchful and keen eye of the dying Highlander, who, with all the provident spirit of his country, 'ruling strong even in death,' groaned out 'hoot man, ye munna tak' that beast, 't belongs to our Captain here.'

The lancer, understanding little of his dialect, and respecting less his writhing gestures, seized on the horse; Donald levelled his musket once more, shot him dead, and the next moment fell back and expired himself. An Officer of the cuirassiers, observing our poor Major still bestirring himself, rode up, and stooping from his charger, aimed to dispatch him with his sword. The Major seized his leg, and still grappled with him so stoutly, that he pulled him off his horse upon him.

Another lancer observing this struggle, galloped up to relieve his officer, and attempted to spear the Major, who, by a sudden jerk and exertion, placed the Frenchman, in the nick of the necessity, in his arms before him, who received his mortal thrust below his cuirasse, and in this condition continued lying upon him with his sword in his hand for near ten minutes. The Major, unconscious that he had bestowed a death wound, expected all this time to receive his own at his hand; at last the French Officer raised himself, ran or staggered a few yards, and then fell to struggle or to rise no more.

Another private of his regiment now came up and asked his Major what he could do to assist him. 'Nothing, my good friend, but load your piece and finish me!' – 'But your eye still looks lively,' said the poor fellow, 'if I could move you to the 92d, fighting hard by, I think you would yet do well.'

With the aid of a fellow-soldier he was moved as the man proposed, and soon seen by an intimate friend, Colonel Cameron, commanding the 92d, who instantly ordered him every succour possible; a blanket and four men carried him a little in the rear. While they were raising him, Colonel Cameron exclaimed, 'God bless you! I must be off; the devils (meaning the lancers) are at us again. I must stand up to them.'

He did so, and in a few minutes, stretched dead on the bed of honor, finished his mortal career of glory in the bold defence of his country. It is a pleasure to add, that the brave Major is still alive, wearing the honourable decoration and marks of sixteen wounds received in this unequal and arduous conflict, and lame from a severe wound received before at the storming of Badajos.

Captain John Kincaid related an incident that took place the day after the Battle of Waterloo:

Two of our men on the morning of the 19th lost their lives by a very melancholy accident. They were cutting up a captured ammunition-wagon for the firewood, when one of their swords striking against a nail sent a spark among the powder. When I looked in the direction of the explosion, I saw the two poor fellows about twenty or thirty feet up in the air.

On falling to the ground, though lying on their backs or bellies, some extraordinary effort of nature, caused by the agony of the moment, made them spring from that position five or six times to the height of eight or ten feet, just as a fish does when thrown on the ground after being newly caught ... I ran to the spot along with others, and found that every stitch of clothes had been burnt off, and they were black as ink all over. They were still alive, and told us their names, otherwise we could not have recognised them; and, singularly enough, they were able to walk off the ground with a little support, but died shortly after.[1]

The following was printed in the *Caledonian Mercury* on Thursday, 27 July 1815:

> The ground being very deep in many parts of the field, the troops presented a frightful appearance, particularly the life guards, from the splashing of the mud increased by the weight of their horses. The French could scarcely dare to look at them. They called them the *Red Lions*.
>
> Among the effective incidents of the day is mentioned an *hurrah* given by an Irish regiment in the act of charging. The shock struck terror into the opposing line, which fled, before it felt the bayonet.

The Irish regiment in question was probably the 27th or Inniskilling Regiment of Foot. It is interesting to note that the Inniskillings included Protestants as well as Catholics with, by all accounts, no problems existing between the two religions.

Napoleon himself took an entirely pragmatic view of religion, fully appreciating its influence upon the masses. It was probably this, and his manipulation of Pope Pius VII, that prompted the following remark:

> On the receipt, in Edinburgh, of the intelligence of the battle of Waterloo, an old woman was passing a crowd assembled to read one of the bulletins put up by the Magistrates, on which she asked, 'What's that ye're a'looking at there folk?' She was told it was an account of a great victory gained over Bonaparte. She then asked when that had happened, and being told on Sunday, she exclaimed – 'Sunday! Say ye: he ne'er minded Sunday, but a troth, he'll no forget it now!'[2]

The next story comes from the *Historical Records of the Eighteenth Hussars*:

> This anecdote of the day may be worth relating: On first encountering the Cuirassiers, Serjeant Taylor of The Regiment made a cut at the head of one of them, which had no other effect on the Frenchman than to induce him to cry out in derision, 'Ha, ha!' and to return a severe blow at the serjeant, which was admirably parried. Taylor then thrust his sabre into the mouth of the Cuirassier, who instantly fell, and the conqueror cried 'Ha, ha!' in his turn, which much increased the ardour of his comrades.[3]

The *Royal Cornwall Gazette* of Saturday, 23 September 1815 shows the degree of animosity that was still evident between Britain and her former American colonies. Some of the British troops that fought at Waterloo had only just arrived back in Europe from the war in America which, after two and a half years of fighting, had recently ended in stalemate:

> American papers to the 13th ult. reached town on Monday. The battle of Waterloo, the abdication of Buonaparte, and the capture of Paris, were all known in America. Many of the papers seem sullen and dogged and will not offer a single comment upon these events. One of them is loud in praise of Buonaparte, whom it compares to Epaminondas and Regulus. Some of these American Editors would do well to go to school again.

Such sentiments had already been displayed in America when news of Napoleon's return to power became known. Unfortunately for the ex-colonists, their news was already out of date. The following note was published in the *London Gazette* of Saturday, 29 July 1815, under the headline 'Miscellaneous Intelligence':

> In the American Papers to the 25th ult. the return of Buonaparte to France is contemplated with extravagant joy – and one paper says, 'Napoleon the Great is popular throughout America since his return from Elba and re-assumption of the throne, and he ought to be, for the system of freedom he is now establishing.' Poor American Journalists! How short-lived will be their joy – how altered their tone, when they know that Napoleon the Great is in the custody of the Lords of this little Island!

It was on Wednesday, 4 October 1815 that the following review (of sorts) was published in the *Hereford Journal*:

> A very interesting memoir is expected to be published in a few days by Marshal Soult, containing a defence of his conduct during the last 18 months. He laid the substance of it some weeks ago before the King, but without effect. It will, however, be very interesting as a history. He proposes giving a detailed review of his administration as Minister of War, and of the short campaign which fixed the destinies of Bonaparte, and of France.
>
> It is said to contain some very severe strictures on the military character of Bonaparte, and particularly of his conduct at the battle of

Waterloo – Soult attended him constantly during the day as Major-General of the army, and frequently remonstrated with him in the most peremptory manner, when the fortune of the day turned in favour of the Allies, but before the close, Soult addressed Bonaparte in the presence of his Staff, and forcibly insisted upon the necessity of retreating before all was lost. Bonaparte replied that he had frequently gained the victory after having been reduced to a situation of greater difficulty. 'Sire,' said Soult, 'you seem to think a battle is a game of hazard, not of skill.' Bonaparte instantly ordered his guard to charge – they advanced in silence – not one cried *Vive l'Empereur*, and at least half remained dead upon the field of battle.

In the very same edition of the *Hereford Journal* this little exchange of words was printed, but the exact reason for the discussion is not made clear:

Excellent Retort. – During the late events, Marshal Ney said to the Swiss Gen. Bachmann, 'Do you know that we fight for honour, while you fight for money?' 'Yes,' returned the Swiss, 'we both fight for that which we have not.' Niklaus Leodegar Franz Ignaz von Bachmann was the Commander in Chief of the Swiss Army and was part of the occupying forces at the time he spoke to Marshal Ney.

The next story, of a rather repugnant nature, was reported in the *Morning Chronicle* of Thursday, 7 December 1815:

Amongst the many new and singular articles of trade recently imported from the Continent, are several boxes, containing an immense number of human teeth for the use of the Dentists, but great has been the disappointment of these traders of this part of the human body, taken from the slain of the Battle of Waterloo, when they heard that this pernicious practice was entirely proscribed [by] this country, and that the only artificial teeth now used are those of mineral composition, made and invented by the celebrated Dentist, Mr. de Chemant, of No.2, Frith-street, Soho-square.

Proscribed or not, some sets of dentures were still made from the Waterloo teeth, at least one example of which can still be seen today at the Army Medical Services Museum, Aldershot.

The use of teeth, and other body parts, taken from the bodies of the dead continued for many years afterwards, as the following staggering article in the *London Observer* of 18 November 1822 reveals:

More than a million of bushels of human and inhuman bones were imported last year from the continent of Europe into the port of Hull. The neighbourhood of ... Waterloo, and of all the places where, during the late bloody war, the principle battles were fought, have been swept alike of the bones of the hero and the horse which he rode.

Thus collected from every quarter, they have been shipped to the port of Hull, and thence forwarded to the Yorkshire bone-grinders, who have erected steam-engines and powerful machinery, for the purpose of reducing them to a granulary state.

In this condition they are sent chiefly to Doncaster, one of the largest agricultural markets in that part of the country, and are there sold to farmers to manure their lands. ... It is now ascertained beyond doubt, by actual experiment on an extensive scale, that a dead soldier is a most valuable article of commerce ... It is certainly a singular fact, that Great Britain should have sent out such multitudes of soldiers to fight the battles of this country upon the continent of Europe, and should then import their bones as an article of commerce to fatten her soil!

As with any battle, there were many acts of bravery played out at Waterloo:

COLONEL COLQUIT. This gallant officer, perceiving a shell that had just fallen in a square which he at that moment occupied, took it up with the most perfect composure, and threw it over the heads of the soldiers, down a declivous bank, by which the terrible effects of its explosion amidst the men were happily prevented. [4]

What is of note here is that similar acts of courage in the Crimean War, the next major European conflict, were recognised by the award of the then recently introduced Victoria Cross.

It is always interesting to learn what great individuals chose to read, especially when they do not expect such information ever to be revealed to the general public. With regards to Napoleon, we are fortunate to know exactly which books he took with him on his final campaign. This list was published in the *Morning Post* of Thursday, 27 July 1815:

The field library carried by NAPOLEON with him during the last campaign, and taken on the 19th June, at Charleroi, consisted of the following works:

The Bible, Homer, Manon Lescant, Bossuet, La Pucelle, the History of Henry IV, the Conspiracy of Rienzi, La Pitie (poem by Delille), the Anarchy of Poland, La Fontaine's Tales, History of the Progress and

Downfall of the Roman Republic, Don Quixotte, Treaties of the Peace by Martens, Gil Blas, Memorial of the Revolution, The Devil upon Two Sticks, the Revolution of Corsica, the Amusements of Spa.

It was not just Napoleon's library that was taken by the Prussians and, once again, it is the *Morning Post,* in this case the edition of Monday, 29 January 1816, that is our informative source:

> At the time that BONAPARTE'S carriage was stopped by the Prussians near Gennape, on the evening of the battle of Waterloo, some of the soldiers, during the confusion, were known to take some of the portable articles, amongst which, it is now discovered, was his splendid diamond snuff box of very considerable value, which was, on his sudden escape, left in the carriage; it is a most splendid article, weighing upwards of six ounces of fine gold, most beautifully enamelled and ornamented with a border, and his initials on the lid in the finest brilliants, 142 in number, on a ground of mat gold; it is made to be held and opened by one hand, and is ascertained to be the same described by LA COSTE, and used by the Ex-Emperor during the battle of Waterloo. It has been purchased by Mr. BULLOCK, and is now added to the exhibition of the carriage and its interesting contents, in the Museum, Piccadilly.

Similarly, the *Caledonian Mercury* of Thursday, 27 July 1815, reported on a list also taken from Napoleon's belongings after the battle:

> Among his papers taken after the battle of Waterloo, was a list of eighty inhabitants of Brussels, whose persons and property were to be respected by the French army on its entrance into that city. Among these was a Flemish Nobleman, who had prepared a splendid supper for Bonaparte on the 18th. Of the remainder, several had prepared entertainments on the same day for his principal officers. Of this junta, the Nobleman, who was to have been Bonaparte's host, has fled. The others remained at Brussels on Saturday last, apparently without fear, although it is well known that the King of the Netherlands is in possession of the list. It is also certain, that several proclamations were found among the papers of Bonaparte, addressed from Brussels, Lecken, &c. all prepared in confident expectation of his success on the 18th, the capture of Brussels, and his irruption into Flanders and Holland.
>
> On the arrival of Bonaparte's carriage in Brussels, a great crowd received it with huzzas, little thinking that it came as a part of the

booty, and presuming that he was in it as a victor. Shortly after the discovery of the mistake, a coach-maker came up, and said he could point out a secret drawer, which might contain something of value. He immediately discovered a box in the bottom of it, containing a very large sum of gold.

Of the attachment of his followers to Bonaparte, the following anecdotes are cited as proofs founded in fact:

A favourite Mameluke, who was taken prisoner on the 18th, having heard of his master's decisive defeat, exclaimed, 'Then I shall never live to see his downfall.' With these words he opened his knife, and cut out his eyes. A French soldier, who had just suffered the amputation of an arm, actuated by a like spirit, requested that the limb should be given to him; when taking it in his remaining hand, and brandishing it round his head, he exclaimed 'Vive l'Empereur! – Vive Bonaparte!'

It is a fact, that at two o'clock on the 18th, it was reported and confidently believed at the Hague, Antwerp, Brussels, and many other places in Flanders and Holland, that the Allies had been completely defeated, and Bonaparte had obtained a decisive victory. This was done simultaneously by previous concert with his spies and secret agents, for the purpose of improving any advantage which he might obtain. By the same agency the road to Brussels from the field of battle was, during the action of the 18th, intercepted by waggons and other lumber and incumbrance: so that had our army been defeated and obliged to retreat, it must have left all its baggage and heavy artillery behind, the road having been thus rendered almost impracticable.

As we have seen, Waterloo became a popular tourist destination. For such visitors it was possible to purchase a commercially-produced *Souvenir de Waterloo* postcard depicting the well at Hougoumont farm which carried the following caption:

Not far from the cart entrance to Hougoumont Farm there is a well. In order to prevent an epidemic, it was used as a mass grave immediately after the battle. According to some, even living soldiers were flung into it because on some nights people apparently heard groans coming from the bottom of the well.[5]

The following brief note appeared in the pages of the edition of the *Chester Courant* printed on Tuesday, 11 July 1815:

BLÜCHER'S TOBACCO BOX. – The favourite veteran, it is said, keeps his tobacco in a large solid box – a little chest – which is carried with him wherever he goes, and placed in his apartment. It has also a solid lid, and upon this he has had fixed a small figure of the Duke of Wellington, that he may never fill his pipe without having a person brought to his mind, worthy of his tranquil recollections.

Another Chester-based newspaper, in this case the *Chester Chronicle*, declared the following on Friday, 7 July 1815 – a statement made with apparent sincerity and utter disregard for the Dutch, Belgians and Germans:

The French fought with uncommon courage, and evinced a fearlessness of death, and sustained an impetuosity in their different charges, which would probably have conquered success if their opponents had not been British.

Some of the many varied stories to emerge after the fighting related to children being born to some of those involved in the fighting, as this account published under the heading 'Waterloo Children' testifies:

A private of the twenty-seventh regiment, who was severely wounded, was carried off the field by his wife, then far advanced in pregnancy: she also was severely wounded by a shell, and both of them remained a considerable time in one of the hospitals at Antwerp in a hopeless state. The poor man had lost both his arms, the woman was extremely lame, and here gave birth to a daughter, to whom it is said the Duke of York has stood sponsor, and who has been baptized by the name of Frederica McMullen Waterloo.[6]

A similar story concerns an ensign called Deacon in the 73rd Foot, who was wounded in the arm at Quatre Bras:

After getting his wound dressed, he went in search of his wife, who, with her three children, he had left with the baggage guard. During the whole night, he sought her in vain; and the exertion he used was more than he could bear, and he was conveyed by the baggage train to Brussels.

The poor wife, in the meantime, who had heard from some of the men that her husband was wounded, passed the whole night in searching for him among the wounded, as they passed. At length, she was informed that he had been conveyed to Brussels and her chief anxiety then was how to get there. Conveyances there were not to be got; and she was in the last stage of pregnancy, she made the best way on foot, with her children, exposed to the violence of the terrific storm of thunder, lightning, and rain, which continued unabated for about ten hours. Faint, exhausted, and wet to the skin, having no clothes than a black silk dress, and light shawl, yet, she happily surmounted all these difficulties; reached Brussels on the morning of the 18th; and found her husband in very comfortable quarters, where she also was accommodated and the next day gave birth to a fine girl, which was afterwards christened 'Waterloo Deacon'.[7]

Some sixty years after the battle, the *Ipswich Journal* of 16 December 1876, reported the following:

WATERLOO – There is now staying on a visit to Captain Kerrich at Geldeston, an old lady who was actually present and took a passive part in the battle of Waterloo. Madame Van Cutsem, now the farmer of Hougoumont, was at the time the gardener's daughter at the Château of Hougoumont, and aged five years. Her father, the gardener, stuck to his post, retaining his little daughter as company. The Château itself was occupied by the British Guards, and was throughout the whole of the memorable 18th June. 1815, the grand and principle object of attack. Madame has a very vivid recollection of the kindness of our soldiers, who treated her as a pet, and kept throwing her bits of biscuit out of her haversacks wherewith to amuse. At last the château was shelled in the afternoon, and was set fire to by Jerome Bonaparte. Madame was then conducted by a sergeant of the Guards to a back gate. And her retreat secured into the forest of Soignies. Madame, a widow, is of course advanced in years, but hale and hearty, and now visiting England for the first time.[8]

The charge of the Union Brigade at Waterloo, and particularly that of the Scots Greys, caught the public imagination and the story was repeated in many of the local newspapers. This particular example was published in the *Chester Courant* of Tuesday, 16 September 1817, having been repeated from the *Carlisle Journal*:

The Scots Greys – Two troops of this gallant regiment are at present stationed in this city; some of them, who were engaged 'mid the din of arms,' at the ever-to-be-remembered Battle of Waterloo, relate the following anecdote of Capt. Cape, who is at present quartered here with his troop: – During the heat of the battle, and after his regiment had been shockingly cut up, he, with a boldness and intrepidity truly characteristic of the spirit of Englishmen, resolutely charged a large body of the enemy's cavalry, at the head of only six men! – waving and cheering them on to the attack, amid the fire and smoke of an infuriated enemy.

If much ink was spilt in glorifying the deeds of the Scots Greys, an equal amount was spent eulogising Sir Tomas Picton, who famously fought at the Battle of Waterloo in top hat and tails as his luggage had not yet arrived at Brussels. He was killed by a musket ball which entered his temple. This anecdote was also printed in the *Chester Courant*; on this occasion it was the edition of Tuesday, 1 August 1815:

> THE HEROIC PICTON. – In the desperate conflict which he sustained, on the 16th of June, at Quatre Bras, against a very superior force, he received a severe wound which he concealed from every one but his own servant, who bound it up for him, and continued his active command, till he perished gloriously in the battle of Waterloo, on the 18th. His first wound, which was never dressed, was so severe that it must have proved mortal in a few days!!!

One day after dinner at Stratfield Saye, Wellington was asked by the Right Honourable Henry Pierrepont about Copenhagen, the Duke's mount at Waterloo:

> 'Many faster horses, no doubt, many handsomer; but for bottom and endurance, never saw his fellow,' replied Wellington according to the journal of the Reverend Julian Charles Young. 'I'll give you proof of it. On the 17th, early in the day, I had a horse shot under me. Few know, but it was so. Before ten o'clock I got on Copenhagen's back.'
> After riding on him throughout a very long day, Wellington got back to his headquarters, '… and thinking how bravely my old horse had carried me all day, I could not help going up to his head to tell him so by a few caresses. But hang me, if, when I was giving him a slap of approbation on his hind-quarters, he did not fling out one of his hind legs with as much vigour as if he had been in stable for a couple of days. Remember, gentlemen, he had been out with me on his back for upwards of ten hours, and had carried me eight and twenty miles besides. I call that bottom! Ey?'[9]

We have read of the exploits and astonishing survival of Colonel Frederick Ponsonby of the 12th Light Dragoons, and to this we can add a touching postscript:

The Baron de Lussat, formally deputy for his department, the Basses Pyrenees, and a gentleman universally respected and beloved by all who knew him, was a major in the [French] Dragoons. After he had quitted the army he travelled in the East for some years, and on his return, at Malta, was introduced to Sir F. Ponsonby, then a Major General and governor of the island. In the course of conversation, the Battle of Waterloo was discussed; and on Ponsonby recounting his many narrow escapes and the kind treatment he had received from a French officer.

M. De Laussant said, 'Was he not in such-and-such a uniform?' 'He was', said Sir F. 'And did he not say so-and-so to you, and was not the cloak of such-and-such a colour?' 'I remember it perfectly', was the answer. Several other details were entered into, which I now forget, but which left no doubt upon Ponsonby's mind that he saw before him the man to whom he owed his life.[10]

The following description is an extract of a letter from an eyewitness to the fighting during the Battle of Waterloo:

I believe you may rely on the following anecdote, which I have not yet observed to have got into print. After the desperate charge of the French in the battle of Waterloo, when our illustrious Chief was actually within a hollow square; Bonaparte finding nothing could shake or move the solidity of the British line, was obliged to retire; and an Officer of our Life Guards, lying on the field, heard him distinctly say, in passing to an Aide-de-Camp – *Ces Anglais sont si grand bêtes, qu'ils ne sauvent pas quand ils sont battus* – 'These English are such beasts, that they do not know when they are beaten.' – What a compliment from such a man in such a situation! He was never seen again on the field; so that it may be called the last speech, confession, and dying words of the bitterest foe that Great Britain ever had.

Though the author of the following piece does not reveal the identity of the cavalry regiment in question, it is highly likely that it is the Duke of Cumberland Hussars which, as we have seen, retired from the battlefield in unusual circumstances:

A very gay regiment of gentlemen light horse volunteers were in the battle of Waterloo; all inhabitants of a continental city, which I shall not name. An opportunity occurred for them to charge the French cavalry, and an aid-du-camp came to them with an order or request to that effect from Lord Wellington. Their colonel, in great surprise,

319

objected the enemy's strength – their cuirasses – and the consideration, which had unaccountably, he said, escaped the Commander-in-Chief, that his regiment were all GENTLEMEN.

This diverting response was carried back to Lord Wellington; who dispatched the messenger again to say, that if the GENTLEMEN would take post upon an eminence, which he pointed to in the rear, they would have AN EXCELLENT VIEW of the battle; and he would leave the choice of a proper time to charge entirely to their own sagacity and discretion, in which he had the fullest confidence! The colonel actually thanked the aid-du-camp, for this distinguished post of honour, and followed by his gallant train with their very high plumes (the present great point of continental military foppery), was out of danger in a moment.[11]

The many accounts detailing Napoleon's actions in the fighting include:

After the battle of the 18th Bonaparte is said to have passed 40 hours without eating or speaking! – On the field of battle was found a PORTABLE OBSERVATORY, on which he was mounted during the action, but from which he very deliberately descended, upon perceiving a storm gathering round UXBRIDGE![12]

In a book containing hitherto unpublished documents, the author claimed that,

The following details of this incident are gathered from the most reliable French and British sources: Captain Harry Wyndham (afterwards General Sir H. Wyndham, KCB, MP) was a son of the third Earl of Egremont, and had already seen eight general engagements in the Peninsular War, although on the day of the battle of Waterloo he was not yet twenty-five years old ... Wyndham is remembered by an incident which occurred immediately after the battle as darkness was falling upon the field.

Pressing on in the general pursuit of the French, he saw one of the Imperial carriages attempting to escape, and soon ascertained that the occupant was none other than Napoleon's brother Jerome against whose columns he had been fighting all day [at Hougoumont]. Quick as thought he opened the carriage-door, only to catch a glimpse of Jerome as he leapt out by the other door and disappeared in the darkness.[13]

More than three years after Waterloo stories such as the following one from the *Caledonian Mercury* of Thursday, 17 September 1818 were still appearing:

At the ever memorable battle of Waterloo, a subaltern of the British infantry was wounded and made prisoner. Shortly after this event, the French regiment by whom he had been taken gave way, leaving the English officer, and one of their own men, who was wounded (his leg broken) on the ground – the Frenchman deliberately collected several of the cartouch boxes of his fallen comrades, seating himself among them with his rifle, placing two or three knapsacks before him as a rest for his piece. In this manner he loaded and fired no less than thirty or forty rounds at an English regiment, which was drawn up at a short distance in his front, bringing down a man at every shot.

At length the British regiment charged over the ground where this determined fellow and the wounded officer lay. Shortly after our informant was removed, and notwithstanding every inquiry he could afterwards make, never could discover what became of this Frenchman, whom he describes as quite a boy, not having been more than sixteen or seventeen years of age.

Even civilians found themselves embroiled in the battle:

All the inhabitants had fled from the village of Mont St. Jean previous to the action, and even Waterloo was deserted; but in a farm-house, at the end of the village, one woman remained during the whole of the day, shut up in a garret, from which she could see nothing, and without any means of gaining intelligence of what was passing, while the troops were fighting man to man, and sword to sword, at the very doors; while shells were bursting in at the windows, and while the cannon-balls were breaking through the wooden-gates into the farm-yard, and striking against the walls of the house.

This woman was the farmer's wife: and, when asked what motive could induce her to adopt such extraordinary conduct, she replied with great simplicity, that she had a great many cows and calves, and poultry, and pigs – in fact, that all she had in the world was there; and that, if she left them, they would be destroyed.[14]

During the retreat from Waterloo Major M. Lemonnier-Delafosse reached Beaumont with General Foy who had been wounded in the shoulder:

We led General Foy to a good looking house and asked the lady there for something with which to make him some soup. 'Alas, gentlemen! This is the tenth general who has come to my house since daybreak. I have nothing left!'[15]

321

Some of those who had been assisted by the local population returned to pay their respects:

> Prince Blücher on his way to the Prussian dominions gave occasion to several fetes. In passing through Belgium, he desired to see again, at Ligny, the place where, thrown from his horse, he lay upon the ground during the pursuit and hasty return of a part of the French army. After remaining there some time conversing with his aide-de-camp, he generously recompensed a miller who had assisted him in his critical situation [when he had been ridden over]. The miller at Ligny, recompensed by Prince Blucher on his return from France, addressed the following letter to the editor of the Brussels Oracle:
>
> Prince Blucher, on his return, called at my house with his aides-de-camp; his modesty concealed his illustrious name, and I did not recollect him. He asked me many questions concerning my losses, and my melancholy situation.
>
> Alas! it was easy for me to answer that I had saved nothing, either in my house, or on the lands which I farm, and that the war had reduced my family to misery, so that I could not pay my contributions. He asked me the amount of them, I told him 80 francs, which he immediately gave me. He departed; and when he got to Namur, he sent me four pieces of 40 francs each, and one of 20 francs.' It was from this messenger, that I learnt the name of this great Prince; his generosity honours him; his modesty ennobles him; and my heart thanks him.[16]

Under the headline, 'The Battle of Waterloo', the following appeared in the *Caledonian Mercury* of Thursday, 27 July 1815:

> A party of gentlemen who returned to town on Tuesday, from a visit to the scene of the late battles in Flanders, relate the following anecdotes:-
>
> A British officer, who was made prisoner in the late battle of the 16th, was brought before Bonaparte, for examination. Being asked by Bonaparte 'Who commands the cavalry?' he answered, Lord Uxbridge. 'No, Paget,' replied Bonaparte. The officer then explained that they meant the same person, and Bonaparte nodded assent. He was then asked, 'who commanded in Chief?' and answered, the Duke of Wellington; upon which he observed, 'No, that cannot be, for he is sick.'
>
> It seems that his Grace had received a fall from his horse, on the 14th, and was reported to be indisposed in consequence, and Bonaparte had received intelligence to that effect. The conversation continued in this line for a considerable time, during which Bonaparte

322

shewed himself perfectly acquainted with the strength and position of the several divisions of the allied armies, and the names of their several commanders. As they were successively mentioned, Bonaparte occasionally remarked, 'Oh! Yes, that division cannot be up in time.' 'This division cannot be up in a day' and so on.

A most unusual story was published in the *Leeds Intelligencer* under the heading, 'Waterloo interesting Anecdote':

> Serjeant Weir, of the Scots Greys was pay-serjeant of his troop, and as such, might have been excused serving in action, and, perhaps, he should not have been forward; but on such a day as the battle of Waterloo, he requested to be allowed to charge with the regiment. In one of the charges he fell, mortally wounded, and was left on the field. Corporal Scot of the same regiment (who lost a leg,) asserts, that when the field was searched for the wounded and slain, the body of Serjeant Weir *was found with his name written on his forehead, by his own finger dipped in his own blood.* This, his comrade said, he was supposed to have done that his body might be found, and known, and that it might not be imagined he had disappeared with the money of the troop.[17]

This narrative, seemingly written at Waterloo, is dated 15 August 1815:

> Opposite the Inn, at a cottage where the Earl of Uxbridge was carried, you are shown a neat garden; in the centre of four paths, a little hillock, with a flower planted thereon, shows the sepulchre of his Lordship's leg in an inclosure, farther behind this cottage, are interred several English Officers; one only, Colonel Fitzgerald, of the Life Guards, has a stone, with an inscription over him; many have been taken up and transmitted to England: you then proceed to Waterloo, the house of Jean Baptiste La Coste, called Belle Alliance, from whom I obtained the following particulars: –
>
> 'About five in the morning, he was taken prisoner to serve as guide, and conducted with his hands tied behind him (that he might not escape as a former man had done) to another house belonging to him, opposite to which Buonaparte had slept. Observing the French soldiers plundering and destroying this house, he cried. Buonaparte asked what he cried for? 'Because your soldiers are destroying all my property, and my family have nowhere to put their heads.' Buonaparte said, 'Do you not know that I am Emperor, and can recompense you an hundred times as much.'[18]

To this account is added as a footnote:

> You are also shown the chair on which his Lordship [Uxbridge] sat during the operation [to have his leg amputated], exactly as it remained; and they still remember the gallant Earl's heroic sentiments at the moment of this severe trial: but he was not seen to wince in the least, not even by contortion of features, consoling those about him in saying: 'Who would not lose a leg for such a victory? It is true, I have a limb less; but I have a higher name in the eyes of my country.'

To some, Napoleon's defeat was unwelcome, as this brief snippet, published under the heading 'Disappointed Belgians', reveals:

> An opulent inhabitant of Brussels felt so confident that Buonaparte would ultimately prove victorious, that he actually prepared a splendid supper for him on the 18th, and similar preparations were made, by other persons, for his principal officers.[19]

'The interesting account given by Ney of the Battle of Waterloo is considered in the British army to be correct,' commented the editor of the *Hampshire Chronicle* on Monday, 24 July 1815. He went to write:

> Napoleon, it is asserted, shewed more pertinacity than on any former occasion. Three messengers were dispatched to him on the hill where he had planted his observatory before he would believe that Bulow's corps was bearing down upon the flank and rear of his forces; and until it was actually engaged with his troops, he had not abandoned the persuasion that it was the division under his Generals Grouchy and Vandamme.
>
> Another mistake is said to have contributed to his destruction on that day. Contrary to all his former maxims, and to the known rules of tactics, he ordered the whole weight of his cavalry to press upon the British before any of their columns were broken or disordered, trusting that the troops under the Duke of Wellington were raw and undisciplined, and were consequently incapable of sustaining this ponderous charge. He was disappointed; and in this stage of the action, his ruin was complete. It is agreed by all persons versed in military science, that such an attempt, if not successful, must be fatal.

An inquest into the death of a Waterloo veteran was reported in the *Royal Cornwall Gazette* on Saturday, 20 July 1816:

Sunday morning, John Moss, a private in the 2d battalion of Coldstream Guards, who was at the battle of Waterloo, was removed in a dreadful state of intoxication from the door of the Rev. Dr. McCloud, in Dean-street, to St. Anne's watch-house, and remained in a state of insensibility for a considerable time. About five o'clock he rose from his stupor, and said he should get finely reprimanded when he returned to the regiment; he afterwards retired to the privy in the lock-up room in the watch-house, and cutting and splicing his belt together, hung himself; he was 29 years of age: verdict, *insanity*.

Described as 'one of the most extraordinary and most likely apocryphal stories of the day', this story concerns a moment during the battle of the 18th. It bore the title, 'The Duke and the Traveller':

For a quarter of an hour, during one of the greatest crises of the Battle of Waterloo, when the Duke of Wellington had sent all his *aides-de-camp* with orders to the different divisions of the army, he found himself alone at the very moment when he most needed help. While watching the movements of his troops through his field-glasses, he saw Kempt's brigade beginning a manoeuvre which, if not promptly countermanded, would probably lead to the loss of the battle. But there was no officer at hand to convey his orders. Just then he turned round in his saddle, and saw not far off a single horseman, rather quaintly attired, cooly watching the strife. The instant the Duke caught sight of him, he beckoned to him, and asked him who he was, why was he there, and how he had passed the lines.

He answered: 'I am a traveller for a wholesale button manufactory in Birmingham, and was showing my samples in Brussels when I heard the sound of firing. Having had all my life a strong desire to see a battle, I at once got a horse, and set out for the scene of action; and, after some difficulty, I have reached this spot, whence I expect to have a good view.'

The Duke, pleased with his straightforward answer, determined to turn his sense and daring to good account, and addressed him as follows: 'You ought to have been a soldier. Would you like to serve your country now?'

'Yes, my lord,' said the other.

'Would you take a message of importance for me?'

Touching his hat in military fashion the traveller replied, 'Were I trusted by you, sir, I would think this the proudest day of my life.'

Putting his field-glass into the man's hands, the Duke explained to him the position of the brigade that had made the false move, and added: 'I have no writing materials by me; see, therefore, that you are very accurate in delivering my message. He then entrusted to him a brief, emphatic order, which he made him repeat, that there might be no mistake.

The orders were barely delivered before the stranger was off at top of his horse's speed, and soon disappeared amid the smoke of the battle. After a few minutes' interval, the Duke turned his glass in the direction of the brigade which was at fault, and exclaimed in a joyful tone, 'It's all right, yet. Kempt has changed his tactics. He has got my message, for he is doing precisely as I directed him. Well done, Buttons!'

The Duke used to say he considered the alteration of Kempt's original movement the turning point of the battle. Wishing to reward our hero for his intelligence and courage, he caused inquiries to be made for him in every direction, but in vain. It was not until many years afterwards that he accidentally heard of the man's whereabouts, and managed to secure for him a good appointment in the West of England, in recognition of his services.[20]

A note from the *Chester Courant* of Tuesday, 18 July 1815, sums up the consequences of the Battle of Waterloo which ushered in forty years of peace (but not internal stability in many countries) throughout Europe:

It is said, that immediately on the receipt of the account of the Battle of La Belle Alliance, the Prince Regent wrote with his own hand a most gracious letter of approbation to the Duke of Wellington. His Grace's acknowledgement of this distinguished mark of favour is said to have been written under the walls of Paris, in which the Duke, after expressing his thanks, concludes by congratulating His Royal Highness, 'on having again saved the world'.

It is perhaps fitting that we leave the last words to Wellington himself, the Duke having made the following statement which was delivered to Lady Frances Shelley in Paris shortly after its occupation by the allied armies:

'I hope to God ... that I have fought my last battle. It is a bad thing to be always fighting. While in the thick of it I am too much occupied to feel anything; but it is wretched just after. It is quite impossible to think of glory. Both mind and feelings are exhausted. I am wretched even at the moment of victory, and I always say that, next to a battle lost, the greatest misery is a battle gained.'[21]

Notes

Chapter 1: Boney Returns

1. *Bulletin des lois de la Republique Française*, Vol.10, (Imprimerie nationale, France, 1852), p.35.
2. John Gurwood [Ed.], *The Dispatches of Field Marshal the Duke of Wellington, K. G., During his Various Campaigns in India, Denmark, Portugal, Spain, the Low Countries, and France from 1799 to 1818* (John Murray, London, 1852), Vol.VIII, pp.1-2 (hereafter, *Wellington's Despatches*).
3. Paul Britten Austin, *1815: The Return of Napoleon* (Greenhill, London, 2002), pp.51-9.
4. David Hamilton-Williams, *Waterloo, New Perspectives: The Great Battle Reappraised* (Arms and Armour, London, 1990), p.54.
5. Reiset, *Souvenirs du Lieutenant Général Vicomte de Reiset, 1814-1836* (Calmann Lévy, Paris, 1902), Vol.III, pp.74-6. The telegraph referred to was a semaphore system invented by the Chappe brothers which first began to be used in 1792 and by 1815 spanned most of France.
6. *The Times*, 13 March 1815.
7. Charles Angélique François Huchet comte de La Bédoyère, *Memoirs of the Public and Private Life of Napoleon Bonaparte, With Copious Historical Illustrations and Original Anecdotes*, Vol.II, (George Virtue, London, 1835), pp.290-1.
8. *Wellington's Despatches*, pp.2-3.
9. *Wellington's Despatches*, p.3.
10. *The Times*, 13 March 1815.
11. *Wellington's Despatches*, pp.5-6.
12. The full text of the Declaration of the Powers against Napoleon can be found in *British and Foreign State Papers 1814-1815*,(HMSO, London, 1839), pp.665-6; August Fournier, *Napoleon The First, A Biography* (Translated by Margaret Bacon Corwin and Arthur Dart Russell), (Henry Holt, New York, 1903), pp.697-9.
13. *Wellington's Despatches*, pp.5-6.
14. T.E. Crowdy, *Incomparable: Napoleon's 9th Light Infantry Regiment* (Osprey, Oxford, 2012), pp.342-3.
15. *The Times*, 13 March 1815.
16. Crowdy, p.342. Saint-Denis, quoted in Alan Schom, *One Hundred Days, Napoleon's Road to Waterloo* (Michael Joseph, London, 1992), pp.55-6.
17. Quoted in Austin, p.270.
18. William Pitt Lennox, *Fifty Years' Biographical Reminiscences*, Vol.I (Hurst & Blackett, London, 1863), p.221.
19. David Chandler, *Waterloo, The Hundred Days* (Osprey, London, 1987), p.19.
20. *The Times*, 11 April 1815.

Chapter 2: Peace and War

1. *Wellington's Despatches*, pp.17-8.
2. *Wellington's Despatches*, pp. 21-3.
3. The Champ de Mai, or Champ de Mars, is a large plot of ground in front of the military school in Paris, bordered on each side with avenues of trees, which extend from the school almost to the banks of the Seine. In the early periods of the French monarchy, the general assemblies of the nation were held in this place. The objects of those meetings were to frame new laws, to lay the complaints of the people before the king, to adjust differences among the barons, and to review the national forces. It was called the Champ de Mars, because the assembly took place in the month of March. In the middle of the eighth century, Pepin transferred it to the month of May, as a milder and more convenient season. After this, it was called either the Champ de Mars or the Champ de Mai, Christopher Kelly, *A Full and Circumstantial Account of the Memorable Battle of Waterloo, etc.* (Thomas Kelly, London, 1817), p.28.
4. Mark Adkin, *The Waterloo Companion* (Aurum Press, London. 2001), p.20.
5. Frank McLynn, *Napoleon, A Biography* (Pimlico, London, 1997), p.610.
6. *Hansard*, HC Deb 22 May 1815, Vol.31, cc309-10.
7. *Hansard*, HC Deb 07 April 1815, Vol.30, cc417-63.
8. Jonathan Crook, *The Very Thing, The Memoirs of Drummer Bentinck, Royal Welch Fusiliers, 1807-1823* (Frontline, Barnsley, 2011), p.133.
9. Cavalié Mercer, *Journal of the Waterloo Campaign Kept Through the Campaign of 1815*, vol. I (William Blackwood, London, 1870), pp.2-17.
10. Marquis of Anglesey [Ed.], *The Capel Letters, 1814-1817* (Jonathan Cape, London 1955), p.102.
11. *Wellington's Despatches*, p.66.
12. *Ibid*, p.24. This was on 11 April.
13. *Ibid*, pp.26-7. This was on 12 April.
14. *Ibid*, pp.27-8.
15. Diary of Captain Digby Mackworth, *The Army Quarterly*, 1937, pp.123-4.
16. Quoted in Ian Fletcher, *A Desperate Business: Wellington, The British Army and the Waterloo Campaign* (Spellmount, Staplehurst, 2001), p.25.
17. W.E. Frye, *After Waterloo: Reminiscences of European Travel, 1815-1819* (William Heinemann, London, 1909), p.12.
18. *Wellington's Despatches*, pp.33-4.
19. *Ibid*, pp.34-5.
20. *Ibid*, pp.38-9.
21. *Ibid*, pp.51-2.
22. *Ibid*, pp.66-8.
23. A.F. Becke, *Napoleon and Waterloo* (Greenhill, London, 1995), pp.6-8.
24. *Wellington's Despatches*, p.89.
25. More details can be found in William Siborne, *History of the Waterloo Campaign* (Greenhill, London, 1995), pp.24-6.
26. Wellington, Arthur Richard Wellesley, *Supplementary Despatches and Memoranda of Field Marshal Arthur, Duke of Wellington, KG*, (J. Murray, London, 1864), Appendix, p.556.
27. Quoted in John Naylor, *Waterloo* (Pan, London, 1960), p.55.
28. Nick Foulkes, *Dancing into Battle, A Social History of the Battle of Waterloo* (Phoenix, London, 2007), p.119.

Chapter 3: Advance to Contact

1. *Wellington's Supplementary Despatches, op. cit.*, Vol.X, pp.464-5.
2. John Booth, *The Battle of Waterloo, Also of Ligny, and Quatre Bras etc.* (J. Booth, London, 1817), pp.251-2.

3. *The Journal of the Three Days of the Battle of Waterloo, Being My Own Personal Journal of What I Saw and of the Events which I Bore a Part, by an Eye-witness, etc.* (Military Chronicle and Military Classics, London, 1816), pp.17-8.
4. La Bédoyère, pp.853-4.
5. La Bédoyère, *op.cit.*, p.856.
6. *Ibid*, pp.856-7.
7. Hamilton-Williams, *Waterloo, New Perspectives*, p.161.
8. Baron Carl von Müffling, *The Memoirs of Baron Carl von Müffling: A Prussian Officer in the Napoleonic Wars* (Greenhill, London, 1997), p.229.
9. *Wellington's Despatches*, pp.142-3. The reference here to 'Alava' refers to General Miguel Alava, the Spanish Minister Plenipotentiary to the King of the Netherlands.
10. John Booth, *op. cit.*, pp.90-1.
11. John Franklin, *Netherlands Correspondence, op. cit.*, p.7.
12. Von Müffling, *op. cit.*
13. David Miller, *Lady Delancey at Waterloo: A Story of Duty and Devotion* (Spellmount, Staplehurst, 2000), pp.169-70.
14. *Wellington's Despatches*, pp.142.
15. Captain George Bowles, *A Series of Letters to the First Earl of Malmesbury, etc.* (Richard Bentley, London, 1870).
16. *Wellington's Despatches*, pp.146-7.
17. Harry Ross-Lewin, *With 'The Thirty-Second' in the Peninsula and Other Campaigns* (Naval and Military Press, Uckfield, 2004), p.253.
18. *The Battle of Waterloo, By a Near Observer* (John Booth, London, 1815), pp.1-5.
19. David Miller, *op. cit.*, p.170.
20. Edward Costello, *The Adventures of a Soldier; or, Memoirs of Edward Costello, Narratives of the Campaigns in The Peninsular and Waterloo Campaigns* (Henry Colburn, London, 1841), pp.283-4.
21. *Correspondance de Napoléon 1er*, Tome XXXI, p.202.

Chapter 4: Quatre Bras

1. John Booth, *op. cit.*, p.51.
2. *Ibid*, pp.255-7.
3. *Wellington's Despatches*, p.143.
4. Becke, pp.301-2.
5. John Booth, *op. cit.*, p.91.
6. Becke, *op. cit.*, p.303.
7. Von Müffling, *op. cit.*, pp.237-8.
8. John Franklin, *Waterloo, Hanoverian Correspondence* (1815 Limited, Ulverston, 2010), p.11.
9. John Booth, *op. cit.*, pp.77-9.
10. A. James, *Retrospect of a Military Life During the Most Eventful Periods of the Last War: Journal of Sergeant James Anton 42nd Highlanders* (W.H. Lizars, Edinburgh, 1841), pp.190-5.
11. John Booth, *op. cit.*, pp.92-3.
12. John Booth, *op. cit.*, p.56.
13. Major S. Rudyard in H.T. Siborne, *Waterloo Letters* (Cassell, London, 1891), pp.230-1.
14. John Booth, *op. cit.*, pp.56-8.
15. Letter from Major Oldfield, of the Royal Engineers, dated Paris, July 1815, quoted in *Waterloo 1815: A Commemorative Anthology* to be published to commemorate the 200th anniversary of the Battle of Waterloo by Extraordinary Editions, London in 2015.
16. John Booth, *op. cit.*, p.90.

17. *Ibid*, pp.51-2.
18. *Ibid*, p.82. Research by Gareth Glover has indicated that this officer is either 1st Lieutenant Orlando Felix or William Chapman, or 2nd Lieutenant William Shenley, see *Waterloo Archive Vol.IV* (Frontline Books, Barnsley, 2012), p.197.
19. H.T. Siborne, *Letters, op. cit.*, pp.230-1.
20. Grouchy, *Mémoires du Maréchal de Grouchy, par le Marquis de Grouchy* (Paris, 1874), pp.102-4.
21. *French Orders and Reports from the Waterloo Campaign: Report of General Kellerman to Marshal Ney on the Charge of Guiton's Brigade of Cuirassiers at Quatre Bras*, provided by Dominique Contant, translated by Marc Moerman.
22. *The Battle of Waterloo, By a Near Observer* (John Booth, London, 1815), pp.233-4.
23. Becke, *op. cit.*, pp.303-4.
24. *Wellington's Despatches*, p.143.
25. J.P. Burrell, *Official Bulletins of the Battle of Waterloo* (Parker, Furnivall & Parker, London, 1849), pp.23-3.
26. *Ibid*, pp.25-6.

Chapter 5: Battle of Ligny
1. 'Prussian Official Account of the Late Battles. Battle of Ligny, June 16', in the *Cambridge Chronicle and Journal*, Friday, 7 July 1815.
2. Reiche, Ludwig von, *Memoiren des Königlich Preussischen Generals der Infanterie Ludwig von Reiche* (Brodhaus, Leipzig, 1857), Vol.II, pp.183-4.
3. General von Ollech, *Geschichte des Feldzuges von 1815* (Berlin, 1876), quoted by Peter Hofschröer, *1815 The Waterloo Campaign, Wellington, his German Allies and the Battles of Ligny and Quatre Bras* (Greenhill, London, 1998), p.120.
4. William Hamilton Maxwell, *Life of Wellington* (Hutchinson, London, 1899), Vol.II, pp.19-20.
5. John Booth, *op. cit.*, pp.201-2.
6. May, Captain E.S. [Ed. & trans.], 'A Prussian Gunner's Adventures in 1815', *United Services Magazine*, October 1891, pp.45-7.
7. La Bédoyère, *op. cit.*, pp.397-8.
8. Quoted at: http://napoleon-series.org
9. John Booth, *op. cit* , pp.255-6.
10. William Seymour, Jacques Champagne, Colonel E. Kaulbach, *Waterloo, Battle of Three Armies* (Book Club Associates, London, 1979), p.200.
11. *Ibid*, pp.200-1.
12. Letter from Count d'Erlon dated 9 February 1829 to the Prince of the Moskowa, quoted in Andrew Uffindell, *The Eagle's Last Triumph, Napoleon's Last Victory at Ligny, June 1815* (Greenhill, London, 1994), p.249.
13. Burrell, *op. cit.*, pp.38-40.
14. This is discussed in John Codman Ropes, *The Campaign of Waterloo, A Military History* (Charles Scribner's Sons, New York, 1906), pp.164-77.
15. Wellmann, Richard, *Geschichte des Infanterie-Regiment von Horn (3tes Rheinisches) No.29* (Trier, 1894) p.99, quoted by Peter Hofschröer, *1815 The Waterloo Campaign, Wellington, his German Allies and the Battles of Ligny and Quatre Bras*, p.311.
16. Anthony Brett-James, *The Hundred Days: Napoleon's Last Campaign from Eye-witness Accounts* (Macmillan, New York, 1964), p.80.
17. Burrell, *op. cit.*, p.39.
18. *Ibid*, pp.17-18.
19. John Booth, *op. cit.*, p.94.
20. Burrell, *op. cit.*, pp.39-40.
21. Franklin, *Netherlands Correspondence*, pp.29-30.

22. Napoleon's Correspondence 22059: To Marshal Count Grouchy. Quoted at: www.wtj.com/archives/napoleon/nap615be.htm.

Chapter 6: Withdrawal to Mont St Jean
1. *Wellington's Despatches, op. cit.*, Vol.VIII, pp.147-8.
2. James Harris Malmesbury, *Letters of the First Earl of Malmesbury, 1745-1820* (Richard Bentley, London, 1870), Vol.II, p.447.
3. *Wellington's Despatches, op. cit.*, Vol.VIII, p.144.
4. John Booth, *op. cit.*, pp.28-9.
5. A Near Observer, *op. cit.*, p.52.
6. *Supplementary Despatches*, Appendix, pp.559-60.
7. John Booth, *op. cit.*, pp.94-5.
8. Burrell, *op. cit.*, p.18
9. H.T. Siborne, *History*, Appendix XXVII.
10. Becke, *op. cit.*, pp.385-6.
11. Burrell, *op. cit.*, p.40.
12. Major-General Sir John Ponsonby, *The Ponsonby Family* (London, 1929), quoted in Anthony & Nicholas Bird *Eyewitness To War* (Summersdale Publishers, Chichester, 2006), pp.42-3.
13. Mercer, *op. cit.*, pp.268-9.
14. Pontécoulant, *Napoleon à Waterloo* (Á la Librarie des Deux Empire, Paris, 2000), quoted in Andrew W. Field, *Waterloo, The French Perspective* (Pen & Sword, Barnsley, 2013), p.32.
15. Le Maréchal Drouet, Comte d'Erlon, *Notice sur la vie militaire, écrite par lui-même et dediée à ses amis. Publiée par sa famille* (Gustave Barba, Paris, 1844), p.96.
16. Mackenzie Macbride, (Ed.), *With Napoleon at Waterloo and Other Unpublished Documents of the Waterloo and Peninsular Campaigns* (J.B. Lippincott & Co., Philadelphia, 1911), pp.181-5.
17. W.A. Scott, *Battle of Waterloo: or Correct Narrative of the Late Sanguinary Conflict on the Plains of Waterloo* (E. Cox and Son, London, 1815), pp.127-31.
18. *Supplementary Despatches*, Vol.VIII, p.501.

Chapter 7: The Battle of Waterloo, Morning
1. George Wrottesley, *Life and Correspondence of Field Marshal Sir John Burgoyne* (Richard Bentley, London, 1873), pp.327-8.
2. Quoted in Gareth Glover, *The Waterloo Archive, Volume IV*: British Sources (Frontline, Barnsley, 2012), p.161.
3. Adkin, *op. cit.*, p.93.
4. *Wellington's Despatches*, pp.147-8.
5. John Booth, *op. cit.*, p.51.
6. La Bédoyère, *op. cit.*, (James Ridgeway, London, 1815), p.51.
7. A British Officer on the Staff, *An Account of the Battle of Waterloo* (James Ridgeway, London, 1815), pp.11-2.
8. Lieutenant Jacques Martin, *Souveneirs d'un ex-officier*, quoted in Andrew Uffindell and Michael Corum, *On the Fields of Glory, The Battlefields of the 1815 Campaign* (Greenhill, London, 1996), p.30.
9. David Howarth, *Waterloo, A Near Run Thing*, (Collins, London, 1968), p.3.
10. MacBride, *op. cit.*, p.378.
11. General Sir James Shaw Kennedy, *Notes on the Battle of Waterloo* (John Murray, London, 1865), pp.100-1.
12. Saul David, *All The King's Men, The British Redcoat in the Era of Sword and Musket* (Penguin, London, 2002), p.470.

13. John Booth, *op. cit.*, p.66.
14. Burrell, *op., cit.*, pp.40-1.
15. Somerset de Chair, [Ed.] *Napoleon on Napoleon* (Brockhampton Press, London, 1992), pp.256-7.
16. *Wellington's Despatches, op. cit.*, p.477.
17. Shaw-Kennedy, *op., cit.*, p.131.
18. D'Erlon, *Vie Militaire*, pp.196-7, quoted in Hamilton-Williams, *Waterloo New Perspectives, op. cit.*, p.261.
19. Ropes, *op., cit.*, p.388.
20. De Chair, *Napoleon on Napoleon, op. cit.*, pp.258-60.
21. Mackenzie Macbride, *op. cit.*, pp. 181-5.

Chapter 8: The Struggle for Hougoumont
1. Franklin, *Waterloo: Netherlands Correspondence*, p.18.
2. *Siborne, Waterloo Letters, op. cit.*, p.269.
3. Franklin, *Netherlands Correspondence*, p.18.
4. H.T. Siborne, *Waterloo Letters, op. cit.*, pp.263-4.
5. Edward Sabine [Ed.], *Letters of Colonel Sir Augustus Simon Frazer* (Longman, London, 1859), pp.555-6.
6. Gordon Corrigan, *Waterloo, A New History of the Battle and its Armies* (Atlantic, London, 2014), p.231. Commanders and their ADCs carried prepared strips of skin on which messages could be written and then rubbed out by the recipient so that a reply could be written. This remarkable survivor is held in the British Museum.
7. Mudford Papers, quoted in Gareth Glover, *The Waterloo Archive, Vol.1: British Sources* (Frontline, Barnsley, 2010), p.143.
8. Reproduced in Gareth Glover, *Letters from the Battle of Waterloo: Unpublished Correspondence by Allied Officers from the Siborne Papers* (Greenhill, London, 2004), p.176.
9. *Journal of the Society for Army Historical Research*, Vol.XLIII, No.174, June 1965.
10. Anonymous, *The Battle of Waterloo, etc.* (J. Booth, London, 1817), p.67.
11. Macbride, *op. cit.*, p.126-32.
12. H.T. Siborne, *Waterloo Letters, op. cit.*, pp.19-20.
13. Mudford Papers, *op. cit.*

Chapter 9: Waterloo: The French Artillery Bombardment
1. Becke, *op. cit.*, p.190.
2. George Simmons, *A British Rifle Man: The Journals and Correspondence of Major George Simmons, Rifle Brigade, During the Peninsular War and the Campaign of Waterloo* (A. & C. Black, London, 1899), p.354.
3. Gareth Glover, *Eyewitness to the Peninsular War and the Battle of Waterloo, the Letters and Journals of Lieutenant Colonel The Honourable James Hamilton Stanhope* (Pen & Sword, Barnsley, 2010), pp.176, 182 & 184.
4. M. Clay, *A Narrative of the Battles of Quatre-Bras and Waterloo; With the Defence of Hougoumont by Matthew Clay* (Ken Trotman, London, 2006), pp.17-8.
5. Nick Lipscombe, *Wellington's Guns* (Osprey, London, 2013), p.369.
6. M. Lemonnier-Delafosse, *Campagnes de 1810 à 1815, Souvenirs Militaires* (Imprimerie du commerce, Le Havre, 1850), p.380.
7. Mercer, Vol.I, p.297.
8. Christopher Hibbert, *Wheatley Diary* (Longmans, London, 1964), pp.64-5.
9. James Hope, *Letters from Portugal, Spain and France* (Michael Anderson, Edinburgh, 1819), p.248.
10. Peter Hofschröer, *1815: The Waterloo Campaign, The German Victory* (Greenhill, London, 1999), p.76.

11. Adkin, *op. cit.*, p.272.
12. Quoted in Martin Cassidy, *Marching with Wellington: With the Inniskillings in the Napoleonic Wars* (Leo Copper, Barnsley, 2003), pp.173-4.
13. Ross-Lewin, *op. cit.* p.270.
14. George Nugent Bankes [Ed.], *The Autobiography of Sergeant William Lawrence* (Sampson Low, Marston, Searle, & Rivington, London, 1886), pp.194.
15. W. Leeke, *History of Lord Seaton's Regiment at the Battle of Waterloo* (Hatchard, London, 1866), vol.1, pp.30-1.
16. Mark Adkin, *op. cit.*, pp.262-3.
17. *A Soldier of the 71st, From De la Plata to Waterloo 1806-1815* (Frontline, Barnsley, 2010), pp.129-30.
18. Anonymous memorandum, 21 June 1815, British Library Add. 34703 folio 32.
19. William Tomkinson (Ed.), *The Diary of a Cavalry Officer in the Peninsular and Waterloo Campaigns* (Swan Sonnenschein, London, 1894), pp.297-8.

Chapter 10: The Attack Upon the Allied Right
1. De Chair, *Napoleon Bonaparte, The Waterloo Campaign* (The Folio Society, London, 1957), p.262.
2. Glover, *Waterloo Archive Vol.IV, British Sources*, p.177.
3. Simmons *op. cit.*, pp.355-6
4. Léon van Neck, *Waterloo illustré, Publication historique, spécialement au point de vue de la Belgique* (Brussels, 1903), No.5 (2/II), pp.41-2.
5. Captain John Kincaid, *Adventures in the Rifle Brigade* (Boone, London, 1830), pp.333-4.
6. Quoted in Hamilton-Williams, *op. cit.*, p.294.
7. Quoted in Stuart Reid, *Wellington's Highland Warriors, From the Black Watch Mutiny to the Battle of Waterloo* (Frontline, Barnsley, 2010), p.196.
8. Quoted in Brett-James, *op. cit.*, pp.115-6.
9. Charles Ainslie, *Historical Record of the First or the Royal Regiment of Dragoons* (Chapman & Hall, London, 1887), pp.158-9.
10. Source unattributed, quoted in Malcolm Balen, *A Model Victory: Waterloo and the Battle for History* (Harper Perennial, London, 2005), p.101.
11. Macbride, *op. cit.*, pp.138-48.
12. H.T. Siborne, *Letters*, p.71.
13. John Booth, *op. cit.*, pp.71-2.
14. Barney White-Spunner, *Horse Guards* (2006), p.333, quoted in David, p.475.
15. Quoted in Ian Fletcher, *Galloping at Everything* (Spellmount, Staplehurst, 1999), p.256.

Chapter 11: Waterloo, The French Cavalry Charges
1. Mercer, *op. cit.*, pp.307-8.
2. John Booth, *op. cit.*, p.51-2.
3. Sergeant Morris, *The Recollections of Sergeant Morris* (Windrush Press, Gloucestershire, 1967), p.77.
4. Hibbert, *op. cit.*, p.65.
5. General Sir Evelyn Wood, *Cavalry in the Waterloo Campaign* (Sampson Low, Marston and Company, London, 1895), p.140.
6. Quoted in David, *op. cit.*, p.477.
7. Tomkinson (Ed.), pp.305-6.
8. "'The Crisis of Waterloo' By a Solder of the Fifth Brigade", *Colburn's United Service Magazine*, 1852, Part II, pp.53-4.
9. Letter to Lieutenant Colonel Robe RA, Waterloo, 19 June, 3 a.m., in the *Journal of the Society for Army Historical Research*, Vol XLII, no.171, September 1964.
10. H.T. Siborne, *Letters*, pp.233-4.

11. *Journal of the Royal Artillery*, Vol.81.
12. Guy Hutton Wilson, *Merely a Memorandum* (Librario, Kinloss, 2005), pp.120-1.
13. Rees Howell Gronow, *Reminiscences of Captain Gronow* (Smith, Elder & Co., London, 1863), pp.95-100.
14. *Caledonian Mercury*, Monday, 3 July 1815.
15. Leeke, *op. cit.*, pp.30-1.
16. Quoted in *The Royal Inniskilling Fusiliers from December 1688 to July 1914* (Constable, London, 1934), p.263.
17. John Booth, *op. cit.*, p.71.

Chapter 12: The Fall of La Haye Sainte
1. North Ludlow Beamish, *History of the King's German Legion* (Thomas & William Boone, London, 1827), Vol. II, pp.456-60.
2. H.T. Siborne, *Letters, op. cit.*, p.407.
3. Abatis (also spelt abattis or abbattis) is a term in field fortification for an obstacle formed (in the modern era) of the branches of trees laid in a row, with the sharpened tops directed outwards, towards the enemy. The trees are usually interlaced or tied with wire.
4. Heymès, *Relation de la campagne de 1815, dite Waterloo, pour server à l'histoire du Maréchal Ney* (Gautier-Laguionie, Paris, 1829), pp.25-6, quoted in Field, p.170.
5. Franklin, *Waterloo, Hanoverian Correspondence*, (1815 Limited, Dorchester, 2010), p.74.
6. Hibbert, *op. cit.*, p.70.
7. Baron Christian von Ompteda, *In The King's German Legion, Memoirs of Baron Ompteda* (Grevel, London, 1894), pp.312-3.
8. James Bogle and Andrew Uffindell [Ed.], *A Waterloo Hero, The Reminiscences of Friedrich Lindau* (Frontline Books, Barnsley, 2009), pp.170-2.
9. H.T. Siborne, *Letters, op. cit.*, pp.408-9.

Chapter 13: The Arrival of the Prussians
1. Seymour *et al, op. cit.*, p.201.
2. *Ibid.*
3. Quoted in Hofschröer, *Ligny and Quatre Bras, op. cit.*, p.325.
4. Seymour *et al, op. cit.*, pp.201-2.
5. *Supplementary Despatches, op. cit.*, p.501.
6. Ropes, *op. cit.*, pp.388-9.
7. Seymour *et al, op. cit.*, p.202.
8. Quoted in Field, *op. cit.*, p.81.
9. De Char, *Napoleon on Napoleon op. cit.*, p.263.
10. Hamilton-Williams, *op. cit.*, p.282.
11. Quoted in Ropes, pp.268-9.
12. Seymour *et al, op. cit.*, p.136.
13. Victor Dupuy, *Souvenirs Militaires de Victor Dupuy, Chef d'escadron de Hussards, 1794-1816* (Paris, 1892), pp.289-90, quoted in Field, *op. cit.*, p.135.
14. Von Müffling *op. cit.*, pp.246-7.
15. Eric Hunt, *Charging Against Napoleon, Diaries and Letters of Three Hussars* (Pen & Sword, Barnsley, 2001), p.245.
16. Von Müffling *op. cit.*, pp.249-50.
17. Ludwig von Reiche, *op. cit.*, pp.212-13.
18. 'Prussian Official Account of the Late Battles. Battle of Ligny, June 16', in the *Cambridge Chronicle and Journal*, Friday, 7 July 1815.
19. Macbride, *op. cit.*, pp. 181-185.
20. Hamilton-Williams, *Waterloo*, p.338.
21. A British Officer on the Staff, *An Account of the Battle of Waterloo*, pp.11-2.

Chapter 14: The Attack of the Imperial Guard
1. John Grehan, *The Age of Napoleon Army Guides, No.1 The French Imperial Guard.* (Partizan Press, Nottingham), p.55.
2. Michel Ney, *Vie du Maréchal Ney, Duc d'Elchingen, Prince de la Moskowa* (Chez Pillet, Paris, 1816), pp.179-81.
3. Kennedy, *op. cit.*, p.127.
4. John Booth, *op. cit.*, p.54.
5. MacBride, *op. cit.*, p.191.
6. A British Officer on the Staff, pp.11-12.
7. Quoted in Lieutenant-Colonel Neil Bannatyne, *History of the Thirtieth Regiment* (Littlebury Bros., Liverpool, 1923), pp.343-4.
8. H.T. Siborne, *Letters, op. cit.*, pp. 254-5.
9. John Booth, *op. cit.*, pp.66-7.
10. Glover, *Letters From The Battle of Waterloo*, pp.186-8.
11. Ludwig E.H. Stawitzky, *Geschichte des Königlich Preussischen 25ten Infanterie-Regiment* (Koblenz, 1857), p.106, quoted in Hofschröer, *The German Victory* (Greenhill, London, 1999), p.145.

Chapter 15: The End of the Battle
1. Quoted in Kelly, *op. cit.*, p.83.
2. *Supplementary Despatches*, Vol.X, p.513.
3. Kincaid, *op. cit.*, p.343.
4. John Booth, *The Battle of Waterloo, op. cit.*, p.104.
5. Stanhope to the Duke of York, 19 June 1815, BL. Add. 34703 folio 23, quoted in Jeremy Black, *The Battle of Waterloo* (Icon, London, 2010), p.149.
6. A British Officer on the Staff, *op. cit.*, pp.11-12.
7. John Booth, *The Battle of Waterloo, Also of Ligny, and Quatre Bras, op. cit.*, pp.72-3.
8. A British Officer on the Staff, *op. cit.*, p.22.
9. Hunt, *op. cit.*, p.248.
10. G.R. Gleig, *The Light Dragoon* (Henry Colburn, London, 1844), pp.81-5.
11. John Booth, *The Battle of Waterloo, Also of Ligny, and Quatre Bras, op. cit.*, p.71.
12. Burrell, *op. cit.*, pp.43-4.
13. *English Historical Review*, vol. xviii, quoted in Brett-James *op. cit.*, pp.171-2.
14. Mackenzie Macbride, *op. cit.*, pp.181-5.
15. Mercer, *op. cit.*, pp.334-5.
16. John Booth, *The Battle of Waterloo, Also of Ligny, and Quatre Bras, op. cit.*, p.68.
17. Kincaid, *op. cit.*, pp.226-7.
18. G.C. Moore Smith [Ed.], *The Autobiography of Lieutenant-General Sir Harry Smith*, (John Murray, London, 1901), pp.275-6.
19. John Booth, *The Battle of Waterloo, Also of Ligny, and Quatre Bras, op. cit.*, p.55.
20. *Hull Packet*, Tuesday, 3 October 1815.
21. Ugo Pericoli, *1815: The Armies at Waterloo* (Charles Scribner's Sons, New York, 1973), p.70.
22. Quoted in Elizabeth Longford, *Wellington, The Years of the Sword* (Weidenfeld and Nicholson, London, 1969), p.490.
23. De Chair, *Waterloo, op. cit.*, p.154.
24. H. Maxwell [Ed.] *The Creevey Papers* (John Murray, London, 1906), p.142.

Chapter 16: The Battle of Wavre
1. Grouchy to Napoleon, Sart-les-Walhain, 11.00 hours, 18 June 1815, quoted in Hamilton-Williams, *Waterloo, op.cit.*, pp.313-4.
2. Becke, *op. cit.*, p.250.
3. Seymour *et al*, *op. cit.*, p.103.

4. Quoted in Hamilton-Williams, *Waterloo*, *op. cit.*, p.355.
5. W. Hyde Kelly, *The Battle of Wavre and Grouchy's Retreat: The Right Wing of the French Army & Prussians during the Waterloo Campaign 1815* (Leonaur, 2010), p.73.
6. P. Berthezène, *Souvenirs militaires de la république et de l'empire* (1855), Vol.2, pp.392-3, quoted in Uffindel and Corum, *op. cit.*, p.295.
7. C. François, *Journal du Capitain François* (1904), Vol.2, pp.888-9, quoted in Uffindel and Corum, *op. cit.*, p.301.
8. Burrell, *op. cit.*, p.50.
9. Bernhard of Saxe-Weimar, quoted in Franklin, *Netherlands Correspondence*, p.99.
10. Burrell, *op. cit.*, pp.51-2.
11. Franklin, *Netherlands Correspondence*, *op. cit.*, pp.98-9.

Chapter 17: The Pursuit
1. A British Officer on the Staff, *op. cit.*, pp.11-12.
2. Philip Henry, Earl Stanhope, *Notes of Conversations with the Duke of Wellington 1831-1851* (Prion, London, 1998), p.182.
3. *Wellington's Despatches*, *op. cit.*, p.149.
4. Hibbert, *op. cit.*, p.73.
5. Quoted in Brett-James, *op. cit.*, pp.179-80.
6. Bob Carruthers [Ed.], *Soldier of the Empire, The Note-Books of Captain Coignet* (Pen & Sword, Barnsley, 2012), p.264.
7. B.H. Liddell Hart, [Ed.], *The Letters of Private Wheeler 1809-1828* (Michael Joseph, London, 1951).
8. *Wellington's Despatches*, *op. cit.*, p.167.
9. Hofschröer, *The German Victory*, p.164.
10. R.D. Gibney, [Ed.] *Eighty Years Ago, or the Recollections of an Old Army Doctor* (Bellairs & Company, London, 1896), pp.223-4.
11. Liddell Hart, *op. cit.*, pp.179-80.
12. Gleig, *op. cit.*, p.103.
13. Quoted in David Chandler, *The Campaigns of Napoleon* (Macmillan, New York, 1966), p.1091.

Chapter 18: The March on Paris
1. Napoleon, *Lettres inédites de Napoléon 1er Tome second (1810-15)*, (Léon Lecestre, Paris, 1897), pp.357-8.
2. *Caledonian Mercury*, Monday, 3 July 1815.
3. Gronow, *op. cit.*, p.201.
4. Müffling, *op. cit.*, p.251.
5. Liddell Hart, *op. cit.*, p.176.
6. Quoted in Brett-James, *op. cit.*, p.207.
7. Lord Broughton, *Recollections of a Long Life* (John Murray, London, 1909), Vol.I, pp.298-9.

Chapter 19: The Fall of Napoleon
1. Fleury de Chaboulin, Edouard, *Les Vent-Jours. Mémoires pour servir à l'histoire de la vie privée, du retour et du règne de Napoléon en 1815* (Rouveyre, Paris, 1952), Vol.II, p.182.
2. Müffling, *op. cit.*, p.272-5.
3. C.W. Vane [Ed.], *Memoirs and Correspondence of Viscount Castlereagh* (H. Colburn, London 1851), Vol.X, p.430.
4. Rear-Admiral Sir Frederick Lewes Maitland, *Narrative of the Surrender of Buonaparte, and his Residence on board H.M.S. Bellerophon* (W. Blackwood, London, 1904), p.56.

5. *Hampshire Telegraph*, Monday, 14 August 1815.
6. *Norfolk Chronicle*, Saturday, 5 August 1815.
7. *La Quotidienne, ou La Feuille du Jour*, 19 July 1815, quoted in Henri Lachouque, *The Last Days of Napoleon's Empire* (Orion, New York, 1967), pp.276-7.
8. Francis Bickley [Ed.], *Report on the Manuscripts of the Late Reginald Rawdon Hastings, Esq., of the Manor House, Ashby de la Zouch* (Historical Manuscripts Commission, vol.3, 1934), pp.308-9.

Chapter 20: The Occupation of Paris
1. *Cheltenham Chronicle*, Thursday, 17 August 1815.
2. Costello, *op. cit.*, pp.297-8.
3. Ian Robertson [Ed.], *The Exploits of Ensign Bakewell* (Frontline, Barnsley, 2912), pp.158-9.
4. John Booth, *The Battle of Waterloo, op. cit.*, p.104.

Chapter 21: The Fallen
1. Chandler, *Waterloo*, pp.171-2.
2. Gronow, pp.74-5.
3. Scott, pp.218-20.
4. *Ibid*, pp.221-2.
5. Quoted in Adkin, *op. cit.*, p.324.
6. *The Mirror of Literature, Amusement and Instruction*, quoted in Adkin, *ibid*.
7. Charlotte Eaton, *Waterloo Days* (G. Bell, London, 1888), pp.30-1.
8. W.E. Frye, *op. cit.*, p.27.
9. *Extract of a Despatch from Lieutenant Colonel Leake to Viscount Castlereagh, dated Pontarlier, July 12*, in *London Gazette Extraordinary*, 21 July 1815.
10. Mercer, *op. cit.*, pp.316-7.
11. Quoted in Gareth Glover, *Waterloo, Myth and Reality* (Pen & Sword, Barnsley, 2014), p.201.

Chapter 22: Survivors' Stories
1. Christopher Kelly, *op. cit.*, p.98.
2. George Simmons, *op. cit.*, 366-8.
3. Edward Costello, *op. cit.*, p.295
4. Major-General Sir John Ponsonby, *The Ponsonby Family* (Medici Society, London, 1929), p.43.
5. Costello, *op. cit.*, pp.295-6.

Chapter 23: Recriminations
1. *Le Moniteur*, 26 July 1815.
2. Murat, Princess Caroline, *My Memoirs* (Eveleigh Nash, London, 1910), p.23.
3. Alan Schom, *One Hundred Days, Napoleon's Road to Waterloo* (Michael Joseph, London, 1993), p.317.

Chapter 24: Travellers' Tales
1. Quoted in R.E. Foster, *Wellington and Waterloo: The Duke, The Battle and Posterity 1815-2015* (Spellmount, Stroud, 2014), pp.84 & 96.
2. Eaton, pp.30-1.
3. John Booth, *The Battle of Waterloo, op. cit.*, pp.65-6.
4. Christopher Kelly, *op. cit.*, p.154.
5. Edward Cotton, *A Voice from Waterloo* (B. Green, London, 1854), pp.38-9.
6. Victor Hugo, *Les Misérables*, quoted in Seymour, *et al, op. cit.*, p.223.

Chapter 25: Honouring the Brave

1. Naylor, Appendix 1. Note that the exact amounts for each band do vary between accounts, particularly in the newspaper reports of the time.
2. *Hull Packet*, Tuesday, 22 August 1815.
3. *Hull Packet*, Tuesday, 3 August 1815.
4. *Hampshire Chronicle*, Monday, 17 July 1815.
5. *Chester Chronicle*, Friday, 11 August 1815.

Chapter 26: After the Battle Anecdotes

1. Kincaid, *op. cit.*, pp.348-9.
2. *Morning Chronicle*, Monday, 18 September 1815.
3. Harold Esdaile Malet, *Historical Records of the Eighteenth Hussars* (William Clowes, London, 1869), p.51.
4. Christopher Kelly, *op. cit.*, p.101.
5. Gilles Bernard and Gérard Lachaux, *Waterloo Relics* (Histoire & Collections, Paris, 2005), p.57. Of note is the fact that excavations carried out towards the end of the twentieth century found no human remains.
6. Christopher Kelly, *op. cit.*, p.99.
7. Quoted in Naylor, *op. cit.*, p.49.
8. Gareth Glover has cast doubt on the authenticity of her claim, see *Myth and Reality*, p.116.
9. Julian Charles Young, *A Memoir of Charles Mayne Young,* (Macmillan, London, 1871), pp.158-9. It must be noted that the full account was not given, as there are elements of this story that are clearly incorrect and these have been omitted.
10. Gronow, *op. cit.*, pp.204-5.
11. *Chester Courant*, Tuesday, 4 June 1816.
12. *Ibid*, Tuesday, 25 July 1815.
13. Macbride, *op. cit.*, p.129.
14. Christopher Kelly, *op. cit.*, p.106.
15. Lemonnier-Delafosse, *op. cit.*, Vol.2, p.404.
16. A Near Observer, *op. cit.*, p.113.
17. *Leeds Intelligencer*, Monday, 21 July 1817.
18. John Booth, *Battle of Waterloo, op. cit.*, pp.153-4.
19. Christopher Kelly, *op. cit.*, p.105.
20. Reproduced in Chandler, *Waterloo*, p.96.
21. Richard Edgcumbe [Ed.], *The Diary of Frances Lady Shelley, 1787-1817* (John Murray, London, 1912), p.102.

Bibliography
& Source Information

Official Documents
Hansard Parliamentary Debates Archive.
British and Foreign State Papers 1814-1815, (HMSO, London, 1839).
The London Gazette.

Newspapers and Periodicals
Bury and Norwich Post, Caledonian Mercury, Cambridge Chronicle and Journal, Carlisle Journal, Cheltenham Chronicle, Chester Courant, Chester Chronicle, Hampshire Chronicle, Hampshire Telegraph, Hereford Journal, Hull Packet, Ipswich Journal, Journal of the Royal Artillery, Journal of the Society for Army Historical Research, Lancaster Gazette, Leeds Intelligencer, Leicester Journal, Liverpool Mercury, London Observer, Morning Chronicle, Morning Post, Newcastle Journal, New York Times, Norfolk Chronicle, Northampton Mercury, Royal Cornwall Gazette, Sussex Advertiser, The Army Quarterly, The Times, United Services Magazine.

Published Biographies, Memoirs and Studies
A British Officer on the Staff, *An Account of the Battle of Waterloo, Fought on the 18th of June, 1815, by the English and Allied Forces, Commanded by the Duke of Wellington, and the Prussian Army, Under the Orders of Prince Blucher, Against the Army of France, Commanded by Napoleon Bonaparte* (James Ridgeway, London, 1815).
A Near Observer, *The Battle of Waterloo, Containing the Accounts Published by Authority, British and Foreign, and Other Relative Documents, with Circumstantial Details, Previous and After the Battle, from a Variety of Authentic and Original Sources: to which is Added an Alphabetical List of the Officers Killed and Wounded, from 15th to 26th June, 1815, and the Total Loss of Each Regiment* (John Booth, London, 1815).
Adkin, Mark, *The Waterloo Companion* (Aurum Press, London, 2001).
Ainslie, General Charles P., *Historical Record of the First or the Royal Regiment of Dragoons: Containing an Account of its Formation in the Reign of King Charles the Second, and of its Subsequent Services to the Present Time* (Chapman & Hall, London, 1887).
Anglesey, Marquis of [Ed.], *The Capel Letters, 1814-1817* (Jonathan Cape, London, 1955).
Anonymous, *A Soldier of the 71st: From De la Plata to Waterloo 1806-1815* (Frontline, Barnsley, 2010).
Anonymous, *The Battle of Waterloo, Also of Ligny and Quatre-Bras, Described by the Series of Accounts Published by Authority, with Circumstantial Details: By a Near Observer. Also Important Particulars, Communicated by Staff, and Regimental Officers, Serving in Different Parts of the Field, with Every Connected Official Document; Forming an Historical Record of the Campaign in the Netherlands, 1815. To which is Added a Register of the Names of the Officers* (J. Booth, London, 1817).

Anonymous, *The Journal of the Three Days of the Battle of Waterloo, Being my own Personal Journal of What I Saw and of the Events which I Bore a Part, by an Eye-witness. Translated from the French. To which is added an Appendix containing the Official Reports of the Allies* (Military Chronicle and Military Classics, London, 1816).

Anonymous, *The Royal Inniskilling Fusiliers from December 1688 to July 1914* (Constable, London, 1934).

Austin, Paul Britten, *1815: The Return of Napoleon* (Greenhill, London, 2002).

Balen, Malcolm, *A Model Victory: Waterloo and the Battle for History* (Harper Perennial, London, 2005).

Bankes, George Nugent [Ed.], *The Autobiography of Sergeant William Lawrence A Hero of the Peninsular and Waterloo Campaigns* (Sampson Low, Marston, Searle, & Rivington, London, 1886).

Bannatyne, Lieutenant Colonel Neil, *History of the Thirtieth Regiment Now the First Battalion, East Lancashire Regiment, 1689-1881* (Littlebury Bros., Liverpool, 1923).

Beamish, North Ludlow *History of the King's German Legion* (Thomas & William Boone, London, 1827).

Becke, A.F., *Napoleon and Waterloo, The Emperor's Campaign with l'armée du Nord* (Kegan, Paul, Trench, Turubner & Co., London, 1936) and reprinted by Greenhill, 1995.

Bernard, Gilles, Lachaux, Gérard, *Waterloo Relics* (Histoire & Collections, Paris, 2005).

Bickley, Francis, [Ed.], *Report on the Manuscripts of the late Reginald Rawdon Hastings, Esq., of the Manor House, Ashby de la Zouch* (Historical Manuscripts Commission, vol.3, 1934).

Bird, Anthony & Nicholas, *Eyewitness To War: The Finest Writing about War by Those Who were There* (Summersdale, Chichester, 2006).

Black, Jeremy, *The Battle of Waterloo: A New History* (Icon, London, 2010).

Bogle, James & Uffindell Andrew [Eds.], *A Waterloo Hero: The Reminiscences of Friedrich Lindau* (Frontline, Barnsley, 2009).

Broughton, John Cam Hobhouse, *Recollections of a Long Life. With Additional Extracts from his Private Diaries* (John Murray, London, 1909).

Booth, John, *The Battle of Waterloo, Containing the Accounts Published by Authority, British and Foreign, and Other Relative Documents, with Circumstantial Details, Previous and After the Battle, from a Variety of Authentic and Original Sources: to which is Added an Alphabetical List of the Officers Killed and Wounded, from 15th to 26th June, 1815, and the Total Loss of Each Regiment* (T. Egerton, London, 1815).

Booth, John, *The Battle of Waterloo, Also of Ligny, and Quatre Bras, Containing the Series of Accounts Published by Authority, British and Foreign, with Circumstantial Details Relative to the Battles, from a Variety of Original and Authentic Sources, with Connected Official and Private Documents, Forming an Historical Record by Those who Had the Honour to Share in the Operations of the Campaign of the Netherlands, 1815* (J. Booth, London, 1817).

Bowles, Captain George, *A Series of Letters to the First Earl of Malmesbury, his Family and Friends, from 1745 to 1820. Edited by his grandson, the Earl of Malmesbury* (Richard Bentley, London, 1870).

Brett-James, Anthony, *The Hundred Days: Napoleon's Last Campaign from Eye-witness Accounts* (Macmillan, New York, 1964).

Burrell, J.P., *Official bulletins of the Battle of Waterloo in the Original languages, with Translations into English* (Parker, Furnivall, & Parker, London, 1849).

Carruthers, Bob [Ed.], *Soldier of the Empire, The Note-Books of Captain Coignet* (Pen & Sword, Barnsley, 2012),

Cassidy, Martin, *Marching with Wellington: With the Inniskillings in the Napoleonic Wars* (Leo Copper, Barnsley, 2003).

Chandler, David, *The Campaigns of Napoleon* (Macmillan, New York, 1966).

Chandler, David, *Waterloo: The Hundred Days* (Osprey, London, 1987).

Clay, M., *A Narrative of the Battles of Quatre-Bras and Waterloo; With the Defence of Hougoumont by Matthew Clay* (Ken Trotman, London, 2006).

Corrigan, Gordon, *Waterloo: A New History of the Battle and its Armies* (Atlantic, London, 2014).

Costello, Edward, *The Adventures of a Soldier; or, Memoirs of Edward Costello, Narratives of the Campaigns in The Peninsular and Waterloo Campaigns* (Henry Colburn, London, 1841).

Cotton, Edward, *A Voice from Waterloo* (B. Green, London, 1854).

Craan, Guillaume Benjamin, *An Historical Account of the Battle of Waterloo, Fought on the 18th of June, 1815; Intended to Elucidate the Topographical Plan, Executed by W.B. Crane ...*, Translated from the French, with Explanatory Notes, by Captain Arthur Gore (Samuel Leigh, London, 1817).

Crook, Jonathan, *The Very Thing: The Memoirs of Drummer Bentinck, Royal Welch Fusiliers, 1807-1823* (Frontline, Barnsley, 2011).

Crowdy, T.E. *Incomparable: Napoleon's 9th Light Infantry Regiment* (Osprey, Oxford, 2012).

David, Saul, *All the King's Men, The British Redcoat in the Era of Sword and Musket* (Penguin, London, 2002).

De Bourrienne, Louis Antoine Fauvelet (Edited by R. W. Phipps Colonel, Late Royal Artillery), *Memoirs of Napoleon Bonaparte* (Charles Scribner's Sons, New York, 1891).

De Chair, Somerset [Ed.] *Napoleon on Napoleon* (Brockhampton Press, London, 1992).

Drouet, Maréchal Comte d'Erlon, *Notice sur la vie militaire, écrite par lui-même et dediée à ses amis. Publiée par sa famille* (Gustave Barba, Paris, 1844).

Eaton, Charlotte Anne, *Waterloo Days*, (G. Bell, London, 1888).

Field, Andrew W., *Waterloo: the French Perspective* (Pen & Sword, Barnsley, 2013).

Fitchett, W.H. (Ed.), *Waterloo 1815: Captain Mercer's Journal* (Pen & Sword, Barnsley, 2012).

Fletcher, Ian, *Galloping at Everything: The British Cavalry in the Peninsular War and at Waterloo 1808-15. A Reappraisal* (Spellmount, Staplehurst, 1999).

Fletcher, Ian, *A Desperate Business: Wellington, The British Army and the Waterloo Campaign* (Spellmount, Staplehurst, 2001).

Foster, R.E., *Wellington and Waterloo: The Duke, The Battle and Posterity 1815-2015* (Spellmount, Stroud, 2014).

Foulkes, Nick, *Dancing into Battle: A Social History of the Battle of Waterloo* (Phoenix, London, 2007)

Fournier, August, *Napoleon The First, A Biography* (Translated by Margaret Bacon Corwin and Arthur Dart Russell), (Henry Holt, New York, 1903).

Franklin, John, *Waterloo, Hanoverian Correspondence, Volume One, Letters and Reports from Manuscript Sources* (1815 Limited, Ulverston, 2010).

Franklin, John, *Netherlands Correspondence, Volume One, Letters and Reports from Manuscript Sources* (1815 Limited, Ulverston, 2010).

Frye, W.E., *After Waterloo: Reminiscences of European Travel, 1815-1819* (William Heinemann, London, 1909).

Gibney, R.D. [Ed.] *Eighty years ago, or The recollections of an Old Army Doctor, his Adventures on the Field of Quatre Bras and Waterloo and During the Occupation of Paris in 1815* (Bellairs & Company, London, 1896).

Gleig, G.R. *The Light Dragoon* (Henry Colburn, London, 1844).

Glover, Gareth, *Letters from the Battle of Waterloo: Unpublished Correspondence by Allied Officers from the Siborne Papers* (Greenhill, London, 2004).

Glover, Gareth [Ed.], *Eyewitness to the Peninsular War and the Battle of Waterloo, the Letters and Journals of Lieutenant Colonel The Honourable James Hamilton Stanhope, 1803 to 1825 Recording his Service with Sir John Moore, Sir Thomas Graham and the Duke of Wellington* (Pen & Sword, Barnsley, 2010).

Glover, Gareth, *The Waterloo Archive: Previously Unpublished or Rare Journals and Letters Regarding the Waterloo Campaign and the Subsequent Occupation of Paris Vol. I: British Sources* (Frontline, Barnsley, 2010).
Vol. IV: British Sources (Frontline, Barnsley, 2012).

Glover, Gareth, *Waterloo: Myth and Reality* (Pen & Sword, Barnsley, 2014).

Grehan, John, *The Age of Napoleon Army Guides, No.1 The French Imperial Guard* (Partizan Press, Nottingham).

Gronow, Rees Howell, *Reminiscences of Captain Gronow, Being Anecdotes of the Camp, the Court, and the Clubs at the Close of the Last War with France* (Smith, Elder & Co., London, 1863).

Grouchy, Marquis Emmanuel, *Mémoires du Maréchal de Grouchy, Par le Marquis de Grouchy* (E. Dentu, Paris, 1874).

Gurwood, John [Ed], *The Dispatches of Field Marshal the Duke of Wellington, K.G., During his Various Campaigns in India, Denmark, Portugal, Spain, the Low Countries, and France from 1799 to 1818 Vol.VIII* (John Murray, London, 1852).

Hamilton-Williams, David, *Waterloo, New Perspectives: The Great Battle Reappraised* (Arms and Armour, London, 1990).

Hamilton-Williams, David, *The Fall of Napoleon: The Final Betrayal* (Brockhampton Press, London, 1999).

Haythornthwaite, Philip, *The Waterloo Armies* (Pen & Sword, Barnsley, 2007).

Hibbert, Christopher, *Wheatley Diary, A Journal and Sketch-Book Kept During the Peninsular War and Waterloo Campaign by Edmund Wheatley* (Longmans, London, 1964).

Hofschröer, Peter, *1815: The Waterloo Campaign, Wellington, his German Allies and the Battles of Ligny and Quatre Bras* (Greenhill, London, 1998).

Hofschröer, Peter, *1815: The Waterloo Campaign, Volume 2: The German Victory* (Greenhill, London, 1999).

Hope, James, *Letters from Portugal, Spain and France, During the Memorable Campaigns of 1811, 1812 & 1813, and From Belgium and France in the Year 1815* (Michael Anderson, Edinburgh, 1819).

Howarth, David, *Waterloo: A Near Run Thing* (Collins, London, 1968).

Hunt, Eric, *Charging Against Napoleon: Diaries and Letters of Three Hussars* (Pen & Sword, Barnsley, 2001).

James, A., *Retrospect of a Military Life During the Most Eventful Periods of the Last War: Journal of Sergeant James Anton 42nd Highlanders* (W.H. Lizars, Edinburgh, 1841).

Kelly, Christopher, *A Full and Circumstantial Account of the Memorable Battle of Waterloo, The Second Restoration of Louis XVIII; and the Deportation of Napoleon Buonaparte to the Island of St. Helena, and Every Recent Particular Relative to His Conduct and Mode of Life in His Exile. Together with an Interesting Account of the Affairs of France and the Biographical Sketches of the Most Distinguished Waterloo Heroes. Embellished with Engravings* (Thomas Kelly, London, 1817).

Kelly, W. Hyde, *The Battle of Wavre and Grouchy's Retreat: The Right Wing of the French Army & Prussians during the Waterloo Campaign 1815* (Leonaur, 2010).

Kennedy, General Sir James Shaw, *Notes on the Battle of Waterloo* (John Murray, London, 1865).

Kincaid, Captain John, *Adventures in the Rifle Brigade in the Peninsula, France, and the Netherlands* (Boone, London, 1830).

La Bédoyère, Charles Angélique François Huchet comte de, *Memoirs of the Public and Private Life of Napoleon Bonaparte, With Copious Historical Illustrations and Original Anecdotes* (George Virtue, London, 1835).

Lachouque, Henri, *The Last Days of Napoleon's Empire* (Orion, New York, 1967).

Leeke, William, *History of Lord Seaton's Regiment, (the 52nd Light Infantry) at the Battle of Waterloo Together With Various Incidents Connected with that Regiment* (Hatchard, London, 1866).

Lennox, William Pitt, *Fifty Years' Biographical Reminiscences* (Hurst & Blackett, London, 1863).

Lemonnier-Delafosse, M, *Campagnes de 1810 à 1815. Souvenirs Militaires* (Imprimerie du commerce, Le Havre, 1850).

Liddell Hart, B.H., *The Letters of Private Wheeler 1809-1828* (Michael Joseph, London, 1951).

Lipscombe, Nick, *Wellington's Guns: The Untold Story of Wellington and his Artillery in the Peninsula and at Waterloo* (Osprey, London, 2013).

Longford, Elizabeth, *Wellington, The Years of the Sword* (Weidenfeld and Nicolson, London, 1969).

Macbride, Mackenzie [Ed.], *With Napoleon at Waterloo and other Unpublished Documents of the Waterloo and Peninsular Campaigns Also Papers on Waterloo by the Late Edward Bruce Low MA* (Francis Griffiths, London, 1911).

Maitland, Rear-Admiral Sir Frederick Lewes, *Narrative of the Surrender of Buonaparte, and his Residence on board H.M.S. Bellerophon, with a Detail of the Principal Events that Occurred in that Ship between the 24th of May and the 8th of August, 1815* (W. Blackwood, London, 1904).

Malet, Harold Esdaile, *Historical Records of the Eighteenth Hussars* (William Clowes, London, 1869).

Malmesbury, James Harris, *Letters of the First Earl of Malmesbury, 1745-1820* (Richard Bentley, London, 1870).

Maxwell, Sir Herbert [Ed.], *The Creevey Papers. A Selection From The Correspondence & Diaries of the Late Thomas Creevey, MP Born 1768 – Died 1838* (John Murray, London, 1906)

Maxwell, William Hamilton, *Life of Wellington* (Hutchinson, London, 1899).

McLynn, Frank, *Napoleon, A Biography* (Pimlico, London, 1997)

Mercer, Cavalié, *Journal of the Waterloo Campaign kept through the Campaign of 1815* (William Blackwood, London, 1870).

Miller, David, *Lady Delancey at Waterloo, A Story of Duty and Devotion* (Spellmount, Staplehurst, 2000).

Moore Smith, G.C. [Ed.], *The Autobiography of Lieutenant-General Sir Harry Smith, Baronet of Aliwal on the Sutlej, GCB* (John Murray, London, 1901).

Müffling, Baron Carl von , *The Memoirs of Baron Carl von Müffling: A Prussian Officer in the Napoleonic Wars* (Greenhill, London, 1997).

Murat, Princess Caroline, *My Memoirs* (Eveleigh Nash, London, 1910).

Naylor, John, *Waterloo* (Pan, London, 1960)

Ney, Michel, *Vie du Maréchal Ney, Duc d'Elchingen, Prince de la Moskowa* (Chez Pillet, Paris, 1816).

Ompteda, Christian Freiherr von, *In The King's German Legion, Memoirs of Baron Ompteda, Colonel in the King's German Legion* (Grevel, London, 1894)

Pericoli, Ugo, *1815 The Armies at Waterloo* (Charles Scribner's Sons, New York, 1973).

Ponsonby, Major-General Sir John, *The Ponsonby Family* (Medici Society, London, 1929).

Reiche, Ludwig von, *Memoiren des königlich preussischen Generals der Infanterie Ludwig von Reiche* (Brodhaus, Leipzig, 1857).

Reid, Stuart, *Wellington's Highland Warriors, From the Black Watch Mutiny to the Battle of Waterloo* (Frontline, Barnsley, 2010).

Reiset, *Souvenirs du Lieutenant Général Vicomte de Reiset, 1814-1836* (Calmann Lévy, Paris, 1902).

Robertson, Ian [ed.], *The Exploits of Ensign Bakewell: With the Inniskillings in the Peninsula, 1810-11; and in Paris, 1815* (Frontline, Barnsley, 2012).

Ropes, John Codman, *The Campaign of Waterloo: A Military History* (Charles Scribner's Sons, New York, 1906).

Ross-Lewin, Harry, *With 'The Thirty-Second' in the Peninsula and other Campaigns* (Hodges, Figgis & Co., Dublin, 1914).

Sabine, Major General Edward, *Letters of Colonel Sir Augustus Simon Frazer, KCB Commanding the Royal Horse Artillery in the Army Under Wellington Written During the Peninsular War* (Longman, London, 1859).

Schom, Alan, *One Hundred Days: Napoleon's Road to Waterloo* (Michael Joseph, London, 1993).

Scott, W.A., *Battle of Waterloo: or, Correct Narrative of the Late Sanguinary Conflict on the Plains of Waterloo* (E. Cox and Son, London, 1815).

Seymour, William, Champagne, Jacques, & Kaulbach, Colonel E., *Waterloo, Battle of Three Armies* (Book Club Associates, London, 1979).

Siborne, H.T., *Waterloo Letters: A Selection from Original and Hitherto Unpublished Letters Bearing on the Operations of the 16th, 17th, and 18th June, 1815, By Officers who served in the Campaign* (Cassell, London, 1891).

Siborne, William, *History of the Waterloo Campaign* (Greenhill, London, 1995).

Simmons, George, *A British Rifle Man: The Journals and Correspondence of Major George Simmons, Rifle Brigade, During the Peninsular War and the Campaign of Waterloo* (A. & C. Black, London, 1899).

Stanhope, Philip Henry, Earl, *Notes of Conversations with the Duke of Wellington 1831-1851* (Prion, London, 1998).

Tomkinson, William, *The Diary of a Cavalry Officer in the Peninsular and Waterloo Campaigns, 1809-1815* (Ed. James Tomkinson) (Swan Sonnenschein, London, 1894).

Uffindell, Andrew, *The Eagle's Last Triumph: Napoleon's Last Victory at Ligny, June 1815* (Greenhill, London, 1994).

Uffindell, Andrew, and Corum, Michael, *On the Fields of Glory: The Battlefields of the 1815 Campaign* (Greenhill, London, 1996).

Vane, C.W. [Ed.], *Memoirs and correspondence of Viscount Castlereagh, Second Marquess of Londonderry* (H. Colburn, London, 1851).

Wellington, Arthur Richard Wellesley, 2d Duke of, *Supplementary Despatches and Memoranda of Field Marshal Arthur, Duke of Wellington, KG* (J. Murray, London, 1864).

Wilson, Guy Hutton, *Merely a Memorandum: From Spain to Waterloo in Wellington's Army* (Librario, Kinloss, 2005).

Wrottesley, George, *Life and Correspondence of Field Marshal Sir John Burgoyne* (Richard Bentley, London, 1873).

Young, Julian Charles, *A Memoir of Charles Mayne Young, Tragedian: With Extracts from his Son's Journals* (Macmillan, London, 1871).

Index

345

INDEX

British Army
2nd Corps, 24, 25, 32, 59, 166
1st Division, 25, 32, 46, 50, 51, 58, 101,
120, 127, 130-1, 139, 261
2nd Division, 25, 32, 33, 46, 50,
58, 101, 143, 205
3rd Division, 25, 32, 33, 46, 50, 71, 79,
101, 121, 138, 139, 164, 165, 199
4th Division, 25, 32, 33, 46, 50, 101,
103, 238-9
5th Division, 46, 50, 52, 56, 62, 68, 71,
101, 141, 148-9, 165, 200
6th Division, 46, 50, 101, 141, 142, 178,
200
Household Brigade, 23, 150, 182, 212,
306
Union Brigade, 107, 150, 155-7, 160,
163, 182, 274, 317
3rd Cavalry Brigade, 49
6th Cavalry Brigade, 195, 213
1st (Guards) Brigade, 68, 203
2nd Brigade, 137, 204, 219
3rd Brigade, 143
8th Brigade, 56, 149
10th Brigade, 78, 141
Royal Engineers, 19, 31, 69, 113, 133
Royal Sappers and Miners, 19
Royal Horse Artillery, 23, 107, 139,
164, 172
1st Regiment of Life Guards, 72, 103,
119, 150, 231, 274, 277, 306, 310, 319,
323
2nd Regiment of Life Guards, 72, 119,
150, 212, 231, 274, 277, 306, 310, 319,
323
Royal Horse Guards, 140, 150, 162,
169
1st (Royal) Dragoons, 151, 161, 163,
277
2nd (Royal North British) Dragoons,
80, 161
6th (Inniskilling) Dragoons, 161, 280
7th Light Dragoons, 169, 231
10th Hussars, 231
11th Light Dragoons, 214, 231, 240
12th Light Dragoons, 152, 231, 318
16th Light Dragoons, 144, 160, 170,
231
18th Hussars, 231
23rd Light Dragoons, 231, 305

1st Regiment of Foot Guards, 119,
131, 175, 207, 244, 305
2nd Coldstream Regiment of Foot
Guards, 68, 120, 125, 130-3, 135, 139,
325
3rd Regiment of Foot Guards, 129,
136
1st (Royal Scots) Regiment of Foot,
62, 73-4
7th Regiment of Foot, 24
14th Regiment of Foot, 143
23rd Regiment of Foot, 23
27th Regiment of Foot, 141, 178, 200,
263
28th Regiment of Foot, 74, 137
30th Regiment of Foot, 167, 202
32nd Regiment of Foot, 137, 275
40th Regiment of Foot, 141, 142, 154,
178
42nd Regiment of Foot, 54, 62, 64, 72,
74, 80-1, 173, 204, 308
44th Regiment of Foot, 62, 73
51st Regiment of Foot, 23, 143, 238
52nd Regiment of Foot, 143, 177-8,
200, 204-5, 213
69th Regiment of Foot, 66, 75, 97, 113
71st Regiment of Foot, 143-4, 165, 204-
5, 213
73rd Regiment of Foot, 165, 167-8, 316
79th Regiment of Foot, 80, 137
92nd Regiment of Foot, 54, 62-3, 64,
73, 74, 80-1, 140-1, 149, 155-6, 309
95th (Rifles) Regiment of Foot, 55, 71-
2, 101, 107, 137, 143, 146, 148-9, 181,
200, 204, 210, 219, 259-60, 276-7, 280-1
King's German Legion, 18, 19, 25, 64,
78, 139, 140, 165, 172-3, 180-8, 266,
298, 304
Brune, Marshal Guillaume Marie Anne,
284
Brunswick
Duke of, 46, 50, 51, 62, 63, 65-6, 69, 70,
97, 272-3
Army, 21, 46, 50, 62, 63, 65-6, 69, 71,
74, 101, 111, 120, 132, 142, 155, 174,
209, 266, 276
Brussels (Bruxelles), xii, 12, 16-17, 18, 27-
8, 30, 38, 45-7, 49-56, 59-62, 65, 67, 69,
72, 78-81, 82, 96, 98, 101, 103-5, 110-11,
112, 114-5, 117-20, 124, 130-1, 135, 138,

346